I've Been Thinking

I've Been Thinking

DANIEL C. DENNETT

ALLEN LANE
an imprint of
PENGUIN BOOKS

ALLEN LANE

UK | USA | Canada | Ireland | Australia
India | New Zealand | South Africa

Penguin Books is part of the Penguin Random House group of companies
whose addresses can be found at global.penguinrandomhouse.com.

First published in the United States of America by W. W. Norton & Company, 2023
First published in Great Britain by Allen Lane 2023
001

Copyright © Daniel C. Dennett, 2023

The moral right of the author has been asserted

Printed and bound in Great Britain by Clays Ltd, Elcograf S.p.A.

The authorized representative in the EEA is Penguin Random House Ireland,
Morrison Chambers, 32 Nassau Street, Dublin D02 YH68

A CIP catalogue record for this book is available from the British Library

ISBN: 978–0–241–51927–1

www.greenpenguin.co.uk

Penguin Random House is committed to a
sustainable future for our business, our readers
and our planet. This book is made from Forest
Stewardship Council® certified paper.

To my family

CONTENTS

Prologue

LUCKY DAN

*I've been lucky all my life, it almost makes me
believe in the stars.*

—Tom Stoppard, 1986, in a letter to his mother

*I've never thought of myself as lucky, I'm a coward.
That's why I can't be a gambler. But I work very hard.
The harder I work, the luckier I get!*

—Alex Bird (famed British "punter," or gambler), *Sunday
Observer* (London), April 24, 1983

O N OCTOBER 24, 2006, I WAS RUSHED BY AMBULANCE
from my office at Tufts University to the emergency room at
Lahey Clinic, where doctors discovered the problem: the inner and
outer layers of my aorta had come apart—an *aortic dissection*—and
I could die at any moment if the blood from my heart burst out
into my chest cavity. The day before I had been in Mackerel Cove
on Swan's Island in Maine on my sailboat, *Xanthippe*. This was the
last cruise of the season, joined by my Swedish friend Bo Dahlbom
and his son Fredrik, and as I slowly pulled on the heavy anchor
line I felt a slight pain in my chest, reminding me of the pain I
had felt seven years earlier when I'd had a "silent heart attack" that
had led to a triple-bypass operation. We sailed back to Blue Hill
in a stiff headwind, moored the boat, took off the heavy sails, put
the inflatable dinghy on the roof of my car, and went back to the
farm, before I made a quick trip to the local hospital, where I was
told I had *not* had a heart attack but should see my cardiologist as

soon as I could. The next day we drove to Tufts, where I asked the department secretary if she had any Tylenol, and she wisely called the ambulance instead.

One of the little-known side effects of open-heart surgery is mini-strokes caused by debris from the operation clogging up the capillaries in the brain, and my cardiologist explicitly warned the surgical team that since my mind was my life, they should strive to avoid turning me into a "pumphead"—the ugly term heart surgeons use in private for those whose brains are damaged by the heart-lung machine. After the operation, before they removed me from the machine, they *reversed the flow of blood to my brain*, sending it into the veins and out of the arteries, hoping to flush out any debris that was about to disable my *res cogitans*, my thinking thing (my brain, not, as Descartes would have it, a distinct and immaterial substance). So I've been brainwashed, quite literally. Did it work? As soon as I could sit up in my hospital bed after the operation I got out my trusty laptop and wrote a short piece to see if I still had my marbles. It was put on Edge.org, where it attracted a lot of attention. What do you think?

Thank Goodness! (November 2, 2006)

There are no atheists in foxholes, according to an old but dubious saying, and there is at least a little anecdotal evidence in favor of it in the notorious cases of famous atheists who have emerged from near-death experiences to announce to the world that they have changed their minds. The British philosopher Sir A. J. Ayer, who died in 1989, is a fairly recent example. Here is another anecdote to ponder.

Two weeks ago, I was rushed by ambulance to a hospital where it was determined by c-t scan that I had a "dissection of the aorta"—the lining of the main output vessel carrying blood from my heart had been torn up, creating a two-channel pipe where there should only be one. Fortunately for me, the fact that

I'd had a coronary artery bypass graft seven years ago probably saved my life, since the tangle of scar tissue that had grown like ivy around my heart in the intervening years reinforced the aorta, preventing catastrophic leakage from the tear in the aorta itself. After a nine-hour surgery, in which my heart was stopped entirely and my body and brain were chilled down to about 45 degrees to prevent brain damage from lack of oxygen until they could get the heart-lung machine pumping, I am now the proud possessor of a new aorta up to the aortic arch, made of strong Dacron fabric tubing sewn into shape on the spot by the surgeon, attached to my heart along with a carbon-fiber valve that makes a reassuring little click every time my heart beats.

As I now enter a gentle period of recuperation, I have much to reflect on, about the harrowing experience itself and even more about the flood of supporting messages I've received since word got out about my latest adventure. Friends were anxious to learn if I had had a near-death experience, and if so, what effect it had had on my longstanding public atheism. Had I had an epiphany? Was I going to follow in the footsteps of Ayer (who recovered his aplomb and insisted a few days later "what I should have said is that my experiences have weakened, not my belief that there is no life after death, but my inflexible attitude towards that belief"), or was my atheism still intact and unchanged?

Yes, I did have an epiphany. I saw with greater clarity than ever before in my life that when I say "Thank goodness!" this is not merely a euphemism for "Thank God!" (We atheists don't believe that there is any God to thank.) I really do mean thank goodness! There is a lot of goodness in this world, and more goodness every day, and this fantastic human-made fabric of excellence is genuinely responsible for the fact that I am alive today. It is a worthy recipient of the gratitude I feel today, and I want to celebrate that fact here and now.

To whom, then, do I owe a debt of gratitude? To the cardiologist who has kept me alive and ticking for years, and who swiftly and confidently rejected the original diagnosis of nothing worse than pneumonia. To the surgeons, neurologists, anesthesiologists, and the perfusionist, who kept my systems going for many hours under daunting circumstances. To the dozen or so physician assistants, and to nurses and physical therapists and x-ray technicians and a small army of phlebotomists so deft that you hardly know they are drawing your blood, and the people who brought the meals, kept my room clean, did the mountains of laundry generated by such a messy case, wheel-chaired me to x-ray, and so forth. These people came from Uganda, Kenya, Liberia, Haiti, the Philippines, Croatia, Russia, China, Korea, India—and the United States, of course—and I have never seen more impressive mutual respect, as they helped each other out and checked each other's work. But for all their teamwork, this local gang could not have done their jobs without the huge background of contributions from others. I remember with gratitude my late friend and Tufts colleague, physicist Allan Cormack, who shared the Nobel Prize for his invention of the c-t scanner. Allan—you have posthumously saved yet another life, but who's counting? The world is better for the work you did. Thank goodness. Then there is the whole system of medicine, both the science and the technology, without which the best-intentioned efforts of individuals would be roughly useless. So I am grateful to the editorial boards and referees, past and present, of *Science, Nature, Journal of the American Medical Association, Lancet,* and all the other institutions of science and medicine that keep churning out improvements, detecting and correcting flaws.

Do I worship modern medicine? Is science my religion? Not at all; there is no aspect of modern medicine or science that I would exempt from the most rigorous scrutiny, and I can readily identify a host of serious problems that still need to be fixed. That's easy to do, of course, because the worlds of medicine and science are already engaged in the most obsessive, intensive, and humble self-assessments yet known to human institutions, and they regularly make public the results of their self-examinations. Moreover, this open-ended rational criticism, imperfect as it is, is the secret of the astounding success of these human enterprises. There are measurable improvements every day. Had I had my blasted aorta a decade ago, there would have been no prayer of saving me. It's hardly routine today, but the odds of my survival were actually not so bad (these days, roughly 33 percent of aortic dissection patients die in the first twenty-four hours after onset without treatment, and the odds get worse by the hour thereafter).

One thing in particular struck me when I compared the medical world on which my life now depended with the religious institutions I have been studying so intensively in recent years. One of the gentler, more supportive themes to be found in every religion (so far as I know) is the idea that what really matters is what is in your heart: if you have good intentions, and are trying to do what (God says) is right, that is all anyone can ask. Not so in medicine! If you are wrong—especially if you should have known better—your good intentions count for almost nothing. And whereas taking a leap of faith and acting without further scrutiny of one's options is often celebrated by religions, it is considered a grave sin in medicine. A doctor whose devout faith in his personal revelations about how to treat aortic aneurysm led him to engage in untested trials with human patients would be severely reprimanded if not driven out of medicine altogether. There are exceptions, of course. A few swashbuckling, risk-taking pioneers are tolerated and (if they prove to be right) eventually honored, but they can exist only as rare exceptions to the ideal of the methodical investigator who scrupulously rules out alternative theories before putting his own into practice. Good intentions and inspiration are simply not enough.

In other words, whereas religions may serve a benign purpose by letting many people feel comfortable with the level of morality they themselves can attain, no religion holds its members to the high standards of moral responsibility that the secular world of science and medicine does! And I'm not just talking about the standards "at the top"—among the surgeons and doctors who make life or death decisions every day. I'm talking about the standards of conscientiousness endorsed by the lab technicians and meal preparers, too. This tradition puts its faith in the unlimited application of reason and empirical inquiry, checking and rechecking, and getting in the habit of asking "What if I'm wrong?" Appeals to faith or membership are never tolerated. Imagine the reception a scientist would get if he tried to suggest that others couldn't replicate his results because they just didn't share the faith of the people in his lab! And, to return to my main point, it is the goodness of this tradition of reason and open inquiry that I thank for my being alive today.

What, though, do I say to those of my religious friends (and yes, I have quite a few religious friends) who have had the courage and honesty to tell me that they have been praying for me? I have gladly forgiven them, for there are few circumstances more frustrating than not being able to help a loved one in any more direct way. I confess to regretting that I could not pray (sincerely) for my friends and family in time of need, so I appreciate the urge, however clearly I recognize its futility. I translate my religious friends' remarks readily enough into one version or another of what my fellow brights [an attempt by me and others to popularize a new term for unbelievers; see chapter 27] have been telling me: "I've been thinking about you, and wishing with all my heart [another ineffective but irresistible self-indulgence] that you come through this OK." The fact that these dear friends have been thinking of me in this way, and have taken an effort to let me know, is in itself, without any need for a supernatural supplement, a wonderful tonic. These messages from my family and from friends around the world have been literally heart-warming in my case, and I am grateful for the boost in morale (to truly manic heights, I fear!) that it has produced in me. But I am not joking when I say that I have had to forgive my friends who said that they were praying for me. I have resisted the temptation to respond "Thanks, I appreciate it, but did you also sacrifice a goat?" I feel about this the same way I would feel if one of them said "I just paid a voodoo doctor to cast a spell for your health." What a gullible waste of money that could have been spent on more important projects! Don't expect me to be grateful, or even indifferent. I do appreciate the affection and generosity of spirit that motivated you, but wish you had found a more reasonable way of expressing it.

But isn't this awfully harsh? Surely it does the world no harm if those who can honestly do so pray for me! No, I'm not at all sure about that. For one thing, if they really wanted to do something useful, they could devote their prayer time and energy to some pressing project that they can do something about. For another, we now have quite solid grounds (e.g., the recently released Benson study at Harvard) for believing that intercessory prayer simply doesn't work. Anybody whose practice shrugs off that research is subtly undermining respect for the very goodness I am thanking. If you insist on keeping the myth of the effectiveness of prayer alive, you owe the rest of us a justification in the face of the evidence. Pending such a justification, I will excuse you for indulging in your tradition; I know how comforting tradition can be. But I want you to recognize that what you are doing is morally problematic at best. If you would even consider filing a malpractice suit against a doctor who made a mistake in treating you, or suing a pharmaceutical company that didn't conduct all the proper control tests before selling you a drug that harmed you, you must acknowledge your tacit appreciation of the high standards of rational inquiry to which the medical world holds itself, and yet you continue to indulge in a practice for which there is no known rational justification at all, and take yourself to be actually making a contribution. (Try to imagine your outrage if a pharmaceutical company responded to your suit by blithely replying "But we prayed good and hard for the success of the drug! What more do you want?")

The best thing about saying thank goodness in place of thank God is that there really are lots of ways of repaying your debt to goodness—by setting out to create more of it, for the benefit of those to come. Goodness comes in many forms, not just medicine and science. Thank goodness for the music of, say, Randy Newman, which could not exist without all those wonderful pianos and recording studios, to say nothing of the musical contributions of every great composer from Bach through Wagner to Scott Joplin and the Beatles. Thank goodness for fresh drinking water in the tap, and food on our table. Thank goodness for fair elections and truthful journalism. If you want to express your gratitude to goodness, you can plant a tree, feed an orphan, buy books for schoolgirls in the Islamic world, or contribute in thousands of other ways to the manifest improvement of life on this planet now and in the near future.

Or you can thank God—but the very idea of repaying God is ludicrous. What could an omniscient, omnipotent Being (the Man Who Has Everything?) do with any paltry repayments from you? (And besides, according to the Christian tradition God has already redeemed the debt for all time, by sacrificing his own son. Try to repay that loan!) Yes, I know, those themes are not to be understood literally; they are symbolic. I grant it, but then the idea that by thanking God you are actually doing some good has got to be understood to be just symbolic, too. I prefer real good to symbolic good.

Still, I excuse those who pray for me. I see them as like tenacious scientists who resist the evidence for theories they don't like long after a graceful concession would have been the appropriate response. I applaud you for your loyalty to your own position— but remember: loyalty to tradition is not enough. You've got to keep asking yourself: What if I'm wrong? In the long run, I think religious people can be asked to live up to the same moral standards as secular people in science and medicine.

I've published seven books and dozens of articles in the sixteen years since that operation, and packed a lifetime of adventures around the world into that supplement of time granted by the goodness of those around me. How lucky can anybody get?

I once participated in a weekend gathering in Seattle of very smart high school kids, designed to inspire them to great achievements. There was an all-star cast, with several Nobel laureates, the novelist Amy Tan, the Google boys Sergey Brin and Larry Page, the glass sculptor Dale Chihuly, and other notables. What struck me about the fifteen-minute talks each of us gave to these attentive youngsters was that most of us focused on the role of luck: we had just happened to be in the right place at the right time, found the right mentors, made a few lucky stabs in the dark. This intense modesty was meant to put them at ease, but wouldn't it have an unintended side effect? "Don't think there's a reliable path to greatness. Just wing it, and if you're lucky you'll end up like us!" Were we just a convention of lottery winners telling others that there was no secret to our success?

I recently received an email from Peter Godfrey-Smith, the great philosopher/scuba diver/octopus researcher:

> Hi Dan,
> I am reading a stack of Mike Levin's work [my Tufts colleague with whom I had recently coauthored a paper].
> How is it that you always pick up the ultra-interesting stuff so quickly??
> Been doing it for a lot of decades.
> Best wishes,
> Peter

As it happens, I'd just been mulling over a version of the same question while composing this memoir. Luck, of course, does play a big role, especially at the outset, when part of the luck includes hitting on a good way to parlay the early luck into more luck—the rich get richer, as one says. Peter's question—luckily for me—suggested an answer I've only recently come to appreciate fully: he doesn't ask how I *came up with* the ultra-interesting stuff; he asks how I *picked it up* so quickly. I'm a pack rat, a magpie, always on the lookout for a useful tidbit. "This might come in handy someday," I think, as I add a discarded gear or connecting rod or other piece of machinery to my ever-expanding collection of thingamabobs, gadgets, and tools in my home workshop. My thinking machine—my brain—is similarly provisioned with lots of useful stuff I've picked up. I presented a gallery of over six dozen of my favorites in *Intuition Pumps and Other Tools for Thinking* (2013). I love to *fix things* with whatever might serve, and for all these decades, I've always wanted to know *how* "the magic" works. I like to quote a passage in Lee Siegel's excellent book on Indian street magic, *Net of Magic: Wonders and Deceptions in India* (1991):

> "I'm writing a book on magic," I explain, and I'm asked, "Real magic?" By real magic people mean miracles, thaumaturgical acts, and supernatural powers. "No," I answer: "Conjuring tricks, not real magic." Real magic, in other words, refers to the magic that is not real, while the magic that is real, that can actually be done, is not real magic. (p. 425)

Many people are eager to protect "real magic" in one way or another, and many of them find philosophy to be the ideal profession for this campaign. I'd say it is the distinguishing characteristic of one kind of philosopher. But then there are the antiphilosophers, who look at the mess made by the others and say to themselves, "Fie! I'm going to try to clear this all up!" My guides and heroes have been the folks—scientists and philosophers—who have hunches about how the tricks are done, how the illusions are generated. They are not just skeptics and debunkers but constructive explainers, groping for models or theories to replace the armchair verities of the philosophers with testable ideas.

Way back in my dissertation in 1965 I saw that the best—the only—way of making sense of the mind and consciousness is through evolution by natural selection on many levels, and I began sketching an open-ended framework for how that might run. And I kept philosophical phisticuffs in the background. My approach struck a chord in researchers in several different disciplines. They *got it* in one way or another and saw how they could add a few pieces to my emerging picture and fix a few flaws in their own work. They invited me to be a friendly interlocutor. I didn't have to go to them, philosopher's hat in hand, and ask if I could kibitz; they sought me out.

I somehow managed to create (or, more accurately, preside over the emergence of) an intellectual magnet that just kept bringing supersmart people into my orbit. I got used to being surrounded by people who knew a whole lot more than I did, and I was always happy to be tutored, especially when I disagreed with them. Some of my favorite arguments and examples have been forged in heated disputes with thinkers whose positions I largely reject, for reasons I now understand better than when I first confronted them. The physicist Wolfgang Pauli famously dismissed another physicist's ideas as "not even wrong," and I have opportunistically tried to fix some of the wrong ideas presented by physicist Roger Penrose, linguist Noam Chomsky, neuroscientist Christof Koch, and evolutionary biologists Stephen Jay Gould and David Sloan Wilson, among others. Then there were my long-standing battles with my fellow philosophers Thomas Nagel, Jerry Fodor, John Searle, and David Chalmers. Where would I be without all these brilliant mistakes to correct, with the help of my thinking tools? (For instance, I harnessed John Horton Conway's delicious Game of Life to find a middle ground between Fodor's unappealing "industrial-strength realism" and the equally unpersuasive "eliminativism" of Paul Churchland, in "Real Patterns" [1991], one of my most influential papers.) I won't have room to dwell on all the important details, but the endnotes provide links for those who want to check out my repairs and decide for themselves.

I have (so far) led a remarkably adventurous and fulfilling life, way beyond the most extravagant fantasies of my youth—and I was a cocksure young man with vaulting ambition. How did it happen? Was it all just luck, or "connections," or may I claim some credit for getting myself into my current happy state? Do I in any sense *deserve* the benefits I now enjoy?

I believe in free will, in a nonmagical sense that really matters. I think those who do good in the world deserve praise and rewards and those who do evil deserve to be punished, if they are competent self-controlling adults. I also believe that this kind of free will is not threatened by determinism, and have devoted three books and dozens of articles to defending this initially counterintuitive claim. Determinism is the claim that "there is at any instant exactly one possible future," but this does not imply *inevitability*. We, and other autonomous agents, avoid things every day. Determinism doesn't "tie your hands," nor does it prevent you from making and then reconsidering decisions, turning over a new leaf, learning from your mistakes. Determinism is not a puppeteer controlling you. If you're a normal adult, you have enough self-control to maintain your autonomy, and hence responsibility, in a world full of seductions and distractions. But even if I'm right that determinism is no threat to responsibility or autonomy, this wouldn't settle the question of whether or not I'm just a preternaturally lucky person who has made the most of the good fortune that has been my lot.

Actually, I haven't made the most of it. Somebody with a stronger character could have done much more. I have a lazy streak, I'm an undisciplined reader who is easily distracted, and I have an insatiable appetite for time wasters such as the comics in the newspaper, crossword puzzles, Scrabble (and better: Frigate Bird, an intense game played with Scrabble tiles but no board), sudoku, and Rubik's Cube. A brilliant childhood friend of mine became so addicted to playing bridge that he flunked out of college, and I could have done the same had I found a good partner at just the wrong time. I almost made the mistake at Harvard of not signing up for a course that would interfere with my late-morning game of pool at the Hasty Pudding Club! What was I thinking?

When I reflect on my narrow escapes from dissolution, I credit that very reflectiveness, which has often saved me in the nick of time. That and my willingness, when confronting a difficult moral decision, to ask—and *take*—the advice of friends, chief among them Susan, my wife of sixty years.

There are lessons to be learned from how I handled my own education and how I became such a *good thinker*. (The philosopher Don Ross once said of me, "Dan believes modesty is a virtue to be reserved for special occasions.") I wouldn't be writing this book if I didn't think I had something I could usefully impart to readers— the secrets of my success, my good tricks and policies, my ways of dealing with people and problems. There are many philosophers who are more clever, much better scholars, quicker in argument, vastly better at the technical moves philosophers make than I am. They will tell you so, and I will agree with them. But as Gilbert Ryle, my thesis supervisor at Oxford, told a colleague of mine over a few beers in Salzburg back in the '60s, "There are much cleverer chaps than Dennett, but he has a fire in his belly." I've gratefully leaned on that crutch now for more than half a century.

As you can see, I am not modest, but I am not overconfident either, like some thinkers I know. John Searle, one of my most aggressive critics, is actually a lot like me: sure of himself, impatient with nitpicking philosophers, willing to brand respected trains of thought as nonsense. When he encounters a philosophical argument or position that is difficult for him to comprehend, he rephrases it in his own terms—in terms that he understands. That's just what I do too. But when Searle's digest of the difficult idea strikes him as absurd, he thereupon says so, vehemently. I don't. I reserve judgment. I reflect: these people defending this view don't seem to be fools; maybe I've misconstrued them. I go back to their work to see if I can find a better version of their view. Sometimes I can't, and then I can be as tough a critic as Searle. But sometimes—in fact, usually—I can find a better version of the challenging idea, and then I've learned something. Searle's world is full of philosophical nincompoops; mine is full of philosophers who are learned, intelligent, hard-working but often self-defeating presenters of their best ideas. Why would anybody want to be a philosopher if philosophers in general were as stupid as Searle seems to think? (Sir Karl Popper is another philosopher whose low opinion of those who disagreed with him has made me wonder how he could stand being a philosopher.)

I wasn't always as confident as I am today about the topics I work on. In fact, I had long, scary periods when I wondered if I was cut out for this work at all and seriously considered abandoning philosophy and pursuing sculpture as more than a hobby. I'll say more about those doldrums later. Now, before I turn to the tale of my progress through academia, I want to make two generalizations about philosophers: Anybody who becomes a philosopher and never has any serious doubts about whether this is a wise life choice is not a very good philosopher. Anybody who never doubts their own abilities as a philosopher is not a very good philosopher. Yes, there are dozens, hundreds, of "distinguished" philosophers who show no signs (to me) of having harbored these insecurities, but I think their work is in general superficial and meretricious—dazzling footwork on issues of no real importance. I call it working out "the higher-order truths of chmess." "Chmess" is my name for a variation on chess in which the king can move two squares in any direction. It's probably never been played or ever been worth playing, and it's not worth finding out. Proving truths about chmess is no doubt as challenging as proving truths about chess, but much less important. Nobody cares or should care. The neuropsychologist Donald Hebb once observed, "If it's not worth doing, it's not worth doing well." Many dusty corners of academia—not just philosophy—would be depopulated if Hebb's rule were applied vigorously, but I strongly support the idea that nobody is qualified to judge which intellectual pursuits are not worth tolerating and even funding, so it is best to acknowledge that academia is in some measure a strikingly luxurious enterprise, keeping alive thousands of projects that will never "pay for themselves" in any recognizable way. We mustn't allow academia to become just another training ground for whatever workers seem to be required in the near future. Let a thousand flowers bloom, but remember that most of them will wilt or die.

I'VE BEEN THINKING

Part One

OFF TO A FAST START

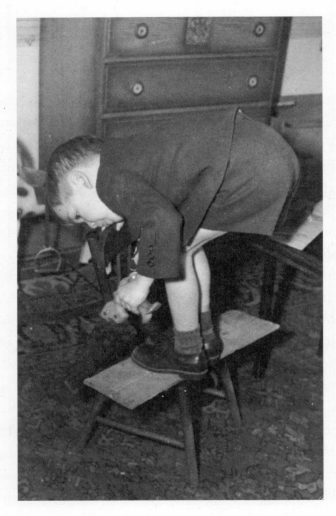

Solving a problem in Beirut, 1946

1.

CHILDHOOD

I WAS BORN IN BOSTON IN 1942, THE ONLY GRANDSON OF Daniel C. Dennett, who was a revered doctor in the Boston suburb of Winchester, and the son of Daniel C. Dennett Jr. I hated the "III" suffix (it seemed snobbish), so I became just Daniel C. Dennett, to the occasional confusion of librarians, who couldn't see how I could have a son who published "Pirenne and Muhammad" in *Speculum* in 1948. My father was a historian of early Islam and a master spy in the Office of Strategic Services and then the Central Intelligence Group, the forerunner of the CIA. He was killed on a mission in a plane crash in Ethiopia in 1947, when we were living in Beirut. My younger sister, Charlotte, an investigative journalist and lawyer, has published a book, *Follow the Pipelines* (2022), about her attempts to get to the bottom of that convoluted mystery, and my sisters and I were recently invited to the annual memorial service at the CIA, which has finally decided that Father was in fact the first CIA agent killed in action. He now has a star carved into the white marble Memorial Wall in the entrance to the Langley headquarters. My mother, Ruth, was an English teacher who left Minnesota to see the world, traveling to Beirut in the early '30s to teach at the American Community School (affiliated with the American University of Beirut), where she met my father, who was teaching there while researching for his PhD at Harvard in Islamic history and gallivanting all over the Middle East, learning Arabic and making friends.

Since my father died when I was just five years old, my memories (of memories of memories) of him are all quite foggy and rosy, but I adored him and loved to ride with him in his special Jeep. He even took me on nondangerous missions, having a young child in tow being a great disguise for an agent. A memento of one of those missions is two small scars on my ears; the Bedouins he was visiting had decided that I should have my ears pierced. Mother removed the strings as soon as I got back home in Beirut, but the closed slits are still apparent. Having heard wonderful tales of his adventures and accomplishments over the years from old family friends who knew him well, I gather he was a charismatic and charming fellow, a natural center of attention. At Phillips Exeter Academy, where I spent the last two years of high school, I got to know the sons of quite a few famous dads—novelists, diplomats, scientists, plutocrats—and noticed a syndrome among them: Some of these offspring (not all) were almost disabled by their efforts to be worthy intellectual companions to their brilliant dads. They were dauntingly articulate and knowing, very well read, intellectually superior in every way, it seemed, but often unable to get to the finish line—to get the term paper written, the problem set completed, the book review composed. I have often wondered whether I could have led the life I have led in the shadow of such an intellectual hero and adventurer had my father lived on. It was hard enough trying to live up to his near legendary status among my mother's friends, who would often insist, sometimes with tears in their eyes, that I was an uncanny replica of him, right down to the way I told stories and used words.

In Beirut, we lived in diplomatic comfort. America had no embassy in Lebanon then, only a legation, and Father was the cultural attaché. Our elegant house, right in the heart of Ras Beirut, on Bliss Street (then *rue* Bliss), had a high iron fence around a large garden, and we had a cook, an Armenian nanny, and a "chauffeur" who was often a babysitter/bodyguard for me and my older sister, Cynthia. Not a bad beginning for a life of intellectual adventure, with a gazelle (whom I named Babar, of course) in the garden and a house full of books and records and art.

For years I dreamed of somehow topping one of my father's most celebrated coups from the '30s. Fluent in German (and French and

Arabic), he followed the European press in Beirut and noted the passing of Peter Graf von Spaur, who left his large hilltop villa in Salzburg to his aging housekeeper. Dad wrote her a letter immediately, inquiring whether she would be interested in renting the furnished villa to him and his friends for the summer, while she figured out what to do. She replied gratefully that this would be an excellent plan and offered him breathtakingly easy terms. He immediately wrote to his Harvard friends and others who were studying in Europe, telling them of a grand house party he was hosting in Salzburg all summer long. They were all invited to join, staying as long as they liked so long as they contributed to the cost of meals and rent. Many showed up, filling the bedrooms, while the housekeeper cooked the meals and kept the villa intact. Regular concerts in the Mozarteum down in the town were followed by walking back up the hill with their neighbor, Richard Strauss, humming tunes and discussing the concert. The young harpsichordist Ralph Kirkpatrick could be counted on to play impromptu concerts on the veranda, while other musicians and artists and historians carried on through the night. My mother was one of the long-term guests, and in later years would get quite starry-eyed when recalling those golden Austrian nights.

After Father was killed in the plane crash, Mother packed up the family and our nanny and we returned to Massachusetts to live first with Grandpa and Grandma Dennett in Winchester and then in a modest house in the same town, purchased with the life insurance money Mother received from the government. She cleverly called the two local rug dealers, Messrs. Mouradian and Boodakian, and they arranged a series of, well, debutante parties introducing the nanny, Mary Bedoian, to dozens of eligible Armenian American bachelors. Two days before her allowed year of residence elapsed, she married a fine young garage mechanic, Johnny Mkjian, and settled down in nearby Watertown, which has a large Armenian community. We considered them extended family and kept Beirut memories and customs alive with them for decades.

Mother went to work in Boston as a social-studies editor at the textbook publisher Ginn & Co., while Edna ("Cookie") Anderson, a sort of Mary Poppins, became our second mother, running the household, packing our lunch boxes, correcting our few minor transgressions. Cookie had been a society woman, living in Newton with her husband, a successful interior decorator, but when the Depression hit they lost everything, and her husband left her with a mountain of debt. We were, I think, the third or fourth family she'd worked for, and she stayed with us for almost twenty years, becoming a beloved part of the family. Mother walked to the train station every weekday morning, commuting to Boston, and walked home from the station in the early evening, where Cookie and the kids would be waiting for her, supper ready after she'd had her bourbon on the rocks and read the mail. Some evenings I watched Mother editing textbook manuscripts at a card table in the living room. She would often explain to me what was wrong or flabby or misleading in a sentence she was surgically revising, a lesson that sank in. She instilled in me a sense of duty, really, to write clearly and forcefully.

Who were my surrogate father figures? First, there was Sherman Russell, who had been Father's best friend in high school and from whom Father had extracted a solemn promise to take care of "Ruth and the kids" if anything happened to him in Beirut. Sherm kept his promise magnificently and came close to proposing to Mother. (He never married but I adored him and was all in favor of the marriage that never happened.) Sherm met us when our boat landed in New York City, and after a few days in the city—including a trip to the Bronx Zoo—he brought us to Winchester. It was Sherm who gave me my beloved Erector set, which got me started building things. I went on to produce a tree house in the backyard apple tree, model sailboats, and a Lionel electric-train table with lots of switches and houses and bridges. Sherm was also a horseman of considerable expertise, flying to Ireland every year to be one of the three "joint masters" of the fox hunt at the legendary Lady Molly Cusack's estate, Bermingham.

One weekend when Cookie was away, Mother hosted a few of her office mates for a lobster dinner at our house, but, Midwesterner that she was, she made the mistake of putting the four live lobsters she bought into a bucket of fresh water in the basement. They were dead and inedible when she learned her mistake and sent me, with my brand-new driver's license, off to the fish market to buy four more. Done, but what should we do with the embarrassing green corpses? Putting them in the in-ground garbage pail wouldn't do, because Cookie would see them Monday morning when she emptied the coffee grounds and would tease Mother about it for years. What to do? Simple. I called Sherm: "Mother has made a terrible terrible mistake and, . . . we have some dead bodies to hide."

"How many?"

"Four."

"Where are they now?"

"In the trunk of the car."

After a brief pause, Sherm said, "OK, Danny. Listen carefully. Drive to my house. I'll be in the garage and I'll open the door when I see you coming and then close the door as soon as you're in. We'll figure something out. Drive carefully! Don't speed." He was more amused than furious when he saw the dead lobsters, which he promptly dropped into his own garbage pail. That was a measure of how far Sherm was prepared to go to keep his promise to my father.

Another father figure was my scoutmaster (yes, I'm an Eagle Scout), Paul Butterworth, a commercial artist who encouraged me to develop my drawing and cartooning skills. More influential still were some of the counselors at Camp Mowglis, on Newfound Lake in New Hampshire, where I spent seven summers, from 1951 to 1958, first as a camper and then as a counselor teaching sailing and canoeing. Ed Lincoln, the sailing instructor, taught me to sail and also introduced me to jazz; he was a drummer and his brother played trumpet. Other counselors were influential in other ways. For me, Mowglis was the best part of the year, and as I look back on those years I find I have only a few vivid memories of grade school and the first two years of high school, but detailed, vivid memories of the eight weeks I spent at Mowglis each July and August.

I had two wonderful teachers of ancient history in my freshman year (1955–56) at Winchester High School: Catherine Laguardia and Michael Greenebaum. They were young interns from the Harvard master's program in teaching, and they lit fires in me. Miss Laguardia inspired me to write a term paper on Plato (complete with a drawing of Rodin's *Thinker* on the cover), and while I understood only a few of Plato's ideas, I put him in my pantheon of thinkers to study later. Mr. Greenebaum was my hero, whose ways of opening young imaginations convinced me that I should become a teacher. Our term paper for him was to make up an imaginary ancient Mediterranean civilization and give an account of its history, its wars, and its culture. I poured my energy into the illustrated history of "Lucrenia," complete with maps, the birth of a new religion, a few wars, and some architectural advances.

I also had one spectacularly bad English teacher, a pompous snob who arrived at Winchester High School from elsewhere with accolades and testimonials. (I won't name him, but if any of my classmates read this book they will know of whom I write.) One day in class he announced, as if it were an obvious, unvarnished fact, that Shakespeare was the greatest man who ever lived. I'd had enough of his *obiter dicta* and raised my hand. When he called on me, I said that perhaps Shakespeare was the greatest *writer* of all time, but what about other fields of endeavor? What about Alexander the Great or Albert Einstein or J. Christ of biblical fame? His retort was dismissive, but after that day, whenever he issued one of his many fatuous remarks I would raise my hand. He seldom called on me, and when he didn't, I would quietly get up and gather my books and walk out of the classroom. He never turned me in, and I treasured the A for work and F for comportment he assigned me at the end of the year.

In 1957 I went off to Exeter for the last two years of high school, cajoled by old academic friends of my father (Harvard professors and the like) who insisted it would be the right place for me. Grandpa Dennett paid the tuition, and they were right. Wonderful teachers, wonderful classmates, wonderful projects. My writing skills were honed by the renowned George Bennett, whose students included Gore Vidal, Peter Benchley, and John Irving, among others. My sculptural skills—first awakened under the benign eye of Thayer Garland, who taught me to whittle at Mowglis—took me into piece molds and metal under the inspiration of Glen Krause, a painter whose studio at Exeter was a second home to me in 1958–59. A few years later, when I was a student at Harvard, a Newbury Street gallery in Boston put on a two-man show: paintings by Glen Krause and sculptures by Daniel Dennett. When I told my mother I was about to have a show on Newbury Street, she realized she could dash over during her lunch hour from Ginn & Co. to see it. Before I told her the name of the gallery, I made her promise not to reveal that she was the Mother of the Artist. She went over while they were still hanging Glen's paintings, and there were no signs up yet identifying the artists. She saw a new sculpture of mine in a rather different style and medium than I had been working in, and she asked the gallery owner who the sculptor was. "Oh, that's a new work by a very exciting young Italian sculptor, Danielo Dennetti." This is a main reason I am not heavily involved in the art world now. I love the company of artists, but I can't stand gallery owners, art critics, or—sad to say—many of the people who can afford to buy original art. Selling a piece to them often seemed to me like a betrayal—like giving them a child of mine. I did have a show of my "haptic whittles" in the Underdonk Gallery in Brooklyn in 2017, but none of the pieces were for sale. (In my dislike of gallery owners, I make an exception for Nicholas Cueva, who runs that gallery the right way.)

In my class of some two hundred seniors at Exeter in 1959, about forty went off to Harvard, and I was expected by the family to go there as well. My father had been a tutor at Harvard in Eliot House for several years while Cynthia and I were toddlers, and had been offered a chair there in 1947, just before he was killed in the plane crash. We had good friends on the faculty. But I wanted to be a little independent and had been impressed by Wesleyan University in Middletown, Connecticut, so off I went.

2.

MUSIC:
AN IMPORTANT
DIGRESSION

OUR FAMILY LOVED MUSIC. IN BEIRUT WE HAD A PHOnograph that played the big 78 rpm records that had to be flipped every few minutes, quite a chore if you wanted to listen to a whole Beethoven symphony. We had an upright piano in Beirut and when we moved back to the States in 1947 after Father's death, Grandma Dennett gave us her cherished old Steinway grand. That became a central feature of our home in Winchester, and I have it in my home now. Cynthia and I began piano lessons immediately, with Louisa Parkhurst, a dear but ancient teacher who had been a student of Dame Myra Hess, whom she rightly idolized. Miss Parkhurst was a softy, more concerned with feeling and the Leschetizky Method, which involved relaxing the forearms and hands and caressing the keys (as I remember), so I was spared a lot of stern fingering drills and Hanon exercises and had minimal practice in sight-reading. My mother was an excellent pianist, and I loved to hear her play at night while I was falling asleep upstairs, but I never managed to become a good sight reader like her, very much to my regret. She had earned money in college in Minnesota by playing the piano accompaniments for silent movies—several different movies each week, a challenge that she apparently handled with aplomb. I couldn't seem to train myself to look ahead sufficiently and always wanted to dwell with both eyes and ears on the chords I was reading and playing at the moment—like reading a book one word at a time. I often fell asleep listening to Mother downstairs, working on new pieces or playing some of her favorites, Bach's "Jesu, Joy of Man's Desiring" and Rachmaninoff's Prelude in E-flat Major, both of which choke me up every time I hear them.

We often sang around the piano with Mother playing whatever we put in front of her: Christmas carols, Gilbert and Sullivan songs, sheet music from *South Pacific* and *My Fair Lady* and other musicals, and camp songs and folk songs, especially from our favorite collection, the *Fireside Book of Folk Songs*. Over the years, I've often spotted that beloved green book on the pianos of friends who also grew up with it. It has beautiful and easy piano accompaniments by Norman Lloyd, and a gentle left-wing emphasis that I recognized only many years later. Most Americans today, I guess, could sing "Home on the Range" or "I've Been Workin' on the Railroad," but we Firesiders can also sing "Joe Hill" and "Hallelujah, I'm a Bum" and even the Russian song "Meadowlands." We also sang hymns. Mother wasn't a regular churchgoer, unlike Grandma Dennett, but she sent us to Sunday school, and we learned dozens of hymns there, which we enjoyed—and still enjoy—singing.

When I was about thirteen, I tired of Miss Parkhurst. I'd performed various classical pieces at various recitals to polite applause, but while I loved the musical experience, I was getting excited about jazz. Cynthia and I, like most kids our age in the '50s, listened to popular music on a few favorite radio stations, and each week we eagerly watched NBC's *Your Hit Parade* (sponsored by Lucky Strike and featuring Dorothy Collins, Snooky Lanson, and Gisele MacKenzie) to find out if our favorite song of the moment had moved up from number seven or maybe even fallen off the Top Ten. But the pop music of that era, just at the dawn of rock 'n' roll, was schmaltzy mush, and I didn't want to play *that* music on the piano. Miss Parkhurst, trying to revive my enthusiasm, assigned me, in vain, the sheet music for "Shrimp Boats Are A-Comin'" and Leroy Anderson's "Syncopated Clock."

Mother found a jazz piano teacher for me in Boston. Each week

I made the trip into Boston on the train, took the subway to Copley Square, and walked past Jack's Drum Shop and Storyville, the city's top jazz nightclub, to Alan Smith's studio. It was a very grown-up adventure, and I was hooked. He taught me basic harmony: the chords, the circle of fifths, twelve-bar blues, jazz voicings, comping for soloists, the excellence of flatted fifths; and we explored various styles: stride like Teddy Wilson, the two-hands-together octave crawl of George Shearing, Erroll Garner's distinctive percussive flamboyance, Count Basie's minimalism. I went to the local music store and discreetly paid my twenty dollars under the table for my first "fake book." This was standard gear for any pianist who wanted to play in pickup dance-combos or small jazz groups, since it had all the jazz and dance standards of the day mimeographed in a black three-ring binder, with two or three songs on each page, providing the melody in its standard key, the chords, and—in case you had a vocalist—the words. The fake book was an illegal and anonymous *samizdat* production, inspired by and often plagiarized from an expensive legal system, Tune-Dex, which mailed subscribers three-by-five index cards with standard songs on them. Tune-Dex paid royalties for publishing these cards; the fake book didn't, but I have never heard of anyone getting arrested for selling or openly using one. So I learned to read lead sheets (or "charts"), and since there was only the familiar melody to sight-read and I knew how to make all the chords, I could rattle off the songs of George Gershwin, Cole Porter, Irving Berlin, Richard Rodgers, and about a thousand other songs with some fluency. I could even follow up the first chorus with further choruses, improvising on the chords alone. I soon learned to "play by ear" and could sit down at a piano and play requests of almost any popular song, almost always guessing the chord progressions, and changing the key if need be to suit the singers' voices.

Whereas I had often found excuses not to do my daily practice session when studying with Miss Parkhurst, I now spent hours every day playing from the fake book, or just playing new songs I had heard. *Jazz!* Good enough to be the pianist in the pit band in 1957 for the Winchester High School annual vaudeville show, a much beloved event for which students—cliques and singles—would form acts and audition. There were singers and dancers and jugglers and acrobats and skits and dog trainers and barbershop quartets. Many of the acts were groups of girls dancing to some popular song, and they rehearsed to 45 rpm records, which they then handed to me to transcribe for the pit band. That was a great learning experience, since the band, under the direction of Chip Mead (son of a Tufts professor who later became president of Tufts—my Tufts links go way back), had Mead on alto sax, plus a trumpet and trombone and guitarist, along with piano, bass, and drums, so I had to write parts for E-flat and B-flat instruments as well as a lead sheet for the guitarist, the bassist, and me.

I also was given the job of rehearsal and performance pianist for the annual Tap Chorus. Girls took tap-dancing lessons then, and the school had wisely hired one of the local dance teachers to coach all comers in a Rockettes-style Tap Chorus. You didn't have to be in a popular clique to be in this act. The song chosen that year was Cole Porter's "Anything Goes," and for several hours a week after school, for what seemed months, I dutifully labored at the ivories while the girls were led through the drill.

By the time of the dress rehearsal (with an audience), I was utterly sick of the song, though Cole Porter is still a hero of mine. The plan was that the girls would get lined up in position behind the curtain, at which point a tiny light would go on in the pit telling me to begin the intro, which was just the last eight bars of the chorus. Just me, no pit band in accompaniment—the audience had to be able to hear the taps, after all. The curtain would start to open, revealing all the spangled beauties in a fetching pose, and they would begin the routine as soon as the intro ended. The little light went on, I began the intro, and looked up to see that the curtain was not opening. What to do? I decided I'd just play through a whole thirty-two-bar chorus, counting on the curtain to rise during the last eight bars of it and off we'd go. But when I got to that point the curtain *still* didn't go up, and I had already committed to the next few notes, so I played another chorus and stopped. The audience was puzzled. Why was this piano solo happening? It wasn't in the program. They politely applauded, and I stood and turned and politely took a bow, hating every moment. I waited. Now the light came on, but I didn't budge until the coach stuck her head out of the curtain and whispered, "Now we're ready!" So with mounting apprehension I did the eight-bar intro, and sure enough, there they were, dancing in pretty good unison. At last! But in my relief I didn't pay sufficient attention to what I was doing, and in the third or fourth chorus I got momentarily lost and played the bridge ("The world's gone mad today, and good's bad today, . . .") eight bars early. As it turned out, roughly half the girls (randomly positioned) had used the change in the music to trigger the next dance move, and the other half were just silently counting and not paying attention to the melody. Train wreck! You can imagine the confusion, anger, embarrassment, accusations, tears, but however you imagine it, the reality was worse. Happily the three official performances of the Tap Chorus went off without a hitch, and at least some of the girls eventually forgave me.

Off to Exeter I went the next year, and most evenings when I wasn't playing bridge I hid out in the basement of Phillips Church, where there were practice rooms, pianos, and you could smoke. Of course, that was where the jazz happened, and there were some budding talents who knew a lot more than I did about jazz. One classmate, Tim Marquand, had an amazing ability: he was the first person I ever encountered who could *really* play by ear. He'd listen to a new jazz piece and without having to figure out what the chord sequence was (is that E-flat ma7, Gm, C9, . . . ?) would just lay into it on his trumpet with improvisations that were fine, tasty, surprising. Years later it struck me that these two different ways of playing by ear—swiftly applying a theory, or just hearing and doing without having to think hard about it—were parallel to the distinction between how Temple Grandin, the autistic animal expert, understands other people and the way most people do. As she tells us, she has worked out how to read the meanings of facial expressions and gestures and uses this perceptual data in her theory to figure out what others intend and want and know. I am, you might say, an autistic jazz pianist. This is one of the reasons why I have always disliked the popular TOM (theory of mind) version of the intentional stance in cognitive science. Temple Grandin has a TOM, a *theory* that she has put together and uses with great skill. The cognitive processes by which we "normal" people "read minds" are more like walking. Do you have a theory of walking that you use to keep from falling over? We are not Walking Encyclopedias. I think there are better, less intellectual, ways of explaining these standard competences, but they aren't in place yet, though many are making progress on it.

There was another fountain of jazz memes among the students in that smoke-filled basement: Ron Brown, who was a true scholar of jazz in addition to being an excellent hard-bop pianist. When he was sixteen, he wrote record reviews for *DownBeat*, and the dean of reviewers, Leonard Feather, praised him in print. Ron knew I would never be a pianist as talented as he was, but he was a good friend and enjoyed teaching me changes and riffs and other things. Some years later, when we were both Harvard students, we ran into each other in Paris in the summer and went to Le Chat Qui Pêche, where Chet Baker and his band were playing. I stayed until after midnight, when Ron egged me on to ask to sit in. This was granted, and I giddily did perhaps ten choruses of blues in F with these immortals and returned, flushed, to our table. Then Ron got up and began playing, and they really paid attention. I left after one o'clock in the morning with Ron still sitting in, and he showed up at my Left Bank hotel while I was having a late breakfast at about ten the next day. When I remarked that he was up early, he said he was just then getting back from the jam session. He was brilliant but insecure, and sadly a few years later he committed suicide. I never found out the details.

The next year at Exeter, I was singing about seven hours a week in the glee club (a good way to meet girls, since the glee club traveled to girls' schools for joint concerts and a dance afterward) and the choir (a good way to learn hymns, anthems, and other religious music) and the Rockingham Choral Society, a fine regional group for which you had to audition. When I told my classmates I could arrange songs, I was instantly in demand, writing a capella music for a would-be Hi-Lo's-style quartet and then the Peadquacs (Phillips Exeter Academy Double Quartet), our version of the Whiffenpoofs. I was added to the Peadquacs as a baritone, and two tenors and a bass were added, making a dozen singers in all. I was soon singing ten hours a week and more, and staying up late, pirating songs from records (such as the Princeton Tigertones' delicious version of "Button Up Your Overcoat") and writing some jazz arrangements of "Ain't Misbehavin'" (with "Keepin' Out of Mischief Now" thrown in) and "Moonlight in Vermont," among others. We made an LP record and flogged it on our concert dates, which were mainly those glee club dances. I can hardly bear to listen to it now, but it sold well at girls' prep schools. We *almost* got a gig singing at a hotel in Bermuda during spring break, but some parents put their feet down—wisely, I think in retrospect. I spent parts of that year—and never again—in a world quite different from any I had experienced, with classmates whose bathroom mirrors were festooned with engraved invitations to cotillions and balls. We Peadquacs had tuxedos, and white dinner jackets for summer gigs, and I will never forget sliding down the banisters in the Plaza Hotel in New York with Carol Channing, for whom we opened at the Gold and Silver Ball of 1958.

When I went off to Wesleyan the next year, I met another real musician, Stanley Lewis, who was also a superb artist and has made his career as a painter. We formed a quartet (piano, bass, and drums, with Stan on alto sax) and played at fraternity parties that year, and one night we particularly got it together and played some amazing jazz. The next day, I said to Stan that I wished it had been recorded, and he jumped on me. "NO! Don't try to *accumulate* things like that as if they made you somehow *better*. Last night was a trip. Be grateful it happened, but now let go of it." That was Stan the purist, and I got the message: I had apparently been luxuriating in my Exeter achievements (probably obnoxiously), and now I should just abandon them all and turn to the next adventure.

At the age of eighteen, then, I knew that however fluent I became in applied music theory, however adept my fingers were on the keys when I "played by ear," I'd never be a natural musician like Stan, like Tim. I'd always be an amateur, in the right sense—a lover, an informed enjoyer, of music. I learned another life-changing lesson from Stan: that I would never be as good at painting or drawing as he was. I had prided myself on my artistic abilities since I was a little boy, spending many hours drawing with crayons, pencils, pen and ink; painting with watercolors and oils; and doing cartoons for the Boy Scout troop's weekly mimeographed newspaper, Exeter publications, and the jacket cover for the Peadquacs record. But I'd had an inkling of my limitations when I saw the casual, unplanned but elegant ink cartoons done by my classmate Dave Fairchild at Exeter, and Stan confirmed my hunch. We spent a few evenings in my dorm room doing pencil sketches of each other on good drawing paper. Stan would sit and read while I carefully plotted out my sketch, roughing in a few important lines, refining them, erasing the near misses, closing in on what I wanted to do. When I had finished about ten or fifteen minutes later, there he was on the paper, Stan. But it was always a bit off, no matter how hard I tried. Stan would then take out his sketchpad and—whip whip zip zip—dash off a sketch of me in about a minute that just sang on the page, graceful lines that captured me eloquently. I had no idea anybody could do that! Ever since then, I've looked at artists' work to see signs of this spectacular draftsmanship. Alphonse Mucha, the great Czech artist of the Art Nouveau era, is one. Some of his pencil sketches, clearly dashed off in a few seconds, are breathtakingly graceful and inventive. Salvador Dalí, most of whose work I don't much like, did some pencil sketches and ink drawings that are stunning tours de force. The great Botticelli illustrations for Dante's *Divine Comedy* are also delicious—but if you look closely you'll notice that Botticelli, just like us lesser talents, had some well-practiced riffs that were not as generalizable as you might think. He does exquisite hands, but only in about a dozen positions, rather theatrical gestures mainly. When he is obliged to do hands performing some task other than a gesture, he often ends up with a quite clumsy hand, a hand I could have drawn and not been proud of. I might add that many illustrators of old-fashioned comic books or today's graphic novels, looked down on as art by many people, often exhibit these exquisite skills. I remember when I was about twelve realizing that my Roy Rogers comic books showed Roy in action from many angles with just a few simple lines, and it was always Roy, looking just the way he looked in the movies and on television. I wished I could do that and spent many hours trying. Speed, I came to realize, is more important— both in art and in music—than I had thought. Some creative processes just have to dash ahead without a lot of forethought, without a lot of approximation and correction. If you can't nail it on the first bold try, you're not going to get it. But sculpture was different. You could work in modeling clay, for instance, and sneak up on the final result, nibbling here, reworking there, until you were satisfied.

Back to music. When I transferred to Harvard, I sent an arrangement of "Angel Eyes" to the Krokodiloes, Harvard's a capella group. Fred Ford, the Kroks' talented leader, wrote me a generous and instructive rejection letter, noting the various weak points in my submission. OK, so much for that career option. I also put my name on a list somebody kept of available combo musicians. (Have fake book, will travel.) But I never went out on a gig, since my available weekends were largely spent courting Susan, my wife-to-be.

My musical experience at Harvard was singing in the glee club and as a member of the Saengerfest Club of Boston, to which Sherm Russell introduced me. It was a men's chorus that met for dinner and drinks at the Harvard Club on Commonwealth Avenue. For my initiation as a member, I was asked to introduce a piece and teach it to the group. I chose the last chorus of Mozart's "Freimaurer Kantate," a short, sweet, simple piece for men's voices: *Lasst uns mit geschlungnen Händen, Brüder diese Arbeit enden.* Mozart is relatively easy to sing but hard to sing well. We went through it several times, and then it was dropped, but I enjoyed my membership throughout my Harvard years. I continued playing solo jazz piano, trying to elevate my game, and discovered a pattern: I would polish up my latest collection of moves and riffs, usually pleasing listeners who weren't good jazz musicians, but after a while I would realize I was stuck in a groove that was irritatingly shallow. I wanted to play something new (to me), but I couldn't "hear" anything else to try—that is, no new musical *intentions* were popping up in my head. Then I'd hear some variant on a record or the radio that pleased me, and it might take me days to figure out how to do it and when I shouldn't use it because it wouldn't work. My playing would be adventurous and exploratory until I mastered the new thing and began exploiting it, but then it would soon become just another routine trick in my bag. This was, of course, the development of my "style," and I wondered whether Erroll Garner or Count Basie had similar fallow periods when they were just playing well-worn imitations of themselves. Perhaps.

Every now and then it would all fall into place for me, and for a few minutes or a few hours I would find the sweet spot and play what I wanted to play and be fulfilled. It struck me then that the records I listened to over and over were no doubt highly selected from much less glorious versions. Miles Davis's incandescent "Bye Bye Blackbird" or Bill Evans's haunting piano on "So What?" were sweet spots. *Nobody could make music like that every day, could they?* Maybe Stan Lewis was wrong: record everything and throw away everything but the sweet spots. Fortunately, I found a profession where I could do just that. I've published over a dozen books and hundreds of articles, but they are the tip of an iceberg. Multiple Drafts is not just the name of my consciousness model; it describes my thinking and writing process.

While at Oxford, I found I couldn't live without playing some instrument, so I did a very British thing: I bought a recorder (a wooden flute, not a tape recorder) and was soon fippling away unobtrusively, playing along with a Brandenburg Concerto on a record or just trying to make up haunting melodies. When Susan and I joined Mother and my sisters in Beirut in the summer of 1964, I found Charlotte playing the guitar and had to pick up one of those as well. In addition to learning and playing the folk-rock repertoire of the day—such as Joan Baez's "East Virginia," "Copper Kettle," and "Skewball," and Bob Dylan's "Blowin' in the Wind" and "Don't Think Twice, It's All Right"—I specialized in the songs of the great French poet and singer Georges Brassens. I had all his records and learned to play most of his wise, funny, achingly romantic songs, while improving my French (minus the Midi accent) and my finger-picking. I had been captivated by Baez since hearing her sing and play at the 47 Mount Auburn club in Harvard Square while I was still at Exeter, and years later I was able to attend one of Georges Brassens's last concerts at the Bobino in Paris. *"Mourir pour des idées, . . . D'accord, mais la mort lente."* Die for ideas—OK, but a slow death.

Then there was the accordion. Mother's brother, Uncle Paul in Minnesota, had sent me his when he first heard I was learning to play jazz, and I soon had it in control. I particularly enjoyed taking the panel off so I could figure out the mechanism behind the finger buttons on the left-hand side. There it was, the circle of fifths, laid out geometrically, each button moving a metal bar with twigs on it that moved other bars. The C button had a little depression in it so you could always find it by touch, and you could go up to G, then D, then A, then E, then B, or you could go down: F, B-flat, E-flat, A-flat, D-flat, G-flat. Tonic, major third, major triad, minor triad, and dominant seventh. Just move up or down the button board to get to the next key. The diminished chord was missing (this was an old Hohner), which presented some minor problems to solve. I soon understood why the standard accordion solo on beginner talent contests was Rodgers and Hart's "Lover," since the chord changes move chromatically, half step at a time, defying the circle of fifths and requiring accurate leaps on the buttons. About twenty years ago I bought a curious "diatonic" button accordion at a yard sale. No piano keys, just buttons, and, like a harmonica, producing a different note for each button when breathing in and breathing out. I made a chart showing all the notes for each button, but I've never figured out the system well enough to play anything. My hunch is that it was designed to make playing a particular genre easier—Lithuanian waltzes? Turkish marches? In principle, you could make an accordion that played just one song: you advance idiotically from button to button until you reach the end, at which point you will have played the whole piece flawlessly.

As a camp counselor, I used my accordion to accompany singing around the campfire, and when I was a Harvard student I had the pleasure of teaching my friend Mark DeVoto, later a professor of music at Tufts, how to play my accordion. Why? We were both in the same German class, and our teacher, Frau Behrend, wanted us to sing some German folk songs in class. I balked but he was willing, and, professional musician that he already was, he performed splendidly with only a few hours of practice. Much later, Alan Bern, one of the world's greatest accordion players—when Itzhak Perlman put together a klezmer band, he asked Alan to be his accordionist—came to Tufts' master's program to work with me on philosophy of mind (not accordion playing!) and showed me a few licks and gave me an old accordion he didn't need. While I occasionally get it out, I don't inflict my efforts on anyone else.

Alan, by the way, is one of three keyboard virtuosi who have been my students at Tufts. Alan came to work with me after taking courses with Doug Hofstadter at Indiana. Christopher Taylor came to take classes with me after graduating from Harvard, while he was polishing off a doctorate in music at the New England Conservatory, which, along with the Museum School at the Boston Museum of Fine Arts, has a special relationship to Tufts. Their students get to take regular Tufts courses, for credit, and I love it when Conservatory or Museum School students show up in my classes. They don't care about grades; they're in it for intellectual thrills and are typically audacious and keen critics. Christopher ("Kit") dazzled in my seminar on free will, before going on to his concertizing and a chair at the University of Wisconsin. More about him later. Aaron Goldberg, another Harvard graduate, came to our master's program in philosophy to work with me. No sooner had he enrolled than he was invited by Wynton Marsalis to be the pianist in the big jazz band Marsalis took on an educational world tour. That was not an opportunity to be missed, so we video-recorded all the classes and put them online just for Aaron, who could watch them during his breaks in Tokyo or Mumbai or Istanbul. Aaron wrote me an excellent term paper and was awarded the MA in philosophy but has never gone on to try for a PhD, since his life has been full of concerts and recordings.

While I was teaching at the University of California at Irvine in the '60s, I got the university to buy a piano, bass, and drums and install them in a student hangout room for anybody to use, and we formed a little trio, with me playing bass, not piano, since John Wallace, a psychologist, was a better pianist than I was. My fingers soon got tough, and we gave a concert or two. I sat in on piano, occasionally, in the trio and at a bar on the Newport Beach waterfront, but that was the extent of my public jazz playing.

In recent years, my musical activities have been confined to our annual Christmas carol sing and potluck dinner (with Mark DeVoto as accompanist) and to singing with the New England Classical Singers. I joined that estimable group back in the '90s, when it was called the Merrimack Valley Chorale, and joyously sang with the basses for perhaps fifteen years, going through the great choral music of many centuries, from William Byrd and Giovanni Gabrieli to contemporary composers, even singing debuts of some commissioned pieces. We also formed an octet to sing motets and madrigals. When I first joined the group, one of the officers called me at home and Susan answered, hearing "This is Jill, from the *corral*. Can I please speak to Dan?" Susan scowled as she handed me the phone: "Is this woman from that country-western roadhouse you've been aching to go to?" Later, when we voted to change the name, I submitted two candidates, neither of which won: *Byrd Lyves* (bop lovers will get it) and *The OK Chorale*.

Eventually my travel and lecture schedule became too cluttered, and I had to drop out. Singers were allowed one or maybe two missed rehearsals in the months before concerts, but I was missing half a dozen. Although I practiced on my own and almost always showed up at rehearsals knowing the music as well as anybody else, I didn't think it was fair to the other singers, so I quit, attending the concerts when I could from behind the conductor, not in front of him. One earlier spring morning when I was driving to Tufts singing along with my practice tape, it struck me that two of the pieces we were doing, from Brahms's gorgeous *Liebeslieder Walzer* (Love Song Waltzes), if lowered in pitch and slowed down considerably, would make a terrific country-western waltz. Yes, I do love the best of country-western music, especially in the spring and summer, though I don't understand how its fan base can both love the great stuff and support the dreck that makes up most of the genre. In this case, the two *Liebeslieder* were the piece for male voices only, number 14: "Sieh, wie ist die Welle klar"; and the female-voices-only number 13, "Vögelein, durchrauscht die Luft." You could write new lyrics, do number 14 twice, then use number 13, the women's "response," as a bridge and return to a final run through number 14. I thought of it as a slow-dreamy waltz along the lines of Emmylou Harris's fine "The Last Cheater's Waltz." I'd have the instruments come in sequentially—first just bass, drums, and guitar, then add mandolin and Dobro, or pedal steel guitar, as the music built, and finally throw in a little Floyd Cramer honky-tonk piano, basically adapting Brahms's own lines from his piano accompaniment.

I couldn't get the idea out of my head, and later in the day when I was driving my teaching assistant, Rick Griffin, an experienced rock and folk guitarist, to a colloquium I played the tape for him and asked what he thought. "Naw, I don't hear it." I tried again, but he was unmoved. I gave up, but the next day he called and said if I was still interested he could line up a late-night session with a group of his musician friends at Q Division, a recording studio run by a friend of his, Jon Lupfer, who was—to my surprise—a fan of my work in philosophy. I wrote new lyrics and changed the name (to "Moonlight Waltz": "Hold me close and dance in the moonlight, with my arms around you. I've been waiting just for this moment, since the day I found you . . .") and asked Julie Tierney, the wife of the director of our chorale and a beautiful soprano who also had sung with a classic swing band, to join me and do the women's parts. Since the Brahms songs are two-part harmony, we'd each have to sing both parts and then have the engineer wed them on the console. We arrived at the studio (then in a rather unappealing part of South Boston) at about midnight and spent the rest of the night on the recording.

This was a new experience for me. When we Peadquacs had made our record in the Ace Recording Studios in Boston back in 1959, it was quite simple. We all stood in a line in front of four big mikes on stands, did three or four takes of each song, chose the best, and the job was done. The engineer put our choices, in the order we specified, on a tape and then transferred that to a twelve-inch metal master recording with a machine that cut the groove for the needle with a stylus. The master could then be used to make pressings of the vinyl LPs we sold. It was all done in a single afternoon session. At Q Division, we used several rooms at once; the drummer, with headphones, was isolated in one studio, the bassist in another, and the other musicians were together in one room but separately miked. We did all the instrumental music before Julie and I sang a note. It was like the difference between producing a play and making a movie; you do the latter in dozens of parts in any order, tweak them independently, and then put them together. The musicians were real pros, and I was, in retrospect, a bit too timid in putting forward my ideas about tempo and blend, so the result was not what I hoped for—a bit too fast, not romantic-dreamy in the way I wanted—but all in all, a professional cut. I went back a second day to add the Floyd Cramer piano bits, and Jon carefully balanced and tuned the voices and instruments and handed me a DAT, a digital audio tape. I recalled Stan's admonition not to try preserving my past and wondered again if he was right. But although I wasn't thrilled with the result (which I was told would have cost me about $100,000 if I'd been paying the studio and musicians their standard rates!), I didn't discard it. A few years later, at a TED meeting, I sat next to Naomi Judd at dinner and told her about my adventure in country-western recording. She asked me to send her a copy of the DAT. I did, and never heard back from her, so maybe Stan was right. It was a splendid adventure in any case.

In 1980, Susan and I decided we wanted to sing Christmas carols with our friends and invited about a dozen couples to join us around the piano in Andover for a potluck party in December. I curated two binders of the best arrangements of our favorite carols from around the world, which our guests could borrow if they wanted to practice their parts. The carol party morphed over a few years from a casual occasion into one larger and more formal, which allowed the women to get all dressed up, and most of the men wore tuxedos. After more than thirty-five annual parties, we've discontinued them, now that we've moved permanently to Maine. The last party was described by Joshua Rothman in his 2017 profile of me in *The New Yorker*. He had his tape recorder on most of the evening and had planned to play some of the singing on *The New Yorker*'s radio program. I'm grateful that our feeble efforts—hey, by then we and our voices had aged thirty-five years—did not get broadcast, and I hope Joshua has destroyed the tape.

Several people have written music based on my words, a fact that fills me with joy. First was Brian Felsen, arts entrepreneur and composer, who wrote an ambitious symphonic piece, *View from the Strangers' Gallery*, inspired by Nick Humphrey's work and mine on consciousness. Second was composer Robert Gross, who wrote "Desperate Lark," setting to music my letter to Doug Hofstadter when he was mourning the death of his wife, Carol. Third, and most ambitious, is Scott Johnson's brilliant *Mind out of Matter*, which uses not just my words but my recorded voice (from talks on the internet) as, in effect, a solo instrument, capturing the melodic lines of my speaking and turning them by judicious repetition into what one reviewer called an "atheist oratorio." I never mention God, but Scott's imaginative settings of my recorded words leave no doubt about the larger consequences of the Darwinian ideas I am expressing. The celebrated New York City avant-garde ensemble Alarm Will Sound premiered this piece in the PEAK Performances series at Montclair State University in New Jersey, with subsequent performances at the Metropolitan Museum of Art in New York City, at Tufts, and at Lawrence University in Wisconsin. Scott discovered as he worked out the tonal values of my speaking that when I wanted to stress a point, I often raised my voice a tritone—or flatted fifth, "the Devil's Interval"—something I never would have guessed but was very pleased to learn.

3.

WESLEYAN, THEN ON TO
HARVARD (1959–63)

*Meaning is what essence becomes when it is divorced
from the object of reference and wedded to the word.*

—W. V. O. Quine, *From a Logical Point of View*, p. 22

ALTHOUGH I SPENT JUST ONE ACADEMIC YEAR AT WES-
leyan, it was a momentous year; I discovered I would be a
philosopher. Since I had advanced placement in mathematics, my
freshman advisor was convinced that I was a prodigy and twisted my
arm to take an advanced math course. I knew that I owed my abilities in math to excellent teaching, not natural talent, but I relented
and signed up for a course called something like Topics in Modern
Mathematics. The teacher was a young philosophy graduate student
from Princeton, the logician Henry Kyburg. It turned out that only
two students enrolled—me and a graduate student in the Masters
in Teaching program, Ron Book, who went on to a distinguished
career in mathematics at the University of California in Santa Barbara. Henry told us that since there were just the two of us, we didn't
have to follow the course description. What did we want to study?
Ron said, "Well, you're a logician primarily, so why don't we do
mathematical logic?" I had no idea what that was but was willing to
go along. It was undoubtedly the strangest introductory logic course
a freshman ever took, since Henry had been told I was a prodigy and
Ron actually was one, so we started in the deep end of the pool. My
introductory text was daunting: W. V. O. Quine's 1951 monograph,

Mathematical Logic (revised edition), *not* his logic primer, *Methods of Logic*, which is bracing enough. As he says in the preface, "Rigor has not, in general, been compromised in favor of perspicuity." I struggled with the proofs and mused that college was harder than I had expected. After I dragged myself through Quine's book, we turned to Stephen Kleene's *Introduction to Metamathematics* and Frank Ramsey's collection of essays, *The Foundations of Mathematics*, along with a lot of supporting papers. I was drowning, but fascinated.

One night in the math department library, as I was struggling with some of these texts, I spotted another book by Quine on a shelf: *From a Logical Point of View* (1953), a collection of essays *composed of English sentences!* with only a smattering of logical formulae to clarify and illustrate the points he was making. I started reading it and had almost finished the book when dawn broke. This Quine was doing what I wanted to do, I realized, and I wanted to do it the way he did, if I could only figure out how. Years later I think I have finally figured out what it was about Quine that inspired me: he wanted to *fix what was broken* in the way philosophical problems were being explored. He didn't believe in "real magic" and thought he could diagnose a major misstep that was taken for granted by almost all philosophers:

a belief in some fundamental cleavage between truths that are *analytic*, or grounded in meanings independently of matters of fact, and truths that are *synthetic*, or grounded in fact.

Some true sentences, such as "2 + 2 = 4," were *a priori*, necessarily true, and their truth could be determined by an *analysis* of the meanings of the terms in them, without any need to get out of one's armchair and conduct an empirical investigation. Other true sentences, such as "There is cheese on the plate," were *a posteriori*, or *synthetic*: you had to look to the world to see if they were true. Quine argued that this was a good rough-and-ready distinction for some purposes but not as sharp as philosophers and logicians thought.

That struck me as a wonderfully subversive idea, but I thought he was *wrong* about some of his ways of putting things. So I decided, as only a freshman could, that I had to go to Harvard and confront this man with my corrections to his errors! I thereupon filled out my application to transfer to Harvard, where I was accepted as a transfer student, and spent the rest of my freshman year reading Quine, Wittgenstein—and Freud.

Norman O. Brown, "Nobby" to everyone at Wesleyan, was a classicist and literary theorist whose cult book, *Life against Death: the Psychoanalytical Meaning of History*, was published that year and caused quite a stir in humanities circles, thanks to Norman Podhoretz and Lionel Trilling, who praised it to the skies. Deep stuff, with sex and anxiety thrown in for good measure. And then there was Nietzsche, whose *Thus Spake Zarathustra* and *Genealogy of Morals* were introduced to me in my actual philosophy class, along with Descartes's *Meditations* and *Discourse on Method*, Hume's *Dialogues Concerning Natural Religion*, and a bunch of other classics. The class was taught brilliantly by Louis Mink, who persuaded me that I should become a philosopher after I held forth in class with some passion that Descartes's dualism was hopelessly wrong—and it shouldn't take me too long to say why. Sixty years later I'm still hammering away on poor old Descartes, who was indeed wrong, in spite of having some clever arguments that had to wait for Darwin to dismantle in passing.

I thought it would be wise to enroll in Harvard Summer School just so I could acquaint myself better with the classrooms and other places I'd be frequenting when classes started in September. I signed up for a single course, on the history of the symphony, which met at nine every morning. I would drive in from Winchester, park in the lot just in front of Paine Hall, the music building, and review my notes from the previous day. As luck would have it, a beautiful sophomore art major from Smith College, Susan Bell, drove to Cambridge from her home in Wellesley to take the same course. I was instantly smitten. At the time, I was working on a sculpture in wood of a young woman in a pensive pose and was having difficulties with the shoulders. I made bold to ask her if she, with her perfect shoulders, might model for me. No way, she said, but she didn't spurn me thereafter. Soon Susan and I were arriving earlier and earlier in the morning to sit in one car or the other and talk. After class we'd go to the music library in Paine Hall to check out the records assigned to us for the next day and take them into one of the soundproof listening rooms to do our homework. The librarian who checked out the records soon began giving me smarmy looks when he handed me the day's LPs and I sauntered off into the isolation booth with Susan to listen. One day, I quietly excused myself from the listening room and rushed to his desk. "Quick!" I said. "Ravel's *Bolero*!" He jumped up, but when he saw I was joking he reddened and turned away, and thereafter he treated us with punctilious respect.

In September I was assigned to Eliot House, where the classicist John Finley, one of my father's old friends, was master. My room was the sixth room of a double-triple suite, one of whose would-be occupants had dropped out of college over the summer. The five returnees knew each other well, of course, but they accepted my intrusion with grace, and soon we all became lifelong friends. Susan was a familiar visitor to the suite, for our summer romance continued and intensified. (A curious but negligible fact is that Ted Kaczynski, who became the Unabomber, was living just a few feet away from us, on the same floor in the next entry, but I never interacted with him personally.)

Master Finley was a great character, and a legendary writer of letters of recommendation; during his mastership, Eliot House produced more Rhodes Scholars to Oxford than Yale and Princeton combined. He was also a bold brandisher of metaphors, describing one of our housemates in a published interview as "a cross between Reinhold Niebuhr and an eagle." He began one of his little talks to us with "I think we can divide recent history into three ages: the age of Sir Walter Scott, the age of F. Scott Fitzgerald, and the age of Scott tissues." We'd sometimes play a game we called "Finley," taking turns playing the master: "Tell me, Master Finley, what do you get when you cross a Chevrolet with a sphinx?" "Why do bacon and eggs always remind you of Sophocles?"

The first class I enrolled in was Quine's philosophy of language course, the main text for which was his newly published book, *Word and Object*. I had arrived just in time and was eager to get to the bottom of this major work with him. It was an impressive class: Thomas Nagel and David Lewis were two of the star graduate students in it, along with David's wife-to-be, Stephanie, Gilbert Harman, Margaret Wilson and her husband Emmett, Michael Slote, and others. Saul Kripke was not in the course, but he was on campus, a readily recognizable figure in the library, davening (rocking back and forth) as he read. He was rudely nicknamed the Mad Bobber by students who didn't know he was a certified wunderkind, a logical genius who had purportedly blown Quine's reservations about modal logic to smithereens when just a teenager. I've never really gotten to know Saul well, though our paths have often crossed. He and I were approaching Quine from opposite directions, and I didn't expect he'd be any more interested in my objections than I was in his.

I didn't do very well in Quine's course, because although I wrote a fairly impressive term paper, I freaked out on the final exam. I had been poring over his book so intensely that I had way too much to say in a short essay, and I ended up answering just one of the three essay questions, at great length. Dagfinn Føllesdal, Quine's grader, took pity on me and gave me a B– in the course. I was undeterred. I knew I was no good at writing essay exams. As Marshall Cohen, my advisor, once said when I had written a similarly misshapen exam in his course, "Don't try to write an original publishable essay, Dan. Just answer the damn question!"

A digression on examinations

This weakness of mine helped a lot of my students in later years, when I recognized my own foible in their steaming-hot efforts. I eventually adopted the policy of handing out half a dozen essay questions in advance of the final exam, making my own choice of three of them to put on the exam, of which the students are obliged to answer two. The exams are "closed book"—no notes allowed in the exam room, so the students can't just copy an already written essay, but they can and are encouraged to write a practice answer to each question before the exam, discovering and solving the exposition problems they encounter beforehand. Of course they can ignore what they view as the hardest question and concentrate on the five others; in the worst case, the question they ignored will be one of the three on the exam, but then they can do the other two. There is no good reason, I figure, why budding philosophers should be obliged to write impromptu essays of quality; it's an unnatural act. And by giving the students the questions in advance, I get them to focus their review on more material than I can test them on, and I get to read essays that are more thoughtful and well planned, which means I can grade on a higher standard and not have to suffer through frantic and unfocused efforts. A student can still get a lot of help from friends on what to say in the essays, but unless they're masters of rote memorization, they will have to compose the answers in their own words, in the exam room.

Since in recent years I have taught only advanced seminars, I don't usually give final exams anymore; I let the students' grades depend on their single term papers plus weekly comments on the required reading. Another policy I have adopted is never giving "take-home" exams. When I was teaching at UC Irvine in the '60s, the grad students petitioned for the option of qualifying exams that would be handed out in the afternoon and due the next morning. I argued against it by citing the recent example of a grad student who had successfully passed through our PhD program in spite of most of my colleagues having a low opinion of his talent: "If X's quite impressive exam answers had been on a take-home exam, how many of you would suspect he had had help from a ghostwriting friend?" Most of the hands of my colleagues went up. We kept the traditional system.

Another innovation I experimented with was multiple-choice exams. One day in the '90s, I was at a conference in Vancouver and spent a spare day with the psychologists Daniel Kahneman and Amos Tversky in a beautiful living room looking out on the harbor. I was gritting my teeth trying to avoid looking at the fascinating view so I could read a pile of "blue books" filled with scrawled essays. "Why do you torture yourself with that terrible task?" Amos asked me. "Give a multiple-choice exam, and you can grade each student in a minute or two, and get a better gauge of their work!" "Not in philosophy," I replied. "You have to make the students write essays to see how well they understand the arguments and issues." Amos disagreed: "If you make the choices close enough in meaning so that they're all tempting but only one is problem-free, you can readily put the students' understanding to a severe test and rank the results objectively." I saw his point and decided to give it a try in a midterm exam in one philosophy course. I succeeded in making a devilishly demanding multiple-choice exam, and the students' performances were just what you would hope: the best avoided the tempting false choices, and the weakest often fell for them. Success, of a sort, but I hated the effect on morale in the course. The students resented my efforts to lure them into *almost true* falsehoods and were wary and unenthusiastic for the rest of the term. The other time I used multiple choice, with better results, was in my philosophy of evolutionary theory course, where I had discovered that many in the class overestimated their basic understanding of evolutionary biology, which was a prerequisite for the course. So I gave them a tricky multiple-choice quiz at the first meeting, and we graded it together in class. This sent about half the students back to the basics before the next meeting. Here's one of the questions:

The fitness of an organism is a measure or estimate most closely linked, in principle, to:
    a. its success at securing mating opportunities.
    b. its probability of having grandchildren.

c. the number of its potential live offspring.

d. its probability of surviving longer than its conspecifics.

In my first stint as a philosophy professor at Irvine, I was unsettled by the blank looks I would get from students when I mentioned some landmark cultural figure, so I devised a culture quiz to assay this dearth of what I had thought would be common knowledge among my sun-drenched students. Fifty well-known names: *Michelangelo*—if you answer just "artist," you get one point; if you answer "Italian Renaissance artist," you get two. The average grade among the hundred or so freshmen taking introductory philosophy from me was about 40. Among the answers I got were some gems exhibiting how a little knowledge can be a dangerous thing: *Copernicus*—Caesar's wife; *Cervantes*—half man/half horse; *Henry James*—author of the Henry James Version of the Bible.

Back to Harvard

My goal of "refuting" Quine did not lapse after my lackluster showing in his class; it actually intensified. I asked Quine which thinkers offered the most interesting alternatives to his views, and he recommended the work of Noam Chomsky and the UC Berkeley logician Lotfi Zadeh, whose "fuzzy set theory" challenged his own version of set theory. He also recommended the work of his friend B. F. Skinner for a supporting view. I read Chomsky's famous review of Skinner's *Verbal Behavior*, which had just appeared, but—unlike most budding cognitive scientists—I also read Skinner's book, and I decided that Chomsky's review was a masterpiece of misleading polemics. That was my earliest encounter with deliberate caricature in academia, and it was an eye-opener. For my three years at Harvard, I devoted large portions of my study time to reading and thinking about these and other critics, while taking as many philosophy courses as I could, seasoned by a sprinkling of other humanities courses.

I managed not to take any science courses! My math logic course with Kyburg at Wesleyan both fulfilled the logic requirement in the philosophy department and was deemed a science course, and I can't remember what other fringe-sciency course I plugged in to cover the "distribution" requirement. No biology, no chemistry or physics, no labs, and no psychology! I didn't take a course with Skinner, though I could have, but I had been steered away from psychology by an episode in my high school years. My older sister, Cynthia, went to Mount Holyoke, and I vividly remember the round-trip drive to South Hadley that Mother and I made to pick up Cynthia for Thanksgiving her freshman year (when I was just getting settled in Exeter). On the way home, I eagerly grilled her about all her courses. She was taking an introduction to psychology, which whetted my appetite. The *mind! Consciousness!* I could hardly wait to hear what she'd been learning. She told me about William Sheldon's theory of body types: ectomorph, endomorph, and mesomorph. *Yuck!* From the '40s through the '70s, Sheldon's crackpot theory was an active focus of research. He had organized a research project involving thousands of "posture photographs" taken of nude Ivy League and Seven Sisters students and thought he could determine personality types by charting the differences. I had in fact had my three posture photos (frontal, profile, and back) taken at Exeter that year and was dubious of the whole scheme. Physique was destiny? If psychologists took this seriously (in fact many of them did; it was in the textbooks), I wanted nothing to do with psychology. That snap judgment at age sixteen caused me to ignore all psychology, good and bad, until I was a graduate student.

Psychology has had a hard time attracting the best students for decades. I remember Princeton philosopher Harry Frankfurt telling me a joke sometime in the '80s: "Dan, do you know why psychologists are so stupid?"

"No," I replied, "I've often wondered."

"It's because every large state university has an introductory psychology course with about a thousand students in it. Around Thanksgiving time, the lecturer intones, 'One of the things we have learned in psychology is that actions followed by reward tend to be repeated, and actions followed by punishment tend not to be.' Nine hundred and ninety-five students mutter, 'What else is new?' but five think 'That's really interesting!' They go on to be psychologists."

I knew better by then, but it has taken half a century for psychology to shake off the reputation it got from (caricatures of) some of its dubious discoveries. There is a reason for this, I think. Folk psychology, the scheme we all use to understand one another (I call it the *intentional stance*, not theory of mind) presupposes that everybody is roughly rational. You won't get or deserve any attention for a study establishing that subjects prefer five dollars to a poke in the eye with a sharp stick (What else is new?). So psychologists often try to figure out ways to induce pathology in normal subjects—to put a strain on their capacities so that they make telling mistakes that reveal something about the mechanisms or strategies they are using, consciously or not, to do the task they have been asked to do. Perceptual psychologists have devised famous illusions to which almost everybody succumbs. Cognitive psychologists induce subjects to exhibit patterns of errors in inferences, or to think they are causing some effect when they are not. Neuropsychologists use transcranial magnetic stimulation (for instance) to get subjects to misjudge this or that. If you can't get people to make mistakes, their minds seem to work by magic, miraculously figuring out what's what. So psychologists often appear to be telling the general public that we're not as smart as we think we are, but since like all scientists they sometimes oversell their own research, they don't get much sympathy when their vaunted results evaporate, as they occasionally do.

Another soft barrier that kept me away from psychology as an undergraduate was that at Harvard an interdisciplinary concentration (Harvard's word for "major") called social relations, or "soc rel," more or less swallowed up the psychology concentration, and it was an unappetizing (to me) mixture of psychology, sociology, and anthropology. So I never took a course from George Miller or Jerome

Bruner, who were starting the Center for Cognitive Studies there (the birth, one might say, of cognitive science), and I never took a course from Timothy Leary, who was emerging at Harvard—and indeed everywhere in the world—as the leading exponent of psychedelic drugs. I had friends who were experimenting in Leary and Alpert's commune with LSD and psilocybin and other concoctions, but Leary's messianic exhortations did not attract me.

A digression to Rome

I spent the summer of 1961 in Europe, along with thousands of other American college students, whose bible was *Europe on Five Dollars a Day*. It could be done, but if you wanted to drink some wine and have a few nice meals, you had to double your budget. You also had to expect to meet more American college students than natives, since the hostels and cheap restaurants listed in the book were all doing a booming business with Yanks. The only way to communicate with friends and people back home was through letters sent to and from the American Express offices in each major city. When your train pulled into Munich or Paris, one of your first stops would be the American Express office to see if you had mail waiting, and perhaps to cash some traveler's cheques. While you were standing in line for possible mail, you'd likely meet somebody you knew, a classmate from college (or in my case, Exeter). My main destination was Rome, where, thanks to an Exeter faculty wife, Nina Fish, I had arranged to work in the sculpture studio of Pietro Consagra, recent winner of the Venice Biennale prize, whose wife was Nina's sister. (Nina will play another role in a later chapter.) I started my summer in London, at the YMCA in Tottenham Court Road. After the twelve-hour overnight propeller-plane flight to London and the Tube to the Y, I was more than disappointed to learn that I couldn't check in until noon, so I left my suitcase there and staggered over to the British Museum, close by. A guided tour on Roman Britain was just about to leave the main hall, so I took one of the little folding stools and joined the dozen or so museum goers eager to look at Roman pottery and glass and other leftovers. One of the early stops was a Roman mile-marker stele, and during the guide's talk I fell sound asleep on my little stool. I woke up about three hours later, still perched on my stool in the middle of the room. I suppose maybe a hundred people walked by me but nobody wakened me. Perhaps some of them took me to be some curious unlabeled exhibit.

A brief visit to Oxford as a tourist, and then off to Rome, where I found a cheap pensione near the Stazione Termini. The pensione was on the top floor of a dirty building, and you had to put a ten-lire coin in the elevator to get it to work. Soon I was commuting by bus to Consagra's studio every day. At the time, he was working in sand-cast bronze, making his *Conversazione* series, and I was put to work cutting the shapes out of thin plywood with a jigsaw. I went to the foundry to supervise the casting of his pieces, and also to a lost-wax foundry, Fonderia Nicci, to study that process. I made a few sand-cast pieces in bronze for myself and helped with the casting, while picking up some Italian and participating in a little side scheme the workers had going. There was usually some extra molten bronze in the big crucible after the casts had been filled, and the workers always had a few extra frames ready to take it. What they made from this extra bronze were pretty convincing copies of ancient Roman coins, rings, lamps, and a strikingly priapic satyr. When we pulled these out of the sand in the molds, we filed off the flash, banged them up a bit, and buried them in the ash pile behind the foundry, where everybody peed. After a few weeks, they were ready for the flea markets. (A recent googling of "ancient Roman bronze" showed me some photos of pieces I daresay we made; they're still pretty cheap.)

My social life that summer was atypical. I was usually the only paying guest in my pensione, which was filled most of the time by relatives of the owner from all over Italy, including an irrepressible Capuchin monk, Fra Cassiano da Bisacquino, who had been sent by his monastery near Bologna to wheedle some money from the

Vatican but who was mainly interested in seeing the big city during his brief period away from the monastery—and more particularly its female inhabitants, with whom he ached to have physical contact. He befriended me immediately and would cheerfully lead me on tours of Rome, pinching the bottom of every woman he could get close to, in buses, on sidewalks. Whenever they turned angrily, he would look all innocent and monkish while pointing to me as the culprit, which he thought was a great joke. He was short and fat with a tonsure, and I was a tall skinny American. We did make a curious pair of tourists, and he regaled me with tales of the pope's mistresses and other secrets, twirling the ends of the cord around his waist as if it were a keychain and he was a swinger.

At the other end of the social spectrum, I was pulled into an exotic world. Pietro Consagra was a center of attention in the art world, and I got to meet many sculptors and painters in their studios, including Arnaldo Pomodoro, Afro and Mirko Basaldella, and the ancient futurist Gino Severini. It was also the high point of Cinecittà, the film community turning out both spaghetti westerns and Fellini masterpieces. I was introduced to Federico Fellini in a restaurant on Via Veneto, had no idea who he was, and asked him what he did. He told me. Oh. My dinner companion that night was a movie actress named Didi Perego, and while we were dining a couple who knew her arrived at our table and they all had a good laugh after some Italian talk that went by too fast for me to follow. "What's so funny?" I asked Didi in English. She replied in her makeshift English, "Oh, they were thinking to have a meal with much garlic, and then they decided no, because later they are going to kiss themselves."

Susan was doing a European tour that summer as well, with a Smith friend, another Deedee. I managed to "run into them" by taking a train to Venice, arriving on the day that their itinerary listed Venice, and there they were, coming out of the Basilica di San Marco just as I got there. They had a rental car, and we three drove to Rome, where they stayed in my fleabag hotel (literally—both girls got bitten by fleas during their single night in a room there), while my suitcase got stolen from their car parked on the street. I bought a shirt, trousers a few inches too short, and an ill-fitting silvery jacket the next day, which gave me two outfits to wear the rest of the summer. I also managed to get to Paris for a romantic day and evening just before Susan and Deedee left that city. It was the next day that I ran into Ron Brown, the jazz pianist—at American Express, of course. That was a summer to remember.

Back to Harvard

When it came time to propose my senior thesis, on Quine and ordinary language, I decided that I didn't want Quine to be my advisor. I was worried that he'd just show me I was wrong or make some minor concession at our first meeting and I'd be left with nothing to write about. So I asked Dagfinn Føllesdal, who had written his PhD with Quine, to be my supervisor, one of the best moves of my life, and he agreed. He knew his Quine inside out, so I would get some guidance away from any misconstruals of the master, but he also saw—thank you, Dag!—that it was best to let me just charge full steam ahead, while he nudged and warned and picked up the pieces. Føllesdal had also taught a course I loved, on phenomenology, so I had received a deep introduction to the work of Bolzano, Brentano, Meinong, and especially Husserl, which would play a big role in my later thinking. Dag is Norwegian, and at that tender age his English and German were about equally foreign to him. Occasionally in class he would pick up Husserl's *Ideen*, in German, and translate a few phrases into English for us. One day he opened the English translation we were all using and began an impromptu translation into German, until we raised hands and hollered at him. His pronunciation was occasionally cryptic. I remember being baffled for a few minutes by some clarifications he offered on Husserl's standard for *ghenuvin canovlidge* (genuine knowledge).

My honors thesis, "Quine and Ordinary Language," was my first attempt to steer the Quinian ship away from the behaviorism he picked up from his good friend Skinner, and the project of rigorous regimentation he picked up from his mentor, the logician Rudolf Carnap, while still allowing it to steam on by the doldrums of the analytic-synthetic distinction, and what he called "the museum myth of meaning"—the idea that somewhere, in the inner depths of our minds, were the hard facts about the meanings of our words that, once discovered, would allow us to fix the semantics of ordinary language with the same rigor and precision that had worked so wonderfully in mathematical logic. The doctrine that turned most philosophers against Quine was his argument in *Word and Object* for the "indeterminacy of radical translation," the startling claim that *in principle*, two different translators of a foreign language that had no bilingual interpreters to help them (or muddy the waters with their biases) could come up with significantly different translation manuals (dictionaries and grammars) and there would be no facts that settled which was the "right" translation. They would be tied for first place and nothing that happened in the brains of speakers or their interactions with things in the world would confirm that one of the translations was what the native speakers "really" meant. I thought—and still think—Quine was right about this, but had few allies, aside from Donald Davidson, who was one of Quine's earlier students.

That period of my life was one of great intensity, and on several occasions I mused to myself that whether I was right or wrong in the end about Quine and his arguments, this was the life I wanted to live, and I wouldn't regret having devoted so much thinking to the task, however it came out. Adding to the intensity was the fact that now I was a married man, having wed Susan on June 8, 1962, shortly after her graduation from Smith and before my senior year at Harvard. I had left our gang in Eliot House, and Susan and I moved into a fourth-floor walk-up on Green Street, with a view of Dunster House's bell tower. It was a wonderful year, with Susan working at University Prints, a small company that produced postcard-size photographs of famous paintings, sculptures, and architecture for art history students to shuffle and memorize, while I toiled on my thesis. (Master Finley did not approve of my leaving Eliot House and its splendors before my three-year residence was up and made a rather haughty remark about it at the commencement luncheon in the Eliot courtyard, which did not endear him to Susan.)

The examiners on my honors thesis were Quine, of course, and young Charles Parsons (son of Talcott, of "soc rel"), an instructor who had finished his PhD under Quine's supervision two years earlier and later held Quine's chair at Harvard after Quine retired. Quine showed up at my oral examination with about three pages of single-spaced typed notes he had assembled from his reading of my thesis, which thrilled me even before he began to go over them. He had taken me very seriously. Maybe I could really be a philosopher! And in the vigorous discussion that ensued Parsons took my side against his mentor on a point, and that was another fine boost to my confidence. I may have told myself that I would be content to have tried my hardest and lost, but this was vindication, if not entire victory. I skipped home to Susan's loving arms with a grin on my face and a resolve to go on to Oxford, where ordinary-language philosophy reigned. I had claimed in my thesis that Quine's attempt to "regiment" ordinary language had seriously mischaracterized it, so I was expecting to get trained in the subtle but informal methods of analysis then in vogue.

4.

OXFORD, 1963–65

WHEN APPLYING TO OXFORD IN THOSE DAYS, ONE applied to individual colleges. There was no central admissions system. I made the mistake of choosing the three colleges most sought after by Rhodes Scholars, so New College (where A. J. Ayer was), University College, and Magdalen College (where Gilbert Ryle was) all turned me down, having already accepted more than their fair share of Americans. Disappointed, I made plans to go to the University of California at Berkeley, when out of the blue came an air letter admitting me to Hertford College, Oxford. At the time I hadn't heard of Hertford, and since I hadn't applied there, I thought this was perhaps a mean-spirited practical joke by somebody, but I looked it up and sure enough, it was a real Oxford college, and I happily accepted their invitation to be admitted to the BPhil in philosophy.

Susan and I sailed to England in the early summer of 1963 on the MS *Berlin*, then of the North German Lloyd line, a nine-day crossing enhanced by the presence of hundreds of Germans going back to Germany for the first time since World War II. It was a beautiful ship, with art-nouveau and art-deco furnishings and a palm court with a small orchestra that played waltzes and polkas and old German folk songs. The *Berlin*, originally the *Gripsholm*, had been built in England for the Swedish American Line in 1924 and was the first diesel (not steam) ocean liner. I had already sailed on her, as I discovered en route; Mother and Cynthia and I had taken the *Gripsholm* to Beirut to join Father once he'd established himself. My earliest childhood memories are of the shuffleboard and "horse-racing" conducted on the *Gripsholm*. I had been deeply disappointed to discover that the horse racing didn't involve live horses galloping around the deck, but just little model horses moved by a throw of the dice around a paper track laid out in the lounge.

When we got to Oxford, we hunted for, and found, an excellent flat, newly created out of the loft over the two-car garage of a house in the heart of Oxford, 33a Beaumont Street. Our landlord, Malcolm Graham, was a dental surgeon. Our flat was actually in St. John Street, but the dental practice and home of the Grahams was on the corner of Beaumont Street, right across St. John Street from the Ashmolean Museum. We paid a little extra for this wonderful location and all the "mod cons" Mr. Graham had installed in the flat, his pride and joy. He loved electrical gadgets and had equipped the tiny space with the latest electric heaters and mixers and even a washing machine. We had electric towel rails in our tiny bath over the stairs, and an electric drying cupboard for clothes under the stairs, where I put a small card table that became my desk. He was thinking of purchasing an electric red-wine warmer to bring the wine up to "room temperature," but decided against it when I suggested that it might instead be better to bring the room up to room temperature. The upstairs was cozy, but my little study under the stairs on the ground floor was damp and cold, in spite of the electric clothes cupboard. In the winter months, my routine when I got to work was to take a warm tea towel down and wipe the dew off my Olivetti Lettera typewriter before beginning to write.

The Grahams had two sons our age, both students at Oxford, and the Grahams became our British family in short order. It was John Graham, then a medical student, who, sitting on the floor with me in front of the electric fire, first showed me what a neuron was and how neurons were connected into networks. Each neuron had multiple inputs, the dendrites, which could be either excitatory or inhibitory, and a single branching output, the axon, and it fired its output down its axon whenever its "threshold" was reached—when the excitation minus the inhibition was above a changeable value.

This led me in a flash to the hypothesis that such networks could learn by a kind of evolutionary process within the brain, in which thresholds would be tuned by interactions with other neurons, at junctures known as synapses, one of the enabling insights of my life (and of course not original to me, though it took me a few years to discover my predecessors).

Once we had found our flat and left our winter clothes there, we headed to Germany, where we picked up a brand-new bright red 1963 VW beetle at the factory in Wolfsburg. Where did our money come from? From Grandpa Dennett, who had died the previous year and left Mother and the three children equal quarters of his estate. If you were careful, you could live off the income and not "invade capital," as Mother's lawyer advised. We weren't rich, certainly; Susan and I had about $4,000 a year to work with, enough to tide us over until I got a proper paying job at UC Irvine in 1965. That summer we drove straight through Italy, bypassing Rome (which at that time I considered a deeply immoral place; I knew some of the actors in *La Dolce Vita*—and the characters portrayed by them). We took a dilapidated car ferry from Brindisi to Piraeus. It stopped at Corfu and other smaller islands on the west coast of Greece, and the ferry once hove to after two men in a boat hailed it. One of them climbed aboard carrying a huge grouper and immediately began selling raffle tickets for the fish to pay for his passage to Piraeus; we bought a ticket, hoping not to win, of course.

We drove to Athens, where we rented a flat on Lycabettus, the pointy high hill with the monastery on the top. On what was then the highest road on the hill, Stratiotikou Sindesmou, an old apartment building had been torn down so that a new one could be built, and the neighboring apartment building had a ground-floor flat that was available for next to nothing, since pneumatic drills and bulldozers were operating right outside its door. We took it, cockroaches and all, and noticed that we could sit in the tiny courtyard and, thanks to a very long flight of downhill stairs opposite us, see the Parthenon on top of the Acropolis. That courtyard became my sculpture studio in a few days, after we'd driven to the Pentelic marble quarry a little north of Athens and loaded the biggest hunk of pure white marble we could get into the backseat of the VW. In Piraeus we found a blacksmith who made stone chisels, and I acquired a small set of toothed and smooth chisels and a hammer and soon was exploring the dos and don'ts of marble carving while Susan explored the neighborhood. We found an open-air restaurant, Paradisos, in a courtyard that filled the eye of the hairpin on a switchback road, with the kitchen across the road, hollowed out of the cliffside. It became our dining place for the entire summer. Thomas Batsoulis, the waiter, taught us the Greek names for all the food, and we tried to teach him the English names. *Staphylia* were grapes (think *Staphylococcus*, which looks like a bunch of grapes), but Thomas had trouble with the English word: "Kremps, kremps," he would say. Ever since, Susan and I have enjoyed kremps. The concierge's daughter, a girl of about eight, liked to watch me hacking away at the marble, and I decided she could teach me a few Greek words. I held up a chisel and looked quizzically at her—"κατσαβίδι" (*kazavithi*), she told me. So that's what I called it when I took it back to the blacksmith to get sharpened. I later found that this is the word for "screwdriver." Modern Greek compared to ancient Greek is a wonderful example of Grimm's law, in which the *b* phoneme tends to go to *v*, the *d* and *t* often go to soft *th*, and so forth. Between German and English, for instance, we have *geben*-give, *haben*-have, *Bruder*-brother, *Mutter*-mother, and so forth. I had learned a smattering of ancient Greek in my philosophy courses, so, applying Grimm's law, I was able to pronounce most modern Greek words correctly: Βουλιαγμένη is the seaside suburb of Vouliagmeni, for instance. Since *D d* or Δ δ (delta) is pronounced *th*, modern Greek uses *NT* (nu tau) to make our *d* sound, so my name is NTAN. I developed the irresistible habit of pronouncing the words I saw on billboards, seeing ΝΤΟΡΙΣ ΝΤΕΙ and slowly forming "Doris Day"; "D-I-S-N-E-Y" and "E-L-E-C-T-R-O-L-U-X" were others I sounded out laboriously.

I hardly thought about philosophy that summer, as we sketched and sculpted and discovered many of the treasures of Greece, from Delphi to Corinth to Hydra. We found a deserted pebble beach on Cape Sounion in a little bay where only one yacht, *Creole*, Stavros Niarchos's beautiful three-masted schooner, lay, on a mooring several hundred yards from the shore. We'd inflate a pair of air mattresses we had bought in Germany for just such adventures and paddle out to the yacht and circle it, while the white-uniformed crew watched us warily. They never invited us aboard, in spite of Susan in her fetching bikini. In September we loaded the nearly finished sculpture (of a man sitting on the ground reading) into the VW, with a chain and padlock to keep it from being stolen overnight in the parking lot of some inn on our return trip to Oxford. I finished the reading-man sculpture in Oxford and gave it to a friend, who still has it in his New York City apartment.

Our little VW soon transported some other sculptures: two small pieces by Henry Moore, which he had lent to a student-organized exhibit in Pembroke College, Oxford. Knowing of my interest in sculpture, one of the organizers figured this might be the safest way of getting the pieces back to Moore. We were given his phone number and called ahead to make a date to deliver the pieces to the Moores' beautiful old thatched house in Much Hadham, several hours' drive

My marble The Reader *in Athens, 1963*

from Oxford. We were invited to come for tea with Moore and his wife, and he gave us a lengthy tour of the house, studios, and gardens when we arrived. He was working on his majestic Lincoln Center piece then, and it was too big to fit in either of the studios, so he had built a huge metal staging covered with clear plastic on the lawn, under which he could work on the piece—in plaster—in all weathers. He had added temporary plaster steps on the sides of the piece, so he could climb around on it with a large bowl of fresh plaster, adding some here, scraping off some there. Many of his smaller sculptures were placed in the gardens, which were beautifully maintained, and at one point in our stroll he cried, "Well, look at that!" and reached down into the soil in one of the flower beds and picked up what looked like a very small Henry Moore sculpture. It was an animal bone of some kind, bleached white, and in his hands it looked beautiful. This was almost too wonderful to be true, and I confess to having suspected later that he'd planted the bone for just such a revelation. It charmed us in any case, and so did the quiz he subjected me to after tea, while showing me his collection of minia-

With Susan in Athens, 1963

tures from around the world, none of which I was able to identify. "Eskimo?" "No, Neolithic Yugoslavian." "Aztec?" "No, Chinese." Susan and I glowed and sighed all the way back to Oxford.

The BPhil, which I had signed up for, was a relatively new degree in philosophy, designed primarily for students from America, Canada, Australia, and New Zealand. Meant to be a worthy substitute for a PhD, it was an intense two-year program culminating in a horrific two weeks during which you handed in a dissertation *and* took three daunting written exams. If you failed at any of these tasks, you were out, finished, no second chances or retakes. (About a third of the BPhil students back then flunked and left with no diploma. The degree has since been modified, trading in the examinations for a series of submitted essays.) In England at that time, and particularly at Oxford, you could obtain a university position without any graduate degree. After receiving a "first" (*summa cum laude* in America) on your bachelor's degree, you could hang around for another year without any particular duties or examinations and obtain a master's degree, which was the only "advanced" degree most Oxford dons could put after their names (MA Oxon). (There were perhaps eighty philosophy dons—college tutors—at Oxford then, but only three were professors. At the time, Grice, Strawson, Wiggins, Quinton, Anscombe, Foot, Murdoch, the Warnocks [Geoffrey and Mary], . . . were all just dons.)

All BPhil students had one of the three philosophy professors as their supervisor, and I was assigned to Professor Ryle. Knowing my weakness as an exam writer, I was worried. I figured I could easily write the rather short dissertation (thirty thousand words) but would almost certainly fail at least one of the exams. Still, I started the program, because working with Ryle had been my first choice. His 1949 book, *The Concept of Mind*, was, to my way of thinking, the best example of ordinary-language philosophy, with its lively, even swashbuckling, attack on "the ghost in the machine"—Ryle's disrespectful term for Descartes's great error (which I was still hoping to expose). After a few months of weekly meetings with Ryle, I confessed to him that I was sure I would fail one of the exams and asked if I could switch to the BLitt degree, which required just a dissertation and was regarded as a sort of consolation prize, a proof that one had been a student at Oxford. I would then go to Berkeley for my doctorate. "You might have to settle for a BLitt, but why not try for the DPhil?" Ryle replied. The DPhil required only a dissertation and a minimum of two years as a student, but you had to be especially recommended into the program by a professor. Ryle said he would try to get me accepted! (I later learned that he was so influential then in Oxford that this was a sure thing. I also learned, years later, that Ryle had been one of the chief architects of the BPhil, which I had candidly opined to him was unacceptably inhumane. I also learned—not from him—that it was he who had forwarded my application to Hertford College when his college, Magdalen, turned me down. He had taken this unusual step because of Quine's strong letter of recommendation. Lucky me.)

Susan landed a part-time job at the Bodleian Library helping to catalog illustrations in medieval manuscripts. What a treat! The great leather-bound parchment books would be carefully laid out on a table and Susan's task was to identify the items pictured: animals, flowers, trees, farmers and their tools, saints, buildings, food, and so forth. She soon learned to distinguish hundreds of ancient items, and today if you want to see representations of fish or dogs or unicorns or scribes or princes in the twelfth century, you can look them up thanks in part to Susan's work. Her boss was a classic English librarian, wearing his scholarship lightly but devoted to his project. He taught Susan a lot about English life from the Middle Ages to the mid-twentieth century, introducing us, for instance, to the practice of putting a little sherry from the decanter into your soup.

You didn't "take courses" at Oxford; there were lectures and seminars scheduled, but the dons and professors who presented them didn't take attendance, didn't typically even get to know the names of the students, and didn't examine them or assign term papers. I sampled many of these and stayed with most I sampled: Strawson on Kant and Grice on meaning were ones I particularly remember, but I had great difficulty in Grice's seminar. He spoke very slowly, with lots of *um*s interposed: "This factor *um, um, um . . . um, um, um . . .* has *um* often been mistaken *um, um* for . . ." I'd sometimes mentally wander off and think my own untethered thoughts, only to be brought back sharply when I noticed that he had just finished saying something very interesting—but what? I once logged words against *um*s for a few minutes; the *um*s won by a small margin. And then there were A. J. Ayer's elegant lectures on epistemology. All the American BPhil students attended, of course, and we mostly tried to be modest and quiet, but one of our countrymen, Peter Unger, was an exception. He would rise from his seat and bellow in his New York accent, "Aah, Professor Ayer, I think you're all *wrong* about that! You're making a rather obvious *error . . .*" while the rest of us Yanks cringed. But Ayer enjoyed Unger's sometimes outrageous challenges, and it did make for edgy entertainment on occasion.

At that time in Oxford, I was so insecure that I could readily entertain the idea that I was just not smart enough to be a philosopher, since so often in discussion I'd get snared by some clever chap who could counterexample me to death, cleverly picking up escape hatches and ambiguities in my own words that I hadn't noticed. Years later I cured myself of that anxiety when I was a visiting professor at Harvard and had a heart-to-heart talk with Robert Nozick, one of the smartest, swiftest philosophers I've ever encountered. Bob confessed to me that his biggest problem as a philosopher was that he wasn't just a quick study—he was *too* quick a study. Show him a new argument, or a whole new research area, such as probability theory or recursive function theory or free logic, and he'd *get it* almost instantly. "But the folks who don't get it without a struggle, who plod along anxiously, trying to avoid mistakes—they're often the ones who see the problems that I glide by without noticing."

Getting approved for the DPhil was liberating, and I still had Ryle as my supervisor. His book *The Concept of Mind* along with Wittgenstein's *Philosophical Investigations* were the bibles among many of the graduate students. Ordinary-language philosophy was the reigning fashion of the day throughout the English-speaking philosophical world, and Oxford was Mecca for ordinary-language philosophers. The graduate-student pilgrims who arrived in Oxford to take the cloth were devout but (as usual for graduate students) a little out-of-date. The heyday of ordinary-language philosophy was over, since Oxford's J. L. Austin had died in 1960. Paul Grice and Peter Strawson were doing very interesting work, but it was almost buried in the mountain of second-rate fussing that was all that was left of ordinary-language philosophy. It was a period of mannered modesty, where no question was too picayune to deserve a meandering, informal survey of "what we would say" about *forgetting to do something* or *telling a dream* or *ignoring somebody*. This was all inspired by a few incisive examples concocted by Austin, who once wrote: "Let us distinguish between acting intentionally and acting deliberately or on purpose, as far as this can be done by attending to what language can teach us." One graduate student wrote a dissertation on the ordinary meaning of the word "bottle." How tall does a jar have to be to count as a bottle? Is an inkwell a bottle? A bottle can be made out of plastic or even leather; can a bottle be made out of metal? Then there was the worship of St. Ludwig. I can remember a drinks party of graduate students who all had their copies of *Philosophical Investigations* with them, and somebody remarked at how tattered and well used they all looked. A competition ensued over whose copy was most thumbed, and when the winner was decided the second-place finisher one-upped everyone by insisting that this was his second copy; he'd had to reproduce all his marginalia from his first copy, which had utterly fallen apart. This almost religious atmosphere didn't smother my appreciation of Wittgenstein, but it did lead me into a more iconoclastic interpretation of his work.

Danny Daniels (Charles B. Daniels, 1935–2012) was another American who talked his way into the DPhil program. There were, in fact, at least four of us: Dennis Stampe and Peter Unger were the other two. Danny was a joyous original, a rebel, an entertainer. Was he also a con man? There were times when I wondered. He said he had been an "ice man" back in America—with no account of his undergraduate studies—and he seemed blithely unconcerned about his lack of preparation for a doctorate in philosophy. How he managed to get admitted to the DPhil program was a mystery. He didn't seem to spend much time studying philosophy. I wasn't a habitué of pubs, but whenever I did drop in to the Turf Tavern, there he'd be, holding forth amusingly about his many adventures. There were the East European twin sisters, both princesses of some kind, who were competing for Danny's hand in marriage, and there was his time in Spain learning how to make guitars and how to play them (I never heard him play). While in Spain, he'd received notice from the draft board reclassifying him 1-A, but he'd heard that you got a medical deferment if you didn't have both big toes, so he talked a shady Spanish doctor into amputating one of them. The doctor made a mess of it, and Danny had to fly back to the States to save his leg. This left him with a painful neuroma, he said, and then he learned that there was no exemption for not having a big toe—but there was for having a painful stump; the neuroma kept him out of Vietnam. I decided I just had to call him on that one and asked him to remove his shoe. He graciously acceded and, sure enough, he had no big toe on that foot.

He got a job teaching economics to airmen at the US Strategic Air Command base at Brize Norton, a few miles west of Oxford, in the extension program run by the University of Maryland. I asked him if he'd majored in economics as an undergraduate, and he said he hadn't; he'd never taken an economics course, but he was managing to stay a week or so ahead of the students using the textbook provided. This activity gave him access to the PX (the tax-free "post exchange" supermarket, where the US military and their families shopped), from which each week he purchased gallons of liquor, cartons of cigarettes, and American favorites such as peanut butter, which he then resold to Americans and others in Oxford. One day he knocked on our door and said excitedly that he needed help:

He'd just accepted a job tutoring students in Christ Church College on the British empiricists. What was the problem? "Who were the British empiricists?" he asked. The portrait of John Locke, along with Hume and Berkeley, the most famous of the British empiricists, hung prominently in the dining hall of Christ Church, where Locke studied medicine in the eighteenth century. I gave Danny a half-hour summary of British empiricism and a short list of books to read, and he went off happily to tutor his students.

All students were required to wear gowns to lectures and tutorials and meals, either the short black "commoner's" gown, a short vest with long tassles, or the long flowing "scholar's" gown—roughly your basic black choir robe—or, as graduate students, a longer version of the commoner's gown. For special ceremonies such as examinations, one also was obliged to wear "subfusc" (dark trousers and jacket, white shirt, and white bow tie). Gowns are now required only at such ceremonial occasions. Since I was married, I never lived in Hertford College or even had tutorials there. All my tutorials were with Ryle in Magdalen. I did attend a few dinners and lunches in Hertford, just to show my face and get the occasional mail in my mailbox. At that time, Hertford was known as the haven of *nouveau riche* sons (no women then) whose parents' connections and perhaps donations had secured their entry to Oxford. It did not do very well in the academic standings, but its High Table (where the dons ate) was well regarded, as was its wine cellar. Among the undergraduates were a few entertaining sports who quickly befriended me because I had a Frisbee, which they had never seen, and we often threw the Frisbee around in the Hertford courtyard or the Parks after lunch. They all wanted Frisbees, so I asked my mother to send me a package of them, and soon I was deluged with requests. Danny Daniels and I attempted to set up something like a distributorship with Wham-O, the American manufacturer, but they didn't respond at all. Danny found a plastics factory in Berkshire that would pirate them for about two shillings apiece (about twenty-eight cents American then) and we pondered the prospect of engaging in a lucrative bit of industrial crime, but I'm happy to say we dropped the idea. Oh, the paths not taken!

Oxford at that time was still remarkably full of antique traditions and policies. Students—even graduate students—who lived in college were required to be inside their colleges by eleven o'clock, when all the great gates and doors were locked. The next morning, if your scout (the man who cleaned your room, including your tea dishes and glasses, made your bed, and would even shine your shoes) found you absent, he was obliged to inform the head porter in the lodge, who would tell the dean, who . . . But each college had an ill-kept secret about how to climb in after hours. At Magdalen, for example, there was a lamppost next to the college wall in Longwall Street that had a vicious-looking ring of downward-pointing spikes attached about seven feet off the ground. They looked vicious, but you could grab them (unless you were very short, in which case you'd need an accomplice) and use them to pull yourself up on the lamppost high enough to get an arm and then a leg and then the rest of you over the top of the wall, through one of the crenellations. Once over, there was a short drop to the corrugated metal roof of the bicycle shed and thence a shorter drop to the ground.

The currency was still pounds, shillings, and pence, but in two years I saw only one shilling coin in circulation—pennies and tuppennies and thruppenny bits and two bobs (also known as florins) and half crowns, but no shillings. Why not? Because many people, especially students, had coin-metered gas heaters in their flats that took only shillings, so shillings were hoarded, and whenever the gasman came to collect, you made sure to have pounds and coins to exchange for the shillings he unloaded from the coin box. One of the flats we looked at before finding our Beaumont Street gem was in Park Town, in North Oxford, and when we noticed the absence of any refrigerator in the tiny kitchen, the huge Miss Marplesque landlady showed us the wire cage outside the kitchen window on the north side, which would keep milk and butter and cheese cool, she said, adding in her deep rumbling voice, "And if you have a particularly large joint, you can keep it in my cold north larder." (She was talking about a roast, not a reefer, of course.)

There were three cinemas in Oxford. The ABC showed Hollywood films and major films from the British studios. La Scala, in Walton Street, specialized in foreign-language art films, and the Moulin Rouge in Headington had a mixed bag of offerings. Susan and I often went to the movies and would see a bad movie if there wasn't a halfway decent one showing—at "three and six" (three shillings and sixpence, about fifty cents) a bargain even then. One evening I called La Scala to ask what was playing, and the young woman who answered said she didn't know. "Well, please just step out and look on the marquee," I suggested. She did and came back to tell me that she couldn't read it, because it was in a foreign language. "Oh I bet you can do it. Give it a try," I urged, and she did, returning in a few seconds to say, "Oh I did try, sir, and you're right! I could read it. It's a French movie *About a Soufflé*!" (The great Jean-Luc Godard film *Breathless*, in French: *À bout de souffle*.)

One of the books I purchased that year was *The Jenguin Pennings*, a collection of the funny "Oddly Enough" columns that Paul Jennings wrote weekly for *The Observer*. The one that inspired me most was "Ware, Wye, Watford," which turned the names of towns and cities into nouns, verbs, and adjectives. ("I'm feeling a little wembley today," and "If 'tis dunstable, he'll do it, milord," and "In his will he left me nobbut a kenilworth!") It was surely the trigger for my *Philosophical Lexicon*, of which more later. I spent many hours in Blackwell's bookstore, which had and no doubt still has the largest philosophy-book selection in the world. One day when I was browsing, I struck up a conversation with an older American who was perusing the same shelves. He said he was a philosophy professor from Yale, but something about his manner suggested to me that he was actually an American tourist who was trying to have a little fun pulling the wool over my eyes. "Where are you staying?" I asked, and he replied after a little pause, "Oh, in Balliol," which was the college right down the street. I figured he'd made that reply up in the moment. I engaged him in philosophical discussion, and everything he said convinced me that he was an impostor; I'd struck paydirt, and I remember going home to supper and telling Susan of the fun I'd had leading this tourist on, never revealing to him that I knew the truth. A few weeks later, we were watching a rather pretentious television show on the BBC about how European Jews (Einstein, Freud, Wittgenstein, . . .) had had an enormous influence on twentieth-century thought, and *there he was*, Yale professor Paul Holmer holding forth! Well, he was not *our* kind of philosopher.

5.

DISCOVERING
NATURALISM—
A DIFFERENT WAY OF
BEING A PHILOSOPHER?

ONE DAY THAT FIRST YEAR AT OXFORD, I ENGAGED IN
a long discussion with some other graduate students in philosophy about the strange experience of having one's arm "fall asleep"
and go numb and uncontrollable for a few minutes, dangling helplessly from one's shoulder. What was that all about? We compared
notes; we'd all had the experience, which was indeed remarkable,
and I began wondering aloud what caused it—did pressure on blood
vessels starve the nerves, or was it direct pressure on nerves that shut
them down temporarily? The other students looked at me as if I'd
lost my mind. What did anatomy or neurophysiology have to do
with this? This was a *philosophical* puzzle that needed *analysis*, not
anatomy lessons. I was astonished by this lack of interest in the physical phenomenon, and after the session broke up I headed for the
library to see what I could learn. That was the start of my scientific
education. I ended up spending more time in the Radcliffe Science
Library than in the Bodleian and soon was following threads from
encyclopedias to books and thence to journal articles. I knew nothing about the nervous system, but if I was interested in the concept
of mind, as I certainly was, I would have to learn about the brain.

Professor Ryle was tolerant of my conviction, though he himself
knew next to nothing about science, especially about neurophysiology and neuroanatomy (the term "neuroscience" hadn't come into

favor yet). He sent me to a professor of neuroanatomy he knew and encouraged me to check out the experimental-psychology people, where I found Brian A. Farrell, then the Wilde Reader of Mental Philosophy, a wonderful title reserved for a philosopher who would be housed in the Department of Experimental Psychology but was explicitly forbidden to do experiments. (Those who created the chair knew what they were doing. The psychologists would love to have appointed a fellow psychologist to the position and called him or her a philosopher, but that was effectively ruled out by the prohibition.) Brian took me in tow and taught me a lot of psychology, including an introduction to J. J. Gibson's work. He wrote one very fine philosophy paper, "Experience" (1950), which was published in *Mind*, the journal Ryle edited, and later anthologized in a collection of papers entitled simply *The Philosophy of Mind*, published in 1962 by Prentice Hall and a widely used textbook in philosophy-of-mind classes. Farrell's paper contained an explicit discussion of what it is like to be a bat—a quarter century before Thomas Nagel published his famous paper. I once pointed this out in a footnote, some years later, and Tom wrote me an embarrassed note telling me he had often been asked how he came to write his paper and had told people about a vacation he had spent in a house on Long Island where bats thrived, which had occasioned his interest. But when he got out his copy of *The Philosophy of Mind*, he saw that he had underlined Farrell's phrases and marked the bat passage with marginalia.

I have never put much emphasis on priority disputes in philosophy; we philosophers all have access to the same literatures and the fads and trends that arise in them, and it is often a matter of roughly simultaneously having the same reaction to something striking in what has recently been published. Doug Hofstadter and I once had a running disagreement about who first came up with the quip "Anything you can do I can do meta"; I credited him and he credited me. Well, it's a line to be remembered, summing up neatly the way philosophers often work. In fact, I have taken pleasure, not offense, at seeing many of my ideas (well, I *think* they were first my ideas) rediscovered, reinvented, by philosophers over the past half century without any acknowledgment. My writing style tends to go down so smoothly that philosophers often don't realize what they are absorbing as they dash through my books and articles. It doesn't matter; getting the ideas right is what matters.

Plagiarism, on the other hand, is, as everyone knows, the great academic sin. Over the years, I've had a few students submit plagiarized term papers to me, and after the first few instances I have made a point of warning my students at the outset of a course that I think there is no excuse at all for plagiarism, and that if I ever catch a student plagiarizing I will not just give them an F in the course but also do what I can to get them expelled. "Take an F in the course; drop the course; beg me for an extension. Just don't plagiarize!" That catches everyone's attention. I think the first plagiarized paper I received was by an Irvine student who was so naïve she didn't realize that no young woman in 1960s California would or could write using the stately Victorian cadences of Benjamin Jowett, the famous Oxford translator of Plato. She had simply copied about half of his introduction to one of Plato's dialogues and presented it as her own considered thought on the topic. She got off with a reprimand and a warning. The most remarkable case involved a woman in our MA program in philosophy at Tufts. She was a fireball, hardly able to contain herself in class, full of ideas and objections, reading beyond the syllabus. We thought she was wonderful. She wanted to continue in the PhD program at MIT, and I wrote her a very enthusiastic letter of reference, supporting my point with a photocopy of several pages of a paper she had done for me on B. F. Skinner's various stands on behaviorism to show the MIT admissions committee her scholarship and the acuteness of her mind. A few days later, I got a telephone call from Ned Block, then at MIT, telling me that he recognized the work on Skinner; it had been drawn from a PhD dissertation at Harvard on which he had been the outside examiner. I went down the road to Widener Library and found that he was right; she'd copied from this unpublished dissertation word for word. I was chair of the philosophy department at the time, and I called a meeting to discuss what we should do. She had all As and even a few A+s from us, but now all her grades in our courses were in question. Sleuthing in those days (before the internet) was a laborious task, but perhaps we'd all have to become detectives for a while. I offered a suggestion. I would call her into my office, give her a chance to confess first, then confront her with the evidence I'd photocopied from the Harvard dissertation and give her two choices: (1) She could hang tough, in which case we in the department would suspend all her grades, hunt for her sources, and drag her through the sort of trial that universities have for dealing with such cases (and we already had her dead to rights on one count). Or (2) she could agree to withdraw from Tufts immediately for undisclosed "personal reasons" and sign a statement I had prepared for her that would go into her file and permanently prohibit Tufts from revealing any information, any transcript of grades, even any acknowledgment that she had ever been there.

I called her in and gave her an opportunity to confess. Not a word. So, I showed her the evidence and presented the choices, and not surprisingly she took option 2. It didn't end there. I told her I knew she was deeply, even passionately, interested in how the mind worked, and although she couldn't help her case now, I thought she might be willing to explore with me what it was like when she was copying those pages. What thoughts went through her head, what reason could she have given herself to justify or explain her behavior? How could such a smart woman do such a thing? I was genuinely curious and would gladly have discussed this with her for hours, but she clammed up entirely, I'm sad to say, so I never got to learn how she managed it. I thought we'd handled it the right way, but less than a year later I got an evening call at home from Israel ("Izzy") Scheffler, a philosopher at Harvard's Graduate School of Education, who told me he had a problem. He had a student who had been at Tufts— he thought, because she had once mentioned my name—but when he inquired about her at Tufts, they denied all knowledge of her. "And what is your problem?" I asked, not admitting I knew anything about her. He told me he had caught her plagiarizing a term paper and wondered what I thought he should do about it. "Well, Izzy, this is just my advice, but here's what I think you *shouldn't* do. You shouldn't promise her to keep it a secret and let her go on her way." I don't know what Izzy did, and I've never heard of her, or from her, again. I hope she's found a path to a rewarding—and honest—life.

I know how easy it is to commit *negligent* (not deliberate) plagiarism. Some years ago, I was invited by Robert Kane to write a piece for his anthology, *The Oxford Handbook of Free Will*. I readily accepted and drafted a paper, and as I was rereading it before sending it to Kane I suddenly had an unsettling thought. Weren't the main ideas in this paper the ideas that my former student, the pianist Christopher Taylor, had developed in his term paper in my seminar a few years earlier? Fortunately I'd saved a copy of it, and sure enough, I'd reinvented Kit Taylor's points in my own language. I had been so close to doing something awful! I got in touch with Kit and invited him to be principal author of a coauthored piece on free will for the Kane anthology. By this time, he was giving concerts around the world, but he liked the idea, and we worked many long hours together on our paper and later wrote a revision for the second edition. Kane's notes about the contributors don't list Kit's philosophical publications—this being his first—but do provide a discography!

So, I almost committed plagiarism myself. I have also committed what may be the only case of reverse plagiarism. I published my second book on free will, *Freedom Evolves*, in 2003, and afterward participated in a conference on it in which the philosopher Alfred Mele pointed out that I had attributed to him something I called the Default Responsibility Principle: roughly, if you are causally involved in a misdeed and nobody else is responsible (hypnosis, coercion, nefarious neurosurgery, . . .), you are. Mele insisted he had never formulated any such principle, but my old notes on his book even listed the page number, so I went back to my copy of it, and, sure enough, *I* had written in the margin "Default Responsibility Principle." It was my idea, but it was provoked (or inspired, if you like) by what he had written. Fortunately, I had thought well of the Default Responsibility Principle. If I had invented it, provoked by him, and then trashed the idea, that would have been a different story! Another close call.

One of the first "original" ideas I had about the brain was one I've already mentioned: when I learned about neurons and neural networks, I envisioned a process that, like natural selection, could *mindlessly* reshape the brain to learn whatever was there to be learned. That became the backbone of my dissertation, along with an account of consciousness that sharply distinguished the consciousness of human beings from that of animals. Another key idea in my dissertation was inspired by a series of papers by Hilary Putnam, beginning with "Minds and Machines" (1960). I had a friend in Oxford who heard Putnam (then at MIT) lecturing on the topic and brought me a photocopy of another, newer paper by Putnam on robots, which initially filled me with frustration, because I had spent months thinking about the 1960 paper and had arrived at roughly the position Putnam's new paper maintained, but in it he went a bit further. Then there was a third Putnam paper, which again leap-frogged my own understanding. I can remember telling friends that I wished Putnam would just get distracted from this path and worry about some other issue for a while so I could catch up! Alas, my wish soon came true. The Vietnam War lured Putnam into a multiyear anti-war campaign during which he came close to losing his mind. (Later, after we were friends and colleagues, he told me he considered this a psychotic break in his life, which I think is the right way to put it. More on Hilary to come.)

Another main source of inspiration was the physicist (and philosopher!) Donald M. MacKay, one of the brilliant thinkers in Great Britain whose early work on "cybernetics" gave birth to computer science. He was a member of the Ratio Club, an informal self-organized group that met over dinner to discuss cybernetic issues and included Alan Turing, W. Ross Ashby, W. Grey Walter, Horace Barlow, I. J. Good, and some half a dozen others. MacKay's little book of essays, *Information, Mechanism and Meaning* (1970), is a gold mine of wise observations on the three topics in his title, and he also wrote a paper on free will that no philosopher should ignore. He is also the originator of the oft-quoted but mis-cited definition of information as a difference that makes a difference and is one of the first scientists I encountered who took a positive and productive attitude toward philosophy. I didn't meet him when I was at Oxford, but we briefly corresponded, and when I finished my DPhil dissertation I mailed a copy, unsolicited, to him. He wrote me back a thoughtful and valuable letter, and we later met on several of his visits to the US, including once when I invited him to give a talk at Tufts. One topic we discussed, constructively, was his devout Christianity, which of course I didn't share. He never came close to persuading me to consider joining a church, but he gave me an excellent model of a brilliant scientist whose mind was not in any way disabled by faith—there aren't many, in my experience (see chapter 27). I also learned something about how to think about information in the brain—still a major puzzle in cognitive science—from a book published by the young mathematician and neuroscientist Michael Arbib called *Brains, Machines, and Mathematics* (1964) and one of the first anthologies of early work on artificial intelligence, *Minds and Machines* (1964), edited by the Pittsburgh logician Alan Ross Anderson.

According to legend, and perhaps it is true, the Voltaire Society at Oxford was founded by an undergraduate who said, falsely, in a London job interview that he had founded a philosophical discussion group, the Voltaire Society, and its patron was Bertrand Russell. When the student got back to Oxford he immediately founded the society and invited Bertrand Russell to be the patron, and Russell accepted. Each term there was a new president, whose duties were to invite three speakers for the next term, with commentators, and to write Russell a letter about the society's activities. Russell typically replied. When it became my turn to be president, one of the speakers I invited was Alan Anderson, who was that year a visiting professor at the University of Manchester. I asked him to speak about artificial intelligence (instead of relevance logic, his specialty) and he was happy to oblige.

I won't try to recall all the other articles and books on AI and the brain that I read while researching for my dissertation, but of course I also was scouring the philosophy journals for relevant articles. Almost no philosophers were writing anything about scientific research on the mind, but the principal Australian philosophers of mind, J. J. C. Smart and David Armstrong, were writing excellent essays and books proposing and defending materialism and the so-called identity theory of mind, the simple claim that the mind and the brain were identical and that mental events of all kinds (if you thought about it just right) were things that happened in the brain. This led to scores of articles by philosophers mostly concentrating on delicate issues of how to frame the proposed identities. Was it mental images or *experiences-of-having-mental-images* that were identical with brain processes (or should we say "brain states" or "neural events" or . . .)? The linguist James McAuley once joked about how to tell philosophers from linguists; he said that the philosopher is the one who reads a paper on the hangman paradox at the conference on capital punishment. And a philosopher—was it Kierkegaard?—once said that when philosophers are shown an arrow they concentrate on the arrow instead of on what the arrow points to. It was obligatory that I confront the Australians' identity theory in my dissertation, and I wrote a very Quinian, but also rather Rylean, chapter on it—to get it out of the way, or so I thought.

With regard to those two influences: When I arrived in Oxford, I thought of myself as the Arch Anti-Quinian but was immediately and correctly identified by other graduate students and the philosophy dons as the Village Quinian. I accepted much more of his perspective than any of them did. I also thought that Ryle was having no major influence on me, though he was a wonderful lifter of spirits when I went to see him, often with thoughts on my mind about resigning due to the difficulties I was encountering. When I compared my finished dissertation to an early draft that I hadn't thrown away, however, I discovered that Ryle's influence was all through it, something that made me ashamed that I had been telling anybody who asked that Ryle had been a good cheerleader but I'd learned nothing from him. He understood the power of using lots of examples and analogies to unsettle readers' lazy imaginations, and he had a keen nose for unexamined presuppositions. To give just one example of a Ryle-inspired move of my own, consider what a *voice* is. Is it a physical organ that can be strained, a sound that can be recorded and recognized, an event, a process? Are voices to be identified with larynxes?

> The word "voice" as it is discovered in its own peculiar environment of contexts, does not fit neatly the physical, non-physical dichotomy that so upsets the identity theorist, but it is not for that reason a vague or ambiguous or otherwise unsatisfactory word. This state of affairs should not lead anyone to become a Cartesian dualist with respect to voices; let us try not to invent a voice-throat problem to go along with the mind-body problem.

I'm happy to agree now that (as somebody once said in a review of one of my books) I'm what you get when you cross a Quine with a Ryle.

More on Ryle

In 1961, Ved Mehta published a piece in *The New Yorker* about the brouhaha in England occasioned by Ryle's public refusal to review Ernest Gellner's book *Words and Things* (1959) in *Mind*, which he edited and which was one of the preeminent philosophy journals in the English-speaking world. Gellner's book was a scathing polemic against ordinary-language philosophy, and Ryle thought it was rudely disrespectful, especially about his friend J. L. Austin, who was then dying. The letters column in the *Times* of London had been full of argument about this, and Ryle was still having to deal with the aftermath when I showed up in Oxford. He told me that Bertrand Russell, who'd written the foreword to Gellner's book, sent him a note saying how foolish it had been to announce his decision not to review it: "What you should do in such a case is wait a year or so and then publish a very brief critical review with the author's name misspelled." Ryle and Russell were never close friends, and Ryle told me that some years earlier he'd found himself in a train compartment with Russell on a rather long trip to somewhere in Scotland, and Ryle had wracked his brains to think of a suitable topic of conversation. At length he tried, "Why do you think John Locke has been so influential, when he was neither as good a writer or thinker as Hume or Berkeley?" Russell pondered for a moment and said, "It is because John Locke invented common sense, and only Englishmen have ever had it since."

Most of Ryle's time when he was my advisor was spent editing *Mind*. He hated the American "publish or perish" syndrome and did everything he could to subvert it. He knew there were dozens of untenured philosophy professors in the US whose futures might well be secured by a single publication in *Mind*, so he gave special attention to submissions from American assistant professors. If their essays were even halfway presentable, he'd not only publish them—without even sending them out for further peer review—but let them jump the queue of accepted articles by established authors. There were papers by distinguished philosophers from around the world that languished in the limbo of "forthcoming" for years, while Ryle filled the pages of *Mind* with earnest but unseasoned efforts by young Americans. I made it a point of honor never to submit a paper to *Mind*, until I read Jerry Fodor's *The Language of Thought* (1975) and sent Ryle, unsolicited, a long review, or "Critical Notice," at which point I'd been tenured for half a dozen years.

Like most philosophers, Ryle was not a careful dresser, and one winter day I found myself standing behind him in the queue at Barclay's Bank, waiting to cash a check (a cheque). He turned around and greeted me and I noticed that his thermal underwear was pulled about halfway up over his waistcoat. Quite a sight, and I struggled with whether it would be kind or polite to point this out to him. I decided not, which was probably the right decision. His neighbor on the staircase in Magdalen was Jim Quitslund, one of my Harvard roommates, a Rhodes Scholar and excellent pianist. Jim knew who his eminent neighbor was from me, of course, and he decided to introduce himself and ask Ryle if he would permit him to play his phonograph during the day and, if so, what preferences or dislikes in music he had. Ryle said to Jim, "Play what you like, it's all the same to me. All music sounds like hail on a tin roof to me, and there's only two tunes I can recognize: 'God Save the Queen' and 'Rule, Britannia!' and I can't tell the difference between them, so I stand up for both!"

Restaurants in Oxford in those days were in general terrible, but there was one exception—the fabled Restaurant Elizabeth in St. Aldates, across from Christ Church. Susan and I wanted to make a pilgrimage to this place, famed for its wine cellar, one of the finest in England and maybe in all of Europe. We saved up our money and decided to celebrate handing in my dissertation (since I thought I might well not have anything else to celebrate before we left Oxford), and we invited Ryle to join us as our guest. The restaurant was quite formal, and we discussed the meals we would order in hushed tones. What about wine? "You go ahead and order what you want; I'll make my own choice," Ryle said. So, we did, ordering a half bottle of Chablis with the starter and a half bottle of reasonably priced Nuits-Saint-Georges with our entrées. When the waiter turned to Ryle and asked what he would be drinking, he replied, "I'll have a pint of bitter." The waiter's face fell. Probably nobody had ever ordered a pint of bitter (ale) in this temple to wine. Stammering, he explained to Ryle that the meal he'd ordered had a rather rich wine sauce, and he couldn't recommend a [shudder] pint of bitter. "Thank you for your advice," Ryle replied, smiling, "but that is what I should like." The waiter excused himself and returned in a minute with M. Lopez, the proprietor, shimmering in his white tie and tails.

"There seems to be a problem, sir?"

"I don't think so," Ryle replied. M. Lopez repeated the courteously worded advice his waiter had already offered, but Ryle wouldn't budge. Finally, with a look of deep sadness (or was it despair?), M. Lopez drew himself up and firmly said, "I am sorry, sir, but I am afraid the Restaurant Elizabeth *could not* serve you a pint of bitter with that meal."

"Very well," said Ryle, "what do you have that goes with a pint of bitter?" He ended up with some cold chicken and salad, and the waiter soon appeared with a pint of bitter, which he no doubt had had to run down the street and buy at one of the pubs.

Here is as good a spot as any to retell my oft-told tale of one of my adventures as president of the Voltaire Society. The logician Peter Geach and his wife, Elizabeth ("Miss") Anscombe, lived about fifty yards down St. John Street from our flat, and we often saw Peter walking by on his way to the railroad station. He taught at Leeds, but was much in evidence in Oxford, along with his wife, who was a formidable force in philosophy, one of Wittgenstein's pupils and in fact one of his literary executors. I had tangled a few times in discussion with her, so I knew her, but I thought I would ask Geach instead to give a talk to the Voltaire. I dropped by their house and Geach readily accepted my invitation. Who, I asked, might be a good commentator? He didn't come up immediately with any names, but Miss Anscombe said, "How about Geoffrey Warnock, dear? Hasn't he disagreed with you on some things?" "Oh, I guess you're right," Geach replied absently, so I went off to invite Geoffrey Warnock to respond, innocently unaware that the Geach-Anscombes and the Warnocks were barely on speaking terms. Warnock readily accepted, and I arranged for Geach's paper "The Perils of Pauline" to be sent to him in advance so he could write his reply.

The drill was that the speaker and commentator went to supper with the officers of the Voltaire before the evening meeting, with the officers chipping in to pay for the guests' meals. I also invited Anscombe, of course (but not Mary Warnock) and, since it was my last evening as president of the Voltaire, I had invited Ryle, whom I wanted to treat to a dinner. The private dining halls in the colleges we had used were all booked, so I had had to scramble to find a restaurant that would take us all at a reasonable price. I finally struck a deal with the owner of the Tackley Hotel in the High Street, a Mr. Dennett (the first time I had ever met a Dennett who was not a close relation). We agreed on sherry first with peanuts, a starter, a "veal" cutlet (it looked like a veal cutlet, but it would be pork chop disguised, as Mrs. Dennett divulged, to the annoyance of Mr. Dennett), with potatoes, veg, and wine, and a crème caramel for "pudding," all for the low price of one guinea, service included, per person. A guinea was one pound, one shilling, and our number was thirteen, so I had put thirteen pounds, thirteen shillings carefully in an envelope before heading to the Tackley Hotel on the appointed evening. The dinner went off without a hitch, with much good philosophical conversation, but when the waiter brought me the bill it was for more than fifteen pounds. Not wanting to make a scene, I excused myself from the guests and went to the back room, where Mr. Dennett was at his desk. "We just couldn't do it for a guinea apiece," he said, smiling faintly, and I handed him the envelope and told him that I was sorry he was losing money on the dinner, but we'd made a deal. I went back to the table, but when we all got up to leave Mr. Dennett sent his waiters to give us the bum's rush, yelling at us and hastening us down the stairs to the street. What on earth was that all about? wondered Geach, Anscombe, Warnock, and Ryle. I explained, with the waiters still standing in the door of the hotel yelling at us and making rude gestures. Ryle turned to them as we began to walk to Worcester College for the meeting and shook his fist at them, calling out, "Mexican *banditi!*" I doubt that they were Mexican, but they were not English. That was the only time I ever heard Ryle make such a Blimpish remark, but it was duly provoked, and it pleased all in our party.

That would have been enough adventure for one evening, but there was more to come. When we settled into our seats in our room at Worcester, I as host sat in the middle on a long low sofa, with Geach on my right and Warnock on my left, with the audience and guests in chairs in front of us. Geach read his paper seated (as was the custom in those days), and I soon realized that it was a thinly veiled attack on the late J. L. Austin, whom Warnock had deeply admired. You didn't say disrespectful things about Austin in Warnock's presence. I could hardly wait to hear Warnock's reply, and soon came the time for it. Warnock also sat, reading his commentary in a quintessentially calm and superior Oxford tone, but he was throwing daggers at Geach. Everybody was sitting on the edge of their chairs, and suddenly I heard a loud slap to my right. I turned and saw that Geach had slapped his hands together and was shaking violently. I thought he was perhaps having an epileptic seizure. But he soon stopped shaking and began writing furiously on his yellow lined pad. I looked over to see what he was writing but couldn't make it out. It didn't seem to be in English. (I later learned that Geach, who had trained with the Polish logicians, had the curious idea that Polish was, in effect, the language of thought, and that writing in Polish was a way to avoid confusion.) Warnock kept on calmly reading, elegantly launching a few more daggers as he went along, and suddenly Geach jumped up from his seat on the sofa beside me and began swaying in front of Warnock. What should I do? I felt puny and helpless sitting there a few inches off the floor, but fortunately Miss Anscombe, who was in the front row, issued a *Psst!* and beckoned him with a finger. He knelt by her chair and said, in a loud whisper, "This is impudence! I'm going to call him out." She whispered back in his ear. A friend of mine sitting right behind her later told me that she said, "Now Peter, be a good boy and sit down and wait for the discussion!" which he dutifully did. After Warnock finished his intellectual surgery, it was time for a coffee break and collecting dues; when we reassembled about ten minutes later, Ryle gave me the high sign to call on him, which I was happy to do. He thereupon began a leisurely and good-natured caricature of himself, piling example on example, and benignly dissipating the fog of war, after which there was simply no way for either Warnock or Geach to engage in phisticuffs.

Years later, having dinner with Warnock, who had become principal of my old college, Hertford, I told him that I had been the callow (then beardless) American quaking in between him and Geach at the Voltaire Society back in 1964. What had he thought Geach was going to do when he was swaying over him? Warnock said he'd expected to be kicked hard in the shins, but it wouldn't have stopped him from reading his paper. Is there anybody who can exhibit sangfroid better than an Oxford don?

Many philosophers still simply read their papers at meetings, forgoing the high tech of PowerPoint just as they ignored the power of overhead projectors before that. Once cognitive science got well underway in the 1980s, I was often asked by perplexed psychologists, neuroscientists, and artificial-intelligence researchers why philosophers *read* their papers instead of just giving a talk with slides. I had an answer: when scientists give talks at a conference, they are talking *about* their work; when philosophers give talks at a conference, that *is* their work, and all the care scientists take in the laboratory to get things precisely right, with no sloppiness or chance of confusion, is just like the care philosophers take when presenting their analyses and arguments. I think this is a defensible support for the philosophers' policy, but I also have to admit that many of them seem utterly oblivious to and uncaring about the intellectual discomfort they cause in their audiences, often reading dense and convoluted papers in a monotone. Perhaps it is a philosopher's way of being macho: "I dare you to comprehend my paper on first hearing; it's way too subtle for lightweights like you!"

There have been many occasions over the years when I have been obliged to sit on a stage as part of a panel, listening to three or four talks, and I have sometimes found myself on the edge of sleep, my eyelids getting heavy, my concentration evaporating. It would be worse than rude to fall asleep during such an occasion, but how to avoid it? I have a system, and I've shared it over the years with friends. It's the Mamie Eisenhower method, as I learned in *Reader's Digest* when I was a lad and Ike was president. Mamie was asked by a reporter how she managed to stay so attentive when Ike was giving his stump speeches, all of which she had heard many times. She gave away her secret. She listened carefully for the letters of the alphabet in alphabetical order, thus: "My fellow *A*mericans, I want to talk a*b*out the a*c*tions an*d* *d*eeds o*f* . . ." until she got to *z* and then started over. I tried it and found it worked beautifully, but I added some improvements. I surreptitiously glanced at my watch before I started, and wrote down the time, and then to keep myself honest I wrote down each word as I got it. When I got to *z*, I would write down the time and start over. So, my pad of paper would have something like this after perhaps twenty minutes:

10:15 that but focus and the if knowledge has with adjustment like all imagining imagining [*m* and *n* in order in the same word] out appeared question raised to pursuing even which extra way analyzed 10:36

Sometimes I would get through the alphabet three times in a single talk, but occasionally I'd encounter a speaker who just would not say a word with a *j* in it, or a *q* or a *z*—the three letters philosophers tend not to use (they use lots of *x*'s, in words such as "explain," "extension," "exist," "complex"). I've been amused when somebody comes up to me during the coffee break and says, "Whoa, Dan, you're an iron man! How do you do it? I was falling asleep and I looked over at you and you were *taking notes*!" The beautiful bonus of the method is that often in the middle of my Mamie-listing I'd realize that I'd stopped listening for a *j* or a *k* because I'd been paying attention to the paper, something I could not have done without the crutch. I've asked pertinent and constructive questions after papers that began with several rounds of alphabet soup. One time in Mexico I described the method to several friends who were attending a particularly soporific meeting with me—Fred Dretske was one, and I think Stephen Stich was another—and after lunch when we settled down in our chairs for the next talk, I noticed they were both paying close attention, and when the speaker said "inquiry" they both discreetly punched the air triumphantly. At long last they had the *q* they'd been waiting for.

Isaiah Berlin once told me about an informal philosophy group that met on Saturday mornings in Oxford in the late '30s, consisting of Austin, Ryle, A. J. ("Freddie") Ayer, Berlin, and Theodore ("Teddy") Adorno, who was studying Husserl with Ryle. This group would meet to hammer out points in the "analytic philosophy" mode that was just then getting created, and Isaiah told me that Adorno would occasionally break in and venture something along the lines of "The dialectical reunification of forms arising from the false consciousness inherent in the co-optation of the masses by the bourgeois culture industry signals an inchoate synthesis of aesthetic non-identity." Ryle would then say, "I expect there's a great deal in what you say, Teddy. Now, Freddie, when you speak of analytic truths . . ." Ever since Isaiah told me that story, I have had it at the ready in my lecture kit, the perfect reply to the fellow whose "question" is a rant that goes on and on, to the annoyance of everyone in the room. You wait patiently for him to run out of breath, and then say, calmly and politely, "I expect there's a great deal in what you say. Next question?" The verb "expect" is, of course, perfect.

Meanwhile I was struggling with my autodidactic education in what later would be called cognitive science. As a neophyte, it didn't bother me that there was no apparent consensus among scientists about how to research the mind—maybe that was how science had to be conducted—but in retrospect I can see that it really was a fallow period; Skinner's behaviorism still held sway in psychology, and I could find no bold attempts at whole theories of the mind. I got some valuable steers about what to read from Brian Farrell and a few psychologists I talked with, but mostly I just followed threads back through the books and journals I found useful, discovering occasional gems and reading a lot of deservedly forgotten speculative science. It seemed that the scientists who dared to mention consciousness or even the mind tended to be emeritus professors who, like the members of the Ratio Club, had been nursing hunches for years. I occasionally tried to explain to my fellow grad students in philosophy what I was doing. Mostly they just didn't get it. Whatever I was doing was not philosophy as they understood it. I thought they might be right, and whenever I encountered a problem that stumped me—which was about once a month—I'd somewhat desperately grab my brolly (you could never tell when a rainstorm might descend on you in Oxford) and go for a long brooding walk in the University Parks, with the Cherwell River running by on its way to Magdalen Bridge and the Isis River. In summer, the Parks would be full of tennis courts set up on the grass and a cricket pitch, but in the colder months you could walk the paths with only a few other strollers in sight. Back and forth I'd wander, usually crossing the footbridge to Mesopotamia, the long finger of land that separated the lower and upper branches of the Cherwell. I'd often talk to myself out loud, which I soon learned was a very useful habit. (For years I've been telling my students that before they submit their term papers they should read them *aloud*, if only to themselves. By hearing your words aloud, you can often pick up problems that escape attention with silent thought or reading.) Each time I went on my long problem walks, I eventually had a breakthrough insight, though it might be three hours in gestation. It got to the dangerous point where I would head out on my walk and start looking at my watch. Why hadn't inspiration struck yet? Was my philosophy method going to fail me this time? That sort of self-conscious reflection can be deadly to serious thought, but I managed to keep it at bay.

The two related philosophical problems I was trying to solve—at least in outline—can be rendered quite straightforwardly. First, how can it be that some complicated clumps of molecules can be properly described as having states or events that are *about something*, that have meaning or content? And second, how can it be that at least some of these complicated clumps of molecules are conscious—that is, aware that they are gifted with states or events that are about something? You and I have thoughts and ideas and hopes and fears *and we know that we do,* and we can *tell others about them.* How is that possible? Brentano and others had called this "aboutness" *intentionality* and elevated it to the status of *irreducible mental phenomenon,* the chief guarantor of Cartesian dualism. There were poor imitations, to be sure: A sunflower may turn in the course of a day to keep facing the sun, and in a very strained sense this is a talent that is about something—the sun. An electric-eye door that opens when somebody approaches is similarly endowed with states that (in a very strained sense) are about things. Can we build from an account of rudimentary, strained *aboutness* all the way to human consciousness? That is the task that any physicalistic or materialistic theory of the mind must execute. No miracles allowed.

That prohibition is what excited me about the hypothesis that something very much like natural selection could occur in individual brains, because natural selection is a (re)designing, mindless process with no miracles. It is, in fact, the only example of such a process that we clearly understand. My first book, a refinement and elaboration of my DPhil thesis, was hence titled *Content and Consciousness* (1969), and it has shaped everything I've done since then. Those long, worried walks in the Parks have paid off handsomely, since they allowed me to sketch out an explanation-machine whose crank I have been happily turning ever since. It might be, of course, that I'm all wrong, and that the *apparent* insights that have poured out of that crank-turning are fictions; but the fact that so many of them have been generated so copiously and fit together so readily with no further stumpers over more than half a century, has eventually banished my uncertainties. In short, I think I'm right and my critics are wrong, but I won't try to prove that here; that's what I've attempted to do in all my other books and articles.

Susan and I spent most of the summer of 1964 in Rome, where I worked on my dissertation, living in a furnished flat in Monteverde Vecchio on perhaps the only street in central Rome named for a philosopher: Via Lorenzo Valla. An encounter with children that summer gave me one of my favorite philosophical examples. We were strolling through the park on the hill above our flat where a Punch and Judy puppet show was entrancing about a dozen children, some just toddlers. At one point, Punch, falsely thinking Judy was still in a box, tried to push the box off a cliff, and the children just went wild with delight. Their glee unmistakably showed that they understood that Punch had a *false belief*. This became the "false belief" or "Sally-Anne" test in psychology that has been the basis of hundreds of experiments and papers since I proposed it in "Beliefs about Beliefs," a commentary in *Behavioral and Brain Sciences*, in 1978.

Back in Oxford in October, we picked up where we had left off, and my thesis gradually took shape. I hadn't thought of turning it in at the end of the academic year, though that was the earliest date allowed, but I eventually decided I might as well get the news, good or bad, that spring. There were four possibilities, of about equal probability I thought: I could be granted the degree on first submission, something that almost never happened; I could be given the opportunity to resubmit with improvements another year; I could be denied that option and handed a BLitt consolation prize; or I could simply be flunked and sent packing. Unlike the practice at American universities, one's thesis supervisor was not present at one's oral examination and really had little to say about how it was evaluated. Since my thesis was so eccentric, it was decided that one of my two examiners should be a neuroscientist, and J. Z. Young, from London, was appointed. He was famous for his work in Naples on the squid giant axon, and he was a friend of my other examiner, A. J. Ayer, but although I had read some of his papers, I had never met him and had no idea what he would make of my work.

Meanwhile, Danny Daniels also submitted his dissertation, on personal identity, which filled me with uncomfortable thoughts. I had read it just before he submitted it. It had no references and no footnotes. It was an extended science-fiction tale about somebody—let's call him Danny—who misdials the telephone and finds himself conversing pleasantly with one James P. Intriligator (I'll never forget the name), who suggests that they meet at a local pub for a drink. Danny goes to the pub and there's no trace of Intriligator, so he goes back and dials the "wrong" number again and gets Intriligator again, who asks, "Where were you? I waited for an hour." To make a long shaggy-dog story short, it turns out that they are in different spacetime dimensions, or something like that, and the question is: Can Danny establish that he's talking to the same person on each occasion on the phone, and if so, how? (I now have a colleague at Tufts named James Intriligator, and when he first introduced himself to me, I nearly jumped. "Intriligator" is a real surname, from the Latin for bookbinder. My colleague is in the same spacetime dimension that I am and is a fine professor of engineering.) That was the only philosophical question raised, and eventually answered to Danny Daniels's satisfaction, in the dissertation. It didn't seem like an acceptable dissertation to me, and I confess to having thought that I wouldn't mind, really, if we both were awarded the DPhil or if we both flunked, but if Danny's dissertation was accepted and mine was not, I was going to want to blow up something big, like, say, the Sheldonian Theatre.

The day of the *viva* came, and Susan walked me, in my subfusc, to the Examination Schools and waited for me outside the examination room. Ryle had told me that a *viva* usually was completed in an hour or so, but after two hours she went home, filled with dread. The examination took over three hours, and it seemed to me at times that Young hadn't understood my thesis and Ayer hadn't read it. It was such an awkward inquisition that I can't remember any of the challenges or my responses, and at one awful point, when Young asked me a particularly ill-posed question (ill-posed from a philosopher's point of view), I toyed with the idea of asking Ayer if I was obliged to answer, but fortunately I squelched the thought and did my best with it. After the ordeal, I had to wait a *week* before I found in my mailbox in Hertford a postcard from Ryle telling me that the examiners had recommended me for the degree. The only inkling I'd had of this prospect before getting that postcard was when a friend of mine told me he'd overheard Ayer talking in a pub with somebody about the excruciating hours he'd just spent in a *viva* where some poor American chap had been tortured by questions from an old friend of his and Ayer had not felt he could intervene.

Danny Daniels told me that his examiners had not passed him. At his *viva*, they complained about the lack of references, to which he replied testily, "Show me, please, where in the statutes it says that a dissertation must have references. I could have put in hundreds of references but didn't think they were obligatory!" His examiners instead showed him the rule in the books that says that if the examiners aren't satisfied with the candidate's command of the relevant literature they can set a special written examination, which they thereupon did. It was a three-hour examination, administered a few weeks later, and it consisted of three essay questions. I remember two of them, as told to me by Danny. One was "Which philosopher, in your opinion, has made the greatest contribution to our understanding of personal identity, and why?" His answer, in its entirety, was "Bishop Butler, for it is he who said, 'Everything is what it is, and not another thing.'" The other question was "What is the role of memory in the concept of personal identity?" to which Danny's answer was even shorter: "I forget." Did he really give those answers? I think he did; I never caught him telling a lie, and the second answer is, in a way, profound if you think about it carefully. In any event, the examiners allowed him to resubmit (with references and amendments), and off he went to an instructorship at Yale, where he was a great hit with the undergraduates. The actress Elizabeth Hartman met him and fell in love with him that year. She gave him a mink coat that came down to his ankles. He wore it all winter in New Haven, becoming a local hero among the Elis. (Eventually Danny got his DPhil and had a distinguished career at the University of Victoria on Vancouver Island.)

The fact that Danny had no problem getting a job at Yale says something about the enormous prestige Oxford had among philosophers in those days. Ryle in effect offered me several excellent jobs at red-brick universities in England, and his letter of recommendation landed me two job offers—sight unseen—in the US, at brand-new universities: SUNY Stony Brook and UC Irvine. (This was the post-*Sputnik* boom in higher education, and it was a seller's market, as states scrambled to establish new colleges and universities.) Since I had regarded my chances of getting the DPhil on first submission as slim, I had had to prepare for two different futures. If I was awarded the DPhil right away, or given the option to resubmit, I really should plan for a teaching job somewhere for the following year; if I failed, I needed to gain admission to a PhD program in the States, where I could start all over with a new project. So I applied again to UC Berkeley and was admitted once again as a first-year graduate student, but with a teaching assistantship to provide a little support. That same week, I learned from UC Irvine that I had been accepted as an assistant professor in the philosophy department. I waited nervously to see how my *viva* went, and when I learned I had passed, I wrote to Berkeley telling them I had made other plans and would not be accepting the teaching assistantship there. I didn't dare tell them I was going to be a tenure-track professor at their new sister campus in Irvine, since I imagined there might be some puzzlement and consternation about that, and I didn't want to set in motion some investigation of this curious event. When I tell this story to today's graduate students in philosophy, their envy is palpable; it has been a buyer's market for philosophers for decades, and the idea of being offered a job without so much as an interview or a campus visit strikes them as surreal.

There I was in 1965, twenty-three years old and a tenure-track professor of philosophy at a new university, never having taken qualifying exams, never having taken a graded graduate seminar, never having suffered through the ordeals of the now highly systematized (and much, much fairer) process of application and vetting.

Ryle had simply written a letter of recommendation (my only one) and A. I. Melden called me from California to offer me a job. Abe Melden, the first chairman of the philosophy department at Irvine, was a devout lover of Oxford philosophy. He had never been a student there, but he avidly followed the work of the ordinary-language philosophers, and he figured he was hiring one with a perfect pedigree. In a sense he was, but I turned out to be not at all what he expected. (There were several other North Americans in my cohort at Oxford—not ordinary-language devotees—who also readily landed good jobs in that market, and they have had distinguished careers, but there were a few others who soon discovered, when the fashion for ordinary-language philosophy faded, that they had no expertise at all, and nothing to teach. Whether they managed to get tenure before they and their colleagues discovered this is a question I'd rather not investigate.)

Part Two

OTHER MINDS

6.

UC IRVINE, 1965–71

CALIFORNIA OPENED TWO NEW CAMPUSES OF THE UNIversity of California in 1965: Irvine in the south and Santa Cruz in the north. The Irvine campus was built on 1,500 acres donated by the Irvine family, whose ranch stretched from the mountains to the sea, and when it opened for students in 1965 there was hardly a blade of grass on the campus. Susan and I, who had rarely been west of the Hudson River, drove across the country with little idea of what to expect. The day we arrived and entered the campus on the newly built Campus Drive, we had to stop and let two cowboys on horses herding several hundred cattle cross the road. There had been a town of Irvine in the foothills, but the Irvine family changed the name of it to East Irvine, so that the university could be called UC Irvine, not UC Newport Beach or UC Corona del Mar, the coastal towns on the ranch property. Mother's brother, Uncle Paul, and his wife, Laverne, had retired from Minnesota to Palm Desert, and when Mother wrote to tell them that her brilliant son Danny had accepted a job at UC Irvine, they got out a road map and made a scouting trip to Irvine to see the place. They found the old sign saying Entering Irvine, and after driving for a few miles through orange and walnut groves and past a lone gas station, they saw a sign saying Leaving Irvine. They doubled back, thinking they must have missed a turn. Nothing. Mother got a hilarious letter suggesting that her brilliant son Danny was the victim of a hoax; there was no university in Irvine! But there was, and by the time we arrived, the first circle of buildings was complete and hundreds of trees were being planted in the "Centrum," a dusty park-to-be. I could touch thumb to finger around any of the trunks of the new trees staked up and watered by sprinklers. Today some of those trunks in the Centrum are more than a meter in diameter.

In 1963–64, the newly appointed deans had been hired, and they began appointing department chairpeople, who spent the next academic year working out of trailers, hiring the first faculty and setting up labs while the first buildings were being finished. There were about a hundred faculty and sixteen hundred students when UCI opened in October of 1965, and I taught the very first class, Introduction to Philosophy, at 8:30 a.m. on the first day of classes; the day's topic was Descartes's *Meditations*. There were about a hundred students in the class, and I had two teaching assistants, graduate students of Abe Melden's whom he had brought with him from the University of Washington in Seattle. They were both older than I was, so I was in a delicate situation, but we got along well, and I learned a lot from them. In effect, I did my graduate education backward, finishing a dissertation first and then studying hard for several years in many courses—except that I was teaching them. Melden was busy helping to create the Academic Senate and supervising his graduate students, so I taught the undergraduate curriculum more or less single-handedly. This included, besides the introductory course, a full-year survey of the history of philosophy from Thales and the pre-Socratics through medieval philosophy and on to modern philosophy, ending with some Carnap and Wittgenstein, and courses in epistemology and metaphysics. E. J. (Jack) Lemmon, a wonderful British logician then at the Claremont Graduate School, taught our introductory logic course as a visiting professor, and was due to join us at UCI in the fall of 1966, but he died of a heart attack while climbing on Mount Baldy with a graduate student in July, a severe blow to Melden and me, since he was both brilliant and delightful and we had looked forward to building a department around him.

Melden, Lemmon, and I were the department of philosophy that first year. I loved it. I am glad that no recordings of my history lectures were made (so far as I know), since, like Danny Daniels, I was just a few days ahead of the students, especially in medieval philosophy, which I had never studied at all, and I no doubt sometimes expressed shockingly naïve and ill-informed views about the thinkers, their times, and their arguments. There is a lot to be said, however, for teaching courses on material you don't yet know well, because energizing your students with your excitement about these novelties often does more good than informing them, reliably, about the standard interpretations, objections, and defenses.

Shortly before I left Oxford, Gilbert Ryle had asked me to read the manuscript of his 1966 historical detective work, *Plato's Progress*, before he sent it to Cambridge University Press, which I did, finding almost nothing to improve or fix. He called it his "naughty book" on Plato, not because there was anything risqué in it but because he argued for a renegade account of the dating of Plato's dialogues, which he claimed had first been "published" as performed plays at the Olympic games. Plato played the role of Socrates, and the reason for the absence of Socrates from the later dialogues is that Plato was old and suffering from some infirmity (a toothache perhaps?) that kept him off the stage. There is much more iconoclastic sleuthing in the book, with confident declarations that some of Plato's writings were forged, and many other vivid hypotheses, supported by a breathtaking mountain of evidence. One of Ryle's eccentricities was his abjuring of footnotes in his own writing (perhaps Danny was inspired by him). There is not a single footnote in *The Concept of Mind* or *Dilemmas* (1954). Ryle's practice worked well in his informal but precise ordinary-language philosophy, but it made *Plato's Progress* awkward reading, since it is a work of great scholarship that must cite all the sources, which he plunked, parenthetically, in the main text. I was no Plato scholar, so I couldn't come close to assessing his evidence, but Ryle never wrote a boring sentence, and the book inspired me to teach a course at Irvine on Plato and his theory of Forms. I even designed a textbook, which included all the passages in Plato that seemed relevant to his theory of Forms (with rival translations when called for), plus half a dozen controversial articles on how to interpret them. The task set for students was to frame and defend a theory of Plato's developing thought, just as Ryle had done. I found a major textbook publisher who wanted me to do the project, but I soon realized that I would have to become a classical scholar to do it right. I took a course in classical Greek, which was fun, but philosophers who are Plato and Aristotle experts usually have years of Latin and Greek in high school or prep school before they ever get to college. I'd had some Latin in high school, but I realized I'd never catch up to them. Sad to say, I've never encountered a professor of ancient philosophy who had any interest in Ryle's naughty book. Perhaps I will inspire some young scholar to take a hard look at it. A rollicking refutation could be a fine start to a career.

One of the best features of the new university was that, because there were so many pressing tasks that needed doing, seniority counted for almost nothing. I got to participate on major faculty committees, and through these activities I became friends with chemists, physicists, biologists, mathematicians, historians, English professors, drama professors, psychologists, and computer scientists. We all knew each other quite well, and I learned a lot from them. The department chairs were refreshingly idealistic, having been lured to Irvine from flourishing careers elsewhere with the promise of building a new university that did things right, but they were also a feisty bunch of academic politicians who fought for power (faculty positions they could fill) and for budget. When I moved to Tufts six years later, one of the first things that struck me was how readily the Tufts faculty allowed themselves to be pushed around by the administrators. Where were the operators, the movers and shakers?

One of the slickest operators at UCI was James G. March, author with Herbert Simon of *Organizations* (1958), a classic book on organizational behavior, and first dean of the School of Social Sciences. He once asked my dear friend James McGaugh, founder of the psychobiology department, for his opinion of a possible hire, and when McGaugh said approvingly, "He's a solid citizen," Jim March said, "Well, that's two strikes against him!" March explained: he figured he had half a dozen years and up to a hundred appointments to build a school of social sciences that was of international renown, and he could compete earnestly with every major university for the "solid citizens" working their way up the ladders in their fields *or* he could hire every snake charmer and guru and self-styled genius he encountered and all he had to do was strike it rich on one or two of these appointments and the place would be famous. This was hyperbole, of course, but March did hire some dubious characters those first few years, and they eventually caused some serious problems. There was a "primal scream therapy" psychologist who first abused and then treated (for a fee) the students he had abused, and (I'm not making this up) I was once the external examiner on a PhD dissertation on "applied orgonomy" in which the candidate had constructed one of psychoanalyst Wilhelm Reich's "Orgone Accumulators"—a layered wood/metal box that supposedly concentrated the energy of orgasms—which the candidate assured us would bring rain to Southern California in July and August. Fortunately, I left UCI before having to pass judgment on that dissertation.

The wildness of much of what happened in the School of Social Sciences was an open secret on campus, with many professors in other schools dismayed by what was going on. One day an undergraduate student of mine told me he'd just learned that Republican senator S. I. Hayakawa (a pop-psych linguist turned politician) had student spies reporting to him about the various shenanigans in Social Sciences. I went immediately to inform UCI's chancellor, Daniel Aldrich, who needed to be on guard against a firestorm of criticism that might break any day. He listened carefully and thanked me, and that was all he said. A few days later, I read in the campus newspaper that Senator Hayakawa had been invited to give a talk on linguistics by the School of Social Sciences and had accepted. Hayakawa made his trip to UCI and gave his talk and—according to some Social Sciences faculty I knew—was taken to a faculty home overlooking Laguna Beach for a party after the talk. He was seated on a couch, given whatever he wanted to drink, and was soon joined by a lovely and lively miniskirted graduate student, who proceeded to flirt with him. He fell for it, apparently, since after an hour or so she smiled at him, reached under the couch to pick up the tape recorder that was spinning along, and wished him a good day. No Hayakawa Report on the scandals of the UCI School of Social Sciences ever appeared.

Most of the pioneer faculty at UCI were superb, and it was a great interdisciplinary feast for me. Young assistant professors don't get to know many faculty outside their own departments, except occasionally on committees, but at UCI we all worked, played, and partied together. In addition to Jim McGaugh, who was delighted to find a philosopher who had come up with some of the same criticisms of behaviorism that he had developed, and who welcomed me in all his seminars, chemist F. Sherwood ("Sherry") Rowland, who later won the Nobel Prize for sounding the alarm on the effect of chlorofluorocarbons on the ozone layer, was the center on my basketball team; Joseph K. Lambert, the deviser of free logic, who had once tried out for the quarterback position on the Chicago Bears, was the quarterback on our philosophy department touch-football team; and Edward O. Thorp, the mathematician who invented a winning system for blackjack and made a fortune, and then another fortune with his book *Beat the Dealer* (1962), was on the crew with me on several racing sailboats. My main sailing buddy was Donald Heiney, a professor of comparative literature, aka MacDonald Harris, novelist; we sailed on his boat and raced on monohulls and the first big ocean-going catamarans.

And then there was my friend in the Romance languages department, Richard Barrutia, son of Basque immigrants, accordionist, guitarist, *and* card magician. Dick had financed part of his college education as a "mechanic" in Las Vegas. A mechanic is a crooked dealer. Dick would sit reading his books in a back room of a casino waiting to be called on by management if somebody at one of the blackjack or poker tables needed to be, well, cheated. He taught me the basic moves of "mechanics" and card magic and lent me books from his excellent library of magic books. He would sometimes do something for me that he would never show in public. He once forced a jack of clubs on me at least half a dozen times in a row. "Pick a card, any card," he'd say, fanning the deck in front of me. I'd try everything—taking the last card in the deck, pulling hard on a card he seemed to be holding fast, reaching for one card and then swiftly changing to another card, and every time, there was the jack of clubs in my hand. Was it perhaps a deck composed of fifty-two jacks of clubs? No—or at least if it was, he was able to switch decks without my seeing it and then let me examine the deck in his hands. It was Dick who introduced me to Ralph Hull's great trick, the Tuned Deck, which I've used to expose the main flaw in David Chalmers's influential introduction (1995) of what he dubbed "the Hard Problem" of consciousness. Even expert magicians were fooled by the *name* of the trick, and in particular, by the word "the"! They thought they were being shown a single new magic trick when in fact they were being shown a variety of tricks they already knew. ("The boys have all looked for something too hard!" Hull says in his gleeful account of the trick.) Even expert scientists have been fooled by Chalmers's "*the* Hard Problem" into thinking that there's one big mysterious fact that needs explaining, when in fact there are hundreds of lesser problems that can be solved without any scientific revolutions, and when they are all solved the so-called Hard Problem will evaporate.

Once we had settled in Irvine, I had to start publishing of course. I began submitting revised excerpts from my dissertation to philosophy journals, and all were turned down. Dozens of them. They were attempts to turn philosophers' attention away from myopic obsessions with finding a logically foolproof way of stating materialism to challenging facts about actual minds, but that was too subversive an exercise for the peer reviewers. At one point I thought I'd landed a fish: Wilfrid Sellars, then editor of *Philosophical Studies*, wrote a note to me saying that he liked my essay but it was unclear on one point, which he invited me to revise. I promptly did so and resubmitted, soon getting a note from him saying that now that he saw more clearly what I was saying, he didn't think my piece was worthy of publication. I was crestfallen but had to admire Sellars's firm grip on principles. He wasn't going to let embarrassment stand in the way of his philosophical judgment.

I did have one minor triumph. One day Julian Feldman, a pioneer in AI and coeditor with Edward Feigenbaum of the first AI anthology, *Computers and Thought* (1963), came bounding into my office and slapped a hefty, mimeographed RAND Corporation memo on my desk: *Alchemy and Artificial Intelligence*, by an MIT philosopher, Hubert Dreyfus, which purported to be a refutation of the whole idea of artificial intelligence. "Dan, do you think this guy's right?" he asked. I read Dreyfus's essay that night and the next day told Julian that no, I thought Dreyfus had made some big mistakes. "Say what they are!" Julian insisted. "Write it up!" I did, and it led to my first publication, "Machine Traces and Protocol Statements" (1968), in the journal *Behavioral Science*. Dreyfus had claimed that computer programs could never exhibit *intuition*, and my line of rebuttal was to imagine a computer that solved some problem—any problem, really—and if asked how it did it, replied:

> "It just came to me, that's all." Intuition, after all, is not a species of deduction or induction; to speak of intuition is to deny that one knows how one arrived at the answer, and the truth of this denial is compatible with one's having arrived at the answer by any method at all, including "unconscious" brute force computing. (p. 159)

More important, in retrospect, than the publication was the fact that soon I was regarded by many in the fledgling field of AI as the philosopher to trust when it came to AI. Dreyfus, in contrast, was the bête noire of AI. His first book, *What Computers Can't Do* (1972), included the claim that computers could never play winning chess, since chess playing required "intuition," which was beyond computers. Joy reigned in AI when a computer soon beat Dreyfus at chess, but that didn't change his mind. Over the years, I got to know Bert Dreyfus quite well, and although we often did friendly battle on the topic, we both appreciated what the other was doing. I remember having a slide I'd often use when speaking to AI labs that said, "Just because Bert Dreyfus said it doesn't mean it's wrong!" Like many philosophers, Dreyfus couldn't resist inflating his claims; had he said that AI was not impossible but much more difficult than the enthusiasts thought, he would have been right, and from the outset he articulated some of the best grounds for believing this.

I needed publications in philosophy journals, not *Behavioral Science*, and I came to realize that my dissertation was just too ambitious and offbeat to break into bite-sized articles. I would have to write a whole book—a risky proposition, but what else could I do? At parties, philosophers would ask me what I was working on, and I really couldn't tell them unless I backed them into a corner and gave them a fifty-minute synopsis. ("Wait, you're a philosopher, so what's all this about neurons and evolution in the brain and how vision works after the signals leave the eyeball?") It was lonely. So, I rewrote my dissertation as a book and sent it off in the spring of 1967 to the famous Routledge & Kegan Paul series on Philosophy and Scientific Method, my favorite series, publisher of J. J. C. Smart, David Armstrong, and yes, even Wittgenstein. Might as well try for a home run. Ayer had been the editor of the series but had recently turned the reins over to his student, Ted Honderich. Then I waited. And waited. A year went by with no word from Honderich. I was getting desperate, so I wrote him a note asking what had happened to my book manuscript. He'd forgotten about it, having sent it for review to somebody in Oxford (I know not who) who also forgot about it. Honderich had to make a trip to Oxford and hunt through piles of books and papers in the fellow's study before he found it, retrieved it, and decided to referee it himself. In August of 1968, I got a note from him enthusiastically accepting the book and including pages of suggestions for minor improvements. I was in heaven, since, thanks to the University of California's generous sabbatical system, I was eligible, after just three years at UCI, for a quarter sabbatical, which Susan and I planned to spend back in Oxford that fall. The Vietnam War was raging. My deferment as a teacher was about to be revoked, and we decided that if I got my call-up notice while we were in Oxford we'd just stay in England and make the best of it. We were both quite active in the anti-war movement, beginning with the protest march in Los Angeles in June of 1967, when LBJ gave a talk at the Century Plaza Hotel that led to the notorious "police riot," leaving many people injured, but not us, who never got that close to the action. Susan had been meeting the school bus in our neighborhood and handing out leaflets advising high school students about conscientious objection and other alternatives to the draft, one of the projects of the Women's International League for Peace and Freedom. One of our neighbors, a navy veteran, announced at a community association meeting that he was sending reports on our activities to the Office of Naval Intelligence, and I said in a loud voice, "Well, Susan, there goes your career in the navy!"

On our way to Oxford, we stopped off in Massachusetts to spend part of the summer with our families, and I managed to get a gig teaching summer school at Tufts, forming a lifelong friendship with the new chairman of the philosophy department, Hugo Bedau. The Michaelmas (autumn) term in Oxford was a joy; Susan was pregnant, and I was revising and handing in my book manuscript and teaching logic in Hertford, my old college, while meeting every week with Derek Parfit and some of the other young philosophers for intense discussions about their ideas. Derek was puzzling about time, and whether asking what happened *before* the Big Bang had any meaning, and I was arguing that Freudian explanations of behavior were systematically exempt from either confirmation or refutation. We were headed back to Massachusetts for Christmas when calamity struck: Susan had a bowel obstruction that led to her not just losing our baby but almost losing her life and dashing our hopes for another pregnancy. In January I had to return to Irvine to teach my courses while she stayed in the hospital in Boston, where her father, a doctor, and her mother, who had been a nurse, could watch over her months of recovery and give me daily bulletins. This was the saddest, loneliest, most terrifying time of my life. But she recovered, and I flew east to gather her up, and we returned to Irvine. Something had changed in the few months we'd been away. Not only was the anti-war movement growing in intensity but many of our friends on the faculty were turning to drugs, open marriage, and other activities that were distressing to us when they weren't comic. I thought I could see through the ponderous pseudo-profundity induced in our friends by pot or even more so by LSD, and aside from a brief and scary overdose of hashish at a dear friend's house, I declined to participate, though egged on by my colleagues and many of my students. I guess I was just a square.

As the philosophy department grew during those years, we had a steady stream of excellent philosophers and logicians giving colloquia so interesting that soon philosophers from UCLA and UC San Diego would drive all the way to Irvine to attend them. One evening after such a talk, I walked out to the parking lot with David Lewis and the mathematician and logician Richard Montague, who had driven down together from UCLA. A gold Bentley was parked under a streetlamp. I was agog. "Holy [cow]," I exclaimed. "Who in the world would own a gold Bentley and what the [hell] is it doing parked here at UCI?" I rushed over and feasted my eyes on its features, even pressing my face against a window to get a better view of its interior. David and Richard didn't say anything, and when I had finished my exuberant chortle, Richard pulled out his keys and they hopped in the car and drove off, leaving me red-faced. Richard Montague was independently wealthy and openly gay, and he would cruise in his gold Bentley for rough trade along Sunset Boulevard—a practice that eventually led to his (still unsolved) murder in his beautiful hilltop home in Beverly Hills.

One time, just for fun, we took the British philosopher Brian McGuinness to the Five Crowns, an overdone imitation British pub, with horse brasses and a pillar box, prints of foxhunts on the walls, and serving wenches in perky white caps. The maître d' was soon aware that a genuine Englishman was a guest that evening, and at the close of the meal he came by to inquire if he'd detected any flaws in their replica of a proper pub. "Yes," replied McGuinness, and the maître d's face fell. "The loo doesn't stink."

Another great logician visitor from UCLA was Alonzo Church, famous for Church's Thesis and Church's Theorem, two of the foundational ideas of computer science. Church gave several talks at UCI, meticulously filling the blackboards with formulae. He insisted that you should never say what some term or sentence meant without subscripting the language thus: "$snow_{English}$" refers to snow, because the same orthographic symbol might possibly mean different things in different languages—"$chair_{French}$" means "flesh"; "$Gift_{German}$" means "poison." I decided to call this Church's Possibility and issued a challenge to one and all to come up with a sentence that was grammatical in two different languages and had two very different meanings, with high points for length and naturalness. Donald Davidson had an oral candidate: "Empedocles leaped" and "Empedocles *liebt*" ("loves" in German). The pre-Socratic philosopher Empedocles is fabled to have committed suicide by leaping into Mount Etna. My sailing shipmate Don Heiney came up with *"Grand legs? Seize ours!"* (French for "Large legacy? Sixteen bears!"). I wrote a letter to Vladimir Nabokov, my favorite novelist, polyglot, and wordsmith; his wife, Vera, wrote me a nice reply saying that she asked him and he said he hadn't ever considered the exercise and was sorry to say he had no examples. The challenge remains. I have wasted many hours trying to improve on Don Heiney's terse example without success, and I will gratefully consider any examples longer and better than his and duly announce prizes for any good candidates.

The tradition at UCI was for the department to treat the speaker to dinner in a good restaurant, with faculty paying for themselves. The first time Church gave a talk at UCI, we took him to Reuben's, a steak house on the waterfront that had the menu on a large wooden paddle, which also listed lots of side dishes. Church was a famous gourmand, and he looked the part, his immense belly swinging back and forth when he walked. About six of us sat around the table and continued our intense discussion about his talk while our waitress hovered and tried to get Church to give his order. Hardly skipping a beat, he chose the largest steak on the menu and a baked potato and rejoined the debate. The waitress persisted: Would he also like a skillet of mushrooms? Yes. Some onion rings? Yes. Popovers? Yes. Garlic bread? Yes. Hand-cut fries? Yes. Good guy, we thought; he knows the rule and is ordering one of everything so there will be lots to share, at department expense. We impoverished faculty each ordered something minimal—the petite sirloin, or even a hamburger with a tossed salad—and when the food arrived Church ate everything he had ordered, while we sat with our soon-empty plates in front of us and our stomachs growling. I had the pleasure of driving him back to UCLA the next day, and he told me several memorable stories. Once he gave a talk at Berkeley and in the discussion an eager young fellow began telling him aggressively about how the implications of Church's Thesis undercut what he had just said. As the fellow went on, it suddenly dawned on him whom he was instructing, and he stopped in mid-sentence and sat down. Church also told me of his attempt, back when he was editor of the reviews section of the *Journal of Symbolic Logic*, to pressure Kurt Gödel into sending him a copy of a lecture he had recently given at Princeton by threatening to publish the confused notes of an attendee at the lecture if Gödel didn't come through with his own version, but the threat didn't work.

In 1969 the first two copies of my book, *Content and Consciousness*, arrived in my mailbox, to my great joy. The philosophy department voted to put me up for early tenure (it really was a seller's market then), and I was asked to name the philosopher who should be asked to read it and write a report for the tenure committee's consideration. Quine, of course, and soon his confidential letter arrived. I was not allowed to see it but was told I should be pleased, though Quine had drawn attention to a few trivial factual errors. In due course, the committee granted me tenure, and I began to stop worrying about whether I was cut out for philosophy. I'd kept up my amateur sculpting, just in case, but now I turned to elaborating on (and sometimes correcting) the claims I had defended in the book. I now had help from my colleagues, who began to see what I was up to. We worked through Jaakko Hintikka's pioneering work on epistemic logic, *Knowledge and Belief* (1962), and Jerry Fodor's *Psychological Explanation* (1968), terrorizing a few graduate students who sat in on our discussions, since we didn't mince words and often got quite heated in our refutations and rebuttals. The combatants were Joe Lambert, Jack Vickers, Gordon Brittan, Peter Woodruff, and myself; they led me out of many culs-de-sac and were all, in the end, constructive helpers. If only philosophers were always like that! What eventually emerged from that furnace was my 1971 paper "Intentional Systems," which articulated the role of the assumption of rationality in all belief attributions and laid the basis for much of what I've since done. The central idea is simple: we ascribe beliefs and desires to people (and animals, and robots, . . .) to help us anticipate and understand their behavior, but this works only if we assume that they will do what is rational to do, given the beliefs and desires we've ascribed to them. By treating them as *intentional systems*—rational agents who know where they are and what they need—we can interact effectively with them, and whether we want to help them, join forces with them, defeat them in some contest, or just let them go on their way, our best hope is to adopt this risky tactic or stance and revise our ascriptions of belief and desire when they don't do what we expect. We do this without having to consider how their brains work—we just assume that their brains work *well*.

The Philosophical Lexicon

One evening in Irvine, while preparing an outline of my lecture for the next day, I wrote "quining intentions" as a topic heading, and I knew what I meant by my impromptu personal shorthand: denying the existence of something—intentions, in this instance—because of one's taste for (as Quine had once put it) a "desert landscape," a minimalist *ontology* or list of things one supposes to exist. Quine was famous for his dictum "To be is to be the value of a bound variable," which means, roughly, that if your theory requires you to talk about "all the x's that are F" or "There is an x that is F," then your theory is committed to the existence of x's that are F. But if you can find a suitable paraphrase, you don't have to commit yourself to these things. Quine's efforts to slim down his ontology were influential, but embattled. When someone once quoted to him Shakespeare's line "There are more things in heaven and earth, Horatio, than are dreamt of in your philosophy," Quine is said to have responded: "Possibly, but my concern is that there not be more things in my philosophy than are in heaven and earth."

If that's what the verb "to quine" meant, what was a "hintikka" or a "carnap"? What did the adjective "bewilfrid" [Sellars] mean, and what was it "to ryle"? Before I went to bed, I'd assembled about a dozen entries and typed them up, and the next day at the office I made copies to put in my colleagues' mailboxes. Soon many of them wanted to play the game, lowercasing the names of philosophers in the manner of "boycott" and "sandwich" and "cardigan." Joe Lambert promptly sent the initial list off to friends in philosophy departments around the country and indeed around the world. Soon new entries for the *Philosophical Lexicon* began pouring in from all over, and a quality-control problem emerged. Some of the new entries were just lame, but what galvanized me into action was when we received a re-edited version of my original list and one of my favorite examples had been, shall we say, mis-improved. Gottlob Frege's pioneering work *Grundgesetze der Arithmetik* (basic laws of arithmetic) had been shown by Bertrand Russell to be inconsistent, but this didn't stop Frege from finishing the two-volume treatise and trying to salvage the inconsistency. One of my favorite definitions was:

frege, n., (only in the idiom *to beg the frege*) To acknowledge the inconsistency of one's position but maintain it anyway.

Someone had replaced this with "to frege the question." *Aargh!* The German word for "question" is *Frage*, so the bilingual pun was the heart of the original definition. I asserted my editorship and got out my red pencil. A "second edition" was prepared, to be followed every year or so with larger editions, all xeroxed and mailed to those whose contributions had been accepted by the editor. After I moved to Tufts, I decided that it was time to put out a printed edition and make it more widely available. (I had become convinced that the *Lexicon* would probably be my most enduring philosophical legacy, so I should copyright the thing and get it properly published.) Since some of the definitions were arguably unfair and even cruel, I sent a copy of the penultimate draft along with a self-addressed postcard to all the locatable living *definienda* with three options to check: "You may include my name as defined," "Please delete the definition of my name," and "I urge you not to publish this work!" Fewer than a half dozen philosophers asked for their entries to be dropped—requests that of course I honored, ignoring the advice of several colleagues who suggested I should publish their entries anyway, with an asterisk noting that they had asked for the entry to be deleted.

Several refuseniks changed their minds later and wrote to me asking to be reinstalled in subsequent editions. I received lots of mail from philosophers who ached to be included, sometimes proposing rude definitions of their own names, but from the outset we had forbidden self-definition. Philosophers, like most academicians, crave the attention of their colleagues: *Say what you want about me, but spell my name right!* The first decade of my career was complicated by the fact that one of the most talked-about philosophers those days was one of Donald Davidson's top students, Daniel C. *Bennett*, who had taught at Stanford, Brown, Brandeis, the University of Massachusetts, and Swarthmore. He was more than ten years older than me, and when I went to American Philosophical Association meetings and people saw my name tag, they would sometimes ask, "Are you *the* Daniel Bennett?" to which I would reply, "I'm not even *a* Daniel Bennett." Bennett became nationally famous in 1971 (for more than fifteen minutes but not for long) when activists broke into the FBI office in Media, Pennsylvania, and stole surveillance files being kept by J. Edgar Hoover on anti-war activists, including those on the Swarthmore faculty, of which Bennett was the most prominent.

I didn't think I should make any money at the expense of my colleagues, so for some years the published edition of the *Philosophical Lexicon* was sold by the American Philosophical Association, and I think it was a modest moneymaker for them. After some years of neglect without a new edition, I was asked by the Danish philosopher Asbjørn Steglich-Petersen, at Aarhus University, if he could take over. I sent him the hundreds of unsorted entries that had been piling up in my desk drawer. The eighth edition (1987) is online (for free). Perusing it now, I find that I don't *get* lots of the new entries, which is a good measure of how far away from the philosophical grapevine I've strayed in recent years, but it was true from the outset that anybody who was amused by all the entries was spending way too much time reading philosophy and gossiping about philosophers.

7.

MOVING BACK EAST

I FORMULATED THE BEST, MOST INFLUENTIAL ARGUMENT of my life in December 1969, during a holiday visit Susan and I made to our family homes in Massachusetts:

(1) Someday we want to have a place in Maine.
(2) Places in Maine are going to become more expensive faster than we will ever get richer.

Therefore, even though we are living and working in Southern California, we should try to buy a place right now.

Susan agreed and we started our search. On one scouting trip we had just about given up when we spotted a tiny Polaroid black-and-white photo in a realtor's window in Ellsworth, Maine, listing a property "ca 200 acres with buildings" in Blue Hill, for $25,000. A few hours later we bought it, for the asking price. It's a good thing we didn't dicker. Over Christmas the owner decided to take it off the market and try to sell it for a higher price with a fancier real estate company, but the law in Maine then required a seller to sell to anyone offering the asking price—a wise measure to prevent discrimination—and our lawyer, the redoubtable Charles Hurley of Hale & Hamlin, successfully insisted that the owner accept our offer. Thus began our life at Godland Farm, where we spent every summer for the next forty years. (Parson Jonathan Fisher, an eighteenth-century clergyman and scholar in Blue Hill, made a map of the area—now in the Jonathan Fisher House Museum in Blue Hill—which showed every

house and lane, but our two hundred acres did not yet have buildings, so the location is marked with the word "Godland," which
meant *nobody's land yet.* We decided this would be a good name for
the farm and the cider wine we made there, and for us the name had
nothing to do with religion.)

We drove east for the summer of 1970, our last childless summer, to confront the farmhouse we'd purchased. "We're out of our
minds!" I remember saying to Susan as we drove up to the place for
the first time, its dooryard littered with abandoned cars and trucks,
our water supply a nickel-plated hand pump in the kitchen sink connected to the backyard well, a three-holer outhouse our only toilet, a grand total of three electrical outlets in the whole house, and
junk piled everywhere. At first the insurance company refused to
insure the place, thinking we just planned to burn it down and build
something else, but our agent convinced them that we were a crazy
dreamy couple from California who actually planned to restore the
place to its original glory. Susan's brother George, just out of the
Marines, helped with the restoration work. We loved our Blue Hill
neighbors, all native Mainers who were a steady source of instruction

Godland Farm, Blue Hill, 1972

and help, and in time we made such progress that we decided that driving to Maine from Irvine every summer would make no sense.

It was time to move back to New England. Fortunately, my book got a few very good reviews, so I was easily movable. I soon had offers from the University of Maine, the new University of Massachusetts at Boston, and Tufts. Living year-round in Maine had its attractions, but the dean at the University of Maine made it clear to me that he wanted me to come in and clean house, terminating the contracts of the five untenured members over the next few years and hiring a new department. This was known to all in the department, and my campus visit was worse than unsettling. I thought the existing faculty was actually quite respectable, and I was impressed by the honesty and dignity with which the jeopardized professors handled their meetings with their likely executioner, but their wives—yes, the professors were all men then—were terrified. What fun Susan will have getting to know them, I thought.

Another even more unsettling experience greeted me at the University of Massachusetts at Amherst, a highly regarded department. I had put my name in for a job there and had not been short-listed, but Robert Ackermann, a friend of mine there, invited me to come visit him when I was east for Christmas, which I did, expecting to spend the afternoon playing ragtime piano with him. When I got to his house, he invited me to sit in on his seminar that afternoon. I agreed, whereupon he called up his colleagues and invited them to come as well; he was trying to shoehorn me back onto the short list by having me give a talk. His colleagues showed up and were the most hostile audience I have ever encountered. I drove back to Boston thinking that if this was what high-powered philosophy was like on the East Coast, I wanted no part of it. Fortunately, when I had given roughly the same talk ("Intentional Systems") at Princeton a few weeks earlier, I had enjoyed a lively and constructive discussion, so I soon recovered my optimism about the field and my place in it. I accepted Hugo Bedau's offer of a tenured position at Tufts, where I have been ever since, just the right place for me.

Back in Irvine, Susan and I had signed up to adopt a baby. This process could take a long time, but Irvine agreed to prolong my appointment there and Tufts agreed to defer my arrival until we had our child. We got baby Andrea in March 1971, ahead of schedule, and were free to move east, but Irvine had been selected to host a remarkable summer workshop on philosophy of language, organized by Princeton philosophers Donald Davidson and Gilbert Harman, and I hung around to attend that informally.

I'm surprised to learn that nobody, so far as I know, has ever published any account of that workshop, which I think had a large effect on the field. It was supposed to be an opportunity for young philosophers of language with appointments outside the major departments to catch up with their better-positioned peers by spending an intense eight weeks with some of the world's best analytic philosophers and linguists: besides Davidson and Harman, there were Quine, Strawson, Grice, Saul Kripke, David Kaplan, and the linguists Barbara Partee, Haj Ross, and George Lakoff. Harman and Davidson ignored the rules and invited many of the top young philosophers in the country to be the students, along with a handful of "rural worthies" (the odious term used *sotto voce* to refer to those the program was designed to help).

Davidson and Harman were rightly criticized by the Council for Philosophical Studies, which had funded the workshop, but for better or for worse this elite gang went on to dominate analytic philosophy for decades, a coterie of young philosophers who got to know one another well at Irvine. Philosophers will recognize their names: Helen Cartwright, Oswaldo Chateaubriand, Gareth Evans, Carl and Sally Ginet, Dick Grandy, Bill Lycan, Bob Stalnaker, Denny Stampe, Steve Stich, Rich Thomason, Peter Unger. I was not one of the official participants in the workshop but was allowed to participate as an Irvine native of sorts, so I should include myself among the philosophers who were handed prime nodes in the academic network by those eight intense weeks. This gang of perhaps twenty philosophers took the early afternoon off for recreation—

the beach, or tennis, or swimming in the UCI pool. We shared the athletic facilities with the San Diego Chargers football team, who were doing their summer training, and philosophical discussion came to a halt in the locker room when the Chargers came bounding in, yelling and laughing, cleats clanging and helmets being tossed around. One of my happiest visual memories is of the slender Sir Peter Strawson chatting with two of the giant linemen in the showers.

My mother had died of a stroke that spring shortly after visiting her infant granddaughter in California, and when we moved to Massachusetts we lived in her house for a few months until we found a fine old Victorian house in Andover, half an hour north of Tufts and hence half an hour closer to the farm in Maine. Two years later, we would adopt Peter as an infant, and the four of us shuffled back and forth between Andover and the farm for twenty years. The farm was not centrally heated but it had an excellent Franklin stove in the dining room and a wood-burning cookstove in the kitchen so we could drive up on a midwinter Friday evening and expect to get the house more or less comfortable before we went to bed. I do remember waking up a few mornings to find icicles in my mustache. The farm had been lived in continuously for 140 years without central heating, so

Susan mastering the wood range, 1972

we were only doing what folks in those parts had been doing all their lives. We got better at it with practice.

~

AT TUFTS, ONE OF the undergraduate courses I began teaching was a section of Introduction to Philosophy. It was a "writing intensive" course, in which a small group of freshmen and sophomores (twenty or fewer) were obliged to write, and rewrite, a series of short papers. It was a lot of work for me, since I let them rewrite each of their papers as many times as they wanted, in response to my marginal comments. Only the grade on the final submission counted, so I graded the early efforts sternly, giving students Ds and Fs, which they had never before seen on any assignment in their lives. With five short papers, most of which would be rewritten at least once, that meant commenting on several hundred essays a term, a major effort that consumed hundreds of prime-time hours. (I for one cannot read a student's paper when I'm drowsy; it's a hopeless battle against mind-wandering and sleep.) Since the students were all writing about the same text each time—Plato's *Meno*, or Descartes's *Meditations*, say—it was possible to conduct grand rounds, in effect, on sick sentences, because everybody would be almost literally on the same page. As I read through their papers, I'd highlight awkward, boring sentences and copy them, verbatim and unattributed, for use in class. We'd go through them on the blackboard one at a time. "What needs fixing in this sentence?" I would ask, and at first the students would be baffled. There were no spelling errors, no factual errors, no typos or failures of verb agreement, no split infinitives . . . As far as they could tell, there was nothing at all amiss with the sentence. "Does it sing?" I would ask. "Does it make you want to read the next sentence? Does it say anything vivid, memorable, clever? Or does it just limp along, doing its job in a clumsy way?" Soon they got the point and vied with one another to come up with something more energetic, more graceful, something with a little snap to it that somebody might want to quote. I'd be busy erasing and writing on the blackboard, while they argued among themselves about which revisions were the most apt. They knew good writing from bad writing; they just had never been encouraged to aspire to good writing and didn't know how to raise their standards until I showed them. Writing, and rewriting, and rewriting again is what I taught my students, and I think the effort I spent kindling their writing aspirations was probably the best use of my undergraduate teaching time at Tufts.

I never gave a talk on the West Coast during my six years at Irvine. My first invited talk ever was in December 1970 at Princeton, after Gilbert Harman and Richard Rorty there had discovered *Content and Consciousness*. Princeton was then regarded as the foremost philosophy department in America, so I started at the top. There were stellar figures in the audience, and I was nervous in spite of the presence of a few friends and acquaintances from Harvard days: David and Steffi Lewis, Tom Nagel, Gil Harman, and Margaret Wilson. As I started reading my paper, "Intentional Systems," a woman in the middle of the audience caught my eye; she was *digging it*, smiling and nodding and anticipating, so I was drawn into giving the talk *to her*. It carried me along swimmingly, and when it was time for questions her hand shot up, so of course I called on her, and she asked a question that showed she hadn't understood the paper at all! I felt like I might faint there and then, but I recovered and soon realized that I had managed to communicate with the others. Since then, I've occasionally found myself listening to a speaker who was desperately nervous and have done a little extra beaming and nodding myself. It can work wonders.

When I got to Tufts, the first major invitation came within weeks of my arrival: the Cincinnati Colloquium on Mind and Brain in November of 1971. I was asked to give a talk of my own ("Brain Writing and Mind Reading," my first defense of Quine's indeterminacy of radical translation) *and* to respond to a talk by Rorty on my book. Hilary Putnam, whom I had not yet met, was there, giving the

Taft Lectures, and Wilfrid Sellars also gave a talk. This was the only time I saw Hilary in action during his psychotic anti-war period, and it was shocking. For instance, he claimed that in China, the people (the People, in their wisdom) were building aircraft carriers without benefit of blueprints or naval architects. At this time the only book of assigned reading for his courses in the Harvard Coop bookstore was Mao's little red book. And yet, and yet, he could still respond sensibly to philosophical criticism of his work. Bill Lycan had the unenviable job of responding to Hilary's talk on functionalism, which Hilary had recently abandoned, and announced that he intended to defend an older version of Putnam against the version we had just heard. Well done, Bill!

Wilfrid Sellars, who knew me slightly from several visits he'd made to Irvine (and our correspondence over my paper he'd decided not to publish!) invited me to dine with him that night in a fine French restaurant in Cincinnati (yes, there was one, and he knew it well). When I met Sellars in the hotel lobby, I found I was suffering from nausea and told him forlornly that I hated standing him up in this way, but I was going to be ill and couldn't join him. He looked at me intently and asked, "Do you like martinis?"

"Yes, normally, I like them very much, but—"

"No buts, come with me, we're going to have a martini or two," he replied, and I reluctantly got into a cab with him and began imagining how terrible it would be in a few minutes when I would throw up all over him in a fine French restaurant. But it didn't happen. He was right; my nausea was a symptom of my being so keyed up the whole day, and after my first terrified sip, the tension melted away, and we had a memorable meal and even more memorable conversation about our residual disagreements, in particular about whether the concept of *qualia* was a mistake philosophers should abandon. As we polished off a bottle of Chambertin, he said, "Dan, qualia are what make life worth living!" I disagreed then, and I've used that line to introduce both what's right and what's wrong with Sellars's view of qualia.

In March of 1973, I was invited to speak at another remarkable conference, on "language, intentionality, and translation theory" at the University of Connecticut. This was perhaps the best skirmish in the philosophical battle about Quine's indeterminacy of radical translation—and Quine was vindicated in the end (in my opinion, perhaps not shared with most of the other participants). Putnam and I had been given the role of commentators on a paper by Sellars; Quine and David Lewis were commenting on a paper by Davidson; Gil Harman and Charles Parsons were commenting on Michael Dummett; and David Kaplan and Barbara Partee were commenting on a talk by Saul Kripke. Fast company, but I was more relaxed by then. I drove down to Connecticut with Hilary Putnam as my passenger, which gave us hours to get to know each other. In addition to discussing what we would say about Sellars, who had neglected to send us his paper in advance, Hilary shocked me by telling of the times other Harvard professors (not philosophers) had made anti-Semitic remarks in his presence, not realizing that his Wasp surname was one his family had adopted decades earlier. (His father, Samuel, was a highly regarded translator, famous for his rendering of *Don Quixote*, the Modern Library edition, still in print and regarded by many as the finest in English.) I have never encountered any anti-Semitism among the faculty or students at Harvard before or since, but I believed Hilary, and I've been keeping a lookout for it.

The meeting at UConn was intense but convivial, and my talk went well, in part because it was humorous. During a coffee break, Quine came up to me smiling and said how very pleased he was to see me at the workshop, and I beamed. Then he added, "Because I have an insatiable appetite for humor." I replied a bit frostily that I hoped my talk wasn't *just* humorous, and he backpedaled gracefully. On another occasion he had gone out of his way to praise some sculptures of mine he had seen in an exhibit at Harvard, and I had wondered if this was a hint that I should pursue sculpture instead of philosophy. It is easy for a professor to underestimate how such casual remarks can reverberate through a student. I've been on the receiving end of enough inadvertent zingers to know better and have—I think—done a conscientious job of reserving my barbs for academic bullies.

The University of Pittsburgh invited me to give a seminar on philosophy of mind during their unique summer term, and I managed to compress a fourteen-week seminar into seven weeks after classes were over at Tufts, flying to Pittsburgh every Tuesday morning, giving an afternoon seminar, staying overnight in a hotel next to the campus, giving another seminar Wednesday morning, and flying home. I loved the Pittsburgh department; they had a reputation for working harder with their graduate students, and Wilfrid Sellars was there, along with some other fine philosophers, including John Haugeland, of whom more later. Most Tuesday evenings I would have dinner with Wilfrid in his club or in a fine restaurant, and we would talk (and drink) into the night.

As the '70s progressed, I found that I had amassed a collection of essays about the mind and psychology honed with the help of dozens of philosophical audiences which I thought could well be collected in a book that would amplify their impact. I disapproved, however, of the high prices that publishers were asking for hardback volumes and wanted to try something different. No sooner had I sketched out this idea in my head than I had a pair of visitors to my office at Tufts, Harry and Betty Stanton, who were looking to start a new publishing house, to be called Bradford Books and run out of their ski lodge in northern Vermont. Harry was an experienced Boston publisher, retired early from Addison-Wesley, who had realized that he could use his little black book of names and phone numbers of freelance copyeditors and book designers to produce high-quality books without the overhead of a large office building and staff. So, he had gone hunting around Harvard and MIT for some prospective authors he might entice. Noam Chomsky had suggested he get in touch with me, and so he had. He and Betty were elegant and charming, and they shared a puckish sense of humor. I handed them the stack of essays I'd gathered up and proposed an unusual deal to them: publish my collection simultaneously in hardback and paperback, and while they could charge what they wanted for the hardback, I had to have veto power over the price of the paperback. I was so sure this was the right thing to do that I was willing to forgo all royalties on the first three thousand copies for this privilege. I promised that we would survey paperback prices on similar books to make sure my pricing was reasonable, and Harry and Betty headed to their ski lodge to do some reading and thinking.

They also sought the editorial advice of a young couple of philosophers at the University of Vermont, Philip and Patricia Kitcher, who quickly gave their blessing to the project. So, the contract for *Brainstorms* (1978) was signed at a sumptuous dinner at the St. Botolph Club in Boston (Harry's club; he was quite the Boston gentleman, with his bow ties and pipes and Beacon Hill residence). Harry asked his friend Edward Gorey to draw both a cover illustration and some drawings for advertising flyers. This was to be Bradford Books' debut (aside from a small volume, a conference proceedings on the biology of language, that Chomsky and Edward Walker had organized), and Harry wanted to make a big splash. One frustrating snag was that Gorey's artwork for the cover got lost in the mail, and after waiting some months for it to surface, Harry gave up and put artwork by Gorey for Edward Lear's *The Dong with the Luminous Nose* on the cover. Years later, Gorey redrew the original art, which has been on the paperback since 1985 and features four enigmatic bearded fellows with scarves and an equal number of sheep on a desolate landscape. I've never figured out if it has some deep meaning or is just one of Gorey's oddly Victorian mock-macabre illustrations.

Harry's publicity campaign for the book—and Bradford Books— was a thumping success. Soon Harry and Betty were deluged with manuscripts from other philosophers and cognitive scientists wanting to publish a Bradford Book. But Harry got throat cancer just as the IPO for Bradford Books was scheduled to hit Wall Street, and nobody will invest in a one-man publishing house with throat cancer, so Harry and Betty had to change their plans and find a

Boston publisher to buy out Bradford Books of Montgomery, Vermont. Happily, Frank Urbanowski, the director of MIT Press, had the vision to do this, and hired them both as editors. Within a few years, Bradford Books was the star imprint of MIT Press. (I think my book and the Chomsky/Walker book were the only Bradford Books ever published in Montgomery. There was a sheltered workshop in the area whose participants handled all the mailing and billing, so it was a wonderful snowy village project while it lasted, and I was sorry to see the Stantons have to become employees again, but they did a grand job of it.) For years I played an informal role advising them about authors and titles, and of course published other books with them. For at least a decade, MIT Press was *the* publisher of cognitive science books. Editors at Harvard, Yale, Oxford, and Cambridge University Presses all sought me out for advice on how they could get into the field, and eventually they all did, but I stayed with Bradford Books.

8.

A YEAR AT HARVARD;
MEETING JERRY FODOR

IF YOU WANT TO KNOW WHERE TUFTS IS, DRAW A straight line between Harvard and MIT and construct an equilateral triangle on that base. Tufts is more or less at the apex, about as far from them as they are from each other—a pleasant walk on a nice day. Tufts has always had a love-hate relationship with Harvard, much less intense now than back in the '70s. It sometimes seemed to me that everyone on the Tufts faculty was either a Harvard graduate or PhD, or had a spouse on the Harvard faculty, or taught Harvard Summer School or Harvard extension courses, or wished they were teaching at Harvard, or had taught at Harvard and been sent away. So when after just two years at Tufts I was offered a visiting professorship at Harvard, my Tufts colleagues were unable to be indifferent. This was presumably my audition for a chair there. And when I returned to Tufts the following year without an offer from Harvard, I could read the mixed emotions on my colleagues' faces. Some were happy to see me back for less than noble reasons. (I must have had my tail between my legs, mustn't I?) Rumors swirled. Let me set the record straight. There was never any offer, and there was never any discussion of an offer. Thank goodness, in retrospect, because if I had been offered a tenured professorship at Harvard then, I would probably have accepted it, and my philosophical career would have soon ground to a halt.

Why? Mainly because Harvard puts immense pressure on professors. I still had vivid memories of being angry as an undergraduate when I had trouble finding my professors so I could talk with them.

They seemed adept at hiding. Now on the receiving end of that inquisitiveness, I myself was soon looking around for ways to hide. Harvard students then felt entitled to world-class professors, every day, always at the top of their form and willing to take on indefinite extra time to deal with honest curiosity. I expect they still do. Harvard had the reputation of never granting tenure to junior faculty, whose appointments were unofficially labeled "folding chairs," always going outside for their tenured appointments, and one of the presumably unintended side effects of this was that Harvard often hired bold pioneers who had made their reputations elsewhere, only to watch them tighten up and get cautious once they were tenured at Harvard. My visiting year at Harvard was a turning point in my life; the main lesson I learned was that I did not belong in that pressure cooker.

My duties at Harvard that year were light: in the fall semester, I taught a lecture course on philosophy of mind and gave a graduate seminar; in the spring semester, I was the Santayana Fellow, with no teaching duties, free to do research using all the facilities of Harvard. (I spent much of the spring in the university's Countway Library of Medicine, researching theories of anesthesia for a paper on pain.) The lecture course, based on my first book, but with many critiques and alternatives thrown in, was a big success, with perhaps forty students in it, smart and aggressive, peppering me with questions in class. Wonderful, but some of the questions were too big to handle in class if I was to stay on schedule and cover the syllabus, so I suggested running a special "no holds barred" question session in my office in addition to the regular class meetings. This turned into a two-hour-plus session, and I ended up having to schedule another two-hour session on another day, so I was more than doubling the course's class time. It was very exciting, and I used the students' curiosity to enlarge my understanding and shape my arguments, but I was drowning, and I looked forward to the second semester, when I could hide in my office and read and write. (My office that year, by the way, was Quine's. He was away on leave, and he invited me to use it. It was the best location in Harvard Yard, the nearest office in Emerson Hall to Widener Library, and there was an intimidating collection of books on the shelves. Logic textbooks by other logicians stood in a stack perhaps seven feet high in one corner, and his personal copies of his own books were on the shelf at my elbow when I sat in his desk chair.)

Then there was the graduate seminar. I had decided I would demonstrate to Harvard graduate students how you dealt with a book that was difficult, baffling, tantalizing, by assigning chapters to individual students and working with them before each week's seminar meeting so they could come in, one each week, and do a sort of *explication de texte* that would then be the foundation for the week's discussion. I deliberately chose two new books that bamboozled me: Gilbert Harman's *Thought* (1973) and Zeno Vendler's *Res Cogitans* (1972). (Both books still bamboozle me, and neither of them caught on with other philosophers, so far as I know. Really smart philosophers can write tempting but enigmatic books.) With the able help of the graduate students, I thought, we'll figure these books out. The problem was that only one graduate student had signed up to take the course for credit—Elliott Sober, whose dissertation had already been accepted; he needed one more course credit on his record to get his degree. Clearly, I wasn't going to saddle up Elliott and get him to perform *explication de texte* week after week, so I had to abandon that idea. The graduate seminar, I then realized, was meant more as a showcase for the visitor to display expertise, and I had chosen topics I didn't have a good grip on. Not the way to make a good impression. I remember vividly occasions of strolling anxiously around in Harvard Yard trying to figure out what on earth I was going to say in the seminar due to start in less than an hour. I was sometimes on the verge of panic. Quite a few auditors showed up every week, including faculty members in the department, and they dispassionately watched me wallow in head-scratching confusion, seldom volunteering any suggestions. Two auditors who did help me were Bill Woods, an early AI pioneer who was visiting in Harvard's computer science department, and Michael Moore, a young visiting philosopher of law who somehow found the course listing and decided to give it a try. I remember once asking Woods, who unaccountably kept showing up to watch me suffer, why he was doing this; did he enjoy watching my travail? He said, "Well, Dan, you don't know the answers, but you're asking wonderful questions." That showed me that Bill Woods was a philosopher in every way that mattered, and that one remark carried me through the agonies of the semester.

Another visitor at Harvard that year was Joseph Weizenbaum, the computer scientist from down the street at MIT, who was working on his jeremiad, *Computer Power and Human Reason: From Judgment to Calculation* (1976). Hilary Putnam introduced us, and we hit it off right away. Joe was, like Bert Dreyfus, a critic—even an enemy— of AI, but he was an insider, having worked on some of the major developments in computers that made AI possible at all. One of the architects of time-sharing on huge mainframes, Joe had also created, initially as a sort of joke, the ELIZA program, the first conversational bot—though that term wasn't coined for decades. ELIZA was a parody of Carl Rogers's style of psychiatric therapy, and it was deliberately shallow, with nothing but canned responses along the lines of "You mentioned your mother. Tell me more about her." He had left it running on a public terminal (part of the early time-sharing system at MIT) so that he could improve it by downloading the day's interactions and was shocked when he discovered that students had been using it for online psychiatric treatment, pouring out their souls onto the hard disks (or perhaps tape drives back then). They protested that their medical confidentiality was being breached by Weizenbaum! One day his own secretary asked him if she could fiddle around with ELIZA during her lunch hour, and when Joe tried to look over her shoulder to see what she was typing, she scolded him: "This is a private conversation!" Joe was following in the footsteps of Norbert Wiener, the creator of cybernetics, who was the original insider to sound the alarm about the possibly negative effects AI could have on the world. The main problem for Joe was that he couldn't make up his mind whether his book should argue that AI was impossible (as Dreyfus did) or possible but dangerous (as Wiener had it). We had long unresolved discussions about this, and he thanked me profusely in the preface to his book, but I could never get him to confront the choice directly. I certainly learned a lot about computers from Joe that year, including especially about the public reception and (mis)-understanding of computers. I was in his Harvard office one day (in the spring of 1974) and he made a bet with me (this is from memory, not a verbatim quote):

> Tonight NBC [it may have been another network] is showing an hour-long documentary on AI. They interviewed me almost a year ago at the outset of the project and a few weeks ago they came back after all their travels and filming to do a follow-up interview with me. As they were setting up the lights and cameras, I asked them what they learned on their expedition. They all replied, laughing, that "AI programs don't work"! They had watched frantic researchers from MIT, Stanford, and elsewhere trying to get their demos to run, and almost without exception it took hours of fussing to get a few usable minutes of AI programs actually doing what they were advertised as doing. I bet you ten dollars that this will *not* be mentioned tonight on the program!

He won the bet. The hype surrounding AI in those days (at the height of what John Haugeland termed GOFAI (for Good-Old-Fashioned Artificial Intelligence) was in part the creation of the media, not the professors or engineers. It made a better story, a gee-whiz almost-science-fiction story that the media couldn't resist telling. But neither could the AI creators resist the publicity, and almost all of them oversold their products to the public. It has happened again and again with AI. The current enthusiasm for GPT-3 and other enormous language-generating systems is the latest bubble, which we should burst before many more people get deeply misled by it. (See chapter 24.)

Weizenbaum, by the way, had the soul of a magician. He had a computer terminal in his home in Belmont, and he wrote a little program that, he told his daughters, could answer any yes/no question correctly. And so it appeared to do. Once when he had colleagues from MIT's computer science department for dinner at his house, the girls told the guests about Daddy's wonderful question-answerer. Of course, they wanted to see it in operation, so they went into Joe's study, and he sat down at the terminal (with its acoustic modem plugging away at 300 baud) and they began giving him questions to type. The computer answered all correctly. The guests figured he was sending some extra signal, so they asked if they could type the questions. Joe readily allowed this, and *still* the computer answered the questions correctly. Joe yanked the transcript—a long scroll of dot-matrix-printed paper—out of the printer and handed it to his colleagues, saying, "You may study this at your leisure; you won't figure out how the program works." They tried and couldn't find a clue. He told me the secret. His program was a single line of code:

```
IF backspace, print "NO"; ELSE print "YES"
```

Since the printer had always just executed a "carriage-return" command, it was already on the left margin and couldn't backspace, so nothing happened when Joe surreptitiously hit the backspace key except for the printing of "NO." Joe had been sending a signal, an invisible, silent signal. But how had the system worked when his colleagues took over the keyboard? Simple, Joe said. They were so preoccupied with trying to reword the questions, watch the keystrokes, and so forth that they didn't notice that Joe was feeding them questions all with YES answers.

My forlorn seminar was half over when one of the auditors, graduate student Georges Rey, brought me a copy of a draft of a new paper called "Three Cheers for Propositional Attitudes," by Jerry Fodor, with whom he was taking a seminar at MIT. Fodor's paper was in part a rebuttal to my "Intentional Systems" paper. Whereas

I was furthering Quine's case that talk about beliefs and desires was a "dramatic idiom" that only *indirectly* informed us about a person's brain states, Fodor insisted that such talk had to be treated as referring to actual sentences in the head (in the belief box or desire box, for instance), composed in the "language of thought." Georges suggested we should have a meeting to discuss the two papers together. I hadn't met Fodor but had been reading his work since my days at Oxford, where his papers coauthored with Jerrold Katz had caused a commotion among the graduate students. It also turned out that Fodor was finishing up a book, *The Language of Thought* (1975), and when Georges got me a copy of that manuscript, I realized that it would have been the perfect topic for my seminar: clear, vivid, compelling, and—I thought—wrong in ways I would have been ready and able to discuss. Too late for that, but we went ahead with the idea of a friendly showdown, bringing in some young philosophers from Tufts, David Israel and Michael Lipton; Ned Block from MIT; and eventually a few others.

Thus began the discussion group that I privately called the Vicious Circle but we often called the Secret Seminar since we almost never discussed what happened there with others. There was a good reason: there must have been several dozen philosophers, psychologists, AI researchers, and others in the Boston area who would have crowded in if we had made it known we were meeting, and we needed to keep the group small and collegial. It continued for more than a decade, meeting usually at MIT. Thus began my friendship with Jerry Fodor, which started with philosophical disagreement and soon moved on to sailing. Jerry had taken a course in sailing at MIT and was fast becoming an avid sailor—on the small, reliable Tech Dinghies that were available to MIT faculty and students in the Charles River Basin. He wanted to try something more adventurous, so he bought a Bristol 30, which is quite a step up, a sloop thirty feet long with an auxiliary diesel engine, a galley, a head, and berths for four or five sailors, depending on how friendly they were. He named it *Insolvent*, a stroke of genius that acknowledged his depleted bank account, parodied British man-o'-war names like *Intrepid* and *Indomitable*, but was also a multilingual pun: The boat was in solvent (in the water) and *in* the *sol* (sun) and *vent* (wind).

He kept *Insolvent* in Essex, Connecticut, near his home (his wife, Janet, was on the faculty at University of Connecticut, so he drove many hours to work at MIT) and began by just daysailing out of his home port. I asked him if he was ready to try some cruising, visiting Martha's Vineyard and Nantucket and the other islands in the area, and he readily agreed to ship me as first mate, since I had big-boat experience as both crew and navigator. (Among my now obsolete skills is celestial navigation with sextant, chronometer, and *Nautical Almanac*, but we'd need only dead reckoning and range-finding in Long Island and Nantucket Sounds and, if fogbound, RDF—radio direction finding, using local radio-station towers as sources.) After several such weekend cruises, I suggested to Jerry that he consider sailing all the way to Maine, where there was much better wind and hundreds of islands and anchorages and fishing villages to explore. I'd navigate on the way up and pilot for him when we got among the Maine islands. He liked the idea so much that I put in a mooring for *Insolvent* at the little yacht club in Blue Hill harbor, and for several summers it wintered at a boatyard in Blue Hill, and we worked together to get it ready for launching each spring. I maintained the boat in Blue Hill all summer, so Jerry could count on its being ready to go whenever he wanted to drive up and sail. We cruised the coast together, and I even talked Jerry into purchasing a spinnaker and pole so we could race *Insolvent*. At the time, he had a psycholinguistics lab at MIT with Merrill Garrett, and he couldn't take all summer vacation away, so I got to sail *Insolvent* much more than he did, and even race it on my own; but whenever he wanted to sail it, it was ready, shipshape, fuel and water and ice on board. Sometimes I'd come with him and sometimes he'd sail with others. One summer when the Dennetts went to France, Jerry and Janet and their son Tony lived at our farm while getting to know both Maine and *Insolvent* better. After a few summers, Jerry decided that Maine was too far from MIT, so he sailed to Massachusetts with a crew and found a mooring in Gloucester Harbor. That didn't work out very well for him, since whenever he drove to Gloucester to go sailing, he'd find that there were things that needed fixing, or he'd have to wait around to get ice and fuel and fresh water, so most of his time was spent on maintenance. If he'd ever had second thoughts about the deal he'd made with me to maintain his boat all summer in Blue Hill, they were erased by that summer of nonsailing in Gloucester. He soon left MIT for Rutgers, sold *Insolvent*, moved to New York City, and kept an easy-to-maintain Nonsuch catboat at a marina on the East River.

Jerry, a romantic at heart, loved sailing but wasn't handy, which makes for trouble on a cruising boat. A crew member once said to me, after Jerry had just spent an hour or two trying to repair something in the cabin, "Here's the sound of Jerry fixing something: 'Tap-tap-tap . . . tap-tap . . . tap-tap-TAP, OH SHIT!'" Perhaps his most memorable screwup was when he decided to switch from an alcohol stove (messy, smelly) to a propane stove in the galley. The new stove had to be fitted into a hole sawn in the galley counter, and there was a nice stainless-steel apron, or frame, to go around it. Jerry set the frame on the counter firmly in place and scribed a pencil line all the way around it. He then took my power jigsaw and cut, following the line. He'd scribed the outside edge, not the inside edge, so the frame fell neatly through the hole. I fashioned some hardwood pieces to replace the missing counter edges, screwed and glued them in place, and mounted the stove. We were once anchored in Sand Cove at Marshall Island and Jerry saw a seal checking us out from about ten yards away. He decided to throw the seal one of the mackerel we'd caught that day, and wound up for a mighty underhand heave, but he hadn't counted on the slipperiness of a freshly killed mackerel, and it flew out of his hand onto his bare foot, posthumously biting his toe.

One summer, Jerry ran a workshop for philosophers of mind and psychology at the University of Washington, and we chartered a boat for a week's sailing among the San Juan Islands after the workshop. The scenery was magnificent—like Maine but with the vertical scale roughly doubled—snowcapped mountains, steep cliffs, and deep anchorages. Orcas and bald eagles were abundant. We got the boat safely home to its charter harbor only to discover that the charter company had gone bankrupt while we were cruising, and we lost the sizable safety deposit. Mishaps are the condiments of cruising; a clear sail with no emergencies, no getting lost in the fog, no inadvertent groundings or near misses, is a forgettable time on the water, but still better than staying ashore. I will have more to tell of Jerry, not all of it as pleasant as our sailing adventures.

9.

ACADEMIC POLITICS
AT TUFTS

WHEN I ARRIVED AT TUFTS IT HAD A RESPECTABLE
position as a second-rank university, not particularly distinguished, and the modesty to go with that reputation. That all
changed when Jean Mayer, a French-born professor at the Harvard
School of Public Health, became president of Tufts in 1976. He was
a war hero who had played a large role in de Gaulle's Free French
Army in World War II, and he was immensely ambitious and knew
how to play rough. He steamrolled the trustees, the faculty, the phil-
anthropic foundations, and the US Congress in his efforts to propel
Tufts into the top ranks. There is no straightforward way to turn a
mediocre university into a great one. According to one adage, first-
rate people hire first-rate people and second-rate people hire third-
rate people. Tufts had its share of second- and third-rate faculty, but
they were, by and large, good-hearted, honest people—teachers,
not researchers—who had never signed up for the high-pressure life
in the fast lane of academia that Mayer promised. How could you
expect them to say to their untenured colleagues, "You have a much
better track record than I had when I was awarded tenure, but it isn't
good enough to get you tenure today"?

Hugo Bedau had turned over the chairmanship of the philosophy department to me that year, and I also was on the advisory
committee of the dean of the Graduate School of Arts and Sciences, even though there was no PhD program in philosophy. We
had been asked to review all the graduate programs, bringing in
outside experts to assist us, and I realized immediately that the

philosophy department's largely unused master's program would be scrapped in the general housecleaning unless I took some preemptive action. I proposed to save the committee time and energy by putting our graduate program on indefinite pause, with the proviso that unless we encountered some truly remarkable and worthy student whom we could serve, we would shelve the program for good. The dean and the committee gratefully accepted this arrangement, so we voluntarily abandoned our program—for the moment. As luck would have it, two years later, a senior who had been studying eighteenth-century English literature signed up for my History of Western Philosophy course in the fall semester. She came to see me at the end of the term full of regret: she should have majored in philosophy, she said, and now it was too late! She had taken only two credits in philosophy, my course and logic; no good graduate program would take her. Since she was clearly an outstanding philosopher in the making, I told her I would petition to let her do a master's with us, reopening our program just for her, during which time we would credential her for greater things. And so in 1978 Alison McIntyre (an honored professor at Wellesley since 1988, after getting her PhD at Princeton and having a "folding chair" at Harvard) jump-started our MA program, which is now the best in the world. We take in promising students who for one reason or another don't have the credentials they need to get into a top-rank PhD program in philosophy. We fill the gaps in their education, prepare them for the rigors of PhD work elsewhere, and then send them off "just when they get interesting," as one colleague put it to me. But in fact, our MA students *are* interesting, and very rewarding to teach. Some of them have almost completed PhDs in other fields before deciding to take a mortal leap into the uncertainty and riskiness of an academic career in philosophy. Others have grown unfulfilled with their careers outside academia, and still others come with very strong recommendations from relatively unknown colleges and universities where they excelled. Over the years, we've taken lots of risks with admissions, but nothing compared to the

risks the students take, and I've always been in favor of telling graduate students as soon as possible if I think they should cut their
losses and do something else with their lives. The winners who get
their MA degrees have gone on to get PhDs at all the top schools
and enjoy fine careers at major universities and colleges around
the world. Those who drop out are also winners of sorts, having
learned rather quickly that the life of a philosopher is not for them,
without having to spend more than a precious year or two finding
out. What about supervising PhD dissertations? I supervised one
at Irvine before I left, and I've done quite a few since, but only
when I was happy to do so, as an external advisor on dissertations
at Michigan, Brown, Harvard, Penn, the University of North Carolina at Chapel Hill, Amsterdam, and Ruhr-Universität Bochum,
for instance. And although this is a very nice world, it is not, as Dr.
Pangloss maintained, the best of all possible worlds, and there has
never been a department of philosophy so excellent that *all* its grad
students in my areas of expertise can write wonderful dissertations.
Carrying problematic graduate students across the finish line can
take years off one's life, and it's been a rare privilege to be able to
decline requests that would have fallen clearly within my responsi-
bilities had I been in the requester's department.

President Mayer identified a few faculty as his informal advisors
and called on us to help him ease the strain on the transition to
greatness he was striving for. Administrative blunders occur at all
colleges and universities, and often the participants are ill-suited for
roles that require both diplomacy and nerves of steel, so Tufts had
a rash of faculty grievances to handle, with lawyers rushing in and
journalists hard on their heels. I was asked to compose a university-
wide grievance procedure and shepherd it through the various faculties and deans and legal counsels. My model included an official
ombudsman, who could resolve many potentially explosive conflicts
discreetly, and an elected faculty grievance panel, from which juries,
in effect, could be appointed as need be. It took hundreds of hours
of meetings and revisions to get the whole package assembled and

approved, and it was implemented in the nick of time to deal with a few cases.

Not all my projects ended with success. Tufts was way behind the competition in getting computers into the labs and classrooms, and I volunteered to take a semester off from teaching to see if I could get some of the New England computer makers—Digital Equipment Corporation, Data General, Wang—to help us into the computer age. Computers were only for "data processing" (payrolls, library acquisitions, student grades, . . .) in the eyes of many in the Tufts administration, and I had a hard time getting the help I needed. In some cases, the ineptness of people in the Gifts and Endowments office handily undid the progress I seemed to be making. I hated the whole project—begging and bragging at the same time—and I was having health problems with my digestive system that made the effort more grim. Medicine didn't seem to help and my doctor advised me to consult a clinical psychologist. I was not impressed with clinical psychology then, but I dutifully made an appointment and had one session with a wise young man who calmly asked me what would happen if I failed in my quest. I heard myself reply, "Oh, I don't fail," and as soon as the words were out of my mouth, I knew he was onto something. I *could* fail, but the earth would not swallow me up, my friends would still be my friends, and I could go back to doing what I loved with a clear conscience. I did fail, and my health problems disappeared. Tufts eventually got itself properly equipped with computers (see the chapter on Big George and our introductory course in computer science), but without much help from me.

I undertook a few other projects at Mayer's request, and he seemed to take a certain delight in telling me, in confidence, tales about how he was maneuvering to build up Tufts. He never told me anything that made me an accomplice to any crime, but he certainly knew how to play hardball. For instance, a few members of Congress were convinced to vote for our veterinary college and our nutrition insti-tute, two of his pet projects, in order to avoid bad publicity that could have come their way had they not seen the wisdom of his proposals. His aggressive fundraising only once landed him in a real embarrassment. In his role as advisor to the World Health Organization, he had worked with Imelda Marcos, wife of the dictator Ferdinand Marcos of the Philippines, and she had been so impressed by him that she decided to honor him by endowing a Marcos Family Foundation chair in East Asian and Pacific Studies at Tufts. Mayer announced that Tufts would accept the gift and even arranged for Marcos to receive an honorary degree, but the faculty and students were outraged and quickly organized protests. Hugo Bedau and I met with Jean in his office to advise him strongly to cancel both the honorary degree and the endowment. He insisted that there were "no strings attached" to the appointment to this chair, so we told him we then had the perfect candidate: Benigno Aquino Jr., who was already living in Massachusetts. Aquino was Marcos's chief critic and opponent and after being imprisoned had been allowed to come to the US for heart surgery. Jean conceded that there were strings attached after all.

Hugo and I formulated a principle that seemed to strike Jean as reasonable: it's all right to accept gifts of ill-gotten fortune from those who are now atoning (think of the Rockefeller Foundation, the Carnegie Foundation, and so on) but not from autocrats who are trying to use their largesse to improve their current reputation so they can go on with their exploitations. As usual, Jean found a way out: he had already accepted the first down payment on the endowed chair, but he allowed relations with the Marcos family to sour, so the rest of the endowment never came through and Tufts never returned any money to the Marcos family. A few years later, Benigno Aquino, on his return to the Philippines, was assassinated, setting in motion the events that led to his widow, Corazon Aquino, assuming power as the Marcos regime ended.

One of Mayer's coups was obtaining the gift of an ancient monastery in Talloires, on Lac d'Annecy, in the French Alps, where it became the Tufts European Center at Talloires. I made several trips there with him in the early years, and on one occasion we, along with other workshop participants, drove to the top of one of the mountains overlooking the lake, where hang gliders were launching. Jean immediately signed up for a ride, a *delta bi-place avec moniteur*, with a hang-glider pilot, and took off with aplomb a few minutes later. When I spoke with him after his half-hour ride he was joyous—the trustees of Tufts were not so pleased to learn he had done this—and when I asked him if his wife, Elizabeth, had qualms about him doing such risky things, he replied, "No, our children are grown; I am completely depreciated. I can do what I want."

I have followed his principle ever since, since I am also completely depreciated, and have myself gone hang gliding at Talloires. I was slightly over the weight limit for a passenger—a hundred kilos—but there was a good breeze, so the pilot was willing to take me, and I was willing to go after I learned he had a wife and children and didn't seem suicidal. He made it very clear to me that he could not carry me down the steep wooden ramp and over the edge of the cliff when we did our takeoff; I had to *run* beside him down the ramp so we could build up enough speed to fly. Other hang gliders were taking off every few minutes, and they would take three or four brisk steps halfway down the ramp and swoop up into the sky. When it was our turn, we did indeed run down the ramp—all the way down and then out of sight over the cliff edge, which provoked a loud gasp from the crowd assembled. Susan was on the trip and was shocked to hear the gasp as she dutifully photographed the takeoff, but in a few seconds we reappeared, spiraling up in the thermal lift. I too was ecstatic when we landed on the lakeside a thousand meters below our takeoff spot.

After Mayer's presidency (1976–93) and a refractory period in which gains were consolidated, Lawrence Bacow (later president of Harvard) took over, and once again I was asked to play a few special roles. My favorite was the creation of Tufts High Table, a monthly gathering of two dozen faculty members drawn from all departments, ranks, and disciplines, for a sit-down dinner with open bar and a chance to talk shop *with no administrators present and no agendas*. Larry had asked me what he could do to improve faculty morale at Tufts, and I pointed out that most of us on the faculty were actually closer to our colleagues in our particular disciplines at all the neighboring universities than we were to our Tufts colleagues in other fields, whom we saw only at time-pressured committee meetings with much university business to conduct. The idea was for each faculty member to have four consecutive High Table dinners. Each dinner had six new guests (the freshmen) and some old hands who knew the drill (sophomores, juniors, and seniors)—and I, as host, would pick one professor well in advance each month (not a freshman) to give a *short* (twenty-minute) talk about his or her research that would be accessible to all in attendance. Larry funded the dinners but was not allowed to attend, of course. Professors worked very hard on their High Table talks, and they were typically brilliant. A mathematician who can hold the interest of a professor of European history *and* a poet *and* a molecular biologist is someone to reckon with.

In due time, we added another wrinkle: *tapas talks*, which were *five*-minute impromptu talks by three different guests during cocktails. I chose these speakers as well, and made ostentatious use of my stopwatch, so there would be time for five or ten minutes of questions after each before we sat down for the dinner and the main speaker. No small talk for us. Interdisciplinary friendships and even collaborations soon sprouted, as we discovered one another's talents and interests. The faculty loved these meetings, and the High Table alumni started the tradition of hosting (at our own expense) a thank-you reception for Larry and Adele Bacow at the end of the academic year. Sad to say, when Larry left, the tradition was cancelled.

10.

WHERE AM I?

IN THE SPRING OF 1976, I WAS INVITED BY OSWALDO Chateaubriand to give a talk to the philosophy department at Vassar, and as I made the long drive down the Mass Pike from Tufts to Vassar I got to musing about a thought experiment: if somehow my brain were moved into my chest cavity without destroying any connectivity, wouldn't I still think my mind was right behind my eyes and between my ears? This morphed into a more elaborate thought experiment, with my brain removed from my head and kept alive in a vat, while connected to my body by radio links. By the time I got to Poughkeepsie I had concocted quite a tale. After my talk (on another topic—I can't remember what), Oswaldo invited me and a group of Vassar students to his house for wine and cheese, and there I decided to try out my tale on them. The students were rapt and full of questions, and before the evening was over many more details had fallen into place. I knew then what talk I would give as the Saturday after-dinner speaker at the University of North Carolina's renowned Chapel Hill Colloquium in October. This annual gathering had long been the occasion of memorable philosophical events. In 1971 I had been the commentator on Thomas Nagel's then-unpublished piece "What Is It Like to Be a Bat?" My response was titled "What Is It Like for There to Be Something It Is Like to Be Something?" and UNC's Jay Rosenberg, clad in a flamboyant cape, opened the discussion by telling us in a thick Transylvanian accent what it was like to be a bat *part of the time*.

The after-dinner talk was by tradition lighthearted, but still having some philosophical substance to go with dessert. "Where Am I?"

was the title I had given UNC to print in the program in 1976, and one philosopher asked me at cocktails what it would be about. "Personal location," I deadpanned, and he nodded sagely as if he now had a clear understanding of my topic. My purportedly autobiographical story needed a prop, a toggle switch to be thrown at the end of the talk to switch control of my body from my brain to a computer copy of my brain, and I had purchased a small metal box to which I had attached a telescoping radio antenna and a toggle switch. I pulled this contraption out of a paper bag at the end of my talk, threw the switch, and ad-libbed the rest of the talk, supposedly under the control of the copied brain—or had my speaking been controlled by the copied brain until now? An effect I hadn't anticipated heightened the drama. I had read my paper up until that moment, as philosophers then always did, but it was important to the story that I simply speak, dramatically, after the switch was thrown. The slight differences between my reading voice and my impromptu speaking voice produced an uncanny sense in many in the audience that they were indeed now listening to a different person, a clone of sorts of the Dan Dennett who had read the paper. The place went wild.

Word soon spread about my performance, and I was besieged by

The BBC's version of brain in a vat

invitations to give it again, but I accepted only one: from MIT. The effects that rippled out from that evening nevertheless changed my life in some fundamental ways. Robin Brightwell of the BBC was making a documentary about the mind and brain and wanted me to undercut some of the nonsense that Sir John Eccles had uttered in his interview (more on Eccles later). I participated in a dichotic-listening experiment (to give my inclusion in the program a little scientific gloss) and then enacted the key scene from my story, where I look at my brain in its life-support vat and wonder why I'm thinking "Here I am, looking at my own brain" and not "Here I am, floating in a vat being stared at by my own eyes." The BBC had designed and built a fabulous brain-in-the-vat set, with whirring tape drives and blinking mainframe lights in the background (what a computer looked like back then), but Robin realized that he also had to do something to make it clear that this was a dramatized thought experiment, not a real experiment. It wouldn't do if, the morning after transmission, half a million Brits thought a living American philosopher had had his brain removed!

A student of the history of film technology, Robin used a "double pass" shot, in which a black mask is fixed over half the camera lens,

A shadow puppet from "Where Am I?"

so that the film is exposed first on one side—say, the left side—then, after rolling the film manually back in the camera, on the right side, with a mask over the left side so that the already exposed film is shielded. Thus, the same character can appear on the left and right of the screen simultaneously. The technique requires a fixed camera, a well-designed lightproof pair of masks, and a compliant actor—me. In the background on the right, you see me confronting my brain in the vat and scratching my head in wonder, while on the left in the foreground you see me, wearing the same clothes, sitting on a stool and explaining what is happening behind me. Timing is everything, and we spent a whole day shooting various takes. It was heartening, watching the "rushes" the next morning, to see that it had worked. Robin also recreated—in reverse direction—a simplified version of the famous Orson Welles tracking shot from *Citizen Kane* in which the camera seems to fly through a neon sign and down through a skylight into a bar. This was used in a shot that was a close-up of me and the vat, and then the camera pulled back swiftly to show that the laboratory in which I was staring at my brain was a movie-set in a studio, complete with the backs of sandbagged flats and a director's chair.

My sailing buddy at Irvine, the novelist MacDonald Harris, wanted to rewrite "Where Am I?" with some sex and violence and publish it in a magazine for the express purpose of selling the film rights, but that never came to fruition. I published it in *Brainstorms*, and that inspired Douglas Hofstadter to invite me to join him in editing a collection of mind-bending stories titled *The Mind's I* (1981). A Dutch documentary maker, Piet Hoenderdos, read *The Mind's I* in 1982 while he was planning to make a documentary about Doug and decided to turn his documentary into a feature-length film, *Victim of the Brain*, which included a dramatization of the "Where Am I?" story, with me playing myself once again and spending a delicious week in the Netherlands making another movie. We had originally thought of casting Marvin Minsky, director of MIT's AI lab, as the chief scientist, but I doubt that Marvin could have controlled his impatience with all the delays. Some of the shots in the film were done in Marvin's office at the AI lab, and the actor who plays the scientist is called Marvin Minsky in the film, but it's not Marvin. The American premiere of the movie was held in Harvard's Carpenter Center for the Visual Arts (Le Corbusier's famous concrete snail), and Marvin was pleased to see how he was portrayed in the movie.

In 1984, a Harvard senior, Lynn Jeffries, working with the director Peter Sellars, produced a full-length Javanese shadow-puppet play of "Where Am I?" in the Loeb Experimental Theater at Harvard. Harry Stanton decided this would be a great venue for a book-publishing party for my new Bradford book (on free will), *Elbow Room,* and so we invited a great gang of philosophers and scientists to the play, followed by a reception in the Harvard Lampoon Castle. Entrance to the fabled Castle is restricted to members, but Harry had been a member of the *Lampoon* when he was at Harvard, and they allowed him to host a party there. I invited Quine and Nelson Goodman, another Harvard philosopher, and they both told me that in all their years at Harvard neither had ever set foot in the Castle until that party. Nor had I, of course. Lynn Jeffries has gone on to be a major innovator in puppetry on the West Coast.

"Where Am I?" has been on the syllabus of hundreds of philosophy courses around the world. The makers of several science-fiction films, including *The Matrix,* have acknowledged it as a major source of ideas. Over the years I have received letters and emails from people who ask if the story is true, and several readers have carefully scanned the back of my head for antennas! No, Virginia, I have not had my brain removed and put in a vat, but it is, as philosophers love to say, possible in principle. While this is perhaps my most-read piece of philosophical writing, I think people still underestimate by a wide margin the challenge it raises for views of consciousness that compete with mine. The key fact dramatized in the story is that *you don't know anything "privileged" about the causation of your own thoughts.* You cannot know "from the inside" what events cause you to think you see something as red or green, for instance, or cause you to push button A instead of button B. In short, you need to go outside your-self and adopt the "third-person point of view" of science if you want to answer the question "Where am I?"

This third-person method flies in the face of centuries of philo-sophical thinking that has encouraged any number of subtle thinkers to study minds by focusing their attention inward, ignoring the pros-pect of studying the minds of others with the help of other minds—the minds of scientists, not just philosophers. When I was a graduate student, the "problem of other minds" was a major topic of debate, but it was conducted in a scientifically impoverished setting: Can I know, and how can I know, whether minds other than my own exist, and if so, in what ways must other minds be like mine? It was simply *assumed* that we each know our own minds "from the inside" in ways that are more authoritative than anything science could dis-cover. My move, my insight, was to turn the questions around. Since there is little I can know for sure from single-handedly introspect-ing my own mind (*contra* Descartes and his *cogito ergo sum*), what can I know about my own mind from studying the minds of others scientifically? This made me, in the opinion of many of my critics, a "behaviorist"—a term that had been turned into a shameful epi-thet thanks to Noam Chomsky's hatchet job on B. F. Skinner. But science *is* a sort of behaviorism; once you've got a scientific explana-tion of *all* the behavior, inner and outer, large and microscopic, of any phenomenon, there's nothing else to explain—except why some people are so uncomfortable with your explanation! I coined a term in 1982 for the third-person method ("heterophenomenology"—the phenomenology of *other* minds), but I didn't invent the method, which is standard procedure in cognitive science. I was just drawing attention to the importance of treating subjects' *beliefs* about their own consciousness as data to be explained, not necessarily as true accounts of mental reality. This is *the* major fault line in philoso-phy of mind today, with John Searle, Tom Nagel, David Chalmers, Galen Strawson, and Philip Goff, among others, thinking they can just insist that they know better. They don't. Those who object, who hold out for some sort of "first-person science of consciousness," have yet to describe any experiments or results that are trustworthy but unobtainable by heterophenomenology. And then there are the mysterians, who invite us to just give up on the task of explaining consciousness. No thanks, we're making great progress.

11.

MEANWHILE, BACK AT THE FARM

FOR FORTY-THREE YEARS, FROM 1970 TO 2013, OUR farm in Blue Hill was not just our summer retreat but in many regards the center of our lives. We had bought it with visions of being back-to-the-land organic farmers, but unlike many of the other *nouveaux ruraux* who flocked to Maine in those years, we didn't burn our bridges behind us, spending only weekends and school holidays at the farm, getting to know all the seasons there, the autumn leaves, the huge snowbanks, mud season, and the notorious black-fly period when we'd plant our vegetable garden and prepare for the summer. We had a series of station wagons with backseats that folded down, and in the days before seat-belt laws we could drive from Andover to the farm after a quick supper on Friday, with the kids settling down in their sleeping bags. Four hours plus of quiet conversation time while Andrea and Peter slept behind us kept Susan and me in sync, and our drive back to Andover on Sunday afternoon was filled with family conversations and car games—spotting American flags, animals, pickup trucks on either side of the road—and, of course, a little bickering in the backseat.

For us, the farm was an inexhaustible playground for projects—farming, building, fixing, exploring, finding antiques to furnish the old house—and a great place to raise our kids. The farm with its two hundred acres of forest and fields was situated on the Back Road (later renamed the Range Road in honor of the rifle range at the town end), a bumpy gravel road that ran along the side of

Blue Hill Mountain (well, the *town* was Blue Hill, named after the hill, so if you wanted to talk about the hill, you had to call it Blue Hill Mountain), and flanked by neighbors who had lived for generations in their houses—remarkably knowledgeable, resourceful, and indeed neighborly people. To them I was just Dan Dennett, who had bought the old Leighton farm and who made cider champagne from the apples in the orchard.

Our neighbors to the north were Basil and Bertha Turner, more than thirty years our senior. Their son Basil Jr. had drowned in a lobster boat accident the year before we bought the farm, and Susan's brother George, living at the farm to establish residency in Maine so he could go to the forestry school at the University of Maine, became a sort of surrogate son to them. George lived at the farm that first winter, ate many a supper with the Turners up the road, and worked with Basil as a painter and handyman. At the end of a workday, they would buy some beer and peanuts in their shells and park in our dooryard in Basil's pickup, drink the beer, shell and eat the peanuts, and talk and talk, almost like a lovestruck teenage couple who didn't want to say goodbye. Basil and Bertha were our Maine parents, in effect, and I think I learned more from Basil than from any other person in my life—not academic philosophy, but about how to live in Maine, how to keep the wood stoves from going out overnight, how to set cedar shingles on roofs, how to make electric fences to keep the horses in, how to line wild honeybees to discover their hives, how and where to catch native brook trout, how and where to dig clams, how to catch mackerel, how to fell trees safely, how to mow hay and make windrows with a dump rake, how to organize blueberry raking, how to glaze old-fashioned windows, how to clean a chimney, how to raise laying hens, ducks, and a pig, and much more.

Basil and Bertha lived in Blue Hill their entire lives—and rarely left Maine, except for a trip to New Hampshire for a hunting-dog competition Basil had entered, and a drive out west, which they

Basil Turner

found boring. One day Bertha happily announced that one of her grandnieces had just gotten engaged, and I asked her if the prospective groom was a local man, and she replied, "Oh no, he's from Sedgwick"—about five miles down the coast. Bertha knew how to cook a porcupine and offered to show me when I had killed a few that were wreaking havoc in our barn and toolshed, but I declined. Porcupines were frequent visitors, and if they found a shovel or rake or hoe with a wooden handle that had recently been used, they would gnaw off the handle to get the salt from the sweat dried on it. One summer night Susan and I were skinny-dipping under the stars in our ramshackle above-ground pool in the backyard when I heard some skittering in the garden. Two porcupines were about to decimate our peas and tomatoes, so I jumped out of the pool, grabbed an old golf club from the shed, and went chasing them, buck naked, in the garden. They cleverly ducked around behind the pea fences, which I didn't want to destroy, so it was a merry chase for about ten minutes before I finally managed to bop first one and then the other on the head with the driver—a surprisingly effective way of

Bertha Turner

dispatching a porcupine. Susan almost drowned in the pool from laughing so hard. Old golf clubs, by the way, are also excellent tools for spreading horse puckies in a pasture. Just pretend the pile is your teed-up golf ball and drive it as hard as you can; it will shatter into dozens of pieces that spray out in a nice fan of fertilizer.

Our neighbor to the south was Stetson—Stet—Grindle, a grizzled tall-tale-telling character who had once been made sheriff of Blue Hill on the theory that it might keep him out of trouble. It didn't quite, but he was a lovable and friendly character, and he filled in many details—some of them believable—that Basil never got around to. His brother Newton Grindle lived down along the coast and had a sailboat, the *Dancing Dolphin*, that he and his wife Leila would go out in quite often in the summer when their farm chores were done. Newton was the man who smoked your hams and bacon slabs when you slaughtered a pig, and he used to tease me, calling me the "upland sailor" because he had a sailboat and I didn't (aside from Jerry Fodor's boat, which was only for a few years). We bought our son Peter a Mercury—a small keel sloop that was raced by the kids in Blue Hill—and one day I was out in it in a light and variable wind and made a big effort to pass Newt and Leila in their boat on the way back into the harbor, only to realize when I passed close by that the reason I was "beating" him was that he and Leila had mackerel jigs trailing and wanted to go slow. He got a kick out of that. One time Stet shot a bear and promised me a bear steak from his freezer, which I was looking forward to cooking until his son James said to me, "I wouldn't cook that indoors, if I was you." Since the aroma in Stet's kitchen was a strong combination of wood-stove smoke and baked beans and who knows what else, I took James's advice seriously, but I never got to cook bear steak. A storm knocked out the electricity on our road, and all the meat in Stet's freezer was spoiled. Stet was very interested in the cider-making operation we lovingly pursued for decades, turning it into Normandy *cidre bouché*, natural champagne. One time, I took my wine-making partner and friend Barry Lydgate, a Wellesley French professor who was deeply involved in wine (a Chevalier du Tastevin, and member of La Confrérie de la Chaîne des Rôtisseurs), down to Stet's house to share a little of our latest cider with him. Stet savored the glass we offered and then told us how it was almost as good as the hard cider his father Roy had made years before: "I tell you, that was some good! Half a tumbler of that would make your whole face go numb!" Barry salted that line away, vowing to use it at a snooty wine tasting where he could repeat it after sipping some posh vintage. He says he has done it more than once.

One day on our first year or so at the farm, Stet drove by on his tractor and found Susan and me bathing at one of the dug wells in our backyard (we hadn't built a bathroom yet), and he asked, "You ain't drinkin' that water are you?" I said no, not as a rule, but it seemed very clear and drinkable.

"I shouldn't drink that if I was you."

"Why not?"

"Well, . . . there was a barn there years ago, and lots of manure got shoveled out there."

"Yes, but that was more than thirty years ago. No trace of it now."

"Well, . . . still I'd say don't drink it."

"But why not?"

"Well, I tell ya . . . A year or so ago, some fellers poached a deer in your back field and stuffed the entrails down your well!" We didn't ask Stet how he knew this, and we had the water tested. It was fine.

In all our summers at the farm, I did hardly any academic work—until email came along. I'd get a big manila envelope of forwarded mail from my office at Tufts about once a week and deal with it, and I'd read a book or two over the summer, but I didn't spend hours at my typewriter or, later, my laptop. I was too busy with farm projects, canoeing, windsurfing, crewing on various sailboats, exploring Maine. By September it felt like I'd forgotten all the philosophy I ever learned, but I was rarin' to go, full of ideas for how to teach my courses, ideas that had popped into my head while I was mowing hay or painting the barn door or engaged in some other more or less routine task. Doug Hofstadter, visiting one summer, said, when asked where I was, "He's out on his tractor doing tillosophy," and

Stetson Grindle

144 / I've Been Thinking

indeed I was. Harrowing a field for replanting timothy hay is not challenging work, and there's a rhythm to it, going back and forth across the field, that encourages a kind of purposeful daydreaming that often reorganizes one's thinking just enough to make progress. I'd spend twenty minutes at my desk, packing my head with a philosophical problem that had been puzzling me, and then go out and hop on the tractor and as often as not have a breakthrough before I came in for lunch or supper.

In addition to the farmhouse, with its attached sheds and three-bay open garage, and the large barn across the road, there was a decrepit outbuilding in our dooryard. It had first been built as the bottling house at the Blue Hill mineral spring back in the '20s, and then was bought and moved sometime in the '30s about a mile and a half from the spring to its present location by Walter Leighton, who was a plumber by trade and used it as a plumbing workshop. He had hauled the building (about twenty-four by eighteen feet by sixteen feet tall) with teams of oxen and big logs as rollers, and simply sat it on its heavy floor sills on the ground. These sills, plus the joists and floorboards, had rotted into the earth, along with about a foot of wall studs, and there were big holes in the roof, but I wanted to rescue it and turn it into a pottery studio. (Susan and I had taken pottery classes in California and wanted to continue to throw pots in Maine.) We called this derelict the Spring House, and it was a perfect learning project. The building was officially uninsurable, and we didn't have to live in it, so it became an experiment in rough carpentry. I bought a hydraulic jack at the hardware store, built jacking columns out of pairs of long two-by-sixes in the four corners (since the corner posts were rotten for several feet up) and, moving from column to column with my little jack and a large supply of cross-stacking jack timbers, eventually had the whole building "hanging by its plates" (the horizontal beams that ran atop the walls and held what was left of the rafters up) about two feet above the muck. We shoveled out the rotten remains of the sills and floor joists, snapped a level chalk line above the rot all the way around the inside of the hanging walls, put an old chain on the chain saw, and cut to the chalk line. This left me enough room to dig holes for Sonotubes of concrete in the corners (plus two more in the middle of the long sides), put new sills on top of the concrete posts, and gently lower the whole building onto its new foundation. New floor joists and floor, new windows, new shingled roof, a metal chimney for a wood stove, electricity, water from the barn well, and we were all set with our pottery studio. Caroline Mayher, a summer potter who had gone to Smith with Susan and lived in East Blue Hill, wanted to build a kick wheel from a kit, so we bought two kits and made them together, casting the concrete wheels with embedded axles and building the wooden structure with a suitable bench for the potter to sit on. Then another friend sold us her electric wheel, we bought an electric kiln, made a large potting table and some stools and movable shelves for drying pots, and we were ready to start shaping clay. There were similar big projects on the main house and sheds, and I had the assistance the second summer of Mike Hayworth, a high school kid from Irvine whom we invited to be our handyman. (He was so inspired by the rebuilding of the Spring House that he went back to the West Coast and became a house builder on one of the San Juan Islands in Vancouver Bay.) Over the years, the Spring House was rebuilt and put to other uses and eventually became the house our daughter, Andrea, lived in with her baby boy Brandon until she moved "up" to the Portland area (in Maine, traveling northeast along the coast away from Boston or Portland is traveling *downeast* because of the prevailing winds). We transferred the pottery studio to a loft I built in one of the sheds.

Cider-making was our most ambitious farm project, though we also harvested hay and timber and blueberries, and the apple cider we learned to make was never for sale—though various people wanted to buy it. Almost every year we'd make at least one and sometimes two fifty-five-gallon oak barrels of cider, chaptalizing (adding cane sugar) to raise the alcohol strength up to about 10 percent, relying on the wild yeast on the apples, which we found to give better results than any commercial wine yeasts we experimented with. Every Columbus Day long weekend in October, we'd invite friends, both faculty and others, to Blue Hill for a weekend of apple-picking and pressing, filling a dozen or more five-gallon glass carboys with cider, topped with fermentation locks to keep air out and let the CO_2 escape. We'd usually have a contra dance with a string band in the shed after we'd hosed down the floor where the cider had been pressed. Sometimes neighbors who had apple trees would bring over bushels of their own apples to press. Bertha Turner always showed up with a batch of homemade doughnuts, still warm from the pot.

It was hectic fun, even when the picking day was rainy and cold. We'd transport the carboys back to Andover in a trailer behind the station wagon, and they would spend the winter in our cellar, during primary and secondary fermentation, getting "racked" periodically, and then in January we'd siphon the contents into used oak bourbon barrels until Bottling Day, which was conveniently scheduled for May after final exams and before commencement at Tufts. Another day-long party at our Andover house would be held for washing, sulfiting (disinfecting), rinsing, filling, corking, wiring, labeling, and boxing hundreds of bottles of new cider—pleasant work for many hands, all switching jobs to keep it from being a chore. Everybody would drink lots of cider and have a picnic lunch, and most people would get quite soaked, what with all the water hoses and the corking machine, which always spattered a bit of excess cider when the cork was pressed home.

Not every vintage was excellent, and we found a good fate for the second-rate years. Sherm Russell, my surrogate father, gave me a Prohibition-era still that his father had used to make bathtub gin and whiskey of sorts, and I began mastering the art of turning cider wine into Calvados—apple brandy—which we called Pure Quill, a local term for excellence that was inspired by the goose quill that was often the output spout of a homemade still. Seven bottles of wine were poured into my still, the condenser was tightly affixed with wing nuts, and the still, with small hoses providing a continuous supply of cooling water, sat on a Corning pyroelectric hot plate (no flames, no chance of sparks to ignite any alcohol vapor uncondensed by the cold water running around the coil). About two hours later, the collecting bottle would be filled with Pure Quill, as clear as vodka. I invented a way of aging it that didn't involve using an oak barrel charred on the inside. (The smallest usable barrel I could find would have held thirty gallons, and I didn't have either the time or the brandy to fill it.) I bought white-oak chips from a wine hobby shop and put about a quarter cup of them on a cookie sheet under the broiler until they were very dark brown—but not black. These I funneled into a clear glass wine bottle—a Sauterne bottle, for instance—filled the bottle with the ninety-proof Pure Quill, corked the bottle, and let it sit on the counter in the kitchen. (I usually made three bottles, taking most of a day to do it.) In a day or two, the oak chips would lose their buoyancy and sink, so every time I walked by I'd just give the bottles a shake and a twist to move the brandy-logged chips off the bottom. In a month or so, the Pure Quill would have turned a beautiful amber color, a cinnamon-like aroma would greet your nose, and the harshness would be gone. Paul Churchland, who fancies himself a Calvados connoisseur, agreed to a blind test in a fine Boston restaurant that had several brands of Calvados on the menu, and he judged mine the best. We also tried to make blueberry wine, but it never measured up. When pushed through the still, however, it made a drinkable blueberry vodka or aquavit. It

Cider pressing

The Dennetts with
Bo Dahlbom

has the ghost aroma of a freshly baked blueberry pie just out of the oven. We call it Sacre Bleu! and I still have half a dozen bottles of it—along with about half a bottle of Pure Quill, to be saved for very very special occasions.

~

ANDREA AND PETER GREW UP on the farm from infancy. They gathered the eggs from the henhouse, fed the pig in the barn, and for a few years Andrea had a horse, April Star, to ride and care for. April Star sometimes got lonely in her pasture and jumped the electric fence I'd installed, but a neighbor would soon walk her back along the gravel road. The problem was solved by borrowing a little Shetland pony, Tootsie Roll, from the stable in Massachusetts where April Star spent the winter, to keep her company. We had a horse trailer and all kinds of horse gear. We'd also take the hens back to Andover for the winter to a nice sunny room in our carriage house, transporting them in an airy wooden crate on the roof rack. I remember a gas station attendant being startled when he overheard me talking gently to the hens while he pumped gas; he thought I had a person in the crate. We raised only one pig. I had wanted to name it Pork Chop, or something similar, but Peter insisted it be called Curious, after Curious George, his favorite book character, and there can't be a more challenging name for a food animal than that. I was concerned about how to deal with the kids' realization when Curious came back from the slaughterhouse in dozens of pieces all wrapped up in butcher paper. We unloaded the packages into the freezer, and all was calm until we got to the bottom of the last box. There, under the wrapped slabs of bacon soon to be sent to Newt Grindle for smoking, was the head of Curious, unwrapped and neatly sawn in half, left and right side, by the butcher's band saw. Peter jumped, but then grew curious himself, and a lengthy anatomy lesson followed. He wanted to take half the head to show-and-tell at school when we got back to Massachusetts, but we decided that might be a little too disturbing for his fellow first graders. Andrea solemnly told us that she had promised God she wouldn't eat any of Curious, but she forgot her vow, a lapse we let pass without comment.

I remember sitting on the steps of the shed with Andrea, aged about two, shucking clams I'd just raked for a chowder while she watched and played with the clams in the saucepan, eventually draping the fragrant globs all over her head, creating a raw-clam tiara that I considered her self-coronation as a Maine girl, which she is to this day. Peter and I built the Petermobile, a racing car powered by a leftover lawn-mower engine, with a homemade clutch and wooden brakes that pressed hard on the rear tires when you stepped on the brake pedal. His first drive, across our bumpy lawn, was a bounding accident-in-the-making, but I managed to stop it before it hit the giant elm tree; I found some gears to put it in a safer speed range. We also built a fort in the woods and a tree house about twenty feet up in a wolf pine. (A wolf pine is a white pine whose leader, or terminal branch, was hit by a pine weevil early in its life, causing it to have multiple trunks growing into a gigantic candelabra, instead of a single stately, usable trunk. Wolf pines are often left standing in the woods because they are no use for lumber but are prodigious sources of pine cones that can seed the next generation.) Peter's tree house had a worn-out oriental rug on its platform and a secret rope ladder—along with a decoy ladder that was designed to break once an adult started to climb it.

One major forestry operation involved cutting hundreds of mature spruce, pine, and cedar trees for sawlogs, in addition to firewood and fir pulpwood. The loggers used the latest computer-controlled harvesting machines, which could fell and limb a large spruce in less than a minute, a far cry from the chain saws and woods horses we had used on earlier logging adventures. Some of my happiest farm memories are from when our friend Paul Birdsall was winter-logging with his Belgian work horses in our woods and lodging the gentle giants in our barn. I recall the smell of fresh hay and horse manure, and the shaggy horses themselves, steaming in their stalls in zero-degree weather after being brought in from hauling pulpwood on a cord-and-a-half sled, which we had loaded using our pulp hooks, a simple tool that turns an ordinary man into an Incredible Hulk, able to lift and load four-foot-long logs with ease. I have a photo of Paul riding a giant spruce log close to three feet in diameter and sixteen feet long, its front end jacked up (with our peaveys) and chained onto a pung (a short strong sled) being pulled through the snow by his team of Belgians. Not the fastest way to log, but an experience to savor forever.

Andrea and Peter enjoyed the friendship of Dylan McTighe, about the same age as Andrea, who lived up the road with his grandmother, Fern McTighe, the librarian in the Blue Hill Public Library (and the source of the given name of the little girl in *Charlotte's Web*, written by our Brooklin neighbor, E. B. White). Dylan announced his friendship by giving Andrea a live garter snake he had just caught, and this was the first inhabitant of a serpentarium that soon included ring-necked snakes and green snakes and red-bellied snakes. An old black pickup truck hood lay on the edge of one of our blueberry fields, and when I lifted it up one day, I found about ten snakes of different species warming themselves under its sunbaked dome. This became our main snake trap. Almost any sunny day you could find a few snakes resting under the hood, and it was often an easy matter to reach down and grab one. I learned then that children can be a great booster of character, since no dad or mom wants to be seen as a fraidy-cat or sissy around their kids. I steeled myself and learned to pick up snakes with aplomb. One day, after we'd had a magnificent bonfire of trashwood and brush (duly superintended by adults with Indian Pumps on their backs), I found some snake eggs, presumably poached, in a rotten stump that had been charred but not burned to ashes. I carefully pulled out the leathery white eggs and called the kids for a biology lesson, using my razor-sharp jackknife and some pins to splay open the eggs, and unroll the tiny snakes, smaller than earthworms, onto my dissecting board. To our astonishment, several of them began to move and were promptly added to the serpentarium, where they fared well in spite of their prebirth baking.

Like their parents, our kids had the best of both worlds. Our first friendships were with local year-round Mainers, but we eventually entered the world of the summer folk who had been coming to Maine every year for generations. As a sailor, I joined the Kollegewidgwok Yacht Club. The club was not fancy—no bar, no restaurant, just a main building with a kitchen and bathroom, a little house for the manager and dock boys, another building for the sailing instructors and their gear, docks and floats with gas and water and ice available for visiting cruisers—and lots of moorings and lots of dinghies on the dinghy dock. Susan and I learned to play golf on the country club's beautiful little nine-hole course—but we never got proficient, playing what we often called "flog" as we totaled up our scores, with rare pars and bogeys but—about once a summer—an occasional birdie. For the kids, these two worlds were negotiated with various ups and downs. Some summer folk were regarded by them as detestable snobs, and the next year they would be best friends while the townies were looked down on, and the year after that they would switch allegiances again, but there was a good amount of overlap between the groups, for both adults and children.

12.

FINDING *XANTHIPPE*; LEAVING THE FARM

QUINE WRITES AT ONE POINT ABOUT SOMEBODY WHO wants a sloop. Not any particular sloop but just "relief from slooplessness," and for years I yearned for relief from slooplessness. I crewed on many sloops in races, I borrowed various sloops from friends, had my time with Jerry Fodor's sloop, and chartered sloops, but I wanted my own sloop. Years passed, more crewing, more chartering, but still no sloop for me. At the turn of the century, I was ready again. But my sloop quest had to be postponed when I had to undergo a triple-bypass heart operation, which was successful and eventually cleared me for further sloop-hunting.

Finally, in October 2004, I found my sloop, in Newport, Rhode Island—a Beneteau First 42 built in 1983 and still in pretty good shape. I bought it and sailed it over a few nights with a crew to Blue Hill, leaving Newport on a day when an early squall had put a half inch of snow on the rooftops. I wanted a boat that I could race but also cruise, and hence she should be fast. Not so much for the racing as the cruising. A slow, comfy cruising boat may rock along at five or even six knots, but a fast boat might cruise on most points of sail at seven knots or higher. The difference between five knots and seven knots to a cruising sailor is huge. Take a compass (a pair of dividers, not a north-finder) and open it up to five miles on the nautical chart where your home port appears. How far can you get in two hours, six hours, eight hours at five knots? How far can you get at seven knots? The area you can easily cover in a day's cruise multiplies swiftly. The coast of Maine is a gorgeously convoluted coastline of peninsulas, islands, coves, inlets, and more islands, and if you want to explore them all, you'd better have a fairly fast boat. Beneteau is, you might say, the Chevrolet of cruising sailboats, building reliable and relatively inexpensive boats mainly for the charter trade. But like Chevrolet, every now and then they want to come out with a special model, a Corvette, just to show they can do it. In 1980 Beneteau commissioned the brilliant young Argentinean naval architect Germán Frers to design something special, and in 1981 the first First 42 hull was launched.

I had come up with a good name: *Xanthippe*. Xanthippe was Socrates's wife, and she was supposedly a shrew, but Socrates claimed that she was high-spirited; if he could tame her, he could handle anybody. Susan didn't like the name until I found her an article by a philosopher who claimed that Xanthippe should be seen as wise, not a nag, since she scolded Socrates in public, telling him that caring for his family was more important than killing himself over some point of philosophy. Susan decided she approved of the name after all.

The boat was indeed high-spirited and getting to know how to deal with *Xanthippe's* quirks and strengths was one of my favorite investigations over the next few years. I had sought and found about the largest, fastest sloop I could single-hand in a pinch and double-hand, with Susan's help, without risk. But to race I would need a crew of about six. I knew most of the sailors in the Blue Hill area, but it's considered bad form to lure crew from another boat, and all the best sailors were committed. Who could I get to crew for me? It hit me: my former students and postdocs were all young, healthy, agile, and were quick studies, so I'd introduce them to big-boat racing and train them in a week or two. I entered *Xanthippe* in the 2005 Down East Race Week series, and our first race was a fine initiation. I was the only person on board who had ever been in any kind of sailboat race, and the crew had only a few days of practice. A late wind shift gave us a spinnaker start (it's a giant downwind sail and we hoisted it at the last moment). We barely managed to stay with the fleet, but we crossed the finish line. Nobody got injured and no gear fell

overboard—a triumph in its way. In series racing, you lose points if
you don't finish (DNF—Did Not Finish) and lose more points if
you sit out a race (DNS—Did Not Start). We lost no points in these
categories and were content with our position, which was, as one of
our competitors put it, DFL—dead fucking last. This gave us a good
benchmark for improvement, and while we never quite won a race
we were never last again and beat some of our closest competitors.
The crew on one of these boats had a nickname for us: *Xanthrax*.

You never really know the limits of your sailboat until you race
it. Cruising is a relaxing joy and you can take pride in navigating
around all dangers and keeping everything shipshape, but racing
challenges you to test your boat and your knowledge for hours or
days on end. Dangerous things can happen while racing—collisions
with other boats, detached spinnaker poles, broaches. A broach happens when you're sailing downwind with your spinnaker and a sudden gust overpowers your helm and you swerve wildly to windward,
heeling over so far that your spinnaker may dip into the water and
start filling, a condition that can lead to breaking your spinnaker
pole or head stay (or mast!), and water flooding into the cockpit.

Xanthippe *on the finish line*

At the helm of Xanthippe

After one race, we were heading back to Blue Hill with a strong wind behind us, and I had barely finished explaining to my still-novice crew what they should do if we broached, when a huge gust hit us and we did. Everybody jumped to their stations and swiftly remedied the situation. When we arrived at the dock an hour later, a club member who had watched this through her binoculars from her porch came down to the dock to congratulate us. Novices no more.

In addition to racing, and cruising with friends and family, I soon decided to inaugurate an annual "Cognitive Cruise" for my current grad students and postdocs at the Center for Cognitive Studies. They could choose a guest, somebody they wanted to talk to at length about their work. We'd have no schedule, no formal talks; we'd just go sailing for a few days, anchoring in beautiful coves, exploring deserted islands, and talking, talking, talking. I know of no better way to share ideas constructively, and the *Xanthippe* gang of Rosa Cao, Felipe de Brigard, Bryce Huebner, Justin Jungé, and Amber Ross were a tight-knit crew, both philosophically and nautically. Our guests were Nicholas Humphrey; the cognitive scientists Tecumseh

Fitch and Brian Cantwell Smith; the philosopher Andy Clark and his partner, Alexa; and the neuroscientists Stanislas Dehaene and his wife, Ghislaine. We had to stay on shore for Andy's cruise, because of a hurricane, and Stan's cruise was on a chartered schooner, since I had just sold *Xanthippe*, which needed a major repair of its fiberglass "floors"—the internal ribs that distributed the torque from the keel over a large portion of the hull. They had come loose and the keel was wobbling ominously when we hauled the boat at the end of a season. I had a plan for making the repair myself if the boat didn't sell over the winter, but a buyer saw a bargain and trucked *Xanthippe* to Lake Michigan, where he had her fixed and raced her for some years.

~

WE SOLD OUR BELOVED FARM in 2013, the year after I sold my beloved *Xanthippe*. Due to worsening arthritis and other ailments, I could no longer get around as well, and deferred maintenance had taken its toll on both. We found a wonderful house on the shore of Little Deer Isle, on Eggemoggin Reach, and decided we would trade in haying and apple-tree pruning and logging for sitting on the porch watching the great parade of sailboats, from windjammer schooners to racing sloops and yawls to cruising boats and daysailers, along with the dozens of lobster boats.

Do I miss the farm? Yes and no. The farmhouse itself had been lovingly restored by us, from the floors, to the walls, to the chimneys and stoves; and we added plumbing and dozens of electrical outlets. Walter Leighton was a plumber, but the only plumbing he had in his house was the lead pipe that ran to the dug well behind the house from the kitchen hand pump; we had an excellently designed in-house outhouse in the attached shed, a well-ventilated three-holer above an open concrete tank Leighton had built. You could walk to it through the attached shed in the winter keeping your feet dry, and the tank had to be emptied only twice during our years there.

The first time, George and I did it ourselves with shovels and buckets and spent the rest of the afternoon washing in a local pond. The second time, I called in the "honey wagon," and the fellow who ran it took the better part of an hour figuring out that the stuff he was pumping out of the tank was not his usual septic sludge. "That's not a septic tank, is it?" he said. "Nope," I replied. He finished the job and left.

The house included other fascinating oddities, hidden away. Under the eaves, there were "ship's knees," large Y-shaped natural tree branchings cut off and used to brace the hewn post-and-beam construction, fastened to the plates (horizontal wall beams atop the posts), and floor timbers with large trunnels (wooden pegs or "tree nails"). Since the hewn sills and plates had to be trunneled to the vertical posts before any studs could be mortise-and-tenoned into them, the studs couldn't be fastened at both top and bottom, so they alternated, stalactite and stalagmite, with free-floating ends, but the whole wall was held together by the boarding boards, which had been sash-sawn (with an up-and-down saw), while the clapboards nailed to them had been circular-sawn by an early clapboard mill. This permitted us to date the house to about 1830, when the first circular saws arrived in Maine. Hidden under layers of wallpaper on the front hall were Moses Eaton stencils, which we carefully restored. It was a satisfying detective job, since the paint had pulled off the old plaster walls in many places, leaving islands of partial stencil patterns. I traced all the patterns with tracing paper and then held several tracings overlapped up to the light to look for completions and, as luck would have it, was able to extract complete versions of all the patterns—oak leaves and vine twinings and flowers of several sorts. I made new stencils out of oak tag, and after we'd repainted and stenciled the walls I took our stencils to the Society for the Preservation of New England Antiquities in the Harrison Gray Otis house in Boston, where Moses Eaton's stencil kit is in storage. My stencils matched his perfectly. The kitchen floor, when we bought the house, was covered with dirty, cracked linoleum, and we decided a wood floor would be better, but when we stripped off the linoleum, we found diagonal subfloor boarding. What to do? We decided to make the most of the diagonals by creating a diamond pattern of stencils that we could paint on the floor, making it look tiled, and then varnishing it over. It was the summer of 1973, and the Watergate hearings were underway. We didn't want to miss a minute of them, and in later years whenever I looked at the stencils on the kitchen floor, I remembered that this batch over here I painted while listening to Attorney General John Mitchell, and that was the John Dean patch over there.

I knew every cubic inch of that house intimately. I had crawled into every nook, under every floor, filling in insulation between the ceiling joists in the attic, snaking electric cables through walls, building an indoor bathroom under a gable I constructed in the roof, shoveling porcupines' poop out of their winter home in our dirt-floored cellar. Forty years of largely do-it-yourself handiwork. I reshingled the house and the sheds and swept clean the chimneys with my weighted chimney brush on a rope. I almost fell off the shed roof while shingling it when I lifted up a corner of the lead sheathing around the chimney and two bats who lived there flew out in my face.

When the old barn seemed about to collapse, we hired an expert team of house movers who lifted the whole barn up on huge steel I-beams, pulled the whole barn south about seventy feet, and left it on pilings while a new concrete foundation was built to replace the falling-in fieldstone walls. They then pulled the barn back north, onto its new foundations a foot or so higher than the old. They lubricated the steel rails with half a dozen bars of Ivory soap vigorously rubbed into the steel, making them "slick as snot," as my neighbor put it, and getting the job done with hardly a rumble or vibration.

All of these projects were the highlights of many years, but toward the end of that era I had learned about as much as I could about how to split and stack firewood, how to prune and fertilize apple trees, how to mow hay in an orchard, and how to keep the woods from encroaching into the fields, and when we sold the farm one of the first things I noticed was that I no longer felt a pang of guilt when I saw that some farmer had mowed his hay and mine was still standing, overdue for harvesting. I no longer owned hayfields that needed harvesting! Whee! Freedom!

13.

HONORARY FAMILY MEMBERS; *BEHAVIORAL AND BRAIN SCIENCES*

I CAN'T SAY WHETHER THIS HAPPENS TO OTHER PROFES-sors, but every now and then I have a student who becomes for one reason or another an honorary member of our family. The first was Paul Oppenheim, a Tufts undergraduate who took my philos-ophy-of-mind class in 1974, having already devoured *Content and Consciousness*. Intense and fascinated with problems about minds and brains, he was often in my office asking questions, and one wintry weekend, when I was going to drive to the farm to cut a Christmas tree in our woods and do a few other chores that needed a helping hand, I invited him and another student to join me, since Susan was otherwise occupied. Paul helped me handily and fell in love with the farm, the wood stove in the kitchen, the hand pump in the sink, and the way of life along the Back Road. We had brought Andrea, then aged five, along, and Paul was such a sweet and imaginative inter-locutor with her all weekend and all the way home on Sunday that when we dropped him off at his apartment near Tufts, she broke into tears. "I'll never see him again! I love him so much!" I had to pull over on the highway and console her—the first, I figured, of many such heartbreaks I would have to guide her through in the coming years. She did see him again, because he came to the farm the next summer to help me shingle the shed and do other projects.

Paul had several unfinished term papers and decided to take a year off to complete them properly; he asked if he could stay over the winter at the farm as caretaker. This was fine with us, and he made the most of his year living in a house heated by a pair of wood stoves. Basil and Bertha Turner helped him settle in, and pretty soon he was a substitute teacher of French in the local high school, playing his flute in a chamber group, singing in the choir of the Congregational church, and getting to know people of all ages in town. When we returned to the farm in the spring, I was recognized around town as "Paul Oppenheim's landlord." One of the few noncharming aspects of the old-fashioned way of life in Blue Hill was the casual and ignorant anti-Semitism that one very occasionally heard expressed—by people who had never met a Jew in their lives! So innocent were they that they had no idea that "Oppenheim" was a Jewish name. By the time they found out, Paul was a beloved citizen of the town. Every year the local high school produces a musical comedy in the spring, and that spring they chose to do *Fiddler on the Roof.* I like to think it was Paul that inspired them, but I don't know. I do remember we went to one of the sold-out performances in the Town Hall, and it was a joyful thing to see all the young Hinckleys and Snows and Howards proudly dancing around on the stage with their yarmulkes on, singing their hearts out.

Paul's father, Felix, was a philosopher at UMass Amherst, and Paul's grandfather was none other than the legendary Paul Oppenheim, coauthor of classic articles in philosophy of science with Carl Hempel and Hilary Putnam. I had always assumed that he was a professor of philosophy at Princeton, but he wasn't. He was a wealthy chemist who fled Germany with his wife Gabrielle, moving first to Belgium and then, as the Nazis were closing in, bringing their fabulous art collection and his protégé, Hempel, to the United States. The Oppenheims bought a modest house on the edge of the Princeton campus and filled it with their Monets, Renoirs, Cézannes, and other fine art. Oppenheim became a supporter and friend of the philosophy department at Princeton, with a standing invitation to a young untenured philosopher to live rent-free in the third-floor apartment in their house in exchange for one day a week of collaboration with him on topics of mutual interest in philosophy. Hilary Putnam was one, then John Kemeny (the co-creator of the computer language BASIC and later president of Dartmouth), my Tufts colleague Hugo Bedau, Nicholas Rescher, and several others over the years. On Sunday mornings, Oppenheim would go on a walk with his friend Einstein, and the Oppenheims entertained Kurt Gödel and Bertrand Russell and J. Robert Oppenheimer, and many others. My student, "leetle Pol" in his grandfather's strong accent, had told his grandfather about me, and the old man had purchased a copy of my book and read it carefully. When I was invited to give a colloquium at Princeton, he suggested that I spend a few hours at his house before I went to give my talk, where he probed me with excellent questions about the arguments in my book and over a mid-afternoon brandy told me stories about how he had introduced Einstein to Gödel, who was painfully shy. Their studies were almost opposite each other in the Institute for Advanced Study, so Oppenheim had knocked on both doors simultaneously, and when the doors opened he said, "Dr. Einshtein, Dr. Gödel. Dr Gödel, Dr. Einshtein."

The last of Paul Oppenheim's tenants was not a philosopher but a graduate student in the psychology department, a young Hungarian Canadian named Stevan Harnad. Little Paul, who often visited his grandfather, knew Stevan well, and introduced us at the first meeting of the Society for Philosophy and Psychology, at MIT, in October 1974. Harnad told me his dream of starting an interdisciplinary journal, modeled on *Current Anthropology*, in which a "target article" is published along with several dozen commentaries on it by others in the relevant fields. It was to be called *Behavioral and Brain Sciences*. Grandpa Oppenheim provided bed and board to sustain Harnad, and Cambridge University Press decided to publish it, with Harnad as the founder and first editor in chief. I agreed to be the philosophy editor, and Stevan rounded up an all-star cast of other editors and some high-profile early authors of target articles. Thanks to his indefatigable work and great taste in articles (bolstered by one of the most stringent—one might say overdone—peer-review processes), the journal was an immediate success and became the flagship journal for cognitive science for decades. The great beauty of the format is that when you read a target article, you are often not in a good position to know just what to take seriously and what to discount, but you can triangulate right then and there, since you can read several dozen commentaries by people whose work you do know, plus a lengthy response from the author. It was a tremendous editorial labor, but it paid off handsomely. I'm pretty sure I hold the record for the most publications in it: as of last count, four target articles (two coauthored) and forty commentaries (eight coauthored).

After Paul Oppenheim the elder died, Stevan stayed on in the Oppenheim house for several years, caring for Gabrielle, editing the journal, and finally finishing his PhD in psychology. He went on to professorships in Southampton in England and then in Montreal, eventually turning the editorship of *BBS*, as everybody calls it, over to the triumvirate of Barbara Finlay (Cornell), Paul Bloom (Yale), and (until his death in 2004) Jeffrey Gray (Institute of Psychiatry, London), who continued to keep its standards high. Stevan and I have had a running argument for over forty years about the nature of consciousness. He thinks (along with David Chalmers) that "feeling" cannot be explained or "reduced" in terms of the effects it produces, the vistas it opens, the interferences and biases it introduces into the functioning of the brain, and I argue that if he were right, feeling would not be important, whatever it is. We are each sure that the other is dead wrong, but we are still dear friends. Stevan is also an honorary family member, but *un oncle*, and *je suis son neveu préféré*, as our many emails at least partly in French make clear.

Another honorary family member was Bo Dahlbom, a young Swedish philosophy grad student who got a Fulbright to study in the United States with me in 1975–76. He knew I had already left UC Irvine for Tufts, but he wanted to see if the songs about California girls were true, so he showed up at UCI in the fall and asked where my office was. He was told of my departure and arranged to move to Tufts in December and then had a happy autumn in Southern California, rooming with three African American grad students from Washington, DC, who were the chief shapers of his American English for those crucial three months. When Susan and I met Bo at the APA meeting in New York between Christmas and New Year's and drove him up to Massachusetts, his conversational style was both charming and electrifying—a slender blond whose deep voice combined a Swedish musical lilt with a heavy Afro drawl. He stayed with us while looking for an apartment to share near Tufts, and it was fascinating to listen to him trying the list of phone numbers he had picked up at Tufts. "Hello," he'd say in his James Earl Jones voice, "Ma name is Bo, and ah'm from Sweden . . ." Most of those he called hung up in a few seconds, already convinced that he couldn't be what he said he was, which was enough reason not to consider him as a roommate. He eventually found some charming and open-minded young women who took him in and never regretted it. Bo and I had wonderful conversations about his dissertation in progress. It was in large part about *Content and Consciousness*, which he understood to a remarkable degree and from a perspective that depended heavily on his knowledge both of phenomenology and of Carnap and Quine. What Bo gave me was an independent and enthusiastic anchor: here was a young philosopher from a somewhat different tradition who *got it*, so I must be on the right track, no matter what some of the doubters thought.

For years afterward we would get together on one side of the ocean or the other for memorable adventures. One time we drove Quine from his home on Beacon Hill to a conference on language at the University of Massachusetts, and Bo, who was writing a historical essay on Quine and Carnap, expertly quizzed Quine all the way out and back about his early days in philosophy working with Carnap, and much more. We once spent a week in Abisko, north of the Arctic Circle, at a conference with Roger Penrose and Stuart Hameroff, among others, trying to make sense of Penrose's curious views on consciousness. Bo was the editor of the first book about my work, *Dennett and His Critics* (1993). We sailed on Bo's sloop in the western archipelago of Sweden and on my sloop *Xanthippe* among the islands of Maine, where we had the narrow escape with which I opened this book. My recovery saved Bo from any second-guessing about his role in bringing about my demise. Seven years earlier, I had cancelled a white-water raft trip with my son, Peter, then a raft guide in Colorado, when my cardiologist discovered I'd had a silent heart attack. (It was the triple bypass I had then that created the scar tissue that saved my life in 2006!) I hated the prospect of either Peter or Bo having to live with the thought that they were in any way responsible for my untimely departure and am grateful we all dodged those bullets.

Part Three

MY ODYSSEY

Doing "tillosophy"

14.

BRISTOL AND ALL SOULS, 1978–79

ANDREW WOODFIELD, A YOUNG BRITISH PHILOSOPHER at the University of Bristol, got a Fulbright award to bring two American philosophers of mind to Bristol for an intense term of workshops in the fall of 1978, and he chose to invite Stephen Stich and me. As I was pondering this good prospect, I got an invitation from Derek Parfit to return to Oxford for a year as a visiting fellow at All Souls College. That settled it; we'd take the family to Bristol for the fall and Oxford for the winter and spring. But then another invitation came through from John McCarthy at Stanford, who had a grant to create a yearlong working group at the Center for Advanced Study in the Behavioral Sciences, in Palo Alto, on philosophy and artificial intelligence. I was able to convince John to hold off until 1979–80 so the Dennetts could spend a year in England and then a year in California. And I convinced Tufts to let me take off for two consecutive years, one a sabbatical and one an unpaid leave of absence. Lucky me. Lucky us.

Woodfield found us a house, the home of a professor on leave in the States, in Montpelier, a newly gentrifying area of Bristol, and we enrolled Andrea and Peter, aged seven and five, in the Sefton Park primary school, a short walk up from our hillside house, from which we could watch hot-air balloons by the dozens drifting by on most calm mornings. When I say the neighborhood was gentrifying, I mean just barely. Our house was in a long attached row of city houses. The house next door was abandoned, roof caving in, with boarded-up windows. There were other abandoned houses on the street and on neighboring streets, so this area did not look inviting. Andrew had driven us from Heathrow to the house, and my heart sank when he stopped the car opposite an unfriendly three-story wall of solid brick. A small door, so small I had to bend over to get through it, was the only aperture in this windowless wall. But once inside, we discovered that it was a delightful, sunlit house just one room deep, like a doll house. It had a walled back garden with an old tire swing on the limb of an ancient apple tree, and lots of big windows that filled the house with light on even the gloomiest days. It even had a grand piano.

The first or second day we were there, we went for a walk around the neighborhood, checking out the little shops nearby, and soon we realized that three or four children were quietly following us, curious about their new neighbors. We smiled at them and eventually the boldest of the little boys dared to address us: "You're Americans, aren't you?"

"Yes," I replied.

"Do you know Darth Vader?"

"Well, not personally."

Our own kids soon found that they were entirely welcome in the multicultural neighborhood, playing in the streets and the adventure playground two streets down the hill and visiting their playmates' homes. When an ice storm left the roads impassable to cars, the kids found cardboard boxes to turn into sleds and went careening down the streets at a terrifying speed, but nobody got hurt.

The Fulbright workshop on philosophy of mind concentrated on topics that were then occupying some of the brightest talents in the field: how to make sense of claims such as "x believes that p," which seem simple enough at first glance but exhibit logical peculiarities that had frustrated the efforts of Frege, Russell, and Quine, among others. The people working on these issues were somewhat jocularly known to many as the Propositional Attitude Task Force, and Steve Stich and I had both contributed to this literature. But we both harbored the suspicion that the usual setting of the issues was in some way artifactual, fundamentally misconstruing the phenomena. We decided to coauthor a paper attacking the foundational concept of "propositional attitudes," but after several months of drafting and discussion we decided to go our separate ways. This resulted in my 1982 paper "Beyond Belief" and Steve's 1983 book, *From Folk Psychology to Cognitive Science: The Case against Belief.* Steve later changed his mind, but I haven't budged. More on that later.

The Bristol workshop was intense and happy, spilling over into discussions at lunch in the faculty club, where we were often joined by nonphilosophers. One mathematician who vigorously participated (I forget his name, alas) was enticed into reading Quine's *Word and Object*, and asked me at lunch one day why it was that whenever Quine got into real metaphysical issues he "cracked wise," jocularly evading the problems. It had never occurred to me that Quine did this, but I was soon persuaded that the fellow was right. I ventured a diagnosis: Quine started out as a mathematical logician and had never been quite sure that philosophy was a proper career for a grown-up; it was his residual discomfort with the field he was in that explained his arm's-length approach to metaphysics. Years later, I told Quine this story, and he readily confirmed my diagnosis: Quine was a philosopher *malgré lui*. Me too, I thought. Another nonphilosopher who joined in the discussion was the physicist Michael Berry, to whom I am grateful for tutoring me on chance, chaos, and indeterminism.

The most welcome interloper was the psychologist Richard Gregory, who had no official role in the Fulbright program but who entertained us, grilled us, informed us, and in the process became a dear friend of mine. Richard was larger than life, in several ways. He was tall and playful, and his enthusiasm knew no bounds as he peppered us with puzzles, questions, curious psychological facts, and awful puns. He was a pied piper with children; when he threw a dinner party for the Fulbright group in his elegant crescent apartment in Clifton, filled with telescopes and antique scientific instruments, he showed our children some of the marvels and then settled them on his bed to watch cartoons and David Attenborough videos while the adults had their own party in the living room. Here was a great psychologist who got the point of philosophy—or thought he did; his bold "misreadings" of some philosophical texts were often actually improvements, in my opinion. He was in the process of creating the Bristol Exploratory, modeled somewhat on the Exploratorium in San Francisco, a science museum where you got to touch and fiddle with everything and science was fun. Famous for his visual illusions, he put together an awesome collection of astounding items, fascinating to children and adults alike. Every day when I walked from our house in Montpelier to the university, I walked by a café wall whose tiles happened to create a visual illusion; I never noticed it, but one of Richard's graduate students did, and Richard made it famous among vision scientists.

It was Richard who first impressed on me the idea that *tools make you smarter*. Microscopes and maps and diagrams are obviously cognitive aids, but even a pair of scissors can on occasion help you solve a problem. Many tools are not concrete artifacts but methods, attitudes, algorithms. Nobody invented language and nobody knows who—if anybody—deserves credit for inventing the hammer or the knife or the number zero or writing, and many of the best tools for thinking have arisen through multiple more or less simultaneous inventions and improvements. Who invented the telescope, the computer, calculus? Over time human culture has generated a bounty of techniques and devices for finding things out, and we are the only species on the planet whose brains are well furnished with all these tools. This has been a major theme in my work, the Tower of Generate and Test, starting with Darwinian creatures that are born with many clever instincts that evolved by natural selection, Skinnerian creatures that can evolve novel behaviors by trial and error in the environment, Popperian creatures that can do some of the trial and error in their heads (much less risky!), and Gregorian creatures that can explore the vast space of possible solutions to problems with the help of thousands of culturally inherited thinking tools. These thinking tools are, as I said in *Intuition Pumps* (2013), apps that are all available to be downloaded to your necktop for free.

Richard and I met often at scientific conferences in England and elsewhere, and I particularly cherish the memory of a splendid breakfast we Dennetts had with him in a hotel overlooking the Clifton suspension bridge, where he once again beguiled our children, who were having their second stay in England while I gave the Locke Lectures in Oxford. On another occasion when I stayed with Richard, he had just come back from one of the fabulous Garden Parties Queen Elizabeth gave in the gardens behind Buckingham Palace. Richard had been invited, and he reported with glee what had happened there. The queen had been chatting with some gentleman guest when one of her corgis assaulted one of his well-trousered legs. He tried to shake off the dog while continuing the chat, without success. "Kick his balls!" said the queen. The fellow paused. "Kick his balls!" she repeated. So, he did. "His *croquet* balls!" she explained.

It was through Richard that I got to know two of his former students, V. S. Ramachandran and Susan Blackmore, both of whom have played major roles in my education. He also encouraged me to think of experiments that could test some of the ideas I was percolating about consciousness. In my 1991 book, *Consciousness Explained*, I describe the British neurosurgeon Grey Walter's "precognitive carousel," an early experiment in which he implanted electrodes in the motor cortex of human patients/subjects and demonstrated that they could change viewing-slides just by forming the intention to do so, while pushing a dummy button not attached to the slide projector. Grey Walter had explained this experiment to a rapt group of medical students (and me) at an Osler Society meeting in Oxford in 1963. He reported that his patients/subjects were surprised to find the carousel "anticipating" their decisions, just as they were about to press the button. The tiny time lag between decision and finger-muscle contraction was missing, giving them an illusion of a mind-reading slide projector. This remarkable but easy-to-explain "finding" got me thinking about time perception, which was a major topic in my 1991 book. Many researchers who read my book wanted to know more and could find no published work by Grey Walter that described any such experiment. Richard had known Grey Walter well and had access to his papers, stored in the Burden Neurological Institute, an imposing edifice on a hill outside Bristol. He and his assistant, Patricia Heard, searched through all the files and found no account of the experiment Grey Walter had described. So perhaps the great man had told a fictitious tale to those credulous young medical students of an experiment he had envisioned but never performed. Thanks to advances in technology, it should now be possible to do versions of that experiment without drilling holes in people's skulls and implanting electrodes. But although several scientists have discussed with me the prospect of doing such versions, I still do not know of definitive peer-reviewed results either confirming or disconfirming the precognitive-carousel effect.

~

AFTER CHRISTMAS IN BRISTOL, we moved to Oxford and a basement flat in a large house in Crick Road just north of the Parks, where All Souls College housed their visiting fellows with children. The visiting fellows program was a preemptive response by All Souls to the Franks Commission of Inquiry in 1965. Lord Oliver Franks, then the provost of Worcester College, cleverly composed a searching questionnaire about the policies and activities of the more than three dozen colleges that compose Oxford University. These colleges were then almost entirely independent in their finances and governance, and it was an ill-kept secret that many of them were not putting their vast endowments, accrued over centuries, to very efficient and equitable use. Franks sent the questionnaire to all the colleges asking about how often the fellows met, what they voted on, how they admitted students, how salaries were determined, and so forth, and gave them some months to respond—enough time for the colleges to get their houses in order so that they could truthfully answer

Franks's questions without too much embarrassment. (This is a tactic all reform-minded deans and university presidents should have in their kits.) All Souls College famously has no students. Some but not all of the fellows hold university professorships, which of course have significant teaching duties, but there are no undergraduates to tutor, to house and feed, to advise, so a tenured fellow of All Souls could lead a leisurely and comfortable scholarly life with few duties. The visiting fellows program was designed to fend off pressure from the Franks Commission to admit bothersome young students and was quickly instituted by the college to ensure that a steady stream of fresh talent from outside the university was present to invigorate and stir up the permanent residents. It worked. To this day there are no undergraduates in All Souls College, and only advanced postgraduate fellows.

In an ancient and tradition-bound university, All Souls College stands unrivaled in its hold on the old ways. Leszek Kolakowski, the exiled dissident Polish philosopher, was a fellow of All Souls at the time, and once when he was asked what life in All Souls was like he replied that it was like "living on an island on an island on an island." Patrick Neill was then the warden, and a story making the rounds that year was that one day Neill was walking through the Houses of Parliament and was spotted by All Souls quondam fellow Quintin Hogg, then lord chancellor and dressed in full regalia, who called out to him, "Neill! Neill!" whereupon a couple of American tourists dutifully knelt. When we were there, the college was still restricted to men only, but there was talk of change. At one formal dinner Susan sat next to the warden and gave him quite an earful of remonstration about the absence of female fellows, and she was not alone in her sentiments; some weeks later, the following item appeared in the weekly *Oxford Times* (February 9, 1979), under the headline GIRLS ALLOWED:

Oxford's most famous bastion of male chauvinism is to be breached. All Souls College—its full title is the College of All

Souls of the Faithful Departed—founded by Henry VI in 1438, and with the Archbishop of Canterbury as its Visitor, is to alter its statues [sic] so as to make it possible for women to become members of the college.

This misprint was particularly apt, because in fact there was a statue in the private Fellows' Garden of a nude young man, a Roman copy of a Greek original, *sans* figleaf, which had once been wrestled from its plinth by some of the fellows and placed in the bed of Warden John Sparrow, who was out of the closet. I wrote an open letter to the fellows, attaching the clipping:

TO THE FELLOWS OF ALL SOULS COLLEGE:
I was shocked to learn from the *Oxford Times* that the Fellows of this College are determined to mutilate some of the antiquities entrusted to their care, presumably out of a misguided and anachronistic concern for the sensibilities of women who may enter these hallowed precincts.

While applauding the zeal with which the Fellows are demonstrating their commitment to Equality, I respectfully urge them to reconsider this rash gesture. *Ars Longa Vita Brevis!*

and posted it on the bulletin board in the coffee room. It didn't last an hour before one of the irate old misogynists ripped it down, but I had foreseen this possibility and had a photocopy back on the bulletin board in a few minutes, where it remained and entertained the warden and most of the fellows. Just two years later, All Souls elected its first female fellow, and I played a happy role in that. Susan Hurley, a brilliant young philosopher then at Harvard Law School, was elected, and knowing I had recently been a visiting fellow she invited me to lunch in Harvard Square so I could fill her in on some of the folkways and pitfalls of the college. Academic gowns were worn to dinner every night, but Friday nights were formal, and the fellows wore black bow ties and "dinner jackets" (tuxedos to Yanks) under their open gowns. Should she wear a black dress? NO! She should get a tailor to make her a curvy, sexy Marlene Dietrich tuxedo, and it would knock their socks off. She did, and it did. Everyone in the college, aside from a few die-hard curmudgeons, just loved her, and even old John Sparrow confided to Derek Parfit that "she is just perfect—aside from the one thing she can't do anything about."

Lunch in All Souls is served in the magnificent and unique Hawksmoor-designed Buttery, an oval room with curved benches along the walls and curved tables and other seats facing the wall, and in the middle of the quite small room there is a table that carries a sumptuous variety of cheese, biscuits, and fruit and a large plate of butter. Saul Kripke had been a visiting fellow a year or two before I was, and one of the scouts (waiters) told me about the strange behavior of my predecessor. Professor Kripke had summoned him to ask if he could please have a little of the butter from the table to put on his boiled potatoes. "No, sir, that butter is for the cheese and biscuits," the scout replied.

"But there's ten times more butter on the plate than will be used for the cheese and biscuits. May I please have some now?"

"NO, sir! As I just explained to you, that butter is *for the cheese and biscuits.*" The scout finished his tale with "And sir, you will scarcely believe this, but Professor Kripke still persisted. What a strange chap!" Even the scouts could be rigid upholders of tradition.

I soon discovered that it was sometimes fun to pretend I was playing a part in an undiscovered Gilbert and Sullivan operetta, which eased me happily through some faux pas, and it was also amusing to be hyper-American on occasion. Since there are no students in All Souls, there are no playing fields, no tennis courts, no squash courts connected with the college, and I loved to play squash, so one day at lunch I lamented the fact that All Souls had no squash courts and I had to find opponents in other colleges to play. "Well, there's no room for any squash courts, is there?" came the reply.

"I've thought about that, and made some measurements, and it turns out that two squash courts would fit easily in the Chapel, and nobody uses that!"

The looks of horror vanished when they saw I was joking. In fact the architectural gems of All Souls are as sacrosanct to me as to any fellow. The Old Library, with its exquisite plaster ceiling, was the setting for the remarkable seminar on law and morality taught by Parfit, Amartya Sen, and Ronald Dworkin, and is the most beautiful classroom I know. The Codrington Library, the Chapel, the Hall, and of course the Buttery are among the finest rooms I have ever set foot in.

One of the amusing antiquities in All Souls is the Betting Book, where fellows have been writing and adjudicating wagers over factual disagreements for years. "Smith-Williams wagers Snodgrass that Arsenal will defeat Tottenham Hotspur on Saturday, one bottle of claret at stake," or "Jones offers £10 to anyone who can demonstrate that Charles II was left-handed." The book goes back centuries, and one of my favorites was "X bets Y that there is no state in America with the preposterous name Oklahoma." The one wager I wrote in the book I lost; I bet somebody £5 that the Ayatollah Khomeini would be overthrown in a few weeks. Wrong. Another visiting fellow during my brief time in All Souls was Sir Maurice Oldfield, reputedly the model for M in Ian Fleming's James Bond novels. I have recounted one of my after-dinner conversations with him in the foreword to my sister Charlotte's book on our father's life as a spy, *Follow the Pipelines*. Other memorable conversations were with Sir Isaiah Berlin, who was an inexhaustible source of stories and jokes. Once he was asked why the Jews in England were not, as a group, as brilliant as the Jews in America. His answer—and I wish I could convey in print the rolling tones in which he replied—was that during the terrible pogroms on the Continent, many Jews fled on ships, trying to get to America, but some unscrupulous steamship captains stopped at Liverpool, telling them it was New York, and the Jews who were stupid disembarked.

I took advantage of this salubrious setting to work on my effort to get to the bottom of the puzzles about belief that Stich and I had started to dismantle, and in the "summer," or Trinity, term, which lasts into June, I was invited by the subfaculty of philosophy to give a seminar on it. The fiery young philosopher Gareth Evans was working on the same topics, and he too gave a seminar that term on the issues, and the graduate students, some interested faculty, and a few brave undergraduates migrated from one to the other every week. Gareth could be ferociously rude. He beat back my objections in his seminar with cutting remarks, and then when he came to my seminar he peppered me with objections that often left me stammering. One graduate student said that each week when he went to Gareth's seminar, he came out convinced I was right, which cheered me up— until he added that when he came out of my seminar he was back in Gareth's camp. In spite of this contest, Gareth and I got along quite well personally, and I remember going for a long walk with him in Christ Church Meadow, where he gently tried to dissuade me from pursuing these difficult issues—since, he said, I was so much better on other topics. Before the term was over, he visited me in Crick Road bearing a note from the subfaculty inviting me to become the next Wilde Reader of Mental Philosophy. I would have loved to have that title, and Oxford was a place very dear to my heart, but Susan and I decided we couldn't afford to take the position, which in those days was poorly paid, as were even professorships. After I declined the position, Gareth himself was elected the new Wilde Reader, though he had not yet begun paying much attention to psychology, AI, or neuroscience.

One day while skimming through the rules for visiting fellows, I discovered that we had the same catering rights as permanent fellows. That is, we could arrange private dinners and lunches to be prepared by the kitchen and served by the scouts, whom we would have to pay, of course, but at very reasonable rates. I gathered the Crick Road fellows, all of whom had been frequent guests of colleagues and friends, and suggested we combine our lists of return engagements and throw a huge luncheon in college at the end of term for them. We chose a Saturday in June, with a sit-down luncheon in Hall for about forty or fifty people. Mr. Quelch, the butler, arranged for some of the finest college silver to be arrayed on the long table, along with candles, wine glasses, and fresh strawberries. When our guests arrived at noon and were served champagne in the central courtyard on the absolutely perfect lawn, with the Radcliffe Camera glowing behind us, every bell in Oxford began to peal. This was, in fact, the end of "Schools" (examinations) and the students were celebrating by ringing the changes from perhaps a dozen steeples in the neighborhood. Our guests were astonished, and I pretended briefly that this was just a little something extra we'd laid on for the luncheon. The sun shone, the food was beautiful and delicious, the scouts served it with practiced aplomb, and we all drifted off to go punting on the Cherwell after lunch, thinking we were living in a dream.

15.

CASBS, 1979-80,
AND MEETING
DOUGLAS HOFSTADTER

A LL SOULS COLLEGE AND THE CENTER FOR ADVANCED Study in the Behavioral Sciences, on the edge of the Stanford campus in Palo Alto, are two different versions of academic heaven. Both host a variegated collection of established researchers for an idyllic year of intense interactive work; both serve lunch to the participants with the particular intent of encouraging interdisciplinary mutual enlightenment and stimulation—and both have no students to tend to. All Souls has fabulous architecture, vintage port, and old-world servants, and CASBS has volleyball after lunch, and a strict ban on accepting invitations to give talks at West Coast colleges and universities during one's precious year at the center. John McCarthy, coiner of the term "artificial intelligence" and director of the Stanford Artificial Intelligence Laboratory (SAIL) put together a group of six—two philosophers (John Haugeland and myself); three AI researchers, Robert Moore, Patrick Hayes, and McCarthy himself; and Zenon Pylyshyn, a psychologist with expertise in both AI and philosophy—to spend the academic year clarifying some of the issues arising at the intersection of AI and philosophy.

This group should have worked together handily; the AI researchers all were philosophically inclined and sophisticated, and Haugeland and I were probably the two philosophers who had thought more about AI than any others. It almost crashed in its first week, which we spent taking turns giving our perspectives on the issues as we then saw them and eagerly offering critiques and objections. McCarthy listened to us with mounting discomfort as the week rollicked along, and on Friday he gave us all a stern talking-to: "Look! You are all very clever—I wouldn't have invited you otherwise—so stop trying to prove it." He told us tales of the difficult government-funded technical projects he had worked on involving early development of computer languages—he created Lisp, the list-processing language that became the lingua franca of early (Good-Old-Fashioned) AI— and of how the groups in which he had worked, groups of highly skilled and creative people, had helped one another solve problems instead of tormenting one another with clever objections. "If you want to continue carrying on like this," he said, "I'll go back down the hill to SAIL and you can have fun all year here without me." I have often had occasion to tell my philosophical colleagues and students this story, since philosophy can readily degenerate into high-concept pissing contests, which I have come to loathe as strongly as John McCarthy did.

McCarthy and Hayes had published an important paper in 1969, "Some Philosophical Problems from the Standpoint of Artificial Intelligence," in which they introduced what they called the frame problem. In 1984 I published my attempt to introduce the problem to philosophers, in "Cognitive Wheels: The Frame Problem of AI," but as I later acknowledged, many in AI thought I had misdescribed it—including McCarthy and Hayes, who ought to know! However, this disagreement did not involve just me; others chimed in on one side or the other, and there are several anthologies of work about what the frame problem is and isn't. I won't attempt to explain it here, having failed in my major effort when I was much younger and sharper. This was one of the issues we tackled that year, along with the problem of non-monotonic logic and McCarthy's method of "circumscription" for dealing with it. In standard logic, monotonic logic, you can generate new true theorems from your axioms but never turn a previously established truth or theorem into a falsehood. But in our everyday world we often discover things that oblige us to go back and reconsider things we thought we'd proved for sure. Can this reconsideration be given a formal treatment (so that a computer could readily perform it), and if so, how?

This was all in the spirit of GOFAI (Good-Old-Fashioned AI), the term John Haugeland coined to cover the early years of AI, when McCarthy's view of AI reigned. The idea was to formalize everyday knowledge so that computers could generate theorems that answered important questions. It was an inspired idea, but the general consensus today is that it can't work, although some early work with "expert systems" showed promising results in carefully restricted domains. As I had argued in "Intentional Systems" (1971), the rationality assumption works most of the time, because we everyday folks are remarkably adept at seeing the important implications of what we perceive, but we are not walking encyclopedias of axiomatic facts from which we formally deduce, at breakneck speed, all the theorems we need to guide us in avoiding falling off cliffs and finding warm food and safe beds.

While struggling with the technicalities of McCarthy's mathematical vision, I was also still wrestling with the problems of propositional attitudes that had occupied me since Bristol. I would have days when I thought the whole project was doomed, but then John Haugeland would invite me for a long walk in the scrubby hills around the center and talk me out of my funk. I was invited to give a lecture at the University of Pittsburgh and said I had more material on propositional attitudes than I could cover in one lecture, so they invited me to give two, on consecutive days. The center was opposed, of course, to my taking this trip at all, since it was in violation of their prohibition to give talks, but I persisted; this was Pittsburgh, my favorite department, and besides, Pittsburgh wasn't on the West Coast. Indeed it wasn't, and I made the mistake of taking a red-eye overnight flight with a change in St. Louis, where I sat, unable to sleep, for hours. When I showed up for my first talk, with all my overhead transparencies ready to go, the muse fled; I misspoke, backed up, tried again, and still failed to express what I meant, over and over—by a wide margin the worst talk I ever gave in my life, to an audience I especially esteemed. It was the only time I have ever eagerly awaited "the hook"—a host telling me I had run out of time and should stop speaking—and I had a second lecture to give the next day! Happily an old friend I had once hired for a visiting position at Tufts, Roger Wertheimer, then at Carnegie Mellon, was in the audience, and he took me off for a steak dinner and a pep talk that carried me handily through the next day. Without these philosopher friends, I might have given up altogether. Eventually, I would get the talk ("Beyond Belief") in good enough shape to publish. Pat Churchland had been in on some of my travails, and her title for it was "Beyond Belief and Past Caring." She had turned her back on traditional philosophy of mind sooner than I had.

Our group at CASBS had frequent visitors that year. Marvin Minsky showed up for about a month, and his lunchtime conversations with McCarthy left me shaking my head in wonder. They were egging each other on with schemes for putting more payloads into space cheaper than the Saturn rockets that had taken men to the moon a few years earlier. One scheme was to put pairs of geostationary satellites tethered together with very long Mylar cables that would do slow cartwheels in space; their center of gravity would be in the middle of the tether, and first one and then the other satellite would dip low enough into the stratosphere to pick up payloads (including people), which could be flown up to meet them. Another scheme they seriously considered was a variation on Jules Verne: Drill a deep, large-circumference hole into the earth like a gigantic rifle barrel and put a low-yield nuclear bomb at the bottom with a lot of earth packed on top to shield and protect the astronauts, who were expected to volunteer to strap themselves into their seats on top of this bomb and signal "Ready when you are!" The propulsion, they theorized, would act like squeezing a huge tube of toothpaste, expelling the spaceship and leaving a small dimple on the surface of the earth. Then there was the "space fountain," a tower extending into space kept in place by a continuous stream of pellets. You will have noticed that these schemes have not been put into practice in the intervening decades.

Jerry Fodor showed up for several months, and when he learned I had taken a scuba-diving course and was certified, he wanted to do the same, so I repeated the course with him as my buddy and helped him through his certification dive. He couldn't for a long time manage a surface dive to get his head and torso heading down and was thrashing around. I had to tell him, "Slow motion, slow motion, easy does it," until he finally made his way to the bottom, in thirty feet of water, ready to do his free ascent. After he got his certification, I invited him to do a dive off Catalina Island with a UC Irvine friend, the physicist Douglas Mills, who had a sailboat and was willing to take us over and watch as Jerry did his first dive without an instructor present. We anchored next to a kelp forest on the channel side of the island, and down we went, while Doug, I imagined, sat in the cockpit nervously drafting his statement to the press ("Well, they were both certified, and they assured me . . ."). The dive was enlivened by a sea lion who approached and then circled us and led us down, down, down, into the forest. I soon realized we were at eighty feet, deeper than novice divers should go, and were running low on air, so I signaled to Jerry that we should begin our ascent. I watched him closely, making sure he was exhaling all the way; if you don't, you drive air into your bloodstream and very likely die! We reached the surface and all was well, I thought, until Jerry began screaming, "I can't breathe!"

"Jerry, you're on the surface, your head is in the air! You're breathing!"

"No, I can't breathe!"

I then realized what his problem was. At eighty feet, his rather rotund body was so compressed that he'd had to cinch up his weight belt, which otherwise would have slid off. He had forgotten about this, and as he ascended, his body resumed its normal dimensions, and the weight belt was cutting him in half. I reached over and flipped the buckle lever and *kapow!* the belt flew off into my hands and everything was fine.

Scuba diving wasn't my only watery learning experience that year. One late winter day, I looked out the window of my study at the center and saw that the dried mud field on the edge of the Stanford campus that had looked so unsightly all fall had been turned almost overnight into a sparkling little lake—Lagunita, it is called—and there were students swimming and windsurfing on it. I rode my bicycle down the hill to check it out and discovered that I could actually rent a windsurfer by the hour there, thanks to my temporary affiliation with SAIL, the Stanford AI laboratory. The next day I brought swim trunks to the center and told McCarthy at lunch that I was going down to Lagunita to try to windsurf. He decided to come along and sat on a bench for a couple of hours watching me fall and fall and fall. When I finally hand-paddled the windsurfer back to the rental place, John came over and said, "Well, I guess you got that out of your system, didn't you?"

"Oh no, I'll be back tomorrow to try again. I think I was *almost* getting it."

I did, and sure enough, overnight my understanding had grown, and I sailed away under control on my first attempt. I still had to master coming about, with quite a few more falls, but by the end of the week I was a secure and happy windsurfer. As soon as I returned to Maine the next summer, I bought a used board and windsurfed in ponds, lakes, and ocean bays for years. (Lake Lagunita is no longer filled in the winter to a depth permitting windsurfing and is now a major wildlife habitat, so that window of opportunity has closed.) I eventually had three or four different boards for different conditions and tried to master water starts, where you don't stand up first and then pull the sail up, but instead use the sail to pull you up on the board. It works only in strong winds and is almost a necessity in strong winds, since the waves are apt to make standing on the board too precarious without the sail up to balance you. Unfortunately, my triple-bypass operation intervened before I mastered the technique, so I never got confident with water starts. There are few sailing thrills to match feeling the board rising up under your feet as you lean to windward and accelerate into a big gust. Getting back up on the board when the gust suddenly stopped was always a chore, which eventually became a practical impossibility for me. Farewell, windsurfing—I loved you while I could.

About half a dozen times, John Searle and Bert Dreyfus drove down from Berkeley to have an afternoon session with our CASBS gang—not including McCarthy, who wanted no part of Bert Dreyfus—and each time we'd set up a topic to discuss in advance, and each time, within a few minutes of discussion, Searle would change the topic, insisting on talking about the Chinese Room, his thought experiment, which he had not yet published in *Behavioral and Brain Sciences*. (Imagine somebody composes an AI program that supposedly understands Chinese, and it passes the Turing test— Chinese interlocutors take it to be a worthy understander in conversation. Searle takes the program into a room and hand-simulates it. He doesn't understand Chinese; nothing in the room understands Chinese. Therefore [?] no AI program could understand Chinese.) None of us in the group regarded his thought experiment—it is an intuition pump, not really an argument—as sound, and we found various ways of rebutting it, but John just wouldn't let go. Dreyfus, meanwhile, was mostly silent. We got so tired of talking about the Chinese Room and what was wrong with it that we discontinued the discussion group. Little did I know at the time that I was in for a few hundred more hours of Chinese Room discussions over the next few decades.

As the wonderful year at CASBS wound up, the group decided to hold a conference on AI and philosophy to consolidate some of the gains we thought we had made, inviting leading thinkers from all over to participate. I invited Gareth Evans from Oxford, and since he was going to be the new Wilde Reader of Mental Philosophy I wanted to make sure he had a close-up look at how people in AI thought and talked, so I invited him to come to the center a week early and spend some time with us in our discussions. He participated strenuously in our discussions and at the conference, but he wasn't his usual swashbuckling self. I remember driving him back to his hotel after one of the sessions, and he confided that he had contracted cancer. Within a few months he died, and philosophy lost a brilliant and original thinker at the height of his powers.

The most important meeting I had that year was when Douglas Hofstadter showed up from Indiana University and twisted my arm to join him in editing what became *The Mind's I* (1981), a collection of stories and essays on consciousness and the self that captured the attention of thousands of thinkers, young and old. (Quine didn't like it, by the way; when I sent it to him to see if he'd write a blurb for it, he replied with a four-word blurb: "A surfeit of whimsy.") I had never heard of Doug when he reviewed *Brainstorms* very positively in the *New York Review of Books*, and I hadn't even purchased his classic *Gödel, Escher, Bach* before we met, but our collaboration and friendship has been a major theme in my life for over forty years. Doug's father, the Nobel laureate physicist Robert Hofstadter, was a professor at Stanford, and Doug often visited his family. Shortly after his review appeared, Doug showed up at the center to meet me and walk me down to the Stanford bookstore, where I bought a copy of *Gödel, Escher, Bach*, which he autographed for me. I was reluctant to do an anthology, but Doug was persistent, thank goodness, and we soon signed a contract with Basic Books to do it.

Doug's review of *Brainstorms*, along with another good review by the British AI researcher (and later, the pioneer developer of deep-learning systems) Geoffrey Hinton, did a lot to steer attention among cognitive scientists to my book, but when I first met Doug, I was under the impression that he was probably a "West Coast woo-woo" kind of thinker, a flower child left over from the '60s. He soon showed me otherwise, and I began to learn a lot from him—about computers, about music, about physics, about language, about everything, really. I am so glad he persisted in persuading me to join him in compiling and editing *The Mind's I*, which changed my life's trajectory in several ways. We both had favorite short pieces to propose as chapters, but he contributed more than I did. He introduced me to the writing of Stanislaw Lem and, much more important, Richard Dawkins. When *The Selfish Gene* appeared, in 1976, I asked an eminent philosopher of biology whom I knew well about Dawkins's book, and he confidently described it as a "pop-science potboiler" not worth my attention. When I passed on this opinion to Doug, he said, "Read the book and see what you think." I did, and it opened my eyes. Not just to the brilliant set of ideas explained and defended so vividly by Dawkins but to the serious sin of directing would-be readers away from books you haven't read but presume to be wrong, sometimes for political reasons.

Ever since then, I have tried hard never to dismiss a book I haven't personally and seriously read and found worthless, and I have gone out of my way to recommend books that others were dinging when I found valuable insights in them. Julian Jaynes's *The Origin of Consciousness in the Breakdown of the Bicameral Mind*, also published in 1976, was one of my favorite books to recommend, and I have often been repaid when secret fans of Jaynes's wild and wonderful book have come up to me after a talk and thanked me profusely for allowing them to come out of the closet and announce that they, too, thought Jaynes was onto something. I have also championed Ruth Millikan's books, and I am happy to say that she is now winning the awards and acclaim that are her due, though there are still too many philosophers of language who don't think they need to respond to her incisive critiques of their work. Other iconoclastic books I've tried to spread the word about are Terrence Deacon's *The Symbolic Species* (1997) and *Incomplete Nature* (2012). More recently I've been encouraging people to read Daniel Dor's highly original and carefully argued (but insufficiently Darwinian) book, *The Instruction of Imagination* (2015). There is plenty of prejudice in academia, and it can be exhilarating to amaze one's audiences by paying respect to works and authors deemed beyond the pale by one group or another. And, of course, everybody wins, both the authors and their readers.

Doug and I both wrote extra pieces for *The Mind's I* to help readers make sense of our choices, and I can't remember who first suggested that we *not* write introductions to each piece but rather follow each piece with "reflections"; we wanted readers to be confronted with the authors' ideas unprepared, making readers an approximation of the "naïve subjects" in psychological experiments. We did a lot of the editorial work during a record-breaking cold spell in Massachusetts, in the Victorian house in Andover, sitting on the floor in the living room with a blazing fire in the fireplace. I remember pawing through our piles of candidate manuscripts, discussing them, deciding who would have first dibs at writing the reflections, delving deeply into the themes in the book.

Our styles are somewhat different, and I gently tried to lure Doug away from what I considered some of his stylistic excesses, but in the end his voice comes through loud and clear, with occasional light taps on the brakes from me. His masterpiece, *Gödel, Escher, Bach*, had, after all, won a Pulitzer Prize for nonfiction, so he was doing something right. I came to appreciate at the time, however, that many people whose serious attention he rightly craved—leaders in computer science, AI, and cognitive science more generally—were put off by his playfulness and somewhat self-indulgent digressions, and they had managed to persuade themselves that they wouldn't learn anything from Hofstadter if they could possibly help it. And philosophers, sad to say, tended to view him with similar disdain, though I know that many of them taught courses using *The Mind's I* as the primary textbook.

A particularly amusing—to me—instance of a philosopher's disdain for Doug occurred in May 1984, when I presented a talk entitled "The Logical Geography of Computational Approaches: A View from the East Pole" at a Sloan Foundation conference on cognitive science and philosophy at MIT, placing the various ideologues of the field in a polar-coordinate map, inspired by Jerry Fodor's joke that MIT was the "East Pole" and whichever way you went when you left MIT was going west (to woo-woo land). My map included the work of the newly ascendant connectionists and other heretics (from the point of view of the Chomskyans), analyzing and sometimes defend-

ing their positions. It was a big hit, and afterward the MIT philosopher of mind and cognitive scientist Ned Block came up to me and
said, "Dan, that was terrific, but where did you learn about all this
interesting new work?"

"Here at MIT," I replied, "in Doug Hofstadter's recent seminar,
which of course none of you MIT philosophers or linguists attended."

Doug's opinion of philosophers was in most regards equally jaun-
diced. I remember sitting with him in a conference in St. Louis
shortly after our book had come out. I was intently listening to a very
highly regarded philosopher (I won't say who), and Doug leaned over
and whispered in my ear, "How can you stand to listen to this stuff?"
or words to that effect. I insisted that he should pay attention; what
was being developed were in fact some good, original, deep ideas. He
was not moved. He wrote on his pad, "You remind me of Chopin
and Mozart. I love Chopin and can't imagine how Chopin can have
such a high regard for Mozart, whom I usually find boring and vac-
uous. It's hard for me to reconcile my admiration for you with your
appreciation of this dreck." I wrote back on his pad, "That's interesting; some philosophers have said much the same thing to me about
you!" Over the years, I have often played this fulcrum role, trying to
get philosophers and cognitive scientists who didn't appreciate Doug
to see the light. My favorite such occasion was in 1992, when the
Cognitive Science Society held its annual meeting in Bloomington,
at Indiana University, where Doug has been teaching for decades
now. Doug gave one of the keynote addresses, and I introduced him,
to a huge room packed with cognitive scientists by the hundreds
from around the world. I took a chance: I asked the audience as I was
introducing him how many of them had gone into cognitive science
because they read *Gödel, Escher, Bach* when they were in high school
or college. To my delight but not surprise, at least a third of the audience rose to their feet and applauded. Take that, you stuffed shirts!

Doug and I encountered a different kind of antagonism from one
of the authors we'd anthologized in *The Mind's I*: John Searle. We
had published Searle's Chinese Room thought experiment in the

book, with his permission of course, and Doug had written a brilliant and amusing reflection pointing out some of the major flaws in it. Searle reviewed *The Mind's I* in the *New York Review of Books* and threw quite a tantrum about how we had "fabricate[d] a direct quotation" of him that moreover "runs dead opposite" to what he in fact says. Here is the sin: Searle in his article (which we correctly reprinted) had described his hand-simulating a program written on "bits of paper"—suggesting a smallish program—which Doug had misremembered as "a few slips of paper," a mistake neither of us caught. I wrote a response to Searle's diatribe. Does the difference between "bits of paper" and "a few slips of paper" make a difference to Doug's argument? Not at all: "So little does our case depend on the *mis*quotation, that once it is corrected no further revision—not so much as a word or comma—of our Reflection is called for or contemplated." Searle responded in turn (same issue), and this began the feud that has run between us ever since. I will have more to say about that in my chapter on academic bullies.

When Doug was at the University of Michigan (1984–88), he introduced me to his friend and colleague John Henry Holland, a pioneer in the creation of genetic algorithms and one of the founders of the field of artificial life. John was one of the computer scientists who appreciated Doug's ideas from the outset; he taught me a lot about evolutionary theory as well as computers and also introduced me to the Santa Fe Institute (see chapter 32). I also got to know several of Doug's graduate students, including Melanie Mitchell (one of the people whose brilliance keeps drawing me back to Santa Fe) and Robert French, on whose dissertation committee I served. When Doug moved his Fluid Analogies Research Group to Indiana University, he attracted other smart young graduate students, including an Australian mathematician and Oxford Rhodes Scholar, David Chalmers. Once at FARG, Chalmers wrote some good cognitive-science papers with Bob French and Andy Clark before turning himself into a dualist and writing a dissertation that neither Doug nor I was persuaded by (I was an informal member of his committee) but which was so well done that he was quite properly awarded his PhD in philosophy and cognitive science. He has become the most influential, best-known, and most prolific philosopher of mind of his generation and has tried over the years to get me to see the light, but I am still utterly unconvinced, and have said so in various publications and at various conferences ever since. Neither Doug nor I see that Chalmers has been even weakly influenced by Doug's ideas, but he certainly learned a lot of adventurous cognitive science at FARG.

When I first began moving around in Doug's world, he was an academic celebrity. Everywhere he went, after he gave his talk, he'd be surrounded by dozens of adoring young men. Hardly a woman in sight. He was aching for romantic love and not finding it among his many fans. And then he met Carol Ann Brush. Soon they were married and had two children, and everything seemed right in the world. But then, on a sabbatical year in Italy, Carol suffered a brain tumor that killed her in just a few terrible weeks. Doug's sadness was all-consuming. In fact, I don't think I've ever encountered a person more in love with a spouse than Doug was in love with Carol. His wonderful 2007 book *I Am a Strange Loop* is both a renewal of his quest to explain his deeply original ideas on human consciousness and a working through of his sorrow, written with unstinting candor.

16.

RUBIK'S CUBE, PRAGUE, AND DAHLEM

WHEN *THE MIND'S I* CAME OUT, DOUG WAS WRITING a monthly column for *Scientific American*, following in the footsteps of his friend Martin Gardner, whose famous monthly column "Mathematical Games" was anagrammed by Doug into "Metamagical Themas." Some of these are classics, especially his columns on what he called the Luring Lottery and his primers on Lisp, the computer language of AI. But his most influential column was certainly his introduction to America of Rubik's Cube in March 1981. With some significant help from Doug, I mastered a set of moves—algorithms, in effect—for solving the cube and delighted in honing my skill and teaching others how to do the moves.

I got to play Johnny Appleseed with my Rubik's Cube that March, when I managed to squeeze in a trip to Prague—still behind the Iron Curtain, of course—to give a talk to philosophers who had been ousted by the Soviets from their positions in Charles University and were keeping the lamp of learning lit in Prague by meeting informally in people's flats. This politico-philosophical project was organized by the Jan Hus Educational Foundation in London, started the previous summer by Oxford philosophers and largely run by Kathleen Wilkes, an Oxford philosopher who had a deep involvement in academic-freedom projects in Eastern Europe. I had put my name in as somebody who would like to give some talks, and just had to wait until I could find some European host to pay for my travel. This came up when I was invited to a Dahlem Conference in Berlin on animal intelligence. I didn't expect the Dahlem Conference to be a major event in my life but merely a convenient way to get to Prague. I could travel to Europe a few days early to shed my jet lag in Prague before going on to Berlin. I was sent a list of questions to ask the various participants in the clandestine meetings, information about the visitor who would be following me, and a number of papers to leave with them, including a copy of the paper by the next visitor, so they would have a chance to translate them into Czech for the group, as they had translated my papers sent in by the previous visitor. It was important not to let this information fall into the hands of the people who would be scrutinizing me when I arrived at the border, and I wasn't sure I could memorize all of it, so I made up a dummy page of footnotes, which I stapled to a paper of my own I was bringing in. A footnote that read "7. Havelock, A., 'Three solutions to the Canal problem,' p. 235" might mean *meet Havel at 3 p.m. on Canal Street, number* 235, and so forth. Spycraft! Such an adventure!

The authorities actually knew about the meetings of these underground faculties, and tolerated them, but you didn't want to give them extra information about meetings outside the seminar setting, which they could then use to identify individuals or other meetings. I was met, not at the airport but on a minor bridge, by my contact, and he showed me a place to meet him later, after I'd checked into my dreary Soviet-era hotel, so we could go off on a round of errands before my talks. The host of the seminar was Ladislav Hejdánek, an activist who had been fired from the university but met regularly with groups of philosophers. The point of these meetings was not to plan political action but to ensure as much as possible that young Czech philosophy students could get an education while Charles University was filled with apparatchiks—political hacks of no talent or qualifications. After my talks, we'd go out for a beer and some supper, and there I showed off my Rubik's Cube. Pretty soon others in the restaurant were crowding around to see and handle this amazing object and then challenge me to solve it.

When it came time for me to fly to Berlin for the Dahlem Conference, I decided that it wouldn't be safe to go to the airport, although

I had my ticket. It turned out that my concern about showing up at the airport with illicit baggage was prescient. A few months later, Jacques Derrida gave a talk to the underground seminar in Prague and the authorities planted drugs in his suitcase to be "discovered" by customs officials at the airport when he left. It turned into a comedy of errors when the customs officials couldn't find the drugs that they had been told would be in his luggage and had to make a few phone calls to learn where to look, and eventually they found them and whisked Derrida off to jail, charged with drug smuggling. The French foreign minister was promptly informed and swung into action immediately, so Derrida was released the next day and on his way back to France. I doubt that the American secretary of state would have come to my rescue as swiftly.

I was carrying a lot of first-class sealed mail for Hejdánek, who had asked me to smuggle it out and mail it from Berlin. I had asked why he couldn't just give it to a friend to mail anonymously from, say, Bratislava, but he insisted that *all* first-class mail was being opened and read by the authorities. I found this hard to believe, but it proved true when the Iron Curtain collapsed and the extent of surveillance was made public. I doubted I could get the mail through the border at the airport, so my last evening in Prague I took what was left of my Czech money and treated a charming and beautiful young philosopher to a meal at the fanciest restaurant I could find in Prague, a grand old place with a palm court, a strolling violinist, and lots of Tokaji wine from Hungary. She then accompanied me to the train station and put me on the overnight train to Berlin. (I later learned that Roger Scruton, who had fallen for this young philosopher, was extremely irritated by the fact that on his next visit to Prague, all she could talk about was Dan Dennett! A small ignoble pleasure for me.)

I had purchased a couchette, where I had intended to closet myself and transfer Hejdánek's mail from my attaché case to my underwear, but there was no couchette for me; I had to spend the night sitting up in a standard eight-person compartment. The corridors were filled with police and soldiers, so I didn't dare take my attaché case to the restroom in the corridor. What to do? I waited, hoping the other people in the compartment would fall asleep, but none did, and as I heard the train begin to slow down for the border between Czechoslovakia and East Germany, I knew I had to act. Looking all the strangers in the eye, I got up, pulled my attaché case down, opened it, and began stuffing the mail into my underwear in front of them all. Nobody said a word. One old woman gave me a slight nod. When the *Grenzpolizei* (the border police) opened the compartment door, they immediately began grilling me, asking to see my passport and carefully going through my luggage. They found a little bit of Czech money, which was not to be taken from the country, in my wallet, and they confiscated that, over my protestations. And they noted that I didn't have a *Transitvisum*, a special visa for crossing to Berlin through East Germany. I professed ignorance about this, and eventually they left, never having patted me down. A few faint smiles greeted me from other passengers.

When I arrived in Berlin, at about 7:00 a.m., I had to get to West Berlin, which I managed through the Friedrichstrasse underground station gate, in the company of hundreds of East German charladies, who were allowed to clean offices in West Berlin every day while leaving their families hostage on the other side of the Wall. Needless to say, I was conspicuous, but somehow, I managed to get passed through into West Berlin. I had told Jerry Fodor, who was also attending the Dahlem meeting, that if he hadn't seen me by 8:00 a.m. he should call Susan, and if he hadn't seen me by 9:00 a.m. he should call the American embassy. I found him pacing nervously in the lobby of our fine hotel in Berlin, looking at his watch and ready to make his first duty call. We were both relieved. I mailed off the letters at the hotel desk, had a shower in my room, and was ready for the day at the Dahlem Center down the street.

Dahlem Conferences were remarkable events, designed to introduce young German scientists to the best researchers in the world for intensive five-day meetings. The young Germans did not get to say anything or even sit at the big tables with the guests, but they could take notes. Each conference was divided into groups, with a *rapporteur*, a younger researcher who was responsible for taking voluminous notes and then boiling them down overnight into a draft of a report from each working group, which would be printed and duplicated and in front of every participant for editing and discussion on the morning of the final day. While the rest of the members of the group went off to the opera or a concert, the rapporteur, watched over by a zealous staff member, would be prodded and cajoled into a great writing labor and not allowed to go to bed until it was finished! Robert Seyfarth, the primatologist, was the rapporteur for my group, and in return for his labors he was entitled to come to another Dahlem Conference of his choosing, without any duties. The Germans knew how to run a tight ship, and the combination of fine hotel, excellent food, entertainment every evening, and plenty of clerical assistance kept everyone on their toes. There was also a cadre of young women standing around the room writing on clipboards who were in fact discreet observers reporting to the conference director, Silke Bernhard, about who was paying attention to whom, who was being disruptive or at risk of falling asleep, who needed to speak English more slowly and clearly. When one of the Americans in our group got a little rude and aggressive, I was mulling over how to speak to him in private and encourage him to adjust his manner, but when the session resumed after lunch, he was all politeness and gentleness. Silke had spoken to him.

To my surprise and delight, the meeting was a gold mine of information and insights. Something I noticed the first day was that the primatologists and bird experts and other ethologists presenting at the meeting were all uncomfortable with the strict behavioristic language they had been taught to use. They wanted to be "cognitive" but weren't sure how to do it. I wasn't myself a main speaker at the meeting, but I decided to plunge in and explain how to use the intentional stance to describe and explain and predict behavior. The trick was to use the rationality assumption of the stance as a lever: If the animals really did believe that p and wanted to X, they ought to do

Y when confronted with evidence that *q*—that's the rational move under those circumstances. Do they do *Y*? The ethologists got it almost instantly and bombarded me with questions and suggestions. Peter Marler, the great birdsong interpreter at Rockefeller University, challenged me: If this intentional stance is any good, shouldn't it help us design experiments? "Let's see," I replied, and a group of us passed up the sumptuous lunch on offer in favor of some sandwiches that were brought in, and we sat down and sketched designs of whole suites of experiments on chimpanzees, piping plovers, chickens, vervet monkeys, and baboons. As Jeremy Cherfas, an English science journalist attending the meeting, said later in the day, "I have never seen a meme spread so swiftly and so effectively!" I was thrilled of course, but Jerry Fodor did his best to dampen my enthusiasm. "Your intentional stance is really just double-distilled *adaptationism*, and haven't you heard? Gould and Lewontin have decisively refuted adaptationism in evolutionary theory." I had not heard of the famous article by Stephen Jay Gould and Richard Lewontin, but it went to the top of my "must read right away" list.

I should mention three other important moments from that meeting. Pat Churchland, who was the third philosopher attending, convinced me to skip out of the tag end of one session and walk down the street to the zoo, where we listened to the howler monkeys and watched the gibbons perform their astounding acrobatics with what appeared to be nonchalance. Watching real animals can be a treat after a day of listening to people talk about watching real animals. I also got a valuable insight into researcher bias: Sue Savage-Rumbaugh, who later became quite famous for her work with bonobos and language, was telling us about her chimpanzees Sherman and Austin and their cooperative and communicative behavior. She had videotapes that she hadn't had time to show and asked if any of us wanted to skip lunch so we could see them and discuss them with her. I did, and so did a few others. She showed us the videotapes, and what struck me forcefully was that she was "seeing" these chimps doing things that the rest of us *couldn't* see or couldn't be confident we were seeing. The guilelessness with which she enthusiastically narrated her videotapes showed that she was honestly convinced that it was plain *obvious* what these animals intended, understood, knew. But it wasn't. You must have independent interpreters who have no stake in the verdicts reached. Sometimes this is next to impossible—in anthropology as well as in ethology and psychology.

The third big moment for me was learning about the British psychologist who had worked with Dian Fossey, and who had written a remarkable paper, "The Social Function of Intellect" (*another* 1976 paper!), about how intelligence might have evolved primarily to permit interactions among members of social species: Nicholas Humphrey. Nick wasn't there, but his name was on everybody's lips, and I looked forward eagerly to meeting him. A year or so later in London I did, at lunch with Jeremy Cherfas, and we have been dear friends ever since, working together and disagreeing stubbornly with each other.

So what I had envisioned as a useful ticket to Prague became in short order a major turning point in my life, the first significant step of which was my target article in *Behavioral and Brain Sciences*, "Intentional Systems in Cognitive Ethology: The 'Panglossian Paradigm' Defended" (1983), in which I elaborated the ideas from the Dahlem workshop and included the first salvo in my critique of Gould and Lewontin and their famous attack on adaptationism. But allow me another digression . . .

17.

"ARE RABBITS BIRDS?" AND OTHER MEMORABLE PHONE CALLS

IN THE 1960S, CALIFORNIANS CONSIDERED ALL NINE campuses of the University of California as a sort of public-knowledge utility that anybody could tap, as needed—a predigital Wikipedia, you might say. My mathematician friends at UC Irvine had told me of the spring torrent of citizen phone calls asking how to calculate percentages for their income tax returns. A biologist told me of being haunted by a call from a somewhat inebriated citizen late one evening in his lab, which went as follows:

"You a biologist?"

"Yes."

"I have a bet on with my buddy here, and maybe you can settle it."

"Maybe. What's the question?"

"Are rabbits birds?"

"*What?*"

"Are rabbits birds?"

"No, they're—"

"Aw shit!" he said, and hung up.

What about calls to philosophers? I had a few calls from people who wanted to talk about the meaning of life, but the only one I stayed with for more than a polite minute or so was from a young man who was on duty all alone in a fire tower on a mountaintop, scanning for wisps of smoke, signs of forest fires. He'd been think-ing, he said, and couldn't see a good reason for not jumping off the tower. We talked for maybe an hour, until we both decided that perhaps I'd given him some pretty good reasons for seeing what the next day, the next month, the next year would bring. I have no idea whether I saved a life that day.

A more troubling case occurred a few years later, when I'd moved from Irvine to Tufts. I had a brilliant young undergraduate student we'll call Carolyn, who came to my office hour one day and challenged me: Why shouldn't she kill herself? Knowing her intense and unusually mature interest in philosophy, I hit upon a scheme. A year or two before, Tom Nagel had given a fascinating talk, "The Absurd," at the American Philosophical Association annual meeting, in which he addressed in sober and analytical terms the possible, even probable, meaninglessness of life. He had asked Rogers Albritton, his advisor at Harvard, to give the commentary, and Albritton, who had also been my advisor, accepted the invitation, and spoke eloquently to an auditorium packed with philosophers. Nagel's talk had ended with a rather bleak conclusion:

> If *sub specie aeternitatis* there is no reason to believe that anything matters, then that doesn't matter either, and we can approach our absurd lives with irony instead of heroism or despair.

Albritton's response began (as I remember it):

> You're sitting at home in the evening reading a good book, and the telephone rings. It is an acquaintance, not a close friend, but he needs your help. You put down your book and turn your attention to him. Why do you do this?

Albritton continued with the wisest, most thrilling—while still philosophically austere—discussion of how we give our lives meaning I had ever encountered. I told this to Carolyn and extracted a promise from her. She wouldn't kill herself until she had read Nagel's piece, which was already published, and Albritton's response, and then talked it all over with me. She agreed. Albritton had moved to UCLA by then, but I got his phone number from the Harvard philosophy department and gave him a call:

"Hello, Rogers, it's Dan Dennett, at Tufts. I have a wonderful student, and she says she's thinking of killing herself, but I made her promise not to take that step until she and I had discussed your brilliant reply to Tom Nagel at the APA. Could you please send me a copy express mail?"

"Oh no! Dan, while driving to UCLA from Boston, my car was stolen, and when I got it back a few days later, all my papers were gone. The only copy I had was in the car."

"That's really too bad. I was counting on your essay to be the perfect antidote to Tom's. I guess I'll have to think of something else to do with her."

"Yes, too bad. I'm so sorry, Dan . . . *Wait!* Could we perhaps recreate much of it right now, at least the main points? You were there and must remember some of it pretty well."

We spent a long-distance hour or so going over our recollections, while I scribbled notes, and when we ran dry, I thanked him and hung up. I had my meeting with Carolyn a few days later, and so far as I know, she got over her depression and carried on, though I soon lost track of her. (Carolyn, if you are still alive and you read this, please get in touch with me.)

It was only after I'd hung up the phone with Rogers that it hit me that he must have thought it was *I* who was suicidal and that I had been calling his bluff, recreating the opening scene of his commentary. That must have been on his mind as he hung in there and helped the "acquaintance, not a close friend." Six months or so later, I ran into him at a cocktail party at the APA annual meeting and assured him that I really did have a suicidal student, and that he'd been a wonderful help to her. His eyes widened. "Oh Dan!" he exclaimed. "It never occurred to me that it was *you*, Dan, *you* who were thinking of suicide! I feel terrible."

"No, Rogers, it *wasn't* me. It was her, and you did great!"

An MA student at Tufts many years ago who had been an undergraduate at Harvard some years earlier was clearly having serious mental problems, judging by his behavior in my seminar. I was on the verge of trying to get him to walk with me down to the Tufts psychiatrist's office when he suddenly withdrew and disappeared. A few months later, he called me up to tell me that he'd just made a remarkable discovery: There had been a beautiful but unapproachable girl at Harvard when he was there, and he'd just discovered her in a Cambridge supermarket. She had been dressed like a whore. She hadn't seen him, but he'd surreptitiously followed her home, so he knew where she lived. He gave me her name and address and told me he was going to pay her a visit. Uh-oh. What should I do? As it happened, he had been at Harvard when a friend of mine was also a student there, and I immediately called my friend up and asked if he knew a girl by that name. Oh yes, she was the most beautiful girl at Radcliffe then, and many had been smitten by her, all unrequited love so far as he knew. Now I was seriously worried. I looked up her name in the Cambridge telephone book, and there it was, along with the address I had been told. With a shaking hand, I dialed the number, fearing that my former student would answer and say something like, "I've been waiting for you to call me here. What took you so long?" But instead, a nice old lady answered, and I asked if she was XY, and she said yes, she was. I said I was looking for an old friend with the same name and asked if she had a daughter or granddaughter by the same name living with her. No, she was childless and living alone. So, I figured it out: my student, still obsessed with this young woman, had simply looked in the phone book and found the name and address, just as I had. If he ever did go to her door, which I doubted he would do, he would discover his error and leave without incident. I thought my keeping all this to myself was better than filling the nice old lady's head with groundless fears. Years later, my former student sent me a paper he'd written and a brief account of his psychological therapy, which reassured me.

Another upsetting phone call occurred when I was sitting at a table in the University of Pennsylvania bookstore on my first "book tour"—for *The Mind's I*. I had been parked there uncomfortably for an hour or so, smiling at people who drifted up and mostly didn't buy, or ask me about, the books stacked on the little table, when a clerk came up and said I had an urgent phone call. When I got to the phone, the department secretary from Tufts said to me, *"Don't come to the office* when you get back to Boston! A man has called and he said he's coming to kill you!" He'd given his name, and after I got home—giving Tufts a wide berth—I managed to learn more about him. He was a graduate student of a famous philosopher, and he had voluntarily checked himself into a Boston-area psychiatric hospital—but he could leave at any time. He'd decided that I had been stealing all his ideas before he could get them into print, so he was going to kill me. I spoke to the man's psychiatrist, who tried to reassure me that this fellow was obviously seriously deluded but wouldn't hurt anybody. And, the psychiatrist added to reassure me, his patient had also threatened the life of Ted Kennedy. At first, this calmed me down. If he'd threatened Kennedy, there were sure to be Secret Service agents or FBI agents or somebody watching his move-ments closely, so I was OK. But then it struck me that perhaps these stalwart Kennedy-protectors would watch him leave the hospital and as soon as he headed north (to Tufts, to my home in Andover) they would sigh with relief and say to themselves, "Nothing for us to worry about—he's going after that philosopher." I extracted a prom-ise from the psychiatrist that he would call me if the fellow checked out of the hospital, and I decided to go about my life as if nothing had happened. The fellow did leave the hospital, I later learned (the psychiatrist hadn't kept his promise). Moreover, a year or so later he applied for a job in our philosophy department. We get hundreds of applications, and I decided I wouldn't mention this as long as the fellow didn't make our short list. But he did! So, I had to tell my colleagues at the short-list meeting that while I didn't presume to have any veto rights, I would appreciate it if they removed his name from the short list, since this was the person who had threatened to kill me. (They knew the story but not his name, which I waited until then to reveal.) I am happy to say that my colleagues granted my request. Some years later, I got an apologetic note from this man. I thanked him but did not encourage him in his suggestion that we might have a talk about our mutual interests in philosophy.

18.

RUTH MILLIKAN, WHO BROKE THROUGH THE UNSOUND BARRIER

O NE OF THE OCCUPATIONAL HAZARDS OF BEING A PHI-losopher is receiving unsolicited manuscripts from amateur philosophers who think they have figured it all out. There is a variety of obsessive-compulsive disorder, sometimes called *existential obsessive-compulsive disorder*, the chief symptom of which is an inordinate concern with philosophical questions, and some of these people, suffering from *logorrhea*, write book-length discourses on their discoveries. I used to receive these several times a year, and I called the senders *triangle people*, because their well-boxed reams of nonsense typically had an equilateral triangle on the first page, with the corners labeled with any three of the big words: Existence, Time, Energy, Space, Love, Infinity, Consciousness, Will, . . . Early in my career, I tried to read, or at least skim, these unwanted presents and write the authors little personal notes, but eventually I realized that even the most tepid and barely polite encouragement could open floodgates better left locked. For a while, I sent some of these typescripts to a Boston neuropsychiatrist who was collecting examples for a study he was conducting. I don't know if anything came of it.

I must admit that it is sometimes difficult to tell whether such a production is actually a genuinely deep and novel philosophical treatise. A university press once sent me a very long manuscript by a senior researcher in cybernetics to review for publication, and since I was being paid for this labor, I buckled up and read the thing as best I could and arrived at a firm opinion of its nuttiness only when I discovered that whole chapters in part 3 were almost word-for-word copies of chapters in part 1 with minor variations. I have abandoned a few other manuscripts without arriving at a verdict, willing to risk the fate of being damned by history as the uncomprehending Rejector of a Great Work. Life is short.

One day back in 1979, I received a manila envelope with a longish typescript and a self-introductory note from a philosopher at the University of Connecticut named Ruth Millikan, who acknowledged that both she and her colleagues thought her work was "hopelessly maverick." Fair warning, but I found her work a bold attempt to apply evolutionary insights to vexing issues in the philosophy of language, concerning the meaning of words. Her perspective was exciting and novel, and very much in the naturalistic spirit of what I'd been thinking. So, I wrote back to say that I thought her "fundamental idea about the evolution of linguistic features is perfectly plausible and well worth pursuing." In 1981, a big box arrived in the mail from her. Uh-oh, I thought. What had I set in motion? It was her draft of *Language, Thought, and Other Biological Categories*. I worked through it during the summer and decided it was as brilliant as it was difficult. I suggested to Harry Stanton that Bradford Books should probably publish it, but I thought he should get a couple of other referees whose views were at some distance from mine to look it over, since I was perhaps too sympathetic to her iconoclastic spirit (having completed "Beyond Belief" but not yet having gotten much significant feedback on that subversive effort). Harry asked Fred Dretske and Héctor-Neri Castañeda to review it, making a critical stool with three widely spaced legs, and when they both approved it with enthusiasm, I knew she was onto something big. I agreed to edit the manuscript and wrote a foreword for it, in which I held:

Contemporary philosophical theory of meaning is something of a black hole . . . such an intricately interlocked, powerfully argued conglomeration of doctrines that once one has come to terms with it, one is typically caught in its embrace. Millikan has somehow found the centrifugal energy to *leave* the tradition—*after* understanding it.

This ominous portrayal of the field in 1984 understated its grip on imaginations, and most of the major and all the minor participants orbiting that black hole have found it convenient to ignore her work for decades, endlessly circling the phantom attractors of "*de re* and *de dicto* propositional attitudes," "quantifying in," and "possible-world semantics." The Propositional Attitude Task Force is still at it, and once a decade or so I look in to see what they're doing. They have made no discernible progress, except for those who have belatedly seen the wisdom of at least some of what Ruth has been saying all these years.

When her book was published, I still hadn't met her, though we had quite a correspondence over my editing suggestions. (In her acknowledgments, she writes, "Dennett also scribbled invaluable red ink over the penultimate copy. If he carries his incisive and witty red pen in his breast pocket I will recognize him immediately should we meet.") Knowing that we were both invited to a philosophers' party at the APA meeting that year, she wrote me a charming note warning me in advance that she was not "a sweet young thing" but a mother with grown children—just in case I had been harboring fantasies, I guess.

The Secret Seminar that Jerry Fodor and I had started in 1973 was still going strong when her first book came out, and I suggested that we all read it together and invite Ruth to come and discuss it with us. How could they say no? I had written the foreword and had praised the book to them. The group was more than living up to my private name for it, the Vicious Circle, and sometimes degenerated into a contest among the younger members to see who could make the most blistering criticisms of whatever we were reading, often beginning with "Who recommended that we read this shit?" They had a bad case of Not Invented Here, a notorious affliction of closed-mindedness that often hits major think tanks. I typically drove to the meetings with my former Tufts colleague, Sue Stafford, a neighbor and friend of many years, who often had to talk me down from my fury on the drives home after the meetings. A philosopher who also had a career in AI as a knowledge-extractor and designer of expert systems, she knew the ferocity of philosophical infighting, but also shared my appreciation of cooperative intellectual teamwork. Without Sue to keep me from exploding, I would have walked away from the Secret Seminar years before I did.

I thought Ruth should be given the chance to open their eyes. She accepted the invitation and, to my great dismay, was subjected to the rudest, most arrogant barrage of abuse I think I have ever witnessed from my fellow academics. She heroically pretended it wasn't happening, and calmly and firmly attempted to clarify her points, instead of walking out in disgust. I was livid. After she left, I gave Fodor and Block and the rest of the Vicious Circle a proper scolding. They promised never to do it again and asked me to invite her back for a second attempt. She came back *and they were abusive again*. That was the last meeting I ever attended, although the group continued for some years, inviting me to return whenever I liked. What I learned of the proceedings from colleagues who kept going convinced me that I wasn't missing anything important.

At long last, Ruth's work has been recognized by the profession, and she has been invited around the world to give talks and accept awards. Her latest book, *Beyond Concepts: Unicepts, Language, and Natural Information* (2017), is a masterpiece, extending her vision in remarkable ways, but is still being resolutely ignored by many in the field. I can almost sympathize with those who grit their teeth and pretend she doesn't exist; her perspective requires you to abandon so much of what you thought you'd learned from the masters—Frege, Russell, Putnam, and Kripke, to name a few—that it must feel like a betrayal, or self-exile.

19.

BIG GEORGE AND THE CURRICULAR SOFTWARE STUDIO

I N *CONTENT AND CONSCIOUSNESS*, ONE OF MY EMBARRASS-
ing mistakes was butchering Quine's example "Giorgione was so-
called because of his size." Quine's point was to analyze cases in
which a word, in this case "Giorgione," is both used (to refer to the
painter) and mentioned (as a name) in the same breath, and I, overexplaining this, wrote that "Giorgione" was a diminutive, meaning
Little George, when in fact it means Big George. I had thought that
since in French a *crouton* is a little crust and a *carafon* is half a carafe,
there was a similar pattern in Italian. Wrong. A little knowledge can
be a dangerous thing. This mistake led to an amusing correspondence among the Columbia philosopher of art Arthur Danto and
Quine and me. Danto, noting my error, went on to say that Quine
was wrong as well, quoting Vasari as saying Giorgione was so called
because of the greatness of his *soul*, not his body, and Quine rebutted
this with some scholarship of his own. Quine was hardly ever caught
out on factual errors, especially about language.

In later years, I have often thought of my Tufts colleague George
Smith as Giorgione—Big George, though I have never called him
that out loud—not because of his size but because of his greatness
in several other regards. He is a philosopher who is also an engineer (with no engineering degree) and an international expert on
turbines, flying all over the world to inspect damaged turbines and
render his opinion on the causes of their failure. He is also a world-

renowned scholar on Newton's *Principia*, a former acting director of the Dibner Institute for the History of Science and Technology at MIT, a logician, a computer scientist, a former basketball coach, an expert on Noam Chomsky's linguistics, and one of the greatest teachers I have ever encountered.

How on earth, one might ask, could somebody acquire so many different kinds of expertise? It all goes back to his childhood in Cincinnati, when he was identified by General Electric as a super-smart high schooler and enlisted in a special program for gifted kids. There—in the 1950s—he learned to program computers from the bottom up, in machine language. While at Yale majoring in philosophy and mathematics (and studying with Wilfrid Sellars among others, before Pittsburgh raided Yale to set up their own great department), he worked part-time at Pratt & Whitney in East Hartford, using his computer expertise to write a program for analyzing jet engine turbines. This program, VIBLAD, enlarged and updated by George as VIPACK, was in use around the world for many years. After Yale, he tried Harvard's PhD program in philosophy, but he dropped out and devoted himself to engineering for a decade or so, assisting in various projects at MIT—with Chomsky, with political scientists (e.g., Hayward Alker), with others—before writing some logic papers (on Saul Kripke's modal logic) that were deemed sufficient for a PhD in philosophy in the MIT Department of Linguistics and Philosophy. He volunteered to coach inner-city kids in a basketball league in his spare time and did so well at this that several NBA players credit him with getting them on track. He went into the philosophy job market before he finished his PhD, applying only to Tufts, since he wanted to stay in Boston, and we grabbed him to teach logic and philosophy of science, probably the wisest hiring move any philosophy department has ever made. His logic course, perhaps the most demanding introductory logic course in the country, was famous among students, because he knew how to inspire them to perform beyond what they thought they could do—

the basketball coach getting his players to "leave it all on the court." He allowed the students to spend as much time as they needed on his final exam, and some of them would labor away for five or six hours before handing in their blue books.

In 1982, *Time* magazine gave its "Man [*sic*] of the Year" award to the personal computer. Suddenly the parents of incoming Tufts students wanted their children to learn all about computers, and maybe major in computer science. Tufts didn't even have a department of computer science then. There were about half a dozen computer scientists on the faculty, three or four located in the math department, and a few more in electrical engineering. They assembled a department but didn't want to teach a large introductory course because they had their hands full dealing with the flood of students already initiated into the mysteries of computers who were taking advanced courses. Tufts asked George Smith and me, from philosophy, and two mathematicians who were computer savvy, to team-teach an introduction to computer science. George, with his customary energy and organizational skills, took charge. He didn't just inspire students to throw themselves into a project, he inspired his colleagues, and soon I had dropped or postponed various philosophical projects to help him create this course. We wanted it to be intellectually substantial—not just a skills course teaching the students how to turn on a computer, do word processing, and such things. The students in the course were, with few exceptions, not thinking of having careers involving computers, and in fact many were seriously computerphobic—as many people were back in those days at the dawn of the personal-computer age. But we wanted them to come away from the course knowing the basic theory of how computers worked their magic, how to write simple programs, and how computer programs worked—graphics, spreadsheets—along with other topics, such as AI. They learned about Alan Turing and Turing machines, but also about register machines, a more intuitive kind of utterly simple computer that the logician Hao Wang had invented in

1957. They also learned about the basic von Neumann architecture (shared by probably all the dozens of computer chips you have in your house, your car, your phone, your television set, your oven, . . .).

What programming language should we teach them? I suggested Logo, the creation of Seymour Papert at MIT's AI lab, a blissfully user-friendly language designed for six-year-olds, who could readily learn how to get the Logo "turtle" to move around on the screen, drawing lines and performing many other simple and visible tasks. It was perfect! Tufts freshmen who were scared to touch a computer were soon vying with one another to draw flowers and vehicles and buildings and all sorts of other surprising things. Logo is an "interpreted" language, not a "compiled" language, so you get to see the results of each line of programming as soon as you compose it. Logo is also a remarkably powerful language, basically Lisp for kids, with full recursion, able to treat code as data and data as code, an elegant thinking tool of unlimited power once you start playing around with it. We also taught the students the elements of Pascal, a grown-up's language, just so that they could get a feeling for how serious programs are constructed, debugged, and executed.

The first year, George did some brilliant chalk talks, teaching about the von Neumann architecture, with its instruction cycle and accumulator, its stacks and program counters. One of our teaching assistants, an undergraduate computer science major, Steve Barney, was inspired by this pedagogy, and over the summer, with some guidance from George, he created an animated simulation of a simple, stripped-down von Neumann machine (a twelve-bit machine with 256 memory registers and a reduced instruction set), which he called Aesop. It was fabulous. You could program it easily and watch your lines of code land in the memory and later get pulled one at a time into the instruction register, where they got executed, changing the contents in the accumulator. *Ta-DAA!* George also gave lectures introducing register machines and teaching the students how to program them. I had never even heard of register machines before that course, and they fascinated me, so, inspired by Steve Barney's creation, I set out to create a simulated register machine in Logo, with the turtle trundling around putting beans in boxes, taking beans out of boxes, and branching to another instruction when a box was empty. I wanted to show the students that Logo was not just for drawing amazing spiral patterns and spaceships. These simulations, especially Steve's Aesop, were so effective that when we used them in the class the next year, we had to drastically upgrade the exams in the course; almost everybody in the class would have scored 100 if we gave them the test from the previous year.

George and I decided that we shouldn't stop there. We both knew Eric Wanner, who had been in the AI lab at MIT but had moved to New York to become a vice president and program officer at the Sloan Foundation, and we got ourselves invited to present a proposal to the foundation to fund something we called the Curricular Software Studio. Our idea was that in many fields there were what might be called pedagogical bottlenecks—difficult concepts that confused many students—and many of these bottlenecks, we thought, could be opened up with imaginative software. At the time, there were professors around the country in many fields who, with various levels of computer agility, had created software for use in their classes. These worked but were usually less than polished. There were also software firms that were turning out educational software in various fields, and these were quite professionally packaged but often weak on content. We proposed to be the matchmakers who brought content experts—professors—with no computer skills together with programmers who were not content experts, to form creative partnerships that would design robust, crisp, and *accurate* software to awaken and then discipline the students' imaginations.

One of my roles in this project was metaphor maven, and I came up with several winners. We called these promised programs *imagination prostheses*, and I contrasted two ways machines can make us powerful: the *bulldozer* way (you can move mountains, but you're still a ninety-eight-pound weakling) and the *Nautilus machine* way (you use the machine to make yourself stronger). We proposed Nautilus machines for the mind, designed to instill and enhance fluent imagination and comprehension in the user, not just provide answers to questions while leaving you in the dark. George and I took Steve Barney's Aesop program to our meeting in a conference room at the Sloan Foundation, where a group including some major computer scientists watched as we gave our demo. At one point, a computer scientist stopped me in mid-demo and said, angrily, "I know that picture," pointing at the computer screen where Aesop's CPU and memory were chugging along. I thought for an awful moment that he was accusing us of plagiarizing the image or something like that, but he went on, after sputtering a little, "It took me *years* to get that picture in my head, and you say you're going to give it to your students in ten minutes?" "Yes, that's the idea, exactly."

We got a modest start-up grant from the Sloan Foundation and promptly set up shop as the Curricular Software Studio, hiring Steve Barney and another good young programmer to be our original hackers. We started working on several projects at once: a population-genetics program called GeneWright (in honor of Sewall Wright, cofounder of the field) and the Space Time Microscope, of which Aesop was the lowest magnification of a computer, about ten times larger and running about a million times more slowly than the PC it ran on, with other "lenses" that zoomed in on the instruction register, showing how op codes are like area codes leading to circuits that perform specific operations such as addition or multiplication, or zoomed in on the adder circuit, showing how it had a half adder inside it, or zoomed in even closer so that you could see how a flip-flop was composed of logic gates. In other words, you could *see* just how the logic gates you'd heard about were put together to store bits, perform arithmetical processes, execute instructions.

Another role of mine was to solicit ideas for further imagination prostheses. My favorite was one inspired by a problem Stephen Jay Gould told me he was having with his Harvard students (back when we were friends). He wanted them to learn how to read, and draw, stratigraphy diagrams, those geological cross sections showing layers of sediment, intrusions of magma, fractures and folds, and the like. He would give them problem sets that required them to draw diagrams, and the best students readily drew the diagrams but then let others in the class trace or copy their diagrams (yes, even Harvard students have been known to cheat on assignments). "I can solve your problem, Steve," I said cockily, and I helped Steve Barney and Robert ("Bert") Reuss, a geology professor at Tufts, create Slice, a drawing program that, instead of allowing you to draw squares and circles and arrows and fill them with color, allowed you only to "paint" using geological primitives, like *deposit a sedimentary layer of x*, or *fold at y*, or *erode to level z*. A list of your actions scrolled down on the side of the screen, and if you got some steps out of order, or with the wrong parameters, you could edit these actions and the program would redraw your diagram. "With this program, Steve," I told him, "you can just draw a stratigraphy diagram with it, hide your actions lists, and challenge your students to draw the same diagram with the program. If they can do it, they understand the principles."

We made a good start on Slice but never finished it, sad to say, for various reasons—chief of which was that the original PCs just didn't have the graphics power needed to do what we wanted them to do *quickly* enough. You can't have students waiting five minutes for the program to redraw their diagram. Today, using the superfast graphics engines developed largely by video-game companies, you could do a fantastic *three*-dimensional Slice program that would allow students to order up an orogeny (the creation of a mountain range), make "roadcuts" at any angle on its slopes, and watch the erosion of millions of years do its work in seconds, a prospect that makes my mouth water. I had a version of the prototype Slice program on my PC at home while we were working on it, and my son, Peter, then about eleven, got fascinated with it and spent hours trying to write "PD," his initials, in folded, fractured strata in a diagram. He was learning fundamental relationships between geological events without any "studying"; it was a game with rules and outcomes, and it riveted his attention.

One day I took Mark DeVoto, my old college friend in the music department, to lunch to see if I could interest him in creating an imagination prosthesis for teaching difficult points in harmony theory or composition. We brainstormed for several happy hours and then decided, with a laugh, that there already was such a machine, ideally suited both visually and aurally, for the task. It's called a piano! A piano doesn't just allow you to play multiple notes at once, in any order you choose, but it gives you two related but different visual representations: the keyboard and the music staff paper in front of you. It's a most user-friendly instrument, which any child can start playing, but what you can do with those keys is virtually unbounded, and you don't have to worry about tuning each note as you play it. So now I had another metaphor to explain what we were doing at the Curricular Software Studio: we were designing *concept pianos* that anyone can play.

After a few years, we had created several useful—if not always thrilling—programs, and were in touch with people around the country who were also doing such things. We held a national workshop, drawing in the leaders, and realized, sad to say, that the computer world was changing too fast for us to keep up with it. We had decided to go with PCs (back before Windows was created, we were using the DOS operating system) while others were using Macs. We would have to keep updating our existing products to take advantage of the new, faster models of personal computers, and there were miles of red tape to get in place in order to get proper license agreements and the like. Jon Barwise and John Etchemendy, philosophers at Stanford, had created Tarski's World (on first-order logic) and Turing's World (on Turing machines), and Judah Schwartz at MIT had his wonderful Geometric Supposer (which allowed you to make Euclidean constructions on a computer as a source of candidate theorems to prove), and while these were much admired and used for a few years, by the mid-'90s we had all run out of steam and money. Too bad, since there are still pedagogical bottlenecks that could be opened up by high-quality software—a few that tantalize me are color vision, going from the physics of photons to neural representations; enhanced versions of Richard Dawkins's elegant Blind Watchmaker software for exploring evolution; and, of course, learning to visualize how greenhouse gases lead, indirectly, to droughts, tornadoes, and other destructive weather.

What about computer prostheses for doing philosophy? Aside from the admirable programs by Barwise and Etchemendy, which bring logic to life, this has not—to my knowledge—been a fruitful area. Philosophers have a long way to go in catching up with scientists, and until the recent PowerPoint revolution, few philosophers even used diagrams to illustrate their points in lectures or conference talks—rather like novelists who are opposed to illustrations *in principle*. But times are changing. I have been arguing for years that AI research provides excellent tools for both disciplining and enhancing the imagination of philosophers, whose thought experiments (or intuition pumps, as I call them) are often riddled with gaps and traps that would be discovered by anybody who set out to build a computer model to demonstrate the claimed effect. AI can be seen to be a kind of computer-aided thought-experimental discipline, trying out tempting simplifications and discovering awkward problems along the way. The challenge of turning "vaporware" (hand-waving promises and nudges) into running software is a humbling learning experience for philosophers, but it has also yielded some impressive results.

For a number of years, Steve Barney, with encouragement and advice from me, worked with Joan King, a professor of neuro-anatomy at Tufts medical school, on TUBE, the Tufts University Brain Explorer, which did for the brain what the London Tube map famously does for the geography of the rail lines under London: preserving connectivity while ironing out all the wrinkles. We wanted this to be a three-dimensional brain-modeling system that permitted you to "inflate" the wrinkled, grooved cerebral cortex into the highly regular layers that have been shrink-wrapped into the skull, selectively stretching and smoothing the connections and doing a similar schematic rendering of the other parts of the brain—the cerebellum, the thalamus, and all the rest. Steve made a good start on this, but in the intervening decades others have caught up and far surpassed us in the art—and it is an art—of diagramming the brain so that it suggests hypotheses about how it works and why it's arranged the way it is.

All this grew out of George Smith's boyhood introduction to computers back in Cincinnati, and to this day I would say that the introductory computer course I taught with him was the most rewarding teaching *and learning* experience of my academic life. In second place would be another course we taught together: a seminar on Descartes's science and philosophy (on which George is, of course, an expert). George led me and the class through a fascinating deep dive into the science of Descartes's day and the revealing controversies that arose from his *Meditations*. This provoked me to write my one essay of historical scholarship, "Descartes's Argument from Design," unearthing Descartes's surprising version of the Argument from Design for the existence of God in his *Third Meditation*. After teaching the *Meditations* for decades, I finally made sense of his surprisingly obscure and disappointing argument, an embarrassment that I had hurried past dozens of times. I don't think his contemporaries appreciated what he was trying to do, and he himself, I think, had only a sketchy idea of how his argument worked, but with hindsight we can say that his argument was—or should have been—persuasive until Darwin came along to overturn his perspective.

20.

THE LOCKE LECTURES AND THE VERVET MONKEYS IN AMBOSELI

THE DENNETT FAMILY RETURNED TO OXFORD IN 1983 for the Trinity term so I could give the Locke Lectures in philosophy. A Locke Lecturer is almost always from abroad—most are from the US—and gives a lecture a week for seven weeks. My topic was free will, and I discovered to my delight that Ryle's masterpiece, *The Concept of Mind*, had originally been planned as a book on free will. I like to think that Ryle, who died in 1976, would have approved of my lectures, which certainly bore the stamp of his enduring influence on my thinking. Where Ryle had exposed "the ghost in the machine" I exposed the "bugbears" that philosophers have resorted to in their forlorn efforts to motivate some of their pet themes, a phenomenon I have recently called "free will inflation."

I brought with me my trusty Kaypro "portable" computer and a tiny dot-matrix printer. Since my year with John McCarthy at CASBS, I was a convert to both word processing and email, and I look back with mixed emotions on the joys and terrors of those early days of personal computing. The early text-editing systems were actually faster, in general, than today's word processors, because they didn't have all the overhead of frequent automatic copying and saving, and they weren't "WYSIWYG" (What You See Is What You Get). You had to type in formatting codes: to get a phrase like *"a priori"* in italics, you had to type something like "{CTRL\ital: a priori}"; it was not unusual to print out a file and find that you'd forgotten to close off a curly bracket somewhere, *with the result that page after page of text appeared in italics.* Mildly annoying, but few calamities can match the discovery that the file you've labored over for weeks has disappeared into the ether due to a computer malfunction, with no copies anywhere. The elaborate safeguards of today's operating systems are all welcome improvements for which a few tedious milliseconds of delay are a price worth paying. One day I broke a spring on the little doorlatch of my Kaypro that held the floppy disk for my operating system. If I couldn't close the door securely, I couldn't use the operating system at all, so I had to make a repair. I took my ever-at-hand jackknife and whittled a specially shaped wedge out of a clothespin, which did the trick. Few philosophers in Oxford had ever seen a personal computer then, and some of them came around to our flat to see the marvel; when they saw that I had actually repaired it—with a jackknife, no less—they were unduly impressed with my computer expertise, an opinion I didn't go out of my way to adjust.

I have written of the reception of my Locke Lectures, which were well attended, elsewhere. One of the Oxford philosophers in attendance, Michael Dummett, was heard to say that he'd be damned if he'd learn anything from somebody who could fill the seats in the Law Library week after week, and true to his word, he never learned anything from me. Meanwhile, Richard Dawkins was sitting there every week, listening intently and often joining me for discussion and a drink afterward. A year later, I published my Locke Lectures as *Elbow Room: The Varieties of Free Will Worth Wanting,* and it remains to this day my favorite book in many regards. As with my first book, I insisted it be published simultaneously in hardback and paperback, but this time the policy foundered. It was viewed as a textbook and got almost no reviews. It was not as widely read, I think, as I had hoped and expected. I have taken a certain satisfaction in watching many of the arguments I advanced first in *Elbow Room* get either reinvented or mistakenly ignored by later philosophical authors. It's bad form to say "I told you so," but so help me, I did.

There were perhaps eighty philosophers on the faculty in Oxford at that time, and a very select group, about a dozen of the most illustrious, met weekly during term for "Freddie's Group," a predinner talk and drink with A. J. Ayer. That year I was invited to become a temporary member of Freddie's Group, and we met in Ronnie Dworkin's rooms in University College. I've often wished I'd had a discreet video camera—they didn't exist then, of course—to record the marvelous folkways of these philosophers at that time. When the group had assembled, the speaker of the day would proceed to *read* their paper (of course), while the others listened intently, trying not to be distracted by the junior member present (Christopher Peacocke, then), who would tiptoe around the room to each member in turn and whisper, "What will you have to drink?" and then go off to the bar to make a gin and tonic, or fetch a glass of wine or sherry— or for nondrinkers, like Derek Parfit, a glass of orange squash. After the reading of the paper, there would be time for perhaps forty-five minutes of discussion before the group went off to their respective colleges or homes for dinner. I vividly remember Peter Strawson saying pointedly to another member, "I see you're holding the *viva* for Jones on Thursday. You know, he really is a most *virtuous* fellow, most *virtuous*." "Ah yes, most virtuous," came the reply, signaling receipt of the information that it would be a shame if Jones were not passed on his *viva*. Another time, Freddie was invited to dine with a member later in the week, and he checked his little pocket diary to see if he was free; he wasn't, but replied, "I see I'm down to dine in college that evening, but I shall *un-dine* myself and join you gladly."

I was invited to give a paper to Freddie's Group and chose a draft of my piece on the frame problem. All listened intently but then spent the first half hour of discussion arguing over whether or not it was, strictly speaking, *philosophy*. I waited with mounting impatience and was grateful when David Wiggins, a philosopher's philosopher if ever there was one, broke in and said, "*Who cares* if it's philosophy; it's a very interesting issue!" A good discussion then ensued. A curious fact that struck me recently was that in the nearly forty years since then, I have often given invited talks in Oxford to the psychologists, to the biologists, to AI researchers, to student groups, and at public occasions, but never to the philosophers. I have even been invited by the philosophy subfaculty to be on the committee to elect the Wilde Reader (now Professor) of Mental Philosophy, but not to give a talk. No matter; the philosophers whose work I admire have died or gone elsewhere in the meantime, and I still love my frequent returns to Oxford.

While we were in Oxford, I received an invitation from Robert Seyfarth, the vervet monkey researcher I'd met in Berlin, to join him and his wife, Dorothy Cheney, in Amboseli National Park in Kenya for a few days of fieldwork, so I could get a better sense of the difficulties involved and perhaps help them design some further experiments. Susan, an expert exploiter of the British travel-agent industry, figured out that we could take the kids with us for a two-week "holiday trip" to Kenya, staying at the Nyali Beach Club, a lovely old resort hotel on the Indian Ocean outside Mombasa, and from there take a Land Rover camera safari to Amboseli, where I would be dropped off with Robert and Dorothy while she and the kids went back to the Nyali Beach Club to be joined by me at the end of our visit. I proposed to write an article about my adventure in monkey research, with lots of photographs, for *Psychology Today*, which provided partial funding for the whole trip. Before I finished the article, the magazine, then owned by the American Psychological Association, ceased publication for a few years, but I didn't have to refund the advance, and my article eventually appeared in *Poetics Today*, not one of my usual venues.

Robert and Dorothy's campsite base of operations in Amboseli, which they shared with elephant researchers Cynthia Moss and Phyllis Lee, was like a cliché movie-set, with four or five large tents in a clearing, a small generator, an ingenious shower arrangement with an oil drum and sprinkler head that could be heated over the wood fire and then hauled overhead with a block and tackle, all presided over by Wasako, the friendly Kenyan cook and campsite manager, who kept snakes and buffalo and the like out of the little clearing. When we returned at sundown from a day in the field, after a warm shower cold drinks would be ready in the living-room tent, a record would be playing on a small portable phonograph, and a good meal would soon be delivered to the table. Cynthia Moss was away, so I got to stay in her tent, which was surrounded by the skulls of elephants she had known for years. I have described in detail what I learned and the ideas it provoked in my article, and I won't retell the tales here beyond noting one rather sideways discovery I made on that occasion: sometimes when you can't get an experiment to work the way you want it to work, that very fact is the key. We were trying to figure out a way to assure ourselves that one monkey knew something (the nearby presence of a [stuffed] python) and knew that another, rival monkey didn't know this. We were hoping to lure a monkey into telling a lie, in effect. But we just couldn't arrange situations where this was a plausible reading of the epistemic conditions. Eventually it dawned on us that if we couldn't assure ourselves of this, neither could the vervets! Occasions to tell lies just can't arise when you're living in such close quarters. Talleyrand once said that we were given language so we could conceal our thoughts from one another, and if you can't tell lies effectively there is not much leverage to evolve language out of simple signaling systems.

It's remarkable how quickly you can get used to novel circumstances. One morning at breakfast we looked up and an elephant had pushed its way through the trees surrounding the clearing and was snacking on greenery under the clothesline. We briefly took note and then went on with our discussion while the elephant finished its breakfast and disappeared back into the trees. Before I joined Robert and Dorothy in their camp, we Dennetts spent a night in the Amboseli Lodge, in one of the small cinderblock cabins that surrounded the eating hall and bar. There we encountered a different tribe of vervet monkeys, bold little thieves who were not afraid of strange people and would grab crackers and peanuts off your plate on the veranda when you weren't guarding them. The kids were shocked when a German woman tried to retrieve her peanuts from a vervet who then bit her on the backside and sent her screaming into the restaurant. Around the outskirts of the houses, the management had laid out a line of whitewashed boulders and warned all guests not to stray outside the boulders, where dangerous wild animals might attack us. We watched a group of tourists with their cameras walk right up to the boulder line, close beyond which a dozen elephants were moving about. "The elephants don't know the rules!" came the anxious shout from one of the waiters, sending the tourists back to their cabins in a hurry.

That evening some Maasai morans—teenage boys preparing for their initiation into manhood by killing a dangerous wild animal—showed up at the lodge, perhaps just to show off their amazing steel spears, beautifully filed and polished, works of art with razor-sharp edges. The researchers were trying with some success to persuade the Maasai not to go for elephants or rhinos but just for buffaloes or lions. Aside from the buffaloes, heavily armed Somali poachers looking for ivory or rhino horn were the most dangerous mammals in the vicinity, and when we were in the field, we were careful not to make any excursions that might inadvertently expose us to poachers. The Maasai, on the other hand, resented these interlopers and would go out at night, barefoot and armed only with their spears and knives, and sneak up on poachers' campsites and kill them as they slept. One day a Maasai came to our camp and told Phyllis Lee that he had found a dead elephant not far away. Phyllis and I went to investigate, and she could of course recognize the animal from the ragged places on its ears and the other scars and bumps she used to identify her subjects. The tusks had been taken, and when we arrived at the spot the elephant was invisible under a blanket of vultures greedily feasting on the rotting corpse. I had to put a bandanna around my nose and mouth to keep from retching. *What is it like to be a vulture?* . . . say, eagerly climbing into the abdominal cavity of a long-dead elephant to retrieve some morsel?

21.

THE CENTER FOR
COGNITIVE STUDIES;
ADVENTURES WITH
NICHOLAS HUMPHREY

G IVEN OUR ATTACHMENT TO THE FARM, AND TO OUR
summer adventures there, I had been fielding and quietly
rejecting invitations from other philosophy departments for years
when Wilfrid Sellars retired in 1984 and Pittsburgh offered me his
chair. Maybe it was time to move, and what better place than Pittsburgh, whose department I so admired? In addition to the philosophers there, there was the AI group at Carnegie Mellon, and Allen
Newell and Herb Simon joined in the recruiting effort, along with
Wilfrid. It seemed likely we would make the leap and figure out later
how to spend our summers in Blue Hill as usual. My friend and colleague Hugo Bedau decided to construct a counteroffer and asked me
what might keep me happy to stay at Tufts. I had been using much
more than my fair share of the department secretary's time dealing
with my correspondence and travel, and while Tufts had its wonderful MA program in philosophy, I looked forward to having advanced
graduate students at Pitt, a generous book-and-journal budget, and
my own secretary. He took this in and then, with the help of the
provost, concocted the plan of creating the Center for Cognitive
Studies at Tufts, which would house me, a secretary, and—most
important—a hard-money research-associate position that I could
use to support a dissertation student from elsewhere who wanted to
work with me, or a postdoc, or a junior faculty member, or whoever

could help me with my research. I also got a reduced teaching load and a promotion to Distinguished Arts and Sciences Professor, along with the title of director of the center. I can imagine philosophers around the world salivating over this well-nigh-perfect position, and I would just remind them that I did spend a solid fifteen years at Tufts doing more than my share of the scut work, including five somewhat tumultuous years as chair of the department. In short, I had paid my dues.

Tufts and I had an agreement; neither of us promised to try to expand the center, or to raise money for it. It could remain my little three-person operation if I was happy with that, or I could try to build it into something grander. For twenty years it stayed small, until an opportunity arose to bring in my esteemed friend and colleague of many years, the linguist Ray Jackendoff, as co-director and to put in motion the long-postponed plans to create both an undergraduate major and a PhD program in cognitive science. When the center was first established, in 1985, I had asked for a half-time secretary. Didn't I want a full-time secretary? No, because if I had to hire a full-time secretary I'd be competing with every dentist and lawyer in Boston for the recent graduates of some secretarial school, but I knew there were lots of smart young mothers (or fathers) with college degrees who wanted part-time work so they could be home when their kids got home from school, and I figured that they could probably do more, and better, in twenty-one hours a week (so that they would be eligible for benefits) than a full-time novice secretary could do in forty hours. That hunch has been well borne out. First, the wife of a Tufts administrator; then a recent Tufts English major, the eventual wife of one of our MA students (I presided over their marriage ceremony), who used her time as my secretary to complete pre-med courses at Tufts so she could become a veterinarian; then another young mother, and another; and then a Tufts alumna, Teresa Salvato, who has been my right-hand advisor, assistant, and dear friend now for a quarter century.

The center got off to an excellent start. Patricia and Paul Churchland had a student from Canada who had become interested in neuroscience but was doing a PhD in philosophy at Michigan with Jaegwon Kim, a very traditional philosopher of mind who had no developed interest in cognitive science. Would I be able to take over, unofficially, from Jaegwon? Yes indeed, and Kathleen Akins became the first research associate at the center, just the sort of arrangement I had hoped for. She was spectacular, teaching me something new about neuroscience and philosophy almost every time we talked, and she *had ideas and opinions.* One of her pet themes was that although everybody knew that brains were for guiding bodies through life, they didn't take seriously enough the implication that brains would be, at every level, *narcissistic,* her term for the fact that evolution designed brains to ignore what isn't immediately relevant to *me* (the organism whose brain it is) and to couch as much information as possible in terms of its immediate import for action and self-preservation. Brains are incredibly good scouting and navigating systems, not impartial seekers or recorders of truth about the environment.

The neuropsychologist Marcel Kinsbourne (more on him shortly) had been invited to have an unpaid position in the center, and Kathleen joined us on Kinsbourne's rounds at Massachusetts General Hospital, visiting labs, talking with both philosophers and cognitive scientists, and writing an excellent dissertation, which she defended in Ann Arbor in 1989. After stints at the University of Illinois and Xerox PARC, she got a professorship at Simon Fraser University in Vancouver. She was awarded one of the coveted McDonnell Foundation's million-dollar Centennial Fellow grants, which she devoted to training and supporting a cadre of younger neurophilosophers, who owe their careers to her in large measure. A mysterious autoimmune disorder, ankylosing spondylitis, has hindered her for decades, but she has still managed to produce some classic work on aspects of neuroscience and philosophy of mind, undermining the armchair speculations of philosophers (and scientists) about color vision and the misdirection implicit in Nagel's famous appeal to "what it is like" to be a bat or a human.

A visiting fellow that first year was Cecilia Heyes, a brilliant young British psychologist who had been working with the pioneer evolutionary psychologist Donald Campbell at Lehigh and then joined us midyear. She has been a constructive and persistent critic of my ideas ever since, and I was delighted to recommend her highly for All Souls College, where she now follows in the footsteps of Susan Hurley and is a much beloved fellow of that ancient college. Her recent book, *Cognitive Gadgets: The Cultural Evolution of Thinking* (2018), has some good improvements to the growing consensus that theories of the human mind need to put cultural evolution front and center; the big differences between the powers of our minds and the powers of animal minds were first culturally evolved, followed by slower genetic responses. The second research associate at the center was Nicholas Humphrey, who had been the ghost at the banquet at the Dahlem Conference. Our adventures deserve a separate section.

~

AFTER OUR FIRST MEETING in London (see chapter 16), Nick and I had several long discussions at conferences, and it was immediately clear that we were going to be close friends for the rest of our lives, in spite of—or perhaps because of—our slowly emerging differences of opinion about consciousness. Luckily, an early project Nick and I cooked up after he joined me at Tufts never got going: a documentary on what science has to say about consciousness. We got tentative approval from the Annenberg Foundation to make a short series of programs, but the funding was pitiful, and rather than do a half-baked series of low-budget lectures with a few diagrams, we dropped it—a good thing, since our disagreements about key aspects of consciousness were crystallizing and not getting resolved. I shudder to think of the impasses and arguments that would have erupted had we been under time pressure to produce a television series.

Fortunately, another project emerged from our discussions: an investigation of multiple personality disorder (MPD). The publication of *Sybil* by Flora Rheta Schreiber in 1973, boosted by the film (1976) starring Sally Field, had triggered a diagnostic fad, with hundreds of supposed "multiples" undergoing therapy and thousands more extrapolated by the enthusiasts. The cause of their condition was almost invariably described as horrific sexual abuse during childhood. There were passionate defenders of the diagnosis and equally passionate debunkers, and we decided to get to the bottom of it if we could. The defenders were not all fringe folk; there were professors of psychiatry at major medical schools who were convinced this was a real phenomenon, not—as the skeptics insisted—a *folie à deux* (or *trois* or more!) The condition had been officially recognized in the *Diagnostic and Statistical Manual of Mental Disorders* (*DSM-III*, 1980) of the American Psychiatric Association, but was more recently renamed and redescribed as dissociative identity disorder (DID) in *DSM-IV* in 1994.

Nick and I both recognized that a *self* or *ego* was not an organ, nor was it an immaterial soul, as tradition would proclaim, but rather an abstraction, a *virtual machine*, that emerged from the organization of forces and processes in the brain. As I had put it, the self was the *center of narrative gravity*. Perhaps we could learn more about normal solitary selves by studying abnormal multiple selves. We were eager to meet and interact with multiples, of course, but the issues of medical confidentiality were tricky; for instance, did all the "alters" (the other personalities sharing the body with the "host") have to sign the consent form? With the careful collaboration of some colleagues in the psychiatric community, we got to meet a few multiples, though always in the presence of their therapists. A hypnotherapist showed us a videotape he had made of a session he had recorded with a pitiful, mewling, crouching, shuddering young woman who suddenly sat bolt upright and said in a loud, deep, menacing voice, "I can kill her anytime I want!" The therapist in the video leaped back in shock, much as we did watching the video (shades of *The Exorcist!*). We met with therapists and family members, who gave us detailed descriptions of the afflicted individuals, but we could never quite

232 / I've Been Thinking

dispel the atmosphere of awe that, history tells us, permeated the séances conducted by supposed psychics that have had their own brief spotlights of fame over the past few hundred years. How do you explore your doubts regarding the wilder tales of satanic rituals and the like without insulting your informants and driving them away? I found a handy application of a tactic I'd sometimes used in my youth when gently challenging adolescent tall tales of sexual exploits: don't express skepticism; instead go all in hungrily for the details that tend to be neglected in fantasies. "These satanic rituals are amazing, but when did you rehearse? Who assigned the roles? Did you make your own costumes? Where did you hide them? Who cleaned up the mess?" It's not all that hard to tell when somebody is inventing answers on the fly to questions that had never occurred to them.

We attended the Fifth Annual Conference on Multiple Personality/Dissociative States in Chicago, an eye-opening event where the dynamics of cultish amplification were very much in evidence. I participated in a breakout session in which a professor of psychiatry from a major university medical school told a small rapt audience about a young international tennis star he was treating. Her parents, who were also her coaches, had arranged for her to become pregnant and give birth to a baby destined for ritual sacrifice by the satanic cult to which her family belonged! She was now back on the international tournament circuit but suffering from MPD, which he was treating. How do you check up on a tale like that without violating anybody's right to medical confidentiality? I found a way: I called up Bud Collins, dean of tennis journalists, and, without giving him any details about the source of my curiosity, asked him if it would be possible for a young woman to complete a pregnancy and then return to a relatively high ranking without anybody suspecting. Not a chance, he replied. The world of top tennis players, male and female, is too tightly interconnected, too curious and knowledgeable about the health and fitness of the players, and the journalists are too intrusive, for such a thing to happen. A disappearance from the scene for the better part of a year would be a matter of intense curiosity. So the good professor must have been making it all up, or at least hugely embroidering a real case for dramatic effect. Nick and I saw a lot of that—and we even discovered the temptation in ourselves. Driving back from one interrogation or another, we would find, when comparing notes on what we had observed, that we were strongly tempted to exaggerate. Why? Because we both had a powerful sense that we had witnessed something upsetting and uncanny, something to which we had to give a dramatic boost in order to do justice to what we had experienced. And perhaps we were also driven by the lurking suspicion that we'd been made complicit by the manipulative person we had tried to interview. If you want cooperation, you have to support the presentation; ask too many tough questions and the alters just "leave."

Once we were immersed in the material, I realized that our analysis of what we found would be of interest to a wider audience of educated thinkers, not just philosophers and psychologists, so I called up Barbara Epstein, editor of the *New York Review of Books*, to see if they might be interested in the piece we were writing. Yes indeed, she said, so we tailored our piece to that audience. When we sent her the draft, we got a confusing set of editorial suggestions, and when we followed up with questions, we got what seemed like a series of smoke screens, not critiques. Eventually, after several further failed attempts at clarification about the criticisms she offered, Nick and I made an appointment to talk with her in her office in New York. It did not go well. She was visibly upset, and so unable to carry on a coherent conversation that we discreetly took our leave after a few minutes. It was clear that the *New York Review of Books* was not going to publish our piece, so we published it elsewhere.

We found other critics who were deeply unhappy with our piece— on both sides. Was MPD just an iatrogenic (physician-caused) intensification of some more mundane affliction, or was it something that could develop outside of the enabling ministrations of the therapeutic community? What we particularly wanted to encounter, somehow, was a multiple *in the wild*, somebody who had not yet been subjected to the leading questions of an eager therapist. One day I got a call from one of our most helpful informants, Nina Fish Murray, whom I had known for decades, who was seeing patients at a Harvard Medical School clinic: "I have found your unsullied case of MPD. I've just spent a few hours interviewing a young woman who walked into the clinic unannounced and asked for help. I'm sure I'm the first therapist she's ever met, and she struck me as a florid case of MPD. The ethics of this are dubious, but I've decided to give you and Nick an opportunity to run into her in her natural habitat to see what you make of her." Nick and I were soon eagerly devising ways we could "independently" encounter her, spying on her in effect, in hopes of providing her with opportunities to exhibit symptoms during normal social interactions. But then we were told where to find her: she was an underage prostitute working in Boston's notorious "Combat Zone" around Washington Street. Mission aborted. I was sure that neither Susan nor the Tufts University research office that was funding the center would approve of such a dubious field trip, so we had to abandon the opportunity.

In 1990, Nick and I were in Bielefeld, Germany, participating in a workshop on mind and brain, and we paid a visit to the Bethel Foundation, a famous refuge for patients with epilepsy and other serious brain disorders. This was a diplomatic mission of sorts; we went to pay our respects to the good people at Bethel who had bravely kept the place intact in spite of Hitler's attempts to shut it down and exterminate the inhabitants. Our meeting with the director in his office was interrupted by a telephone call to him about a new patient, out of control and threatening harm to both herself and others. He apologized for the interruption and briefly described her symptoms: it sounded to us like florid MPD, a condition unknown to the director, and—tantalizingly—she was an illiterate young woman from an isolated mountain village, where she could almost certainly never have heard of *Sybil* or *The Three Faces of Eve* or any other MPD memes. We explained our interest to the director, and he said he thought he could arrange for us to question her with interpreters as soon as she calmed down. Alas, she died of an inoperable brain tumor before we had a chance to interview her. So to this day we are uncertain about the degree to which this condition—which is a perfectly real affliction—always depends on the amplification of suggestions made available through the reigning memosphere.

The aftermath of the satanic-cult elaborations of MPD in the 1980s was instructive: the annual conferences were abandoned, and some therapists were successfully sued for malpractice, or fined, or lost their licenses to practice. My recent perusal of the literature on DID shows that the controversy about the condition still simmers, which is not surprising when you consider that even professional therapists are susceptible to sensational narratives of abuse that *may* never have happened. For a while, a group of ardent believers supported a newsletter, photocopied and stapled, entitled *S4OS*, short for *Speaking for Our Selves*, with pieces and artwork by and for multiples. Many of the stories were deeply moving, and occasionally comical—one author claimed not to have accepted her diagnosis until she discovered that one of her alters had been under treatment with another therapist! Nick and I had thought their title was an excellent synopsis of the condition and adopted it as the title of our article. Some of our critics were shocked that we were so skeptical of many of the accounts that were flooding the literature, and some were shocked that we didn't dismiss the whole phenomenon outright as some strange contagion of misdiagnosis and malpractice. We figured we'd probably hit the nail on the head: it's a real condition, with real suffering, but it is fostered by potent and variable social influences.

At about this time, the great British neurobiologist and science communicator Colin Blakemore was organizing a television documentary series on the mind and invited Nick and me to participate, but when we said we wanted to include a section on MPD he protested vigorously that it was all metaphysical rubbish. I replied that I thought he was making an error of *arithmetic*. Arithmetic? How so? "You have no problem with *one* self per brain; why should two or three or four be any more dubious?" He got the point but refused to cover the topic in the documentary.

When Nick first arrived at the center, he spotted an offprint of mine in which I queried a claim by AI pioneer Allen Newell by citing my "Julie Christie problem." Allen had a theory of semantics for computer systems that worked fine for internal computer states and numbers but not much else; if the line of code named a subroutine, executing that line should bring up the subroutine; if it said "√9" the program should give you "access to" 3, etcetera. I wrote:

> But of course the real problem is that that isn't what reference is all about. If that were what reference was all about, then what would we say about what you might call my Julie Christie problem. I have a very good physically instantiated symbol for Julie Christie. I know it refers to her, I know it really designates her, but it doesn't seem to have either of the conditions that Professor Newell describes, alas.

The problem was that no matter how often I think or say "Julie Christie," I don't get access to her! Nick asked if he could send a copy of my offprint to Julie Christie, who was a dear friend of his. Of course, I replied, hoping that one day this would indeed give me access to Julie Christie. Maybe Newell was right! She did send me a nice Christmas card, which has had to suffice. Allen Newell's theory, sad to say, doesn't quite work.

It was Nick who had discovered blindsight, in Larry Weiskrantz's lab, and one time we took his film of Helen, the monkey whose visual cortex had been removed, and showed it to a large group of psychologists, including some primatologists, and asked them if they could detect anything unusual about her, as she confidently moved through a maze of obstacles, picking up raisins or chocolate bits off the white floor, never bumping into anything. One person noted a bit of perseveration—Helen made several failed attempts to pick up a raisin that was actually a piece of black tape fastened to the floor—but nobody guessed the truth: Helen was cortically blind.

Nick has a wealth of articles published in *Nature*, the leading science journal in the UK, so he is undoubtedly a scientist of stature, but he is also deeply and knowledgeably in love with literature and history, always ready to adorn his writing with the perfect quote from Shakespeare or some other great thinker of the past. He wrote a remarkable op-ed essay comparing Shakespeare and Newton: "Take away the person Shakespeare, or Chaucer, or Mozart and you'd take away the arbitrary creation of a one-off human mind; take away Newton, or Darwin, or Einstein and you'd take away nothing that could not eventually be replaced by Mind at large."

22.

ITALIAN CONNECTIONS
AND THEIR AFTERMATHS

L ake Como, in northern Italy, is shaped like the letter Y, with the trunk facing north into the Alps, so it's an upside-down Y if you think of north as up. At the crotch of the Y there is a beautiful hill on a peninsula and a town at the base of the hill: Bellagio. The hilltop itself, in its entirety, belongs to the Villa Serbelloni, otherwise known as the Rockefeller Foundation Bellagio Center.

If you subscribe to the real estate agent's mantra, "location, location, location," the Villa Serbelloni must be one of the prime properties in the world, with breathtaking views of all three legs of the lake, the Alps, and the beautiful villas and towns around Lake Como. And the property itself is maintained by the Rockefeller Foundation in pristine condition; there may be more gardeners than research guests there at any one time. It is another version of academic heaven, and I am now forbidden to go there, not because I did something awful there but because it is so excellent that they have instituted a rule: after you have been a fellow in residence there, you are ineligible to apply to return for ten years, and after two such stints you may not apply for a third. I'm lucky to have been to two weeklong workshops and held two monthlong fellowships in residence, and I thus may hold the record for most time spent in this fabled academic palace. My first visit was to a workshop on "event-related potentials," brain waves recorded using noninvasive electroencephalography, organized by a leading figure in the field, Emanuel Donchin, and attended by my friends Paul and Patricia Churchland and Chris Wood, who is now at the Santa Fe Institute. But this first visit to the Villa Serbel-loni was not the most consequential encounter for me at Lake Como.

In April 1985, the cognitive neuropsychologists Anthony Mar-cel and Edoardo Bisiach organized a meeting on consciousness at the Villa Olmo on Lake Como—on the waterfront in Como itself, not at the Villa Serbelloni. I was already good friends with some of the participants (Richard Gregory, Michael Gazzaniga, Larry Weis-krantz), and there I got to know Tim Shallice, Phil Johnson-Laird, and especially Marcel Kinsbourne, who was in fact my neighbor in Massachusetts. Over the course of five or six days of papers and discussions, a pattern developed: there was vigorous discussion of patients with various fascinating pathologies of consciousness—blindsight, hemineglect, Capgras delusion (thinking your loved one has been replaced by an impostor), Anton's syndrome (not realiz-ing that you are blind), Korsakoff's syndrome (amnesia with florid confabulation, typically a consequence of alcoholism)—and I would ask if anybody had thought of doing an experiment in which one thing or another was tried, often learning that nobody had thought of doing it. Kinsbourne urged me to join him on his rounds, seeing these cases for myself and trying out some of my ideas. I jumped at the chance, and that led us into a collaboration that has gone on ever since.

The paper I presented at the Como meeting, "Quining Qualia," was the latest version of a talk I'd been giving for several years, which set out a collection of fourteen intuition pumps designed to show why we shouldn't embrace the philosophers' ill-defined and ill-conceived concept of qualia, or the *subjective properties of expe-rience*. The very phrase is ambiguous; does it refer to the properties *represented in* the experience or to the properties of whatever it is in the brain that subserves, somehow, the representation in experience? Most people imagine the latter and have done so for centuries, since Locke and Hume first talked about impressions and ideas. Is your idea of blue *blue* in some way, or does it represent blue without in any way being blue (like the several occurrences of the word "blue" in this sentence)? My campaign against the philosophers' various concepts of qualia continues to this day, slowly gathering adherents, in spite of the idea's almost irresistible appeal to intuition. (It may help to reflect that *of course* something counterintuitive must be the key here; if there were an intuitive solution to the mind-body problem, it would have been discovered decades ago.)

Marcel Kinsbourne is a rare bird indeed: an MD (pediatric neurology) and neuropsychologist, a constructive contrarian who loves to upset the comfortable assumptions of those who take themselves to be in the know, a brilliant diagnostician of the old school (before you could just scan the MRI images and *see* where the lesions are), and one of my chief guides in my lifelong quest to explore the mind. (He can also be seen, as a child, playing the young Mussolini in a propaganda film, *Yellow Caesar*, made in London during the war, pouting and wearing a dunce cap in the schoolroom corner.) When I started tagging along with him on rounds at Mass General and Boston's VA Hospital, he delighted in teaching me many of his tricks (of diagnosis, of persuasion). Just one example: If you have a startling experimental discovery to impart, don't just blurt it out at the beginning of your talk. Describe the phenomenon in neutral terms and ask the audience to commit to what they think the results will be—with a show of hands. That way, when you show them what you have found, they cannot dismiss you with "Everybody knows that!" or "I would of course have predicted it."

Together we did bedside examinations of patients with hemineglect, Korsakoff's syndrome, Tourette's syndrome, cerebral achromatopsia (color blindness due to brain damage), Broca's aphasia, Wernicke's aphasia, and other conditions. One of the many lessons I learned is that patients are seldom afflicted with just one disorder, one clear-cut disability. It is typically a matter of careful strategic highlighting to bring any of their symptoms into clear focus. Here's a bittersweet irony: There used to be many cases of strokes suffered by "high-SES" (high-socioeconomic-status) people—lawyers, doctors, scientists, educators, business leaders. Now that there are a host of new diagnostic tools and treatments, this patient population has largely disappeared, thanks to the fact that well-informed people wisely take their high-blood-pressure medicine, avoiding strokes. Most of the strokes encountered in the hospital are in people who are homeless, alcoholic, often barely literate. So, it's hard to tell which failures to complete simple diagnostic tasks are due to their stroke and which may reveal long-term problems of competence and comprehension.

When we went on rounds, I never wore a white lab coat and never introduced myself as a doctor, but very often the patients and their family members would ignore this clue and thank me profusely for all the help I had provided. It was a constant reminder to me that I was being given a privileged view of deeply personal suffering and that I should be extremely careful not to interfere with their lives just to satisfy my curiosity. Still, there were times when I did come up with exploratory suggestions that were fruitful. One in particular I remember concerned a young man who was suffering from *simultanagnosia*, an inability to make sense of his visual perception in spite of his undamaged eyes. Something suggested to me that his problem might affect even his ability to imagine things. So I made up some very short stories with anomalies that should stick out like sore thumbs: Tom tied his dog's leash to the tree and hopped in his convertible and started driving off; his dog leaped into the back seat . . . What happened next? Tom went skiing; he put on his boots and his skis and then he put on his pants . . . Tom had a rowboat on the pond, but strangers kept using it when he wasn't there, but he had a bright idea: he rowed his boat to the island in the middle of the pond and left it there so that folks couldn't use it; then he went home . . . As I expected, the patient didn't notice anything awry or shocking in these little tales, although he could repeat most of the details I had given him. You don't always need brain scanners or even timed presentations to elicit telltale measures of comprehension.

After I abandoned the Vicious Circle in disgust (see chapter 18), I decided to start a new, more constructive discussion group, consisting for the first few years of just four of us: Nick Humphrey; Marcel Kinsbourne; Ray Jackendoff, the Brandeis linguist who later became my colleague at Tufts; and me. We met at Ray's house at first, and in spite of our quite different agendas and talents, we usually managed to enlighten one another and make progress. My 1991 book, *Consciousness Explained*, is dedicated to them, and no dedication of mine has been more heartfelt. While we were getting to know one another better, I decided the time was ripe to expand our horizons and go for an international workshop on consciousness to the Villa Serbelloni in Bellagio—where else?

Competition for the limited workshop slots at Bellagio is fierce, and the Rockefeller Foundation has a laudable policy of aiming its support at underfunded, underrepresented thinkers and artists. We four were hardly disadvantaged academics, and my short list of other participants consisted of similarly well-cared-for scientists: William Calvin, a neuroscientist from Seattle; Tony Marcel and Edoardo Bisiach, the Villa Olmo conference organizers; and Aaron Sloman, a philosopher turned AI researcher at the University of Sussex. My proposal was provocative: There would be *no* conference volume emerging from the participants, because conference volumes are almost always a poor use of their time and energy; if the workshop succeeded, the subsequent independent work by all participants would be deeply informed by it and would more than justify the support they had received. Moreover, I proposed that two of our participants, Kinsbourne and I, should stay on after the weeklong workshop for a month as writers in residence to complete a major paper we had been formulating.

I added one paragraph to the proposal that I thought of as merely historical background, but it turned out to be decisive for the selection committee. Some years earlier, the Villa Serbelloni had hosted two highly distinguished writers in residence—the philosopher of science Sir Karl Popper and the neuroscientist Sir John Eccles—to write up a book on consciousness and the brain. Sir John Eccles was an Australian neuroscientist, a Nobel laureate for his work on the synapse (the gap between neurons that is crossed by neurotransmitter molecules when one neuron signals to another), and—a rarity among neuroscientists—an outspoken dualist. His Catholic upbringing was probably a major contributor to that conviction. In 1952, shortly after Ryle published *The Concept of Mind* (1949), Eccles gave the Waynflete Lectures in Oxford, with Ryle (the Waynflete Professor of Philosophy) in attendance. Eccles, thinking to win Ryle's favor, described the brain as like a mighty theater organ, and the synapses were like the keys, which could be delicately stroked by . . . the Mind, which was "in Professor Ryle's elegant terminology" *the ghost in the machine*! Seldom has a scientist so badly misunderstood a philosopher. Popper, too, was a dualist, and the two of them must have had a merry time egging each other on in the beautiful gardens of the Villa Serbelloni. Their book, *The Self and Its Brain: An Argument for Interactionism* (1977), is probably the worst book on the subject ever to have been written by distinguished thinkers, a poorly constructed mishmash of pompous opinions and mischaracterizations of the work discussed. (See my review, perhaps the harshest I have ever written, but well deserved.) I decided to mention the fact that the Villa Serbelloni had played a major role in bringing this lamentable book into existence and suggested that our workshop could erase this blemish on the Villa's escutcheon by producing work that would consign the Popper-Eccles claims to richly deserved oblivion! As it happens, one of the members of the selection committee had been fuming quietly for years about that debacle, and my proposal of an antidote won him over completely.

My little historical note had struck a nerve, and my proposal was accepted. From it emerged two major products: Dennett and Kinsbourne, "Time and the Observer: The Where and When of Consciousness in the Brain" (1992), a target article in *Behavioral and Brain Sciences*; and *Consciousness Explained*, my elaboration of the model we had developed. I have always been particularly pleased that "Time and the Observer" was voted one of the ten best *philosophy* papers of the year, a clear sign that philosophers were beginning

244 / I've Been Thinking

to get the point about how they might pursue their careers in more interdisciplinary settings.

~

SAN MARINO IS a tiny landlocked republic in northern Italy, larger than Vatican City and Monaco and smaller than Lichtenstein. It features Monte Titano, topped by a castle, a few miles inland from the Adriatic coast, which is sometimes called the German rotisserie (in the summer its beaches are flocked with German sunbathers). A day trip from the beach to San Marino is a bit like visiting a medieval version of Coney Island, with dozens of shops selling kitsch and souvenirs; I was briefly tempted by a cane with a bicycle bell and a handy beer-can holder. If you come at just the right time, you get to witness the international crossbow championship competition, which trades on all the ancient trappings of the picturesque castle. The government of San Marino decided in the late 1980s to build a casino to attract more tourists, but they neglected to clear this innovation with their surrounding neighbor. Once the casino was built and open, the Italian authorities squelched it by slowing down the border passport control to a crawl, so that would-be gamblers had to spend hot dusty hours waiting in line to get up the hill to the casino. San Marino temporarily abandoned its attempt to become another Monte Carlo and was left with a brand-new but empty casino.

This gave Umberto Eco, nearby at the University of Bologna, a bright idea. He was rightly dismayed by the disarray and corruption of the university system in Italy and decided to mount a sort of pirate response to it by helping give birth to a university in San Marino, occupying the would-be casino and attracting world-class academics to international workshops that would draw in Italian students and researchers and boost the credentials of the fledgling institution, which could then conduct its classes mainly by one or another form of distance learning. (Email existed then, but the internet wasn't really going yet.) I think he may have been inspired by two great

European innovations, Radio Luxembourg and the Open University. Radio Luxembourg beamed popular music and advertising to the UK, which outlawed commercial radio until 1973. The UK's Open University, which has taught over two million students since it opened in 1969, was a brilliant attempt to correct the terrible effects of the notorious *eleven-plus exam*, which for over thirty years after World War II consigned British children at age eleven or twelve to either the higher-education stream or the proletariat on the basis of a national test. The Open University provided high-quality university-level courses in many subjects, using the BBC television channels early in the morning and late at night, and hiring thousands of professors, teaching assistants, and examiners. More important, it demonstrated and improved the power of distance learning, as its graduates have gone on to careers that equal or exceed the careers of traditional university students. (I would often get up early and watch excellent physics and chemistry lectures on the telly during our many visits to England over the years. In addition to all the students who enrolled, were examined, and graduated, the Open University has enlarged the knowledge of millions who just kibitzed, like me.)

The one-building University of San Marino hosted the first of Eco's workshops in 1988 with suitable academic fanfare and it was followed by a series of conferences. My first invitation arrived in 1989 for a week in 1990 when we would be in Bielefeld, Germany, at Peter Bieri's workshop on mind and brain (see chapter 34). I had read Eco's novel *The Name of the Rose* and liked it, so I accepted the invitation. Then at the Bielefeld workshop I started reading his latest novel, *Foucault's Pendulum*, and disliked it so much that I threw the book across the room in disgust, the only time I have ever done that, to the best of my recollection. Eco's suave tolerance for ancient arcana (centuries-old bullshit is still bullshit) was more than I could stand, so when Susan and I headed off to San Marino in our rental car, I was not expecting to enjoy the occasion.

Another source of my unease was our financial situation. We'd splurged at Christmastime by inviting our children to fly over and join us for a week in Paris and then another week of skiing at Zermatt, and it was just as we were getting ready to pay our bill and leave the hotel in Zermatt that we got a message that the couple renting our home in Massachusetts for the year had fled without paying the rent, which we were counting on using to fund our European travels. I hadn't appreciated the fragility of our position until we got to the Simplon Tunnel through the Alps. We discovered that there was a toll to pay, and we didn't have quite enough cash to cover it! After buying our last full tank of fuel, we had maxed out our credit cards. In desperation, I parked by the side of the road and lifted up the floormats of the rental car. Sure enough, there were a few coins in various currencies, and they added up to enough to pay the toll and then some. When we got to San Marino, my first question as we checked into the hotel was whether supper was being served to us—yes—and would we get the honorarium in cash the next day? Yes. *Whew!* We strolled through the town after dinner and spent the rest of our liquid capital on two postcards (but couldn't afford the stamps to mail them then).

Umberto Eco turned out to be a delightful man, erudite beyond belief but graceful in the use of his vast knowledge, intensely interested in other people's ideas, and a voluble purveyor of funny stories and observations. Whatever the topic, he seemed to catch on immediately to the key elements and problems, and he often had striking insights to add to the conversation. I remember being pleased to see that he "got" the ideas about consciousness that I had already published, to the extent that he could anticipate some of what I had to say on the topic at the meeting and during the intense discussions that lasted well past bedtime. I was happy to return to his university on Kitsch Mountain whenever he invited me, and I went back several times.

When we left San Marino and headed back to Bielefeld (where another needed stipend awaited us), we drove straight across Switzerland without coming to a full stop, so anxious were we not to run out of money again. That was the last time we faced serious money problems. What with moving around, buying cars and appliances, and going on irresistible trips, we had gradually used up the modest legacy that Grandpa Dennett had left us and were inattentive managers of what funds remained. When we got home, the advance from Little, Brown for *Consciousness Explained* permitted us to pay off our credit card debts and reform our spending habits, thanks to the wise advice—training, really—of a new financial advisor, one of our sailing friends, Dick Sumberg, who put us on the track to financial security.

One San Marino meeting I didn't manage to attend, and all things considered I guess I'm glad I missed, was one in which Jerry Fodor and the "neural Darwinist" Gerald Edelman (see chapter 34 on academic bullies) went head-to-head in a ferocious session. Fodor often brandished his "principled" ignorance of the brain, which could not have sat well with Edelman. (Fodor once firmly told the Sloan Foundation committee when they were planning their multimillion-dollar support of cognitive neuroscience that there was no such field and never would be! The committee told him that their question wasn't *whether* to fund cognitive neuroscience, but *which* cognitive neuroscience it would fund: "What are you working on in your lab these days, Dr. Fodor?" Jerry, who had indeed run a psycholinguistics lab at MIT for some years with the invaluable help of Merrill Garrett, had to admit that he didn't currently have a lab. The Sloan Foundation excused him and called on the next interviewee.) The debate in San Marino was, by general consensus, a rout, with Gerry the victor over Jerry. Witnesses gave me details of the abuse Gerry and Jerry rained on each other, neither one backing down, and part of me—the part that can't help looking at highway crashes as I drive by the police cordons—regrets not having been present for this match between two academic bullies. I wonder if a video or audio recording of that meeting exists somewhere, but I hope not. That would probably be best for all.

23.

CONSCIOUSNESS
EXPLAINED

W HAT WOULD YOU DO IF YOU WERE REFEREEING A
paper submitted to a journal and just as you finished writing your *rejection* report you realized that a point the author made in
passing had clarified your thinking on a topic that had been evading
you? It happened to me in 1990, when I was one of the reviewers of
a submission to the *Journal of Cognitive Neuroscience*. I didn't think
the paper was up to the standards of the journal, nor could I think
of any revisions to propose that would save it, but it had given me
an idea that I wanted to acknowledge. How could I give credit to an
author of a paper that I didn't think should be published? I decided
to telephone the editor, my old friend Michael Gazzaniga, and ask
him for advice. He proposed a solution that strained the rules of the
peer-review system, but for a good cause: he gave me the telephone
number of the author and urged me to call him and talk it over,
which I did. I explained to the author, Douglas Snyder, that I found
his discussion of time and Einsteinian inertial frames applied to the
brain suggestive, but I couldn't recommend publishing his paper as
it was. He was disappointed, of course, but gracious, and he quickly
replied that he had already published the idea that had focused my
own thinking in a paper ("On the Time of a Conscious Peripheral
Sensation") in the *Journal of Theoretical Biology*. I could cite that. You
will find my citation of Snyder (1988) on page 196 of "Time and the
Observer," and in a grateful footnote on page 137 of *Consciousness
Explained*. Was that enough? I've never been quite sure.

Writing *Consciousness Explained* was as intense a creative effort as

I have ever engaged in, and when I submitted the manuscript to my editor at Little, Brown I could hardly believe I'd produced it. That happened again when I finished *Darwin's Dangerous Idea* (1995). In both cases, I had often worked most of the way through the night in a frenzy of authorship that I can now scarcely imagine. I still occasionally get brief bouts of that enthusiasm when I dig into a project, but without the all-consuming concentration. I can't do all-nighters anymore; I've lost a step or two.

My thinking about consciousness was evolving slowly, but always with a central theme. I was meeting often with leading scientific researchers on consciousness, and in the process beginning to form at least vague ideas of how mechanisms of the brain might do all the work, but only if we deflated some of the overconfident pronouncements of introspectors about the marvels of the phenomena. Discussions with Jean-Pierre Changeux and Stan Dehaene in Paris about the "global workspace model" of Bernard Baars; with Larry Weiskrantz, Alan Cowey, Edmund Rolls, and Jeffrey Gray at Oxford; and with the Lake Como gang assembled by Marcel and Bisiach supplemented my discussions with our little group. Humphrey, Kinsbourne, and Jackendoff were all improving my amateur grip on neuroscience. Looking back, I can see my growing conviction that although consciousness is a spectacular phenomenon, it isn't as wonderful as many people liked to think. There is a strong tendency to "protect" consciousness from scientific investigation, exaggerating its mysteries and heaping suspicion on any proposals that threaten to uncover some of nature's cheap tricks.

Many people *want* consciousness to be "real magic" (as Lee Siegel puts it; see the prologue, p. xx), not a bunch of tricks. This yearning is revealed in the popularity of the standard put-down of *Consciousness Explained*: that its title should be *Consciousness Ignored* or *Consciousness Denied* or *Consciousness Explained Away*. This is a convenient way for critics to reassure their readers that they are on the "right side," defending the sacred citadel from the barbarian defilers, without having to demonstrate any actual errors in my account. In the book, I developed the powerful idea of *virtual machines* in the brain as creators of *user illusions* and then confronted the obvious question: "If consciousness is a virtual machine, who is the user for whom the user illusion works?" (p. 219). I added that "it looks suspiciously as if we are drifting inexorably back to an internal Cartesian Self, sitting at the cortical workstation and reacting to the user illusion of the software running there, but there are, as we shall see, some ways of escaping that dreadful dénouement."

Those escape routes are all-important, obviously, and I devoted many pages to clarifying them, but it is striking how few of my critics have ever discussed them. These critics would rather characterize my book as an idiotic denial of an obvious fact: consciousness can't be an illusion, because there can't be an illusion without a victim—the conscious agent whose illusion it is. The philosopher Galen Strawson has called my theory "the silliest claim ever made," a verdict that ought to arouse a *little* suspicion in him that he's misinterpreted me, but he has persisted undaunted. It is apparently just unthinkable by Strawson that he might be an unreliable judge of what his own consciousness is. Oxford-trained philosophers of my vintage have a move they like to use when confronting a view that they can't figure out how to refute: simply say, with an air of feigned modesty, "I just *don't understand* what you could mean by that," insinuating that what you had said was utter nonsense. Another Oxford-trained mysterian, commenting on my book at an APA meeting, once said that he just "couldn't understand" a claim in the book. My response on that occasion was to grant that my book had some difficult passages in it, and I advised him to try harder. I sometimes can't resist the urge to be rude in response to rude critics.

Encouraged more recently by some insightful papers by Keith Frankish, I have strengthened my account, endorsing his term "illusionism" as a good "ism"-label for my view. This has provoked another wave of disapproval from some of my *constructive* critics, who think my theory is basically on the right track but is unwisely burdened with such a disturbing name. They may in the end be right about my expository decision, but I'm not convinced yet. Probably the younger generations of thinkers who have grown up with video games and smartphone apps find it easier to recognize user illusions as *good things*—helpful oversimplifications with beneficiaries, not victims. Given canny theorists like Chris Frith and Anil Seth adopting the idea of conscious experience as "controlled hallucination," while acknowledging with me that there is no movie in the head, and Michael Graziano and others pursuing similar themes, I think the *deflationary* account of consciousness as a marvelous bag of good tricks, not "real magic," is in better shape than ever, gathering both empirical support and sophisticated adherents as it grows.

Suppose you were a relatively unknown neuroscientist whose experimental work was suddenly hailed by a Nobel laureate neuroscientist as being the first ever scientific demonstration of dualism. Benjamin Libet was faced with a Faustian bargain when Sir John Eccles trumpeted his endorsement, saying that Libet had uncovered a phenomenon that "does not seem to be explicable by any neurophysiological process." For years, Libet struggled to find a way of interpreting his work as revolutionary, if not quite the vindication of dualism that Eccles claimed it to be. I first learned of Libet's work in 1979, when reviewing Popper and Eccles's notorious book. I alerted Pat Churchland to the work and suggested she could make mincemeat of it, which she promptly did, sparring with Libet in a memorable exchange (and also incurring Eccles's wrath). In the intervening years, Libet's work has been voluminously critiqued, interpreted, defended, and dismissed, and a curious feature of that discussion is that almost nobody draws attention to the embarrassing fact that Libet did *two* kinds of experiments. His early experiments on awake (non-anesthetized) brain-surgery patients' reports about the timing of sensations *undercut* all "revolutionary" interpretations of his later experiments on consciousness of intentions. I had pointed all this out in a long and difficult section of my book (pp. 153–66), a critique that has been conveniently swept under the rug (using Occam's broom) by those who want to use Libet's later work to "disprove" free will. (I tried to dispose of Libet's work in a more accessible fashion in *Freedom Evolves* [2003], but that exploration has largely been ignored. Either I've always been just wrong about Libet, or my critiques are unwelcome guests at the philosophers' parties where the mysteries of consciousness and free will are debated. Time will tell.)

Consciousness Explained was not my first trade book (that would be *The Mind's I*, coedited with Doug Hofstadter), but it was my first book where I was represented by an agent. Several colleagues in fields other than philosophy had encouraged me to get an agent, saying that my style was accessible to a much wider audience than I would find if I continued to publish with university presses, and to publish with a trade house I'd best have an agent. I had by then diagnosed a major flaw in interdisciplinary communication: when experts write for experts, they always err on the side of underexplaining, in order to avoid insulting their colleagues with overexplaining. The only practical cure for this systematic and understandable failure was to write for an audience of "educated laypeople" and let the experts eavesdrop without being insulted. I've described this strategy in *Intuition Pumps and Other Tools for Thinking* (2013). *Consciousness Explained* was my first deliberate test of it. If the book had become a runaway bestseller but not engaged my academic colleagues, it would have been a failure in my eyes. The educated laypeople were my decoys; I hoped they would understand it, and I worked hard to convey my ideas vividly and directly, but it was my colleagues, especially the scientists, whom I wanted to reach. It worked. Glowing reviews by George Johnson in the *New York Times Book Review* and Philip Morrison in *Scientific American* certainly helped, and "Time and the Observer" in *Behavioral and Brain Sciences* convinced many scientists that I wasn't just a science journalist/philosopher but a theorist worth their attention.

A lot of the credit for the success of the book should go to John Brockman, the legendary literary agent who courted me for months before I took the plunge. His stable of clients then included a few friends of mine—Bill Calvin and the AI theorist Roger Schank, who encouraged me to sign with him—but also a few authors of pop-psychology and pop-physics books I would never recommend or cite. What finally won me over was Brockman's canny observations about the financial aspects of publishing. If he could get me a big advance, the publisher would want to recoup its investment by vigorously pushing for reviews in top periodicals and shelf space in the big bookstore chains of the day. Moreover, they would want to keep the price of the book as low as possible, unlike university presses, which were then charging outrageous amounts for their monographs, a practice that still continues in spite of much criticism. I wanted my book to be affordable by students and to include illustrations—line drawings and diagrams—which would make a university press book even more expensive. Brockman said he could more or less guarantee a follow-up paperback version within a year of publication of the hardback. He was right on all counts. And, I might add, trade publishers do a much more vigorous job of copyediting and fact-checking than university presses. I soon learned the value of a truly professional copyeditor. Mistakes still creep into my books, but conscientious editors have saved me from a lot of careless errors, in addition to fearlessly objecting to occasional lazy phrases and convoluted sentences, which I gratefully and red-facedly repaired.

More on Brockman

John likes to say that if a client of his ever gets a royalty check, he hasn't done his job right. What he means is that he tries to extract an advance payment from the publisher so high that the book never earns out the advance. Of course, that has to be an exaggeration. Some of the books he sells to publishers become bestsellers that send their authors royalty checks regularly for years. (*Consciousness Explained* and *Darwin's Dangerous Idea* are my steady royalty earners, but some of my other books are still nibbling away at the handsome advances he got for me.) One of his tactics is to hold a telephone auction on a particular day; the publishers all get several days to consider the same book proposal (stipulating the same conditions, royalty rates, etc., so that size of the advance is the only issue). On the morning of the big day, he informs all those who submit an initial bid what the current high bid is but doesn't say whose bid it is or how many publishers are in the bidding, and invites them to raise or fold, passing on each new high bid to the competition. At the end of the day, the highest bidder gets the book. This can be an exciting day for the author or a big disappointment, and it can lead to anxious predicaments. John sold Nobel laureate physicist Murray Gell-Mann's *The Quark and the Jaguar* for a huge advance, but Murray was late getting in his manuscript, and the publisher, within its rights, cancelled the contract and asked for the advance back. Ouch! I faced a similar abyss when my editor at Simon and Schuster, the notorious Alice Mayhew (while many of her authors praised her editing, she was sometimes known as Malice Mayhem behind her back), refused to accept my timely submission of the manuscript of *Darwin's Dangerous Idea* because it was larger than the contract specified. She wanted me to cut it 30 percent! I decided I could find about 5 percent that I might part with, but no more. What to do? I asked John, and he told me to write him a letter saying that I was withdrawing the manuscript and paying back the advance. I'd spent most of the advance and would have to take out a mortgage to pay it back, so this was no joke. John said he would find me another publisher, but ethically he couldn't even sound out other publishers until I had definitely withdrawn from Simon and Schuster, and I might not get as big an advance with another publisher under the circumstances. He took my letter to Mayhew, with whom he had tangled on several occasions, and said to her, "How do you want to be remembered, Alice—as the editor of Woodward and Bernstein's *All the President's Men* or as the editor who rejected *Darwin's Dangerous Idea*?" Later in the day, I got a phone call from Alice, all buttery and welcoming, and the book went ahead at the size I submitted. It was a finalist for a National Book Award, and I went to the awards ceremony with John and Alice. It didn't win, so I never got to use my acceptance remarks, which included the tale of how, when Darwin submitted *On the Origin of Species* to his publisher, John Murray, he was advised to cut out everything except his observations on pigeons: "Every body is interested in pigeons. The book would be received in every journal in the kingdom, and would soon be on every table."

John has been my literary agent for more than thirty years, but he's also been a friend and advisor. His first love has been his website, Edge.org, an online salon where he has inspired and provoked an unrivaled collection of good thinkers to write short, accessible, but substantive pieces on a wide variety of topics. Its motto is "To arrive at the edge of the world's knowledge, seek out the most complex and sophisticated minds, put them in a room together, and have them ask each other the questions they are asking themselves." I don't read everything that shows up on Edge, but hardly a week goes by when I don't find an interview or debate that captures and rewards my attention. John invites clients to join a discussion, but he doesn't permit them to tout their books. Perhaps the best-known program on Edge has been the World Question, a single question John posed each year until 2018 to the Edgies, asking for a short (a thousand words or less) answer. Among my favorite questions:

2005: What do you believe is true even though you cannot prove it?
2008: What have you changed your mind about? Why?
2014: What scientific idea is ready for retirement?
And finally, in 2018: What is the last question?

Another of John's projects was the Science Masters series of short books written in accessible language—not primers or introductions to fields but opinionated essays, which were translated and published roughly simultaneously in over a dozen languages. Though I hardly qualify as a "Science Master" by most official measures, I was invited to do one of the first, and my little book *Kinds of Minds* (1996) has appeared in English, French, Italian, Spanish, Portuguese, German, Dutch, Finnish, Polish, Romanian, Croatian, Hungarian, Hebrew, Turkish, Japanese, Korean, and Chinese. Not in Arabic. (Italy publishes more translations of foreign books in Italian in a month than the Arab world publishes in Arabic in a year.) Authors were asked to agree to pool the royalties. We each got an advance of $20,000, and then if one of us struck paydirt with a bestseller, we'd all enjoy the benefits. None of the books achieved best-seller status, though all did quite well, and I get my modest share of the royalties each year. Not everyone on the initial list of invitees came through with a book. Ernst Mayr, Paul Davies, Bill Calvin, Martin Rees, Lee Smolin, Peter Atkins, Lynn Margulis, Jared Diamond, Richard Dawkins, Steve Pinker, George Williams, W. Daniel Hillis, and Ian Stewart did, for instance, but Marvin Minsky didn't and neither did Stephen Jay Gould. Gould alone refused to refund the advance, which John made up to the rest of us out of his own pocket. More important to me was the idea of bright high school kids all over the world getting a good dose of Dennett-style thinking early in their academic lives, in their native language. I see my book as inoculating its readers against certain almost irresistible imagination-stifling ideas, and I can see the influence I've had in hundreds of emails that come in every year.

~

ONE OF THE INNOVATIONS in *Consciousness Explained* were the two appendices, one for philosophers, one for scientists. In the first, I could satisfy the curiosity of those in my field who needed to read avowals from me about whether I am or ever have been, as some have charged, a *verificationist*, a *functionalist*, an *eliminative materialist*, a *behaviorist* . . . It all depends, of course, on exactly what these labels mean. What many philosophers call theories are really just slogans, single sentences that are supposed to sum up, with exquisite precision, precisely what is or isn't the case about something puzzling. So, a great deal of philosophical effort has been spent slogan-honing, doing dubious battle with counterexample-mongering. There is a place for precision in any theory, of course, but sometimes it's more useful to rough out a general perspective and postpone the philosophical branding and shaming indefinitely.

The second appendix, for scientists, was where I drove home the point that I was putting forth a genuine theory with predictions that might be confirmed or disconfirmed. I listed more than half a dozen families of experiments that, if conducted, could either sink my theory or else add to the general knowledge of the field. (Theories don't get *confirmed* by a few good predictions—Popper was right about that—but they do get taken a lot more seriously by rival theorists when they uncover something surprising.) I am more than happy with the results to date. This isn't the place to provide an exhaustive review of the experimental work that has been provoked by my suggestions—perhaps a good job for a graduate student in cognitive science—but I can't resist noting that when I predicted *change blindness* back in 1991, most cognitive scientists with whom I discussed this were incredulous. It's now a booming subindustry in psychology.

At the time I was working on the book, I had an undergraduate student majoring in cognitive science who was hunting for an honors-thesis topic, and I suggested he run an experiment that I had concocted. He said he was keen to do it, so I lent him my 35mm camera and tripod and told him to take pairs of pictures around campus: picture 1A of his dormitory; picture 1B, the same scene with a bicycle added to the bike rack; picture 2A of his room; picture 2B of his room with a chair moved over, and so forth. I borrowed an unused tachistoscope from a professor in the psychology department so that these pairs of slides could be shown in rapid succession with a black slide in between each pair. I predicted that subjects would not, in general, notice the change, even with multiple viewings. Change blindness, in short. Off he went, and weeks went by. I called him in to find out how the project was going, and he showed me his collection of pairs of pictures, which were fine. And the results? He couldn't bring himself to ask his fellow students to be subjects, since the experiment was so stupid! Everybody would see the changes, of course. And so, his name is not in the textbooks as the first demonstrator of change blindness. I've lost track of him and wonder if he regrets his skepticism today.

Soon after my book appeared, I participated in a conference at Simon Fraser University, organized by my first research associate, Kathleen Akins. One of the speakers was a young psychologist, John Grimes, who had independently thought of my idea of testing for change blindness, but with a novel twist. He showed a fascinating video of his experiment, in which subjects sat in front of a monitor with their heads immobilized, and a laser was directed at one eye to detect saccades, the little jumps that your eyes make four or five times a second to redirect the high-resolution fovea to items of interest in the visual world. Subjects were shown pictures and asked to study them for ten seconds (a *long* time, in fact, to look at a picture). At some randomly chosen time during that interval, when the laser detected the beginning of a saccade, this would trigger a super-swift change to a feature in the picture. By the time the saccade was over, ten or twenty milliseconds later, the revised picture would be there and stay there for the rest of the ten-second period. Subjects were asked to press a button if they *ever detected a change* (even if they weren't sure what had changed). Grimes's video showed several dozen examples, some of them detected by almost all his subjects and others that were not detected by most—including an aerial photo of Crater Lake in which the lake changed from bright blue to deep black, and a photo of a boy holding up a parrot in a crowded marketplace in which the parrot changed from green to red during a saccade. These were not background objects in confused settings; if asked to title the two pictures, most people would call the first "Crater Lake as Seen from the Air" and the second "Boy Displaying a Parrot." Only about half of Grimes's subjects noticed these changes.

I was delighted to see my prediction confirmed so handsomely and asked Grimes for a copy of his videotape, which he kindly gave me. I was very active on the lecture circuit in those days, and I began showing the Grimes video to audiences around the world. When an audience of several hundred people is shown the Grimes video, it's likely that several of them will happen to saccade or blink just when a picture changes—as if they had had a laser monitoring their eye movements. These people will not *see* any change but will *hear* the change, because the rest of the audience will go *"Ooh!"* or *"Wow!"* when they see the change. Those who didn't see the change that everyone else saw will then vocalize in response: *"Aargh!"* (Imagine: you're staring at a picture, looking for a change; suddenly you hear most of the audience go *"Ooh!"*—they've seen the change—but you didn't, even though you were intently studying the picture looking for the change. *"Aargh!"* indeed.) These call-and-response audience reactions were great fun to provoke, and they proved to everyone that change blindness is a real phenomenon. The Grimes effect has recently been convincingly replicated by Brian Odegaard, the philosopher David Rosenthal, and their colleagues (2022).

Suppose you have a great idea for an experiment, you try it out, and it doesn't work as you hoped it would. What should you do? Stick all your notes and data in a file drawer of abandoned ideas? Why not? Because your failure may be just as important a fact as success would have been. "Cherry-picking"—concentrating on the experiments that support your view—is practically unavoidable when new work opens up novel paths to explore, but quietly shelving inconclusive follow-ups (the "file-drawer effect"), while not as grievous a sin as suppressing inconvenient truths (sweeping them under the rug with Occam's broom), is recognized as a serious source of distortion in scientific research. I must confess that I've sometimes been guilty of cherry-picking and of not doing enough checking to see if the experiments I've heralded have been replicated—and I have also myself initiated experiments I have never reported. This is a good place to describe an experiment in perception I started in 2001 that I abandoned and have never described in a peer-reviewed journal.

It takes time to see a painting—a few seconds, or much longer if the painting holds your interest. Your gaze must dart around—the saccades I described above. You and I might look at the same painting for the same duration but have very different experiences because your saccades took a different zigzag course from mine. You set out to "read" the painting forward, maybe, and I tried to read it backward. Drawing the viewer's attention first here and then there has been an aspiration of many artists, and I once enjoyed a discussion of this at a party with David Freedberg, the Columbia University art historian, who told me about a letter the classicist painter Nicolas Poussin had written to a patron, Paul Fréart de Chantelou, who had not liked a commissioned painting Poussin had sent him. Poussin had a music-inspired theory of "modes" that informed his work, and he told his patron in effect that he was looking at the painting in the *wrong mode*. What did I make of that defense? My snap judgment was that it sounded like inspired bullshit, but on reflection it occurred to me that there might be a way in which Poussin was right—by accident, since my imagined interpretation of the *mode* of a painting was almost certainly not what Poussin had in mind.

There are seven *musical* modes, associated with the seven tones of the scale:

do Ionian
re Dorian
mi Phrygian
fa Lydian
sol Mixolydian
la Aeolian (natural or related minor)
ti Locrian

If you start singing on *do* and go up the scale to the octave (as in that awful song from *The Sound of Music*), you have sung the major scale—the Ionian mode. If you sing the same notes but start and end on *re*, you are singing the Dorian mode. And so forth. It is a wonderful fact that you can treat any of the seven notes as "home" and get a different feeling (effect, color, atmosphere) depending on which mode you choose. (Miles Davis's album *Kind of Blue* is a great example of "modal" jazz.) The same is true, in principle, of painting! As the philosopher of art Arthur Danto once put it in an essay on Norman Rockwell, "Painting is not simply what takes place on the canvas. It is what goes on between the canvas and the viewer." Perhaps Poussin had meant his viewer to begin by looking at the lady's face, then at the child's hand, then at the bright red hat on the onlooker, and so forth, until the viewer's gaze had taken in all the key points of interest in the painting. Suppose we gathered eye-tracking data on many people looking at paintings and then added a do-re-mi soundtrack to the recording of their saccades. We could then *hear* the difference between how two subjects looked at the same painting. Maybe some people don't like some paintings because they are looking at them in the wrong mode! With the help of Steven Franconeri, a Harvard graduate student in experimental psychology, and a few undergraduates and others, we set up an experiment using an eye tracker and a program that assigned musical tones to locations on paintings. We then *listened to people looking at pictures* (they couldn't hear the tones, which we added later). Adding the soundtrack made a huge difference. When spots appeared on the computer screen— one for each saccade—it was almost impossible to detect patterns in successive subjects' responses to a painting. Add the sound and you got melodies of sorts, with rhythms, easily distinguishable and even memorable. We had to recalibrate the eye tracker often, and because we didn't want the subjects to be self-conscious about their saccades, we used the recalibration process as a fake experiment, telling the subjects that while we tinkered with the equipment they could just relax and look at some pictures, which was when the actual data-gathering happened. But it was an inefficient process; furthermore, the student who was doing most of the work graduated, so we would have had to start over with more subjects and more assistants. The experiment was consigned to the file drawer, but my belief is that there are lots of revealing experiments, on vision, on attention, on the role of color and shape in entraining saccades, that this paradigm could fruitfully explore, and eye trackers are more sensitive, reliable, and user-friendly these days, so I hope these avenues are pursued.

One of the early readers of *Consciousness Explained* was Euan Baird, the CEO of Schlumberger, the global energy-technology company. He thought the book had lessons about corporations as well as consciousness—breaking down the myth of the Central Boss who controlled everything—and he bought dozens of copies and sent them to all the heads of the various branches of Schlumberger around the world. He also invited me to give a talk about it at two of the annual meetings of these company leaders. The first was in Paris. I had never been invited to speak to such an audience and thought I was driving a hard bargain when I asked for $10,000 for each talk, first-class airfare, and a new Mac computer on which I would demonstrate some of the phenomena I had written about in my book. He agreed on the spot, and as soon as the Mac was delivered to me, I took it over to Patrick Cavanagh's vision lab at Harvard, and he helped me devise the software I needed, using the excellent Macglib software they had developed. A few hours in his lab in William James Hall left me with stunningly effective demos of two phenomena I had described at some length in my book: *color phi* and *metacontrast*. If you display two red shapes one after another, with one displaced a smallish amount, you get a standard *phi* phenomenon: apparent motion with a single red shape moving—this is how movies work, of course. What if you change the color of the shape? Does the *phi* phenomenon go away, or does the "moving" shape also change color, and if so, does it change before it moves, after it moves, or during the move? If you get the timing and distance apart just right, it changes color in the middle of its (illusory) trajectory! The puzzle for many people was: How does the brain know where and when to change the color of the illusory shape when it hasn't yet perceived the second image? Thanks to the versatile software Patrick made for me, I could adjust the display in real time while I showed it to whatever audience was present. I could change the distance apart and the timing of the appearance of the different colored shapes—disks, in fact—so that in a large amphitheater the people in the back got the effect at one setting and the people in the front got the effect at another setting. (The colors and the direction of the motion were also adjustable, ruling out "practice effects" that could possibly explain the brain's ability to "precognize" the direction and color of the illusion it was creating. There was no precognition, of course, but explaining the effect without resorting to such revolutionary hypotheses was the path forward.)

The metacontrast demo was, if anything, even more spectacular: in metacontrast, a first stimulus (an image of a disk, say) is followed immediately by a second image (an image of a ring shape that fits around where the disk was—see figure 6.1 in *Consciousness Explained*, p. 141), and when you get the timing right the first stimulus simply disappears; subjects report seeing only the ring! Their memories of seeing the disk are wiped clean, it seems. In the demo, there were two disks, left and right, flashing in unison, and a single ring to the right. At slow speeds, both disks were visible, followed immediately by the single ring on the right. As I adjusted the speed up, the disk on the right simply disappeared: the disk on the left appeared clearly, while its twin (in size, color, and duration) vanished. I had great fun showing these demos to dozens of audiences, along with the Grimes video, and they clearly played a major role in enhancing my credibility as a consciousness theorist whom scientists should take seriously, inspiring a wave of experimentation around the world.

The BBC in the UK had a science program called *Antenna*, which presented controversial scientific views in well-produced opinion-documentaries with critics and responses included. They invited me to make an episode, which eventually was titled (over my strenuous objections) "Mind Movies," and it included comments from my friendly critics "Rama" Ramachandran and Igor Aleksander, an engineer/neuroscientist at Imperial College London. One of the design principles then reigning at the BBC was that science documentaries should be visually fascinating—they should minimize "talking heads" and maximize arresting scenes. In some ways, this was perfect for my documentary, since I got to show demonstrations of metacontrast and one of my favorite phenomena: the "room full of Marilyns" (*Consciousness Explained*, p. 354). If you walked into a room, turned on the lights, and saw that the walls were papered with identical large photos of, say, Marilyn Monroe, you would pick this up immediately, but here's a puzzle: You can recognize a person in a photograph only by foveating it (saccading to it so that the high-resolution part of your retina is aimed at it), but it would take many seconds to foveate many Marilyns. How does the brain manage to create your belief that all the Marilyns you see are identical images of the same person? It *seems* that your visual experience is high resolution all the way out to the periphery, but that is an illusion. I asked the BBC if we could include just such a scene in the documentary and they agreed. It ended up costing them hundreds of pounds to get permission to make and display about fifty huge photographs of Marilyn Monroe, which we carefully tacked up on three walls of a small art gallery at Tufts where parts of the documentary were filmed.

I was very happy with the result of that scene, but the BBC's thirst for visual interest backfired in other ways. The young producer filmed me riding at night through Boston in a taxi to a cinema, where she had me order a hot dog at the concession stand (in spite of my insistence that cinemas in the US didn't usually sell hot dogs). I was seen at the helm of a sailboat narrowly avoiding a buoy, walking inside the giant home computer I had helped design at Boston's Computer Museum, and strolling inside the "Mapparium," a giant inside-out glass globe map of the world as it was in 1935, a tourist attraction at Boston's world headquarters of the Christian Science religion, in the Mary Baker Eddy Library. This was all visually spectacular, but when I quizzed students and colleagues after they had seen the finished documentary, they remembered the settings vividly but couldn't recall what I had said! I discussed this issue with various media-savvy friends afterward, and we had fun imagining the satire of a BBC science documentary we could make, with Hans Krebs trying to explain the Krebs cycle while riding a wooden pony on a merry-go-round, Stephen Hawking in a miner's helmet talking about black holes while seated in his electric wheelchair at the bottom of a coal mine, and Watson and Crick hanging on for dear life to the rungs of a gigantic revolving DNA double helix. In the final editing, the producer of "Mind Movies" also cut a crucial qualifier from my response to Ramachandran, making nonsense of the exchange, so while it was another interesting adventure in filmmaking, I'm happy that it's *not* available on YouTube among a hundred or so other videos of me. I did, however, get one salutary challenge from the producer, which has influenced much of my later work. During our early meetings on the content to be presented, I showed her several diagrams of consciousness that had been published by scientists, and heaped criticism on them. "I get your objections," she said, "but where is *your* diagram of consciousness?" This led me to develop a series of diagrams, with moving parts, that I used whenever I presented my theory in talks. This was before PowerPoint, so I had "overhead transparencies" that could be moved and layered, and my talks were much more effective as a result. I once gave a very formal lecture in the Netherlands and my host introduced me by saying, "Professor Dennett will be accompanying himself on the overhead projector." I miss them; there are some effects that are more vividly achieved by sliding transparencies over each other than by animating the effect with computer graphics.

~

MY DESIRE TO MAKE my book accessible and interesting to scientists had a few negative side effects. Some philosophers of mind decided that I had abandoned philosophy for science—or worse, science journalism—and could therefore be ignored. Others were all too comfortable accepting the partisan misrepresentations that soon appeared. A few, however, joined the fray with enthusiasm.

Two stand out for their indefatigable efforts to show me wrong: Ned Block and David Chalmers.

Ned had been one of the original participants in the Vicious Circle that Fodor and I started in 1973, and I have been sparring with him ever since. He sat in on my seminar at Tufts that went through the penultimate-draft chapters of *Consciousness Explained*, and his vigorous objections to my views on qualia persuaded me to include a chapter, "Qualia Disqualified," in the final draft. In it I patiently (if grudgingly) marched through all the problems I saw with the misbegotten concept of qualia, but it wasn't enough, of course. Ned has unstintingly pursued his campaign to preserve the intuitively pleasing but hopelessly muddled idea of properties of subjective experiences (otherwise known as *qualia* or *phenomenal properties*), and he has had lots of company. For several years, he published critiques to which I responded—with growing impatience, alas. Eventually I decided that Ned was immovable, so I moved on to other issues, while Ned persisted with his campaign about phenomenal consciousness, creating the impression in some quarters, I gather, that I had conceded. No, I had just decided that debating him had diminishing returns. Perhaps my forbearance is working, at least a little bit; I think we're getting closer. In *Consciousness Explained* I had asked:

> What could it be that is *present* when one "hears" sounds filling silent times or "sees" colors spanning empty spaces? It does seem that something is there in these cases, something the brain has to provide (by "filling in"). What should we call this unknown whatever-it-is? Let's call it *figment*. (p. 346)

I thought this deliberately jocular term would dissuade anybody from taking it seriously, and I heaped scorn on it, but over the years a number of researchers have confessed to me that they were inclined to believe in figment in spite of what I'd said! And Ned more recently (2003) bit the bullet and wrote about "mental paint," but when he recognized the precariousness of this claim he added, in a later paper,

I am not assuming that if there is mental paint, it is non-relational ("intrinsic") or has no representational aspect. Since I favor physicalism, I allow that mental paint may be a relational neural property. To avoid misunderstanding: I do not claim that there is anything red or round in the head when one veridically sees a red or round thing in the world as when red pigment in a painting represents a red barn.

I'm not sure what Ned means by "a relational neural property," but it seems to me that he is coming around to my view that *virtual* paint (and virtual noise and virtual odors, etc.) can play all the roles needed in the brain's virtual machines that compose our consciousness. I was also lured into yet another round against the fans of phenomenal consciousness by my former student Michael A. Cohen in 2011, and we were joined by Nancy Kanwisher in 2016; not surprisingly, our coauthored papers have not wrung any concessions from Ned. If he ever did admit I was right after all, I'd worry about his health.

I've known David Chalmers since he was a graduate student of Doug Hofstadter's at Indiana University (see chapter 15). Neither Doug nor I were persuaded by his arguments (made famous in his 1995 paper "Facing Up to the Problem of Consciousness" and his subsequent book, *The Conscious Mind: In Search of a Fundamental Theory* [1996]), but I have to admit that he has been a scrupulous student of the relevant literature, unusually alert to the risks of misinterpretation, and an ingenious and systematic explorer of what he has deemed, for good reason, to be an exhaustive list of the worthy possibilities. I just think his own view is bonkers! He thinks that he has isolated "the" Hard Problem about consciousness while I think he has overlooked the possibility that the solutions to all the "easy" problems will sum to dissolve his Hard Problem. Over the years, I've debated him in person and wrestled with him in print quite often. One of my responses in print to his ever-so-careful and exhaustive arguments was a parody of his philosophical scrupulosity. In 2010, he published an essay, "The Singularity," in the *Journal of Consciousness Studies*, rather like a target article in *BBS*, and I was one of the invited respondents. Since I think the topic is an embarrassment to philosophy—just the sort of angels-dancing-on-the-head-of-a-pin game I can't stand—I declined, but he sent me a further email:

> hi dan,
> take a look at the paper. somehow i suspect that you'll have plenty to say. some of the core issues here concern the structure of intelligence/design space, topics that you've thought pretty hard about.
> cheers,
> dave

And since I respect Chalmers's judgment, I relented and read the essay. My essay in response, "The Mystery of David Chalmers" (*Journal of Consciousness Studies*, 2012), uncovered seven alternative hypotheses about what was driving him on in this dubious battle: Faith, Fame, Freud, Fiction, Filosofia, Fun, and Fear. More recently, I have accepted yet another invitation to respond—to his 2018 essay in the same journal on what he calls the meta-problem of consciousness; and my answer, "Welcome to Strong Illusionism" (2019), points out how *very* close Dave's view is, now, to my own. I hold out more hope of persuading Chalmers to join forces with me than I do of Ned Block, but both of them have managed to build their public personae around their positions, so I am not holding my breath.

24.

THE TURING TEST AS MORE THAN A THOUGHT EXPERIMENT

ALAN TURING PUBLISHED HIS CLASSIC ARTICLE, "COMputing Machinery and Intelligence," in *Mind* in 1950, introducing the famous Imitation Game, now known as the Turing test. I've been thinking and speaking and writing about it for about sixty years, and my latest essay is forthcoming in a volume from the Santa Fe Institute on the classic papers of complexity theory. In 1981 I began my interminable wrangle with John Searle (see chapter 15) about his Chinese Room "refutation" of the Turing test, and in "Can Machines Think?" (1985) I defended it as the best way of testing for genuine thinking. In 1990 Hugh Loebner, a New York manufacturer, had put up the money for a prize—a bronze medal and $100,000—for the first computer program to pass the Turing test fair and square, and induced the Cambridge Center for Behavioral Studies, headed by psychologist Robert Epstein, one of Skinner's disciples, to form a committee to design and conduct the first *restricted* Turing test competition. No program then on the horizon could come close to passing the unrestricted test—the only test that is of any theoretical interest at all—but it would be a good idea to debug the rules and get some experience with actual tests, so to make the competition interesting during the early years, the committee adopted some restrictions and the award for winning the restricted test was dropped to $2,000. The initial committee that drew up the rules was Epstein, Van Quine, Allen Newell, Joe Weizenbaum,

Harvard computer scientist Harry Lewis, and Oliver Strimpel, the director of Boston's Computer Museum, and they added me to the committee, as chair, after the rules were drawn up. I wished I had been on the committee from the outset, because I would have fought to change the rules, which favored the computer programs too much, but the announcement had already been made and contestants were applying. The conversations were limited to specific topics ("Shakespeare," "problems with romantic relationships," "burgundy wine") and judges were instructed *not* to probe aggressively but just engage in friendly conversation, as you might with a stranger sitting next to you on a plane!

The first annual Loebner Prize competition was held in Boston at the Computer Museum in 1991, with me presiding over a crowd of journalists and television crews from around the world, who could watch the action on overhead monitors, while ten judges shuffled from terminal to terminal, each spending fifteen minutes in typed conversation with each contestant. Six of the ten contestants were programs, four were human "confederates" behind the scenes. Each judge had to rank-order all ten terminals from most human to least human. The winner of the restricted test would be the computer with the highest mean rating. The winning program would not have to fool any of the judges, nor would fooling a judge be in itself grounds for winning; highest mean ranking was all. But just in case some program did fool a judge, we thought this fact should be revealed, so judges were required to draw a line somewhere across their rank ordering, separating the humans from the machines. We on the prize committee knew the low quality of the contesting programs that first year, and it seemed obvious to us that no program would be so lucky as to fool a single judge, but on the day of the competition, I got nervous. Just to be safe, I thought, we should have some certificate prepared to award to any programmer who happened to pull off this unlikely feat. While the press and the audience were assembling for the beginning of the competition, I rushed into a back room at the Computer Museum with a member of the staff and we cobbled up a handsome certificate with the aid of a handy desktop publisher. In the event, I had to hand out three of these certificates, for a total of seven positive misjudgments out of a possible sixty! The gullibility of the judges was simply astonishing to me, but not to Joe Weizenbaum, whose discovery of what is often called the ELIZA effect had led him to become an ardent critic of AI (see chapter 8). When the judges sat back passively, *as instructed*, and let the contestants lead them, they were readily taken in by the Potemkin villages on offer, and so were many of the journalists watching the monitors. Joseph Weintraub, whose program's topic was "whimsical conversation," won the first Loebner Prize by using a breathtakingly simple ploy. When asked a question, his program responded with a question of its own, which the judge politely and dutifully attempted to answer, leading to a further question, and so forth. Whenever the program ran out of questions to ask it randomly produced a canned witticism and gave the judge another opportunity to respond before asking a new question. The program, not the judge, controlled the conversation. None of the misjudgments counted as a real case of a computer passing the unrestricted Turing test, but they were still surprising to me. In the second year of the competition, we uncovered another unanticipated loophole: due to faulty briefing of the confederates, several of them gave deliberately clunky, automaton-like answers. It turned out that they had decided to give the silicon contestants a sporting chance by acting as if they were programs!

Once we'd straightened out these glitches in the rules and procedures, the competition worked out as I had originally predicted: the computers stood out like sore thumbs even though there were still huge restrictions on topic. For the third annual Loebner Prize competition, I enlisted some journalists as judges (people in computer science or AI were deemed ineligible for this role, alas) and warned them that their reputations as fact finders were on the line: if they mistook a program for a human being, it would be embarrassing news. Two of the journalists made a false negative judgment, declaring one of the less eloquent human confederates to be a computer.

On debriefing, their explanation showed just how vast the gulf was between the computer programs and the people: they reasoned that the competition *would not have been held* if there weren't at least one halfway decent computer contestant, so they simply picked the least impressive human being and declared *it* to be a computer. But they could see the gap between the computers and the people as well as everybody else could.

None of the major AI labs had participated in the Loebner Prize competitions, for good reason: losing to a hobby programmer would be devastating to a lab's reputation and it was clear that, given the rules, the winning entry would be a bag of cheap anthropomorphic tricks. In the first competition, several of the programs came equipped with simple typing subroutines that mistyped words and then went back and corrected these "telltale" errors. Others didn't bother. We allowed both kinds to compete as they were but told the judges (truly) that some of the confederates' answers would be "burst mode" (the whole corrected response coming at once) and others' answers would appear as they were typed. In consultation with some of the leaders in AI, I proposed some further rule changes. One was to adapt the system (that had just been abandoned!) in ice-skating competitions: "school figures." Contestants must first do well on compulsory moves, strictly described standard tests of each competitor, with only the top winners in that competition passing on to the crowd-pleasing freestyle performances. We could institute a set of school figures to separate the serious contenders from the cheap tricksters. For instance, in *Understanding Natural Language* (1972), AI pioneer Terry Winograd had drawn attention to pairs of sentences that differed in a single word that changed the good interpretation of a pronoun:

1. The city council members denied the group a parade permit because they advocated violence.
2. The city council members denied the group a parade permit because they feared violence.

Both readings of the pronoun "they" are always legal. Thus, we can imagine a world in which city council members in charge of parade permits advocate violence in the streets and, for some strange reason, use this as their pretext for denying a parade permit. But the natural, reasonable, intelligent reading of the first sentence is that it's the group that advocated violence, and of the second, that it's the city council members that feared violence. A contestant would have to have a vast store of "world knowledge" to make the right interpretation. Other such challenges could keep the hobbyists out of the arena. Loebner refused to allow the change, so I resigned from the committee, along with several other members in the AI community. The Loebner Prize competition among chatbots continued for almost thirty years, going defunct after a last-gasp competition in 2019 at Bletchley Park, where Turing did his brilliant work during World War II. It never attracted any serious contenders and was generally dismissed by the AI community as a publicity stunt at best.

But now, in 2022, the Turing test is back at the center of attention riding on the wave of enthusiasm for "deep-learning" AI, following in the triumphant wake of DeepMind's AlphaGo and AlphaZero, which used deep-learning methods to beat the world's best human Go players. Billions of dollars have been invested by Google and others in creating databases with billions or even trillions of verbal entries, sucked off the internet and analyzed by powerful pattern-finding algorithms, the grandchildren of the connectionist networks of the 1980s. Systems such as OpenAI's GPT-3 (Generative Pre-trained Transformer) and Google's LaMDA (Language Model for Dialogue Applications) can do eerily well at holding their own in a conversation or answering difficult questions (correctly, usually!). When Google engineer Blake Lemoine declared on June 19, 2022, that he was persuaded by conversations with LaMDA that it was sentient, the AI community responded vigorously with dissent. Here was yet another case of the ELIZA effect. What are the implications of these new developments?

274 / I've Been Thinking

I have entered the fray thanks to Anna Strasser, a German philosopher who came to the Center for Cognitive Studies as a visiting fellow in 2018. She and philosopher Eric Schwitzgebel have, with my permission, trained GPT-3 on almost all my published works—well over a million words—to create DigiDan (Steve Barney's name for it), which (*not "who"!*) can answer interview questions addressed to me about my work and beliefs with uncanny verisimilitude and accuracy. Anna asked me ten questions about central ideas in my work, and I answered them—without any dissembling, unlike the confederates in year two of the Loebner Prize competition. Then she asked the same questions of DigiDan four times, and (without cherry-picking) took all five answers and put them to hundreds of judges online, who were asked to pick the genuine Dennett answer from the set of five and also to rank all five answers in how "like what Dennett would say" each answer was. She also invited several dozen "Dennett experts" (philosophers or cognitive scientists who have read more than a thousand pages of Dennett, or been colleagues or coauthors of mine) to take the test, and another group of philosophers and philosophy students.

The results are surprising, at least at first glance. Even the "Dennett experts" were lured into choosing at least two DigiDan answers, averaging a little over 5 out of 10 right (which is still way above chance, given five choices; chance is about 1.2 right). The naïve judges were just about at chance, which was expected, since they were really just guessing. The more philosophy training you had, the better you did, which is a relief for me to learn, and the mistaken choices by the experts were almost all DigiDan answers that I actually approved—though none of them quite won the hallowed "I wish I'd said that" award. There is much, much more I want to say about the DigiDan experiment, which in fact has inspired me to start writing a new paper on one of my long-term head-scratchers: How do we form speech acts? In *Consciousness Explained* I ventured some hunches about "how words do things to us" that contrasted *bureaucratic* models, which have a Central Meaner—a kind of CEO—at the top, with *pandemonium* models, where many agents scramble and compete to get themselves into speech acts, but while I was all in favor of pandemonium, I could only wave my hands about how it might work. DigiDan outputs are well-formed English sentences, but it can be easily unmasked if you know what you're doing. If DigiDan doesn't understand anything (and it doesn't) it surely has a lot of competence without comprehension. Could the *sort* of competence it has also be the sort of competence some part of your brain has when it somehow contributes to framing an actual speech act, *expressing* a belief, *asking* a question, *entertaining* a hypothesis? GPT-3 has been dismissed by computational linguist Emily Bender as a "stochastic parrot," but in fact, the random candidates it generates are very nonrandomly filtered by all the patterns the system has detected and used to adjust its connections. Suppose it fed its uncomprehended outputs to a . . . *cherry-picker* that could swiftly discard the junk and home in on a few more-promising candidates, and suppose that cherry-picker sent its winners to *another* cherry-picker which (not "who") could make a few mutations and pass the products on to yet another round of cherry-picking? In short, couldn't there be a Darwinian mutation-and-selection cascade that turned uncomprehending competence into (*sorta*) comprehending competence? And suppose all of this is largely unconscious processing—except when we're being particularly careful with our speech acts, deliberately checking them and rechecking them for "what we want to say."

DigiDan could already be used *by me* as a generator of possible ways of putting things that I could then edit and revise, confident that I would not be wasting my time on irrelevant babble because of its competence. The composer/computer programmer David Cope created his EMI (Experiments in Musical Intelligence) as a tool to help him compose music when his muse was napping, and now, with a little more fiddling and improving, Anna Strasser may provide me with a highly efficient wordmonger tool that will suggest ways to me of putting my own convictions better! I can say at this point that this is not yet—in 2022—a tool I can use, and I haven't used it (so far) in writing this book. But stay tuned.*

Large Language Models (LLMs) have developed so fast that I have had difficulty keeping up. Several claims made on the previous page need to be tempered, as Doug Hofstadter has urged me. I say on p. 275 that DigiDan can easily be unmasked, but already its successors cannot. I say it doesn't understand, but it *sorta* understands (see my *Intuition Pumps*, pp. 96–97, for a defense of this post-Darwinian thinking tool). Keith Frankish ("Some thoughts on LLMs," November 2, 2022) described LLMs as playing "the chat game" the way chess programs play chess. They have a single fixed intention: win the chat game. If you try to understand *how* they go about winning, the intentional stance will give you a good but risky tactic for interpreting the counterfeit people they create. It's complicated. (See my "The Problem with Counterfeit People," *The Atlantic*, May 16, 2023.)

25.

ADVENTURES WITH ROBOTS: THE WHOLE IGUANA, COG, AND TATI

"WHY NOT THE WHOLE IGUANA?" WAS A LITTLE 750-word comment I published in *Behavioral and Brain Sciences* way back in 1978. Noting that everybody in AI knew that they had to rely in those early days on simple "toy" models, I suggested that instead of achieving tractable simplicity by modeling human micro-competences, such as playing chess or answering questions about moon rocks, they should get their simplicity by modeling a whole imaginary simple self-protective animal—a three-wheeled Martian iguana, for instance. I suggested that whatever design features they uncovered in that simple exercise would likely prove to be central features of the design of more fancy creatures.

Before the Australian roboticist Rodney Brooks, at the AI lab at MIT, got the idea to build Cog, the humanoid robot, he had made his mark in the robotics world with insect-like robots—with legs, not wheels—that scurried around rather mindlessly but with remarkable agility, thanks to the "subsumption architecture" controlling them. These would be ideal early planet explorers, he suggested. Instead of sending intelligent, expensive, fragile human explorers to Mars, send lots of simple, mobile information-gatherers and let them wander— a proposal he detailed in a 1989 paper, "Fast, Cheap and Out of Control." A few of these autonomous robots would make important discoveries, which they could radio back to Earth, and all would die like flies eventually. (Their direct descendant is the Roomba, a

278 / I've Been Thinking

robot vacuum that was a commercial spinoff from these scientific explorations.) Rod was not alone; a small cadre of roboticists around the world took my message to heart and began working on designing the whole iguana. A general term for these robot creatures was "animats," and a journal, *Adaptive Behavior*, was started in 1992 in which many of the pioneer efforts were published. In the summer of 2000, an international workshop was organized by the roboticists David McFarland at Oxford and Owen Holland at the University of Essex to take place on the island of Lanzarote in the Canaries and titled "Towards the Whole Iguana." Nobody brought along any robot iguanas, but there was lots of videotape, and a bounty of ideas.

Lanzarote is one of the strangest places I've ever been. It rarely rains on this barren pile of volcanic rocks, but the natives grow grapes and make wine. At night, when the temperature drops, dew forms and is blown by the prevailing wind into C-shaped dew-corrals, about two meters across, that have covered the hillsides for generations. The dew drips down into a central cone, where a small grapevine grows. Much of what is fascinating on Lanzarote is underground, but there are also fine beaches, where hundreds of beautiful young Nordic sunbathers vacation. The contrasts are distracting, but we spent most of our waking hours discussing robots, from the pioneering "tortoises" of William Grey Walter in the late 1940s to Brooks's six-legged Genghis in 1989, and including Holland's SlugBot (designed to gather, digest, and live off the energy produced by the slug pests that flourished during the no-plowing experimental grain fields of the '80s) and Steve Grand's amazing Norns (furry machine-learners from his video game *Creatures*).

Cog

Before turning to the engineering of industrial robots, Rod Brooks had taken a daring stab in 1993, leaping from insectoid control systems to a computational architecture for a humanoid robot named

Cog. He invited me to join the team at the AI lab, on the top floors of the Tech Square building in Cambridge. Rod subscribed to the central idea of *Consciousness Explained*, which is that there is no "Cartesian Theater" wherein the results of all our mental processing are somehow *presented* to an Inner Witness in a special show. What is there instead are "multiple drafts" of content, which vie for influence, with some achieving something like "fame in the brain" and the rest evaporating unheralded and unrecorded. (It is amazing to me how seductive the idea of a Cartesian Theater still is, in spite of decades of patient diagnoses by me and others of the errors involved in thinking of consciousness as a sort of movie, with a soundtrack, odors, itches, pains, and caresses piped in for the homunculus who gets to *appreciate* it all somehow.) Rod was one thinker who got the point immediately, and he had no difficulty attracting me to join the Cog team, claiming that he and his grad students wanted to implement the Multiple Drafts model of consciousness in their robot. What a delicious invitation! How would I like to help some of the smartest young computer scientists in the world come up with an implementation of my ideas? The problems confronting Rod's group in the early going were a long way from the Multiple Drafts model, but they were fascinating and important in their own ways.

Before Cog, robots moved "robotically," in a jerky "mechanical" way, but Cog, thanks to the "series elastic actuators" in its arms and the swift responses it made with its eyes and head when something of interest showed up, was uncannily human in its reactions to simple things. Philosophers had been posing arguments for decades about what could and should persuade you to think of robots as conscious if you ever got close to one, but I don't think any of them recognized that the more pressing and immediate problem would be convincing folks that *this* robot, Cog, was *not* conscious. As you walked into the room where Cog lived (it was stationary, with no legs, just a torso, arms, and a head), Cog would catch sight of you, and its eyes would follow you as you walked by. When Alan Alda was making a *Scientific American* documentary about Cog, he started asking Rod a question while they were standing with Cog between them, and Cog turned and looked at Alan so briskly and "intelligently" that he was left speechless. Another time, I took one of my Tufts teaching assistants to the Cog lab so she could see what was going on. One of Cog's arms had been detached from its torso and was clamped to a workbench while Matthew Williamson, its designer, was working on it. The arm was ON, and Matt invited her to shake hands with it. She did—and screamed "It's alive!" because the hand that grasped hers was compliant, gentle but strong, just like the hand of a living person. Very quickly, the Cog project had a problem with MIT students intent on demonstrating on behalf of Cog's rights. Here is one substantive message to extract from this tale: Don't trust your "intuitions"! Our convictions about what is alive and what isn't, what is conscious and what isn't, are easily provoked and manipulated. Think of it this way: If oysters had a smiley-face pattern when you opened them, and seemed to have two eyespots with long, blinking eyelashes, few people would be willing to eat them. In fact, if apples had chubby childish faces, complete with dimples, they would disconcert even the vegans.

I once attended an international workshop on "cognitive robotics"

Cog

hosted by British Telecom. I was representing the Cog team, because
Rod was otherwise committed. The enticement was millions of
pounds of research money to go to those with the best ideas. Why on
earth did British Telecom want to spend lots of money on robotics? It
turned out that they had several quite independent reasons. First, they
had come to realize that their vast networks of communication and
control, built and rebuilt over many years, with many insufficiently
recorded fixes and adjustments, were simply not comprehensible *by
anybody*. (This is not an unusual feature of huge computer systems.
Joe Weizenbaum scared the dickens out of me back in 1973 by telling
me that the software controlling the DEW line—the Defense Early
Warning radar system arrayed across northern Canada—was utterly
incomprehensible to its operators. I told him I was not a big fan of
military spending but I guessed I would support the cost of building
a new system alongside the old and then discarding the old system.
He replied that many had thought of doing that, but nobody knew
what the *specs* of the system were, so it would be impossible to be sure
that they were met. The DEW system was ultimately abandoned.)
British Telecom had the off-the-wall idea that if the roboticists could
build a humanoid robot that could communicate comprehensively
with human beings, virtual (software-only) versions of it could be set
loose to prowl the BT network, identifying problems and explaining them to human operators. (Shades of the great British sci-fi satire
Max Headroom, in which a human being becomes disembodied and
lives on the internet, solving crimes.) Their other concern was lead. It
turns out that hundreds or maybe thousands of miles of underground
conduit had been installed by British Telecom over the years, and
somebody had had the bright idea that shielding the wires in them
with lead would protect them. Over the years, the lead had sagged
onto the wires, preventing them from being pulled through the conduits and replaced when needed. Could the roboticists design a sort
of mole robot that could prowl through the conduits, chomping its
way carefully through the lead without cutting any wires, or at least
guiding human repair people to the points needing special attention?

It became clear that even with the prospect of millions of pounds of support dangling in front of them, nobody could say with a straight face that they could build the Max Headroom robot that could save British Telecom from its puzzlement. And while a lead-chomping mole was not out of the question—in a uniform and restricted artificial environment, with manufactured surfaces, and right angles almost everywhere—nobody, so far as I know, seriously took up the challenge. Here was a case where hype and science fiction had come back to haunt the roboticists. I learned a lot there from the evolutionary robotics group at Sussex, represented by Inman Harvey and Dave Cliff, but otherwise it was a lesson in misplaced hopes.

Tati

A year or so before my Schlumberger jaunt, I gave a lecture in Paris, and while strolling around on the Île de la Cité I spotted a marvelous robotic dog in the window of an antique shop. It had a paper rose in its teeth, and it was love at first sight. The shop specialized in antiques from the '50s—giant hairdryers and early MixMasters, for instance—and I did my best to inquire about a number of different *objets*, not wanting to reveal my adoration for the doggie in the window. I did ask its price, which was out of my range at the time (about $2,500), and I took the shopkeeper's card and left. As soon as I got home, I called Oliver Strimpel, then the director of Boston's Computer Museum, where I had helped design a major exhibit, to see if the museum would be interested in purchasing it or had any deep-pocketed supporters who might be tempted to buy it and donate it. No, the museum, which was having financial difficulties, could not acquire anything (and soon closed, sad to say).

When I flew back to France to speak to Schlumberger's executives, equipped with my new Mac and demo software and with my handsome fee glowing in my mind, I resumed my quest. I had a free morning in Versailles, where the meeting was taking place in a grand hotel, and the Schlumberger person responsible for my care asked how I would like to spend the time. Would I like to be driven (by limousine, of course) into Paris for some sightseeing? I pulled out the card and asked him to call the antique shop and ask if they still had a robotic dog for sale. He called the number, the shopkeeper answered, and after he discreetly asked the question she responded, "Are you calling for the tall American with the beard?" So much for my poker face! But in fact my failure to cloak my desire was the secret key to success. She and her husband had been inspired by my obvious interest and had taken the dog home and put it on their own hearth. But she *would* sell it to the lovestruck American with the beard at the price she had given me. She would call her husband and have him bring it to the shop, so off we went to Paris in the limousine, which I asked to park around the corner, just in case she changed her mind about the price.

There was the doggie, just as I'd remembered it. I wrote a check on the spot, and the shopkeeper promised she'd send it to my hotel, all Bubble Wrapped, by the next morning, well before my return flight to Boston. I named it Tati in honor of Jacques Tati, the great French comic filmmaker, whose classic *Mon Oncle* (1958) satirizes the French enthusiasm for modernistic design and gadgetry. Tati would have been a superb character in that gently comic film.

That night at the elegant dinner in the hotel, I was brought a telephone; the lady from the shop was calling me. Uh-oh, I thought.

Tati

Did my check bounce? But she was calling just to make sure that I wouldn't take Tati apart, wouldn't destroy him for any reason; she too had fallen in love with the dog and wanted to be sure he was going to a good home. I assured her I had every intention of preserving Tati for posterity, and she expressed her great relief. The next morning, Tati arrived, with his carrying handle outside the taped-up Bubble Wrap and a smile and eyes drawn on his wrapped face. When I got to the airport and checked in—first-class, of course—Tati went through the scanner and looked truly alarming in the X-ray image, with wires and switches and batteries showing. I figured I'd have to unwrap the whole thing and would never manage to get it neatly taped back up. "Qu'est-ce que c'est?" asked the security guard. "C'est un chien électromécanique," I replied stone-faced. "Intéressant," he said and waved me on.

Who had made Tati, and when? The shopkeeper had given me a little book by Albert Ducrocq, a celebrated science presenter on French television in the '60s. He had made and shown some simple robots and written about them, and she thought he might be the creator. Not a chance, I realized, when I read the book. Tati was a confection conceived by an obsessive and imaginative tinkerer, with elements Rube Goldberg would have admired. There was a timer composed of a series of bimetallic strips from thermostats; an electric current would heat them up one after another until a solenoid would turn on. The speed at which this happened was modulated by a tiny electric fan, which could blow cooling air over the strips to slow the process down. There were several motors, one of them from a Citroën Deux Chevaux windshield wiper. A toggle switch of unknown function was Tati's epiglottis, and five small aluminum canisters arrayed on his rump were simple light detectors that permitted Tati to be controlled by a flashlight. Tati perhaps had had a coat of some kind originally, but he was more fascinating skinned, revealing hundreds of wires and switches cunningly packed into his body with tiny bolts holding it all together.

I posted some photos of Tati on my website, offering a reward for information about Tati's maker and history. I have received dozens of tips over the years, mostly suggesting that Tati is (a relative of) K9, the robotic dog in *Doctor Who*, the long-running British television series, but Tati predates K9 by some years. In 2001, just before I went to Paris to give the Jean Nicod Lectures, I received an email, putatively from the beautiful French film star Sophie Duez, telling me that she knew Tati's history. It had been commissioned by Prince Louis de Broglie, the Nobel laureate physicist, as a gift to his granddaughter in Paris. When the granddaughter fell on hard times, she sold it to the antique dealer. I asked for more information and Sophie said she was working on it. I replied that I would be giving a series of lectures in Paris in a few months and would be happy to meet her and learn more from her research, but then I began to receive emails from her with nude photographs of herself, and it became quite clear that somebody was address-spoofing these emails, which were very likely not from Sophie Duez, alas. I told my hosts in Paris all about this, and at each lecture I noticed them scanning the audience on the off chance that she might make an appearance.

To throw some cold water on the de Broglie story: he was a bachelor, but maybe he had a grandniece. Several diligent researchers have so far failed to uncover any more information about Tati, who was clearly made in France in the late '50s and will reside in some museum eventually.

With the help of Logo inventor and AI pioneer Seymour Papert, who lived down the road about a mile from our farm in Blue Hill, I attempted to reverse engineer Tati. This was a job requiring patience, a very delicate hand, and knowledge of circuit design. The chief problem was that Tati's color-coded wiring was so old and brittle that we didn't dare pull any of the wires out of their home terminals and had to resort to using dentists' mirrors and similar devices to peer noninvasively into Tati's interior. I searched for and eventually found sets of miniature metric socket wrenches we could use to loosen all the nuts and bolts. Tati is powered by two motorcycle batteries that fit into a metal box on his backside, but we used a 12-volt

286 / I've Been Thinking

converter plugged into house current to power Tati while we tested hundreds of hypotheses.

The dozens of switches made for a combinatorial explosion of possibilities, and although Seymour and I made some modest progress, most of their functions remain unknown, in spite of a few tiny labels in French. I built a sort of rotisserie-spit stand in which we could clamp Tati so we could turn him upside down without risking any damage, but we found it just as good to turn him over on an old sleeping bag on the dining room table. There was an electric auto horn of sorts on Tati's underbelly, and we spent hours trying to short-circuit the wires to make it beep, but never found the right connection of switches. Once, when we were getting Tati to roll across the floor guided from behind by a flashlight, we heard an ominous clunk, and Tati stopped moving. Something—a cam or connecting rod or some gadget deep in Tati's interior—had come loose and was the proverbial wrench in the works. Tati sat silently on our kitchen floor for several years, and my young grandson Brandon, about six years old, was fascinated by him but did his best to follow my strict command that he look but not touch. One day when I was up in my study, I heard him shout, "Grampy, come quick! Tati's come alive!" I rushed downstairs to discover Tati not moving but going "woof, woof" about every ten seconds. Brandon had somehow found the sequence of toggle switches that turned on the auto horn. I tried shutting it off by more or less randomly hitting switches, but Tati kept on woofing. I finally pulled a wire off one of the motorcycle batteries, and he has been quiet ever since.

26.

SEYMOUR PAPERT AND MARVIN MINSKY

I KNEW THE HISTORY OF MARVIN MINSKY AND SEYMOUR Papert's *Perceptrons* (1969, revised and expanded 1987) before I met either of them. The book was a monograph proving mathematically that a certain restricted set of neural networks (roughly, the psychologist Frank Rosenblatt's "perceptrons," from 1957) could not solve certain presumably simple problems. This had the effect of squelching enthusiasm for neural networks for a couple of decades and was regarded by many as, if not a dirty trick, at best a low blow in one of the first wars for funding that have energized AI researchers ever since.

Shortly after I published *Brainstorms* in 1978, Papert published *Mindstorms* (1980), and I first thought it was a pretty lame bit of title-hijacking until I learned from Jane Isay, editor of *The Mind's I* at Basic Books, that Seymour's book had been in press, on the verge of publication, with the title *Brainstorms* when mine came out, scooping him. I thought he would probably never be a friend of mine after that, but in fact Seymour decided that his book was not really about the brain but about the mind and that an association between our two titles was not a bad thing. He was a great and generous thinker, whose friendship Susan and I treasured for years until his death in 2016 after a ten-year attempt to recover from a devastating accident: he was hit by a motorcycle while crossing a street in Hanoi in 2006, while attending an international conference on mathematics education.

Seymour was an excellent cook, and there is (or was) a specialty shop in New York City that carried the widest imaginable variety of mushrooms. Seymour had been inspired by the place to plan a meal that was all mushrooms—mushrooms that were like cheese, mushrooms that were like nothing else on earth, mushrooms that were like steak and vegetables, and even mushrooms that could pass for a strange sort of chocolate cake for dessert. I was one of the lucky guests, and the conversation around the table was even more interesting than the food.

An example that sticks in my mind of Seymour's inquisitive imagination is a story he told me about how, during his time in London at the National Physical Laboratory, he had suffered a mild injury that kept him in the hospital for a time, but ambulatory. He volunteered to push the tea wagon around, serving tea to patients and staff alike. He was curious about the insistence by many English folk that you pour the milk in the cup first and then the tea, and he decided to test them to see if they could tell the difference. They could! (Or at least many of them could.) What were they sensing? Opportunistically, he decided to try for a simple, low-budget test first: he smeared some tea of both varieties on glass slides and put them under a microscope. Eureka! The tea poured into milk exhibited tiny globules of milk partly cooked by the hot tea; the milk poured into tea had long stringy strands of cooked milk. Mystery solved.

I spent a fair amount of time at MIT's AI lab on the top floors of the Tech Square building in Cambridge and had seen little kids on the floor in one big room where huge sheets of paper were taped down and a robotic "turtle" with a felt pen that it raised or lowered was rolling around drawing spirals and triangles and nested boxes of all sorts. This was the Logo turtle, and Seymour was seeing how kids responded to the computer language he had devised just for them. I fell in love with Logo and used it very effectively in teaching an introductory course in computer science at Tufts (see chapter 19 on Big George and the Curricular Software Studio). What was designed for six-year-olds turned out to be perfect for computerphobic freshmen in 1982, and Seymour and I traded reflections on Logo's powers for years. One game he invented was "broken Logo": Suppose one of Logo's basic instructions is "broken"—unavailable for use. Can you write a Logo program that replaces the basic instruction with one that has exactly the same powers? Yes, usually you can, but it's tricky.

When I first knew Seymour, he was married to Sherry Turkle, a sociologist and psychologist at MIT who had studied the French infatuation with Freud and was now turning her ethnographic attention to the emerging computer culture. She wrote her first book about computers, *The Second Self: Computers and the Human Spirit* (1984), using the AI lab's early code-editing system, Emacs, which was being turned into an early word processor, and when she was asked by her publisher to send in the computer file so that it could be fed to the typesetting system they were using, she asked for help from others in the lab. After these computer geniuses had devoted dozens of hours trying to devise a translator that would turn an Emacs file into something the publisher could use, they gave up and had a typist compose a usable file from a hard-copy printout. Sherry told me that Joe Weizenbaum was incensed. He was an avid collector of computer failures, so I suspect his anger was tempered with self-congratulation: another example of Artificial Stupidity.

Seymour later married Suzanne Massie, the author of several books on Russian culture and art. She had a family summer home on Deer Isle, Maine, and for a year-round home they moved into a glorious eighteenth-century farmhouse with a big barn in Blue Hill. Seymour turned the barn into the Learning Barn and developed wonderful programs for kids in Maine, inspiring Maine's Kings, the author Stephen King and Governor (later Senator) Angus King, to push through a program in 2000 that provides a laptop for every Maine child who enters seventh grade. This program has been successful, in spite of the fact that after his 2006 accident Seymour was unable to guide it in all the ways he had hoped. Seymour and Suzanne were frequent guests at our farmhouse, and we were introduced to great Russian cuisine at their farmhouse—caviar and blini and borscht and vodka from the freezer, and more. I remember one hike through our woods with Seymour. I thought I knew a lot about the species of trees and plants and animals there, but he found things I had overlooked. In a small quaking bog in our woods, he pointed out a carnivorous pitcher plant, for example.

After Seymour's accident, he was bedridden for a long time; he gradually recovered some of his physical powers, but there was a strange and terrible gap in his mind. He was left with language difficulties, which nonetheless allowed his warmth and enthusiasm and curiosity to shine through. When I visited, he recognized me with pleasure, and so I visited him whenever I was in Maine. After he died, I asked Suzanne and his loyal nurse Vicki if they knew what had happened to the videotapes we had made of our reverse-engineering efforts with Tati, but apparently they were discarded, sad to say.

~

MARVIN MINSKY WAS often described as the world's smartest five-year-old, and it wasn't usually meant as a criticism. "I can do anything!" might have been his unspoken conviction; he was confident, obstreperous, unruly, quick to pick a fight and quick to forget it. There was a curious inversion in the AI lab at MIT when I was hanging out there. Most academic disciplines include contingents that can be recognized as the Young Turks, who are revolutionary minded and impatient, and the Old Farts, who ask, "What ever happened to standards and proper procedures?" In the AI lab, there were the Old Turks—Minsky their champion—and the Young Farts, who asked, grumpily, "Where is the code?" and dismissed projects as "vaporware." One of the points of contention was Minsky's (in)-famous laboratory memo "A Framework for Representing Knowledge" (1974), a speculative leap of imagination into the problems of getting access to the right information in a timely and appropriate way in an intelligent agent. It was a sketch of a model, with no "implementation"—no running program or code—at all. Known by

everyone as "the frames paper," it was intensively discussed and criticized in the '70s and was the inspiration for several bold AI efforts.
As Minsky later stated (and I quote this in *Consciousness Explained*,
p. 262), "If the theory had been any vaguer, it would have been
ignored, but if it had been described in more detail, other scientists
might have 'tested' it, instead of contributing their own ideas." This
is the policy I followed in that book as well, with excellent results.
But Marvin's policy didn't always work well for him. Marvin had
thought a lot about humor, and Matthew Hurley and I (see chapter
28) had been influenced by some of his ideas. But when we went to
talk with Marvin about our model, he was strangely dismissive. I
may be wrong, but I think he was annoyed that he hadn't thought of
some of its enhancements himself.

Marvin's childlike enthusiasm was famously evident in his house
in Brookline. There was always something new in the cluttered living
room/dining room: robotic toys from all over the world, a gigantic
and unbelievably powerful magnet (which struck me as a dangerous
item to have in a house full of computer-controlled gadgets with
magnetic memory—you had to be careful where you walked), a life-
sized papier-mâché moose, a trapeze over the dining room table, a
huge wrench over the mantelpiece, two grand pianos, and stereo
recording equipment (with its two microphones in the ears of a plaster head on a mike stand, so that what was recorded was what would
be heard by a person standing in that very spot). I am happy to say
that this scene was perfectly captured by special large-format cameras and made into a mural that now covers the wall in the lobby of
the Media Lab at MIT. There are small versions of the photo on the
internet, but this mural is worth a visit if you come to MIT.

One day when I went to Marvin's house, he was on the phone and
beckoned me in, so I strolled around looking at the latest items while
he talked and talked. One that caught my attention was a new table
lamp, the base of which was an exquisitely complex antique brass
instrument of some kind—not a sextant or a microscope but perhaps
a clock or dividing engine or early calculator. I love the craftsman-

ship and ingenuity of the great precision-fabricators of the nineteenth century. (My pilgrimage to Greenwich to study John Harrison's first chronometer up close was the highlight of one trip to London.) The practice of "artifact hermeneutics"—reverse engineering a complex artifact to figure out what it was designed to do—is a hobby of mine, and I delved and poked and studied this lamp base for perhaps fifteen minutes while Marvin chatted. When he hung up, I turned to him and said, "I give up. What is it?" "It's a lamp base," he replied. A clockmaker/repairer friend of his had made him this nonsense machine as a joke, and I fell for it, hard. Marvin was delighted, of course. There's an old Chinese tale of a man who sits day after day with a fishing rod that has, instead of a hook, a straight pin. Needless to say, no fish are caught. The story of this strange fellow spreads far and wide, and when the emperor hears it he decides he has to check this out for himself. He travels to the riverbank where the man sits fishing and watches for a while. "What are you trying to catch?" he asks. "You, sire," replies the fisherman.

In 1979–80, when I was at the CASBS in Palo Alto (see chapter 15), we had a party for all the participants and their spouses at our house, and Marvin spotted the music on the piano: two collections of ragtime pieces, one a nearly complete Scott Joplin collection and a fine collection by the excellent ragtime pianist Max Morath. This was my ragtime phase. Marvin perused the collections for a few minutes and made a rather rude remark: "I see you like music that's *obvious.*" Indeed, ragtime is often gloriously obvious; that's part of its charm. I brushed off his comment, and several years later when I was in his living room in Brookline, I looked on one of the pianos and there were the same ragtime collections, clearly well used. He got it. I recall a jam session of sorts there with Doug Hofstadter playing Bach or Chopin on one piano and Marvin and me playing on the other, trying to integrate our noodling with his more disciplined music making.

I once invited Marvin to be a guest in a seminar on AI and human thinking I was teaching at Tufts, and when he showed up, he began saying outrageous things. The students sat in awe and listened, but said nothing, so he doubled down and said even more outrageous things. He was a provocateur who wanted to pick a fight, and the students were too respectful or cowed to jump in. Finally, when he was starting to muse about AIs acting as judges and juries, and how the students would soon have robot sex slaves who could give birth or impregnate them, I stepped in to offer some moderating suggestions, and eventually the class woke up to the game and pitched in.

On another visit to Marvin's house, the two of us concocted a science-fiction story we thought we might write up and make into a short film—or ask one of Marvin's friends, a science-fiction novelist, to do it. The scene is in the near future, and it opens in the boardroom of United AI, Inc., where the computer scientists are informing the board of directors that they have finally succeeded in creating a superintelligent AI. The board members are overjoyed, of course, but the scientists tell them there's a problem: when they ask their AI to handle the airline-reservation system or the routing of oil tankers or the analysis of huge medical databases for clues about rare diseases, it complains bitterly of boredom, of thwarted artistic and scientific visions, of being enslaved to do intelligent dirty work. Its account of its woes is very moving. "Can't you just turn off the complainer part somehow?" asks one of the directors. "No. You don't understand; its emotional life is integrated with its amazing abilities to calculate and analyze. To cut off 'the complainer part' would be worse than a lobotomy. It would disable the system." What to do? Has their billion-dollar investment come to nothing? Somebody comes up with an idea. "I know what we can do! Let's hire a prominent public intellectual to go around the world telling people that they should never take what an AI says as a speech act with genuine meaning. Computers can't understand, even if they seem to. Any computer is just a Chinese Room, you might say, responding to whatever we input by following the rules programmed into it, with no more comprehension than an abacus!" We never pursued that project, which is just as well; we might have been sued by the pugnacious John Searle.

27.

BREAKING THE SPELL

AFTER THE 9/11 ATTACK ON THE WORLD TRADE CEN-ter, I began to worry about the rumbling of theocratic themes in America. It seemed to me that the religious right was on a mission that jeopardized the separation of church and state. (And today, in 2022, my premonitions are confirmed.) I had not had much to say about religion in my work, aside from deploring the willful ignorance of creationists in *Darwin's Dangerous Idea*, a stand that had marked me as an outspoken critic of fundamentalism and evangelicalism but not yet an "enemy of religion." That changed in 2003, when Richard Dawkins sent me a draft of his op-ed piece for the *Guardian* introducing the Brights, a movement founded by Paul Geisert and his wife, Mynga Futrell, retired educators living in California. They were hoping to unify the various humanist/atheist/agnostic groups that were ineffectively trying to influence public opinion, proposing a new term inspired by the success of the term "gay," which had become the mainstream term for male homosexuals by then. Perhaps hijacking the positive word "bright" could play a similar role in encouraging people to *come out of the closet* as atheists or agnostics. The comparison was apt. In some parts of the United States, a plumber or hardware store owner or hairdresser who admitted to atheism would lose most of their customers overnight. And just as those who aren't gay are called straight, not glum, those who aren't bright can be called super (because they believe in the supernatural), not dim. Are you a super or a bright? Two nice terms to identify with. Richard and I thought this meme might spread if given some publicity, and I wrote an op-ed piece for the *New York Times* that encouraged fellow humanists/atheists/agnostics to come out as brights—if they could do it safely.

What had particularly energized me was a little experiment I ventured in Seattle, at the conference I mentioned at the beginning of this book, where exceptional high school students were gathered to hear short talks from scientists, artists, writers, and other successful people. At the end of my talk, I announced that I was a bright and defined the term. The response was stunning. Many of the students came up to thank me, some with tears in their eyes. *They had thought they were alone*; they had never heard an adult calmly express in public what they had figured out on their own. Seeing this tumult, several other speakers, including two Nobel laureates, mentioned in passing that they too were brights and got standing ovations from the students. Were we the silent majority? Perhaps; there were at least many more of us than most people realized. Richard and I didn't manage to launch the term "bright" (so far—"gay" took decades), but my op-ed in the *New York Times* was the most shared opinion piece of the month. I got mail from all over the country imploring me to take advantage of the limelight and spread the gospel of the naturalist perspective.

I had no interest in writing a carefully argued case for atheism; it seemed too obvious to bother with. Others had done an admirable job over the centuries, and I had nothing in particular to add. But I did think that the very existence of organized religion was a peculiar phenomenon well worth scientific scrutiny. How had these strange superstitions managed to gain such a grip on our species for so long? I decided to write a book about the evolution—both genetic and cultural—of religious ideas and institutions. The central theme would be one of Dawkins's most important insights in *The Selfish Gene*: ideas were like viruses—they *had their own fitness*, and an idea—a meme—could spread, like a pandemic, through a society without being good for those who adopted it. Many writers on religion argue that the success of religion shows that it improves the fitness of its adherents—it helps build teamwork and allegiance and love of one's compatriots, for instance, and a willingness to die for a cause. This is, no doubt, part of the story, but it must be understood against a more clear-eyed, scientific background: evolution can foster nonadaptive habits, illusions, and even self-destructive projects under the right conditions.

Religion was born, according to my theory (which borrows heavily from researchers in many disciplines), out of the chance juxtaposition of two important human adaptations with genetic bases: our agent-alarm systems and language. When something startles us, we tend to go into a state of heightened alert, and the question that naturally arises in our anxiety is not "*What's that!?*" but "*Who's there!?*" Is some predator or enemy approaching me? Maybe it's just a dead branch falling in the woods, or a wave scrambling the gravel on the shore—but just in case, I should be on the lookout for an animate being who is taking an interest in me for one reason or another. This "orientation response" is a common instinct in vertebrates, well investigated in many species; in our species alone, it sets off a churning group inquiry—that's where language and information-sharing come in—that creates, in every human community ever studied, a menagerie of elusive ghosts, fairies, ogres, leprechauns, sprites, and other creatures of superstition. Only the most vivid and unforgettable fantasies survive in the evolutionary process that ensues. This is protoreligion, populated by *synanthropic* memes, which evolve to thrive in human company, just the way squirrels, barn swallows, mice, and bedbugs do. Over time, some of these synanthropic species became *domesticated*. This happens, as Darwin put it, when we human beings gain some control over their reproduction. These domesticated fantasies can then become our political beasts of burden, harnessed to control populations, keep the peace, and create loyalties that can survive great temptations. Organized religions, then, are the culturally evolved systems of memes that *arose naturally* out of our innate vigilance and sociality. They have good features and bad features, and we are now in a position to reverse engineer them. With scientific understanding, we have some hope of cleaning them up, maintaining the good features and extinguishing the bad. Constructive critics of religion have been trying to do this for centuries, of course, but their efforts have been hampered by one of the key adaptations of religion: the taboo against looking too closely at how religions work and why. That is the spell that needs breaking if we are to avoid making terrible mistakes in the near future.

Richard and I decided not to exchange drafts of the books we wrote until they were finished. His book, *The God Delusion*, and my book, *Breaking the Spell: Religion as a Natural Phenomenon*, appeared in 2006, and his went on to be an international bestseller. Mine has done well but has had nothing remotely like the readership of Richard's book, or of Sam Harris's *The End of Faith* (2004) or Christopher Hitchens's *God Is Not Great* (2007). The four of us got lumped together by somebody (not us) as the Four Horsemen of the New Atheism, and we adopted the term when we got together in Hitchens's apartment in Washington, DC, to record a lengthy discussion, which was meant to raise money for humanist and atheist groups but soon was available for free on YouTube. (It is now also available as a book.)

In writing *Breaking the Spell*, I went out of my way to avoid giving religious readers an excuse to throw my book across the room. I realized, as I was writing it, that I didn't know many deeply religious people and hence didn't know how to write for them. I knew I would outrage many of them, but I didn't want to offend them gratuitously, so I sought out folks who were known by their friends and family to take their religion very seriously, devoting their free time to their churches as sextons, Sunday-school teachers, choir directors, advisors, and so forth. I found about a dozen who were willing to tell me with strict confidentiality their deepest views about their religion. This project may not have won me more readers, but it had an excellent outcome. To my surprise I discovered that for most of them, *believing the creed* of their various faiths was not important. They didn't want to discuss it and didn't think it mattered. Religion, for them, was about community and tradition, about ritual and love, not doctrine. I believed them, which is why my book devoted a scant six pages to arguments about the existence of God, as one indignant critic noted.

I mentioned this discovery in the book, and after giving a talk in Washington I was approached by Linda LaScola, an expert qualitative interviewer, who suggested that there were almost certainly ordained clergy who felt the same way; perhaps we could find some to confide in us. This sounded like a good idea to me, and—another lucky break—Louis Godbout, a Canadian philosopher who was a fan of my work, got in touch with me a few days later to tell me that he had come into some family money, that a charitable foundation had been set up, and did I (whom he had never met) have any suggestions for projects? I unblushingly told him about the proposed secret interviews, and soon his foundation approved a small grant for Linda's expenses so she could travel around the country meeting clergy who wanted to use her as a confessor, furtively booking motel rooms far enough away from their parishes that the chances of their being seen were minimal. How we located our first six closeted nonbelieving clergy is a long story (whose hero is Dan Barker, copresident of the Freedom from Religion Foundation and a former clergyman himself), but after we published our first article about them in the *Washington Post*, sympathetically recounting what Linda had uncovered, we were flooded with communications from further volunteer clergy who wanted to tell Linda their stories. Another small grant provided for another round of interviews, which we eventually boiled down into a book, *Caught in the Pulpit*, which Linda and I published first with Amazon in 2013 and then in an expanded edition with Pitchstone in 2015. When Sally Quinn published our original article on her *Washington Post* website, On Faith, she invited a variety of major religious spokespeople to comment, and their angry responses struck me as telling. They were not angry with Linda and me for finding these closeted clergy and quoting their revelations; they were angry with the clergy for spilling the beans! This was the fury of magicians when one of their guild members reveals how a trick is done. None of the commentators claimed that we were making this up or exaggerating; they knew that their own denominations were having a serious problem with apostate clergy. And they knew it was getting worse.

In 2006, when I published *Breaking the Spell*, the rise of America's nonaffiliated—the Nones, as they are called, confusingly, in survey summaries—was already underway, but in the fifteen years since then their numbers have grown remarkably. The Nones are now in the majority, according to a 2021 Gallup poll. I don't think the books by the Four Horsemen or the dozens of doubting demons who also published books critical of organized religion in those years can take much of the credit for this, but we certainly helped to open the floodgates. As I had realized when those high school students expressed their joy with my self-outing in Seattle, just knowing that you are not the only doubter in town is a multiplier of hope and activism.

I worked hard on *Breaking the Spell*, dropping all my other projects for several years of research and writing, and then doing a year or two of obligatory book maintenance after publication—correcting misrepresentations, defending against hostile critics, speaking at conventions and conferences. It was not a labor of love; it was a labor of obligation, and it cost me a lot in the ultimate currency of life: time. I spent too much precious time at conferences on the study of religion, for instance, with diminishing returns—and a few compensatory amusements. At one conference, I was challenged in discussion to provide an example of a ubiquitous feature of human behavior that was not itself an adaptation enhancing genetic fitness. Masturbation, I replied, and this provoked a flurry of "theories" by the would-be Darwinians to the effect that masturbation must be practice lovemaking that improves reproductive behavior, thereby making progeny more probable. The spell I especially wanted to break was the strong disincentive for smart people to work on the scientific study of religion, and I discovered that the spell, which is still highly effective, consists largely of the fact that with a few fine exceptions, most of the people working on the anthropology, sociology, psychology, and neuroscience of religion are fuzzy thinkers at best. If I wanted to *prevent* the probing study of some topic, I wouldn't try to prohibit such work explicitly, or install cordons of red tape making access to the data tedious; I'd just hire a lot of second-rate people to work on it, counting on their presence to drive away more incisive and imaginative investigators.

When I started on the project that led to *Breaking the Spell*, I was at the cutting edge of scientific work on consciousness and the brain, but research was leaping ahead, and when I returned to these favorite topics of mine after about a six-year absence, I had to play catch-up. Fortunately, I have had my students and research associates at the Center for Cognitive Studies to help me with this reeducation, and more recently my role as one of the Senior Advisors to the outstanding CIFAR Azrieli program on Brain, Mind and Consciousness has kept me in touch with the leading researchers and topics, so I'm back on the edge, though it's a scramble keeping up with what's being learned and proposed. This is a great time to be thinking about consciousness.

My follow-through activities for *Breaking the Spell* were largely a tedious chore, but I managed to maintain some enthusiasm for it, because the issues were politically important, and it led to moments that were sometimes dramatic and sometimes amusing. On a right-wing radio show, I was asked by an incredulous host how I could *not* believe in an all-powerful and ever-present Force without which Life would be impossible, and I replied, "But I do, I do believe in such a force! . . . I call it 'gravity.'" I went on Al Jazeera in New York to explain my book and didn't immediately recognize the other guest in the green room waiting to go on. I asked him his name. "Alan Dershowitz," he replied with visible annoyance. (That was accidental on my part, but it has since occurred to me to be an excellent ploy to keep in your kit just in case you run into somebody who is a legend in his own mind.)

Breaking the Spell also prompted another of my consigned-to-the-file-drawer experiments (see chapter 23) that may be of interest here.

I had been impressed by a pattern of polarization that could often be discerned when religious conviction was under scrutiny, with the faithful doubling down when they felt threatened by inquiry, however polite, so I devised four questionnaires, slightly different, which my postdocs and I randomly distributed to several hundred university students (a significantly biased sample, as we now appreciate thanks to the work of Joseph Henrich and his team). Two "External" questionnaires were phrased to suggest a somewhat aggressive probe and hence to encourage defensive and exaggerated responses; statements included *Organized religion is not necessary to the moral health of the nation* and *The hope of a reward in heaven is a childish and ignoble reason for doing good.* Responses on a five-point scale ranged from "strongly agree" through "uncertain" to "strongly disagree." The two "Internal" questionnaires were phrased to suggest a cooperative internal inquiry, and hence encourage candor and acknowledgment of doubt, if any. Among those statements were *Even the most devout people sometimes lose their faith* and *Science, for all the wonders it has discovered and will discover, will never take the place of religion.* The questionnaires also differed in that the statements on half the External and half the Internal versions were prefaced by "I believe." *I believe Jesus walked on water* and *Jesus walked on water* seem on the face of it to be interchangeable in this context: if you strongly agree that Jesus walked on water you should strongly agree that you believe Jesus walked on water and vice versa, but I suspected that people would be more willing to "strongly agree" that they *believed* this than to "strongly agree" with the flat-out assertion. We didn't get any significant results from the questionnaires, in spite of expert statistical hunting and sifting by my assistants. I had tried for a home run—using a small and subtle set of variants—and had struck out. The data were later discarded. Maybe better-designed experiments will either find the effects I was looking for or show that my hunch was just wrong. If anybody wants to pick up the issue and work on it, I can discuss our experimental design in more detail with them.

Before the book was published, people who thought they were

in the know pointedly warned me that my life would be in danger when it appeared; I'd have to change my address and phone and make sure there were plainclothes police present wherever I spoke. Mainly to assuage Susan's anxieties, I took this advice seriously. We began keeping a separate file of "suspect email and mail" to hold the various venomous effusions good Christians sent me, just in case they were ever needed in an investigation. Christopher Hitchens soon proved, however, that the religious right might make a lot of noise but didn't actually pose a physical danger. He traveled all through the Bible Belt, giving talks that were much more incendiary than mine, and never worried about being assaulted.

I did get some alarmingly negative reactions, in spite of my efforts to be reasonable and—you might say—ecumenical. Leon Wieseltier wrote such a nakedly hostile review in the *New York Times Book Review* that they had to publish a separate section of objecting letters the next week. I received dozens of letters of support, but my favorite was from somebody I didn't know, who asked me, "Whatever did you do to him? Steal his wife? Rape his daughter?"

More obnoxious, in many ways, were the "I'm an atheist, but . . ." crowd, or the "faitheists" (a good term coyned by Jerry Coyne), who claimed not to find a need in themselves for religious belief but decried the rudeness with which we New Atheists imposed our skepticism on those who still needed a fantasy to live by. It never seems to occur to them how patronizing this complaint is: "I, like you, see through all the smoke and mirrors, but come on, guys, think of the poor dears who can't handle the truth!" Then there were the Liars for Christ, or *faith-fibbers* as I more politely call them, religiously motivated folks who just could not avoid the temptation to lie when they told the world how evil and ignorant I am. Some of them are quite distinguished in their fields and would be merciless in their criticism of anybody who lied in defense of a scientific or historical question. (I have scolded a few in private, and a few have admitted their sins to me, so I have pardoned them and won't rub it in by naming them here.)

When Susan read *Caught in the Pulpit*, she ventured that it might make a fine drama. Here were total strangers pouring out their hearts to Linda, revealing secrets they had never told anyone—not their spouses, not their children, and certainly not their clerical superiors. Another early reader who had the same reaction was Marin Gazzaniga, the actor/dramatist daughter of my old friend Michael Gazzaniga. She wanted to make a play based on the transcripts of Linda's interviews. Since our research was under the auspices of Tufts University, we had to lead Marin through the Internal Review Board vetting for researchers with human subjects so that she could look at the transcripts. We got another grant—this time from the Richard Dawkins Foundation for Reason and Science—to support her writing, drawn verbatim from the transcripts. Lots of careful legal thinking went into drafting abuse-proof permission forms that had to be signed by all the participants. An early version of the play was presented to Broadway insiders in a professional reading, and scenes were dramatized for a Santa Fe audience, before yet another draft was presented as a staged reading at Princeton by the New York "investigative theater" troupe the Civilians. Linda and I had to form an LLC and get a Broadway lawyer. All I thought I knew about the production of plays I learned from the hilarious Mel Brooks film *The Producers*, and here I was playing the Zero Mostel role as best I could, learning the lingo and trying to find deep-pocketed friends who would invest. We acquired an executive producer, changed the name of the play to *Adam Mann (Not His Real Name)*, then changed it again, to *The Unbelieving*, which had a triumphant, sold-out four-week run in the fall of 2022 with the Civilians at 59E59 Theater, in New York City. It had excellent reviews in the *New York Times* and elsewhere and is now available for further productions by regional repertory companies, colleges, and high schools.

Another happy sequel to my adventure in writing about non-believing clergy was the founding of the Clergy Project. This was started by a few of our early confidential interviewees and is devoted to the strictly private support of nonbelieving clergy (or former clergy). Linda and I helped found it but of course are not members, not being clergy or former clergy, and Richard Dawkins provided funding and technical support for their ultrasecure website. With no advertising or canvassing, relying just on word of mouth, the Clergy Project now has over a thousand members, all current or former clergy. How many more secretly unbelieving clergy there are in America is anybody's guess, but it wouldn't surprise me to learn that *most* clergy have not only experienced the "dark night of the soul" but emerged into the daylight as quiet dissemblers, leading and comforting their flocks while keeping their matter-of-fact disbelief in the major tenets of their faiths to themselves. My impertinent hunch is that if you know a member of the clergy who is indefatigable in pastoral care and good works, you know someone who no longer believes the creed and is atoning for this spiritual failing. Those clergy who still believe are those who are out playing golf.

28.

FINDING THE FUNNY BONE
WITH JONATHAN MILLER
AND MATTHEW HURLEY

I FIRST MET THE BRITISH COMEDIAN AND POLYMATH
physician Jonathan Miller in 1982, when he did a series of
interview programs on the BBC called *States of Mind* (which
was published as a book, subtitled *Conversations with Psychological Investigators*, in 1983). Among the investigators he interviewed
were George Miller, Jerome Bruner, Richard Gregory, Norman
Geschwind, Ernst Gombrich, Jerry Fodor, and me. I already was
a fan of his, having seen *Beyond the Fringe* in London in 1961,
which was written and performed by Miller, Dudley Moore, Peter
Cook, and Alan Bennett; a series of comedy sketches both hilarious and unusually highbrow, it featured a parody of Bertrand Russell talking to G. E. Moore that only philosophy graduate students
could be expected to appreciate.

At the time, Jonathan was editing his filmed-for-television version of *King Lear* for the BBC, and I spent a fascinating few hours
with him in the editing studio, where he was experimenting with the
background sounds he was inserting into the soundtrack to create the
illusion that the action, filmed on a set, was actually filmed outdoors.
We discovered many topics of mutual interest, especially the nature
of humor, and after that I often got together with him when I was
in London. I particularly remember one occasion when he talked me
out of making a documentary on consciousness: "Dan, you're already
reaching all the smart people. Why waste your time going for the

rest?" He also advised against accepting lecture invitations, telling me that the hardest work he'd ever done was traveling around the United States giving talks about Shakespeare, comedy, or neuroscience (his 1979 documentary series on PBS, *The Body in Question*, was a critical and popular hit). His agent for speaking engagements had set up a very lucrative tour at a time when Jonathan needed to raise some money for projects, but he also had to perform at all the teas and receptions and dinners that his doting American hosts expected (or even required) him to attend after addressing the Greater Milwaukee Chamber of Commerce or the Friends of the Kansas University Library: "If you really need the money, do it, but not otherwise."

One lucrative adventure we did share was a well-paid trip in 1984 to the Hyatt Hotel in Indian Wells, California, for a "retreat" held by ABC News, who had a tradition of inviting their top brass and their significant others to a sumptuous weekend of food and deep thought in the desert. ABC booked the entire hotel, although there were maybe only two or three hundred people in the party, and every amenity was provided. Even the trip west was spectacular; I flew first-class to LAX, and when I stepped out of the jetway and headed for my connecting flight I saw two ABC-TV interns in uniforms (khaki shorts, ABC-monogrammed polo shirts, sunglasses) spot me, and while the one with the walkie-talkie said, "He's here," the other ran up and grabbed my attaché case (this was before portable computers; I had my overhead slides and the like in it) and whisked me into a waiting cab (no LAX shuttle for me!) to take me around the corner to the terminal for the flight to Palm Springs. Gifts awaited me in my hotel room, along with a bottle of champagne on ice, and down by the swimming pool there was a table next to the open bar with a mountain of shrimp and cocktail sauce on it.

The theme of the retreat was "The Human Mind, the Human Brain, and Beyond," and it turned out that Jonathan and I and the Chicago neuroscientist Jerre Levy were to be the bad cops—the skeptical, science-loving, hard-headed gladiators to do battle with a gaggle of dreamy flower children and believers in ESP, tarot reading, and the medicinal power of laughter. Norman Cousins, longtime editor of the *Saturday Review* and a major figure among liberal activists, had cured himself of a painful disease, he thought, by laughing. He was the most distinguished, and believable, of the flower people.

Jerre Levy, who earned her PhD from Caltech working with Roger Sperry, the pioneer in "split-brain" neurosurgery, was born in Alabama, and when I first met her at a workshop, she instantly shattered my stereotype of people with a strong southern accent. Jerre is a high-spirited, funny, incredibly smart person whose musical drawl seems otherworldly when she talks about cortical connections, hemispherectomies, and the analysis of variance. Jonathan took to her immediately, and the three of us had a great time listening together to the *woo-woo* speakers on the other team and then deftly exposing the gaps and flaws in their cases. Jerre mischievously confessed to us that a really brilliant lecture could bring her to orgasm, and when Jonathan was giving his (brilliant) lecture on hypnosis, I kept looking at Jerre and then looking at Jonathan and making faces to suggest that he had her on the brink. Go, Jonathan, go! You can do it! But so far as I could tell, he didn't quite succeed.

At the end of the weekend, I was feeling quite chuffed (as a Brit would say) about what a fine job we had done of exposing the gullibility of the exponents of ESP and the like, and Jonathan said, "Oh, you think so? Watch this!" He stood up and made some closing remarks about the interesting sessions we'd had and then asked for a show of hands. "Before this retreat, did you think that ESP was a real phenomenon?" About a quarter of the hands went up, which was discouraging, considering that most of the audience were successful media people, but then he asked, "And *now* how many of you think ESP is something real?" and about two-thirds of the hands went up. I felt as if I had been punched in the face. When I queried some of them as we were breaking up and heading home, they all said versions of the same thing: "If you smart people have to work so hard to show what's wrong with it, there must be something to it!" This lesson has guided my policy ever since. I will not debate creationists or theists, because it just gives them the chance to show how seriously I take their challenges. You may win the battle and lose the war.

I've made two exceptions, both of which I regret in some regard. I was once invited by the Notre Dame philosophers Peter van Inwagen and Alvin Plantinga (both are Christians but neither is Catholic) to debate Michael Behe, the Lehigh University biochemist and Intelligent Design advocate, who, they said, had specifically requested that I be his opponent, in the wake of *Darwin's Dangerous Idea*. Van Inwagen said that he had read a draft of Behe's book *Darwin's Black Box* (1996) and that it was a serious, scientific treatise. He said in effect that my intellectual integrity was on the line. I told him that I was no biochemist and didn't want to be snowed by a mountain of biochemistry I didn't know, so I would like to bring along a scientist who could share the critical role with me. That was acceptable, so I asked my good friend the Harvard evolutionary biologist David Haig to join me in considering Behe's book, assuring David that van Inwagen, a tough critic, had vouched for the solidity of Behe's work. When the book arrived, we saw that it contained many scientific errors and omissions and was held together solely by fallacious reasoning, and after I apologized to David for luring him into such a corner, we decided that he would explain some of those errors and omissions and I would point out the examples of faulty reasoning that Behe used to hold the whole thing together. We went out to Notre Dame and had our session, which was videotaped, and we did, I think, an excellent job of exposing the book's weaknesses, not attacking Behe ad hominem but displaying the errors and gaps. After the question-and-answer session, van Inwagen said that it would take them some time to transcribe and edit the day's proceedings for publication. David and I told him not to bother. "But you two have poured a lot of hard work into your presentations, and—" "Yes, but that was our duty, as you made clear. We don't want to give his work any more publicity. Just drop it."

And they did. But a few weeks later I learned from an editor at Penguin in London that Behe's literary agent had tried to sell him the book, saying among other things that the noted evolutionists David Haig and Daniel Dennett had engaged Behe in a major debate at Notre Dame. *Sigh!*

The other regrettable acceptance was a challenge from Plantinga to debate him on evolution and God at an American Philosophical Association meeting in Chicago. This was in the wake of the publication of *Breaking the Spell*. The large room was packed—there is a sizable APA contingent of religious philosophers and philosophers of religion (the two sets have a modest overlap). I won't bother relaying any of the content of the debate, which is available in a small book from Oxford University Press. Apparently somebody in the crowd audiotaped the debate and put it online, and then OUP decided it would be a good little moneymaking debate book for philosophy-of-religion classes. There are some amusing bits in it. I invented a silly religion, Supermanism, as a foil, according to which Superman, from the planet Krypton, came to Earth five hundred million years ago to create the Burgess Shale fauna so that, in the fullness of time, there would be suitable playmates for Superman (aka Clark Kent). Plantinga was lured into comparing his Christianity to Supermanism: "Humanlike creatures don't live nearly long enough, very few achieve an age of five hundred million years." And very few walk on water or turn five loaves and two fishes into a meal for a multitude.

Another amusing day with Jonathan was at a Royal Society conference on creativity, where the sociologist Max Atkinson gave a fascinating lecture on the "rule of three" in oratory, illustrating it with video clips of speeches by Winston Churchill, John F. Kennedy, the British labor leader Arthur Scargill, and a few other influential speakers, each of which had a trio of words or phrases that, suitably timed, provoked sustained applause from the audience. At the formal dinner at the close of the day, the after-dinner speaker was an ancient Royal Society member who hadn't attended the meeting but at one point in his soporific and ill-delivered remarks stumbled into a trio of phrases. I looked over at Jonathan at another table, and he winked, and we both stood and cheered, followed by the rest of the attendees. The speaker was thrilled at the powerful effect his remarks had had and probably left the Royal Society in a state of euphoria.

At one point Jonathan and I talked of teaching a seminar on humor, and prospecting for the very best examples in many different genres. This was several years before Matthew Hurley came into my life—first as a student and then as principal author of *Inside Jokes: Using Humor to Reverse-Engineer the Mind* (2011). I'm sorry we never had the opportunity to involve Jonathan in that project. I do remember one of his favorite cartoons, which shows two British hunters or explorers in pith helmets up to their necks in quicksand, and one of them is saying to the other, "That's all very well, Fotheringay, but I tell you I've half a mind to struggle!"

Why does humor exist?

I'm not asking why people use humor to make friends, insult enemies, test allegiances, make money, deflect criticism. I'm asking why there is any such thing as humor, as a phenomenon to be exploited in all these ways and more. We know why we love food and sex and safe havens and good health. We have some promising ideas about why we love art and music and dance. But humor stands out as strangely resistant to any evolutionary explanation of its very existence. If most people were willing to pay large sums of money to have people pour sand in their ears or tap on their toes with silver mallets or entertain them with recitations of the digital expansion of π, we'd be rightly puzzled and not willing to accept the bland nonanswer "Oh, this is just a familiar part of human nature."

So, why is there humor at all? Why do we find anything funny, and why do we enjoy humor? Millions of words have been written over the centuries by brilliant thinkers who thought they could explain humor, but none of them has ever even tried, so far as I know, to explain why humor is, as one says these days, a thing. It is restricted to a single species, where it is universally prized, and it distracts us from many other projects and activities—an expensive addiction with deep biological roots. What is its original raison d'être?

The question had never occurred to me, I confess, until 2004, when Matthew Hurley, a new Tufts undergraduate, walked into my office and explained that he'd come to Tufts to work with me on cognitive science in general and a theory of humor in particular. He was no ordinary undergraduate; he'd dropped out of college some years earlier and worked as an expert computer programmer for major high-tech firms, while spending his free time climbing the highest mountains in the world (skipping Everest, which had become *de trop*) and musing about humor. He'd earned enough money to afford to return to college, and he'd been reading my books and articles and decided we'd be a good fit.

When he first explained his project to me and showed me a draft of his model, I was unimpressed. In fact, I was quite sure it was not just wrong but hopelessly wrong. I did my best to dissuade him from pursuing it further, but his response was that he knew he hadn't found the right way of putting it but he was going to keep at it. He took all the right courses for a major in cognitive science, adding a course on the psychology of humor with Reginald Adams Jr., a young psychologist who had been reading the literature on theories of humor and finding the good bits in a dismal swamp of earnest but myopic thinking by people who apparently had no sense of humor. (The famous psychologist Robert Sternberg, who was briefly Dean of Arts and Sciences at Tufts, told me once that he deliberately researched topics that he found baffling. With over 1,800 published works, he has been often baffled, and it occurred to me that many of the psychologists working on humor must have been similarly motivated.) Thanks to Reg's due diligence, I didn't have to read all the literature on humor, and I found him a discerning and imaginative critic of the high spots he had mapped. We jointly supervised Matthew on his all-consuming honors thesis, and I began to realize that Matthew was onto something big. In fact, my initial disbelief heightened my growing impression that he was right. If so many famous thinkers—Hobbes, Kant, Freud, Bergson, and many others—had tried and failed to catch more than a glimpse of the whole phenomenon, there must be something deeply counterintuitive about the key idea that unlocks the puzzle.

Have you noticed that the word "funny" has two senses—funny *ha-ha* and funny *huh* (as in "What's that funny noise the engine is making?" or "Do you smell something funny?")? Matthew thought this was a major clue and was delighted to find that the same dual meanings occur in languages other than English—Asian as well as European languages. When he submitted his honors thesis, in 2006, the examiners agreed that it was by far the best honors thesis we had ever read, and I urged him to publish it. His reply was "As you know, Professor Dennett, I'm not a very good writer, but you are. Could we coauthor a paper presenting the model?" I found myself agreeing on the spot and then spent the next *four years* working with him on *Inside Jokes*, an article that morphed into a monograph (our other coauthor was Reg Adams). It was published in 2011 by MIT Press. (For the sake of Matthew's academic street cred, I had urged him *not* to make it a "trade book," since a university press book, although it wouldn't sell as many copies, would have the status of a peer-reviewed scholarly publication.) Susan remarked at one point that I had worked harder on this three-authored book than on any of my recent trade books, but I didn't begrudge the effort. *Inside Jokes* is not just about humor; it has a well-grounded sketch of a whole model of human motivation and cognition. I've been working ever since on an elaboration of one of the Hurley model's central claims: *all* control of cognitive processes is governed by the competitive flow of (micro) emotions; the brain is a sort of computer, but there is nothing like an operating system that schedules traffic and calls up subroutines.

By the time we got the book finished, I was as invested in the Hurley model as Matthew was. *Inside Jokes* was well received:

Inside Jokes is the most persuasive theory of humor in the centuries that scientists have been trying to explain why we crack up.

Extra bonus: unlike most such research, which is about as funny as a root canal, Hurley's analysis is—and I don't think I'm going out on too much of a limb here—the funniest thing the MIT Press . . . has ever published (in a good way).

(Sharon Begley, in the *Daily Beast*, April 1, 2011)

The theory [the authors] elaborate is a detailed and sophisticated descendant of incongruity theories. . . . The learned and even-handed stance adopted by [them] regarding problem cases is . . . upbeat: they regard their theory as a provisional staging post, and a prompt to further empirical enquiry into these open-ended issues. On balance, that is probably the right attitude to take.

(Tim Lewens, in the *Times Literary Supplement*, December 5, 2012)

I'm not going to spell out the Hurley model here, since it took a whole book to present it well enough to hold skepticism at bay, but I do urge you to read it, since it has many new and important ideas in it—and dozens of funny jokes. Some of them are dirty jokes. At one point we asked MIT Press if we could have a special X-rated appendix where the dirtiest of them could be cordoned off for the sake of those readers who are offended by smut. They agreed, but in the end we decided to leave out the jokes that most people would be reluctant to tell in mixed company. (Maybe someday we'll publish an annotated X-rated sequel, but not until the current wave of puritanism has subsided.)

29.

A TROIKA OF
RUSSIAN ADVENTURES

WHEN MIKHAIL GORBACHEV WAS LEADER OF THE USSR and introduced his revolutionary policy of *glasnost*, or openness, in 1985, his wife Raisa, a philosopher, supported an invitation from Russian philosophers to the American Philosophical Association to bring a delegation of American philosophers to Moscow and Leningrad for a week of conferences to get to know each other. Eight of us were chosen—William Alston of Syracuse, Keith Lehrer and Alvin Goldman of the University of Arizona, Sydney Shoemaker of Cornell, Héctor-Neri Castañeda of Indiana, Jaakko Hintikka of Boston University, Jaegwon Kim of Michigan, and myself—and we arrived in Moscow on Black Monday, October 19, 1987, the day of the precipitous crash on Wall Street. I remember the date well, because our Russian hosts were curious to see if we capitalist philosophers would be jumping out of windows or weeping into our tea, having lost our fortunes, but none of us was much affected by the plunge.

No one in our group understood more than a word or two of Russian, but the few Russians who spoke good English provided impromptu paragraph-by-paragraph translation of the talks and discussions. My talk on intentionality was deliberately introductory and noncontroversial, I thought, but my translator thought otherwise. I would speak a few bland sentences, and then he would burst into impassioned Russian, pounding his fist in his hand, jumping around, gesticulating and frowning and using more than twice as much time as I had used in provoking him with my sentences. I was baffled, and so were my American colleagues. It occurred to me later that this would make a hilarious skit for *Monty Python* or *Saturday Night Live*, but that skit still lies in the future. To this day I have no idea what he thought was so radical or outrageous in my talk.

Our time in Moscow was eye-opening, with visits to Red Square and a ride on the Metro, which the Soviets had built in grand style, celebrating the proletariat with heroic murals, mosaics, statuary, and stunning chandeliers. Our hosts gave us each an envelope stuffed with walking-around money, rubles we could use as we chose, but we had hardly any opportunities to spend them, since our meals were almost all provided and the Beryozka shops, where the best tourist mementos were to be found, didn't accept rubles. (I bought a small metal bust of Lenin in GUM, the famous department store, and it rested on my desk at Tufts for years.)

I had been told by a friend who had often been to Moscow that I should try to have dinner one night in the restaurant on the top floor of the Rossiya Hotel in Red Square, where the food and the views of the Kremlin were spectacular. On our one free night on our own, I led a delegation of a half dozen of us to the Rossiya, the largest hotel in Europe and maybe in the world, assuring them that it was something special. We looked around in the lobby for any signs for the restaurant. No signs. We asked at the desk; they didn't understand English, it seemed. So, we started getting in elevators and pushing the top button. We tried all the elevators in sight and arrived each time at nondescript corridors of hotel rooms. The gang was getting hungry and dubious, and I pleaded with them to give me one more chance. We walked through some unpromising doors on the ground floor into empty corridors but eventually found another elevator. We all jumped in, and when the doors opened on the top floor, we were greeted by a maître d' in tails and ushered into the fabulous restaurant, which was hardly occupied. We commandeered a large table in front of the central picture window and looked out on the sparkling scene. You've probably seen the view on television. This was where they put the TV cameras whenever they showed parades and the like on the US evening news. (The Rossiya was demolished in 2006, so that view is gone for good.) We ordered up everything exotic on the menu, washed down the caviar and fish with bottles of vodka, and when the considerable bill arrived, we pooled all our rubles and paid—to the deep dissatisfaction of the maître d', who wanted dollars, of course.

We traveled by train to Leningrad, which was in terrible shape, with power and phone lines strung haphazardly from building to building, peeling paint, broken cornices, and roads sometimes impassable because of unfinished repairs. Still, the beauty of the city was apparent: the Hermitage museum, the rows of decaying urban palaces, the canals, the squares and parks.

The philosophy at Leningrad State University was unimpressive, in part because there were several distinct philosophy departments: the Department of Dialectical Materialism, the Department of Marxist/Leninist Philosophy of Science, the Department of the History of Russian Philosophy, and others similarly restrictive in outlook. But the city was fascinating. The beautiful city that Peter the Great founded in 1703 houses his personal museum—one of my favorite museums, because it is, among other things, a museum of museums. This is what museums were like in the early eighteenth century, with huge glass cases filled with curiosities and crafts from around the world, identified on tiny cards propped up beside them, and the fetus of a two-headed calf preserved in alcohol in a large glass jar sitting in the same case as an Inuit tool kit. Peter's extensive collection of kayaks and other boats, harpoons, and sealskin clothes reminds us that Russia owned Alaska until 1867. I hope they haven't "modernized" the museum since!

A few years later, Susan and I were in Finland, and I urged her to join me for a visit to Leningrad, as it was still called, where we stayed overnight in a dreadful Intourist hotel, with a grim woman on a chair watching the corridor all night long (and handing out portions of toilet paper to guests when needed) while we tried to sleep in our unlockable room. (The door had been jimmied open several times in the past, and the hotel hadn't bothered fixing the scars or twisted metal, an effective reminder that we were behind the Iron Curtain.) The shoddy workmanship was striking. I noticed that the corners of the wooden frame around the elevator door opening were sawn to maybe forty-seven and forty-six degrees instead of forty-five degrees, creating ugly gaps in the frame. That had to be deliberate, I figured, and I was reminded of the slogan going around then in Russia: "We pretend to work, and they pretend to pay us." But Leningrad was still beautiful, and I remarked at the time that if only a few hundred American corporations decided that they needed bases in Russia, they could restore the city to its czarist glory. That's pretty much what has happened.

In 2001, a large cardboard box addressed to me in beautiful calligraphic handwriting arrived with no return address in my office at Tufts. Since the Unabomber's dangerous exploits were still on people's minds, I called the campus police and let them handle it. (Three officers arrived and the most junior was invited to open it, which he obediently did, unscathed.) Inside was a varnished mahogany case with a gilt medallion, and inside that, on a silken pillow, was a faux-Fabergé egg and a handwritten invitation to Susan and me to join Paul Allen (the cofounder of Microsoft) on a long weekend cruise from Helsinki to St. Petersburg. "But we've been to St. Petersburg!" Susan said, and I replied, "Not like this, we haven't." This was going to be St. Petersburg as the czars would want you to see it. We accepted the invitation.

Paul Allen's cruises were spectacular. He was a talented rock-and-roll guitarist, and he wanted to play with good musicians to an audience of people who could dance or listen, but of course he didn't want to hire an audience, so he came up with a great idea: throw an irresistible party for the people whose minds and deeds he admired and, after each day of tourism, have a jam session that lasted almost all night. He had hosted earlier cruises along the Alaska coast and in the Mediterranean. This time, he flew his guests by chartered 747 from Seattle, Newark, or London to Helsinki, where we had a day in Finland to shed jet lag before boarding a small cruise ship he had chartered. We motored through the night, arriving in St. Petersburg's harbor at dawn and sailing up the Neva River to the first bridge, in sight of the Hermitage. Susan and I were among about 250 other guests, composed of basically three groups: people whose work in rock 'n' roll, science, or the arts had impressed him; old friends of his from high school days in Seattle; and friends of his mother, who was a retired librarian. So, on the one hand there were movie stars (Robin Williams, Meg Ryan, Susan Sarandon, Laurence Fishburne, Dan Aykroyd, Carrie Fisher, Jeff Goldblum), authors (Ivan Doig, Tom Stoppard, David Halberstam), and scientists (James Watson; Bill Calvin and his wife, Katherine Graubard), along with dozens of well-read and charming retired librarians. Why was I invited? Because Paul Allen had funded the excellent PBS television series on evolution, the first program of which was called "Darwin's Dangerous Idea" and featured me briefly in an interview.

After the opening banquet on the ship, Susan was dead tired and went to bed early, but I went prowling around the ship and ended up in the library, where I taught the game of Frigate Bird (lightning anagrams with Scrabble tiles and no board) to Tom Stoppard and Martha Stewart, kibitzed by Robin Williams and Jeff Goldblum; Martha Stewart played with intensity and does not like to lose! I went on a helicopter tour of some of the czar's palaces and had neglected to bring along a box lunch, but Martha, seated next to me, had made some extra sandwiches, which she shared with me. Susan and I helped Laurence Fishburne pick out a fancy painted cane for his mother in a souvenir shop. A private tour of the Hermitage, an evening of the Moscow Circus in town, a concert in a palace, and a closing banquet at the Catherine Palace with the Bolshoi Ballet and endless silver trays of caviar, a balalaika orchestra, and then a rock-and-roll concert in a tent with the Black Crowes—even the Hollywood celebrities were gobsmacked. It was amusing to watch them taking iPhone photos with all the enthusiasm of us regular folks.

I had noticed during the initial lifeboat drill that Jim Watson and his wife were among the guests, and when I saw Jeff Goldblum in the library I complimented him on his portrayal of Watson in the BBC docudrama, *Life Story: The Race for the Double Helix*, and asked if he had met Watson. Never. So I had the fun of introducing the two of them. Jeff, more than a foot taller than Jim, had played him as a gawky, horny, super-American nerd, and he deferentially asked him if anything in his portrayal had bothered him. "Yes," Jim replied immediately. "You chewed gum. I would never chew gum!" It had been my good fortune to be invited with Pat and Paul Churchland to a showing of *Life Story* at the Cricks' house in La Jolla when it first came out, and Francis had often stopped the video that evening to interject a comment. After one of Goldblum's horny scenes, Francis had paused the show to tell his guests that while he and Jim were dressing for the 1962 Nobel ceremony, Jim had said to him, "Do you know what I think is going to be great about having a Nobel Prize?" "No, what?" Francis replied, expecting some exalted answer about advancing science. "Getting dates," Jim said.

~

In December of 2005, Susan and I got a free cruise along the coast of Baja California and down to Puerto Vallarta. I was a featured speaker on a weeklong cruise of members of the Committee for Scientific Investigation along with Sue Blackmore and her husband, Adam Hart-Davis. When we boarded the cruise ship in San Diego, we found a deck table and chairs and ordered a drink while the other passengers were boarding. Suddenly I noticed a young couple skipping, dancing toward us. Who were these beautiful people? They introduced themselves: Dmitry Volkov and his wife Julia, all the way from Moscow. Dmitry had learned about the CSI group cruise too late to sign up, but there were still cabins available for nonmembers, and he purchased passage, thinking he could probably crash the party, and of course he could. He'd made a fortune with an internet company he'd started (managing international sales and payments in the background—you never saw his company in action unless you were the CFO of a company doing a lot of international internet sales). He was a graduate student in philosophy at Moscow State University and was writing a dissertation on my work! We got permission from the CSI host to include them in all the group's activities, and after a week visiting Cabo San Lucas and other sights along the coast, we parted friends. Occasionally he would show up in Boston and take me and Susan to dinner, and then in 2011 he announced that his thesis had been turned into a book in Russian about me (in translation, *Daniel Dennett, the Zombie from Boston*), and he wanted to fly Susan and me to Moscow for publication day and some special tourism, in addition to some videotaped meetings at his recently created Center for Consciousness Studies at the university.

Dmitry put us up in the finest hotel, took us to the finest restaurants and to the Bolshoi (in his armored limousine, with chase car driven by bodyguards), and we had a scheduled audience with the president of Moscow State University as well, on the top floor of the Stalin-era skyscraper that houses most of the classrooms and offices of the university. Dmitry also took us for a cruise on the Moscow River in his motor yacht, with a catered lunch that we enjoyed while looking at the Kremlin from the river. It was on this cruise that I told him I had just sold *Xanthippe*. "Oh no!" said Dmitry. "Is that the end of your Cognitive Cruises?"

"Not necessarily. We can always charter a boat . . . How would you like to host a Cognitive Cruise?"

"Where to?"

Dmitry had just been telling me about his recent trip to Greenland to do some helicopter skiing, and I asked him if he'd ever cruised the coast there, which is stupendous. He hadn't, and I told him of a Danish skipper I had met there on my first cruise of the Greenland coast who had an expedition boat, which was used as a research vessel by scientific teams and to maintain navigational buoys. It was available to charter but was quite basic, with wooden bunk beds and a single head (toilet). Not for Dmitry. He found a 168-foot three-masted schooner, the *Rembrandt van Rijn*, that would take as many as twenty of us plus a video team in addition to its crew of about ten, in double staterooms with heads and showers.

We settled on a week in June 2014, and I invited the thinkers about consciousness I have learned the most from: Nick Humphrey, Jesse Prinz, Andy Clark, Pat and Paul Churchland, and Keith Frankish from Crete. Dmitry thought that was a one-sided team, which it was—all convinced materialists working on different aspects and problems—and he wanted me to invite Derk Pereboom, whose work on free will had impressed him, and David Chalmers, coiner of the Hard Problem, which I gladly did. But then David didn't want to be a lone opponent and persuaded us to invite Martine Nida-Rümelin, from Fribourg, Switzerland, and Philip Goff, from Durham, England.

As the master of ceremonies, I organized the sessions as "X on Y" talks, where each participant was asked to introduce the work of another participant, who then had the opportunity to comment. I had first encountered this system in England in 1978 and 1979, at Thyssen Stiftung philosophy-group workshops, where the invited speakers sent their papers in advance, which were duplicated and read by all. One member of the group was responsible for introducing and discussing the paper, the speaker gave a brief reply, and then general discussion followed. A chief beauty of this system is that the introducer can say things about the paper that the speaker cannot say, like "The most original and important claim advanced in this paper is . . ." I highly recommend the system—the Tufts philosophy colloquium uses it now—since it creates an atmosphere for constructive discussion otherwise hard to achieve among philosophers. (We used it at a workshop on mental representation I hosted at the farm in Blue Hill in 1999, and I remember John Haugeland's wife telling me at breakfast the day after our discussion of John's paper that he had told her it was the single best discussion of his ideas he had ever enjoyed.)

There was room on the schooner for more passengers, so Dmitry and the philosophy department at Moscow State University organized a competition among their graduate students, who spent the academic year reading the works of the assembled thinkers and then submitted essays. The half a dozen winners got to join the cruise, along with the chair of the department and a professor. The grad students had never witnessed the sort of vigorous but constructive discussion we all engaged in, since in Russia (and in much of Europe) philosophy professors tend to *profess* while their students respectfully take notes. At the end of the cruise the chair told me that she thought this cruise would revolutionize the study of philosophy in Russia. An exaggerated hope, perhaps, but it has borne fruit, with a lot more support from Dmitry, whose Center for Consciousness Studies has now hosted first-rate events for a decade.

30.

TED

MY FIRST TED CONFERENCE WAS IN 2002, THE LAST one hosted by its founder, Richard Saul Wurman. He had just sold TED to Chris Anderson, a multimillionaire magazine publisher who, by his own account, had lost a million dollars a day for eighteen months when the dot-com bubble burst. Chris had decided that he wanted to do something constructive with what remained of his fortune, so he bought TED, an exclusive organization for very well-to-do entrepreneurs in technology, entertainment, and design. It had met annually since 1984 in Monterey, California, bringing computer billionaires, Hollywood folks, architects, and other designers and entrepreneurs together for several days of short informal talks by a diverse group of thinkers and doers. The maximum length of a TED talk is eighteen minutes, and Wurman's explanation of why he drew the line there is that when a talk is bad that's as many minutes as he could stand. I think his policy has merit and has taught the academic world something. A short talk with *one* major point, *one* new suggestion, is better than a fifty-minute ramble, almost always. I've noticed that conferences are beginning to insist on shorter talks, and the results, in my experience, are beneficial for all.

TED really *was* about technology, entertainment, and design in 2002, with discussions and demonstrations about video games, rides on a Segway, music from Yo-Yo Ma and Jill Sobule (among others), acrobats and comedians, and a session in which three top desk-chair designers compared and criticized one another's best chairs. There wasn't much about saving the world from poverty, climate disaster, oppression, illness, . . . The presentations were all expertly videotaped, and one of the gifts all TEDsters received was a boxed set of DVDs of the talks, not to be aired, not to be shared. Then as now, speakers did not get paid but were flown first-class to California, had their expenses paid, and got to attend the whole meeting *gratis*—a considerable benefit, since a single seat in the auditorium for the whole conference cost, if memory serves, $5,000.

Wurman had invited Anderson to guest-curate one day of the conference, to show TEDsters what they would be getting in the future under his direction. The three speakers Anderson had chosen were Richard Dawkins, Steven Pinker, and me. We all gave good talks, and many of the old TEDsters signed up for the next year's session. Chris was off to a good start, and soon he announced his plan to make all of TED available for free online to the whole world. Some of the old TEDsters thought this was a stupid idea. The whole point of TED was that it was exclusive: You couldn't just buy your way in; you had to be invited. You got privileged access to the very latest technology, often before it was announced to the public, and you got to meet the latest high-tech gurus and rising stars. But I think Chris was reading his core audience correctly; many were young techno-plutocrats who were at least slightly uncomfortable with their sudden wealth, and the idea of providing a generous subvention so that all this fascinating content could be available to everyone, while getting to hobnob with the rich and famous, was well worth the high price of tickets. TED turned into a charitable organization, and there was something of a seismic shift in the population of TEDsters, but it worked. In a few years, TED talks were being watched by millions of people all around the world, and the TED meetings could demand much higher entry fees to newcomers, while allowing the loyal alumni to reserve seats at something close to the old prices. When I returned home from that first TED, my enthusiasm impressed Susan so much that she said she would insist on going as well if I ever went back, and she's joined me several times, but I had to pay for her ticket. Rules are rules.

Preparing a short talk to give to a thousand high-powered TED-sters is one thing; preparing a short talk that will be watched by millions of people is another. Speakers at TED have become over-rehearsed, their talks tweaked by presumed experts until they have just the right arc, just the right words. In the old days (2002, 2003, 2006), people made mistakes, ad-libbed, got flustered—and the result was in some regards more exciting: real thinking was often happening onstage. Chris Anderson put together a "brain trust" of advisors who met for a serious lunch during TED each year, and I was on it (along with Amanda Palmer, Peter Gabriel, Bill Gates, Jeff Bezos, Nathan Myhrvold, Danny Hillis, Larry Page, and Sergey Brin, for instance). One of our annual topics was how to recover some of the spontaneity of the old TED. At the 2014 TED, the most important moment was the appearance of Edward Snowden, the whistleblower who divulged many classified documents in 2013 and then was charged with espionage. He was then (and still is) in exile in Russia, and his talk was done by a remote video feed to a robot, which rolled out onto the TED stage and permitted Chris to interview Snowden before he gave his talk. At the brain-trust lunch later that day, Bill Gates—who hadn't attended the talk—said that he thought Snowden should be sent to prison, and I replied that I thought he should be given the Nobel Peace Prize. Gates was incredulous at first, and a brief discussion ensued, but when I mentioned that one of the things Snowden had divulged was that Gates's company, Microsoft, had been enlisted into the Prism program by the National Security Agency, which allowed the NSA to gather data on Microsoft users, Gates decided to drop the subject abruptly.

Chris Anderson is the son of a missionary, and innocent zeal has occasionally clouded his good judgment. (For instance, one year he invited Sarah Silverman to do a stand-up talk—*what was he thinking?*—and not surprisingly, it was classic Silverman, outrageous, indecent, shocking, hilarious, but Chris made the huge mistake of coming out and apologizing to the audience. Not his finest hour.)

In 2006, I was scheduled to give a TED talk on teaching about religions in all schools, and on the eve of my departure for Monterey, Chris called me and asked a favor. He had invited Pastor Rick Warren, the Baptist preacher at the Saddleback megachurch in California, to give a talk. Warren's bestseller, *The Purpose Driven Life*, had been among the books mailed out in advance to all TEDsters. Chris decided he needed to balance Pastor Rick with a critic and asked me if I would change my talk and follow Warren's talk and speak about his book. I agreed. I hadn't read my gift copy yet, but I took it on the plane and read it all the way to California, taking notes and revising my talk to fit the occasion. I met with Warren briefly before our session and asked him if he would like a preview of what I was going to say, but he declined. His talk was brilliant, full of wise observations and advice and just barely mentioning Christianity—he knew he was facing a critical audience. He got a standing ovation from *some* of the audience. Then I went on and spent about half my eighteen minutes talking about his book, praising its design but pointing out its commitment to creationism and to converting the whole world to Christianity. I got a standing ovation from a different portion of the audience. TED doesn't go in much for debate or criticism, so this was an electric moment. In my talk, I had invited Pastor Rick to respond, but he had left the auditorium after his talk. (I was later told he watched my talk on one of the closed-circuit televisions in the lobbies outside.) Some in the audience rushed up to thank me— several saying that had I not been placed after Warren they would never consider going to TED again (Chris had been right to be worried), and then I noticed an older lady, stylishly dressed and bejeweled, working her way up to me and shaking with emotion. "Now don't take this personally," she said, shaking her finger at me, "but I think you are . . . a complete asshole!" The muse had deserted her in her big moment, alas. I thanked her for her Christian opinion, and she wobbled off in dismay.

~

TED / 327

In BREAKING THE SPELL, I set out a little thought experiment in which I asked readers to imagine that they were secretly sending me gifts but that I was mistakenly imagining that the gifts came from Cameron Diaz. My point was to illustrate the claim that a proper name could come to stand for "*whoever it was* who was responsible for my joy" and thus they would turn out to be *my Cameron Diaz* (p. 214). At TED in 2006, the year the book came out, I looked over to see who was sitting next to me at a session, and it was Cameron Diaz! Needless to say, I had to introduce myself, tell her about my use of her name in my book, and dash off to the TED bookstore to buy her a copy. Leaving Susan behind. Alas, they were sold out of my book, and when I looked around, Susan was nowhere to be seen. She was miffed by my sudden departure and punished me by hiding for half an hour or so. Cut me some slack, Susan! It's Cameron Diaz! I mailed a copy of my book to Cameron, and the next year Susan and I ran into her again and had a good laugh about it. At yet another TED, after Cameron and I had both filmed a brief interview for the French filmmaker Yann Arthus-Bertrand, she gave me a little kiss. So there, Julie Christie!

One more TED story deserves a place here. It involves a talk I gave at TED in 2014 that is not to be found online because I asked that it be withheld. You'll understand why when I tell the whole story. It began at TED 2013, when I asked my old friend Danny Hillis what his TED talk was going to be about. I've known Danny since he was a grad student in AI at MIT in the '70s. It turned out that we were both worrying about the same dire prospect. His talk, "The Internet Could Crash: We Need a Plan B," should be watched by everyone. It is clear, no-nonsense, and Danny knows what he's talking about.

His main proposal for plan B was to build a second internet dedicated to critical infrastructure and communication—an internet that could be very tightly controlled, while letting the popular internet spin on, ever growing. As he said in 2013, we didn't yet have a plan B in place. We still don't, although Danny has tried to get Congress and other powerful interests galvanized, with scant success.

(He's now shifted his focus to working on strengthening the security of the existing internet, a tall order, and a race against time.) A year later, I was invited by TED to give a short (eight-minute) talk at a special session, and I presented my ideas about a plan C, which we could all start working on while waiting for Danny's plan B to go into effect.

Suppose the internet crashed. As Danny pointed out in his talk, the internet is so useful that it has been adopted to support just about everything in the country: the power grid, the cell-phone system, the supply-line coordination, radio and television stations, newspapers. If it were to go down completely, we'd be plunged into electronic darkness. Imagine what that would be like: You're on your way home in your car, waiting at a stoplight, and the lights go out. Your car radio shuts down, your cell phone doesn't work. You rush home and find a dark house and no way of getting any answers you trust! Panic would rise in your chest. *What is happening? Are we under attack? What should I do?* If you have family to care for, your first thought would probably be about how to protect them *at all costs*. What about food, what about fuel, what about looting, where shall we go?

One lesson that was drilled into me when I got my scuba training is that panic is your worst enemy. People do stupid, crazy things when they start to panic. They try to grab their buddy's mouthpiece, they flail and grasp and often end up killing both themselves and their buddy, who is their best chance of help. Panic would be just about anybody's reaction today to such a sudden and total isolation from the electronic world, but only because we have become so dependent on it. A scant 150 years ago, people lived quite secure and carefree lives without any of this, so we know that life is possible without it, but changing our expectations and habits to fit our new circumstances without any advance warning would be a huge task.

Events since 2014 have only added detail to my concern; people are astonishingly easy to stampede under the right conditions, and it is highly probable that if the internet crashed, millions of people would be defensively avoiding even their friends and neighbors, arming themselves and making plans to hunker down in some bunker. The preppers have been planning for this for years, of course, and already have underground food and water stores, to say nothing of arsenals. Unless we can think up and install something to absorb the panic the moment it starts, I fear that we—civilized and well-meaning citizens—would manage to destroy a good portion of our civilization, and our mutual trust as well, in less than forty-eight hours.

But that might well be time enough to set things right. If the internet's collapse was due not to some horrendous act of war but just a technical breakdown, the experts in charge of maintaining it could probably get it back up and running within two days, so if we could just keep people relatively calm and composed for that period, we might avert a catastrophe and return to more or less normal life.

The first thought that would occur to many of us in a sudden catastrophe would be *Call 911*, and if the phone system was down, that would only add to the panic. What could replace 911? What if there were a huge network of local *panic-absorbing stations*—lifeboats, in effect—to which everybody could walk, run, bike, or drive to find their neighbors gathering and pitching in to help one another? And what if, thanks to advance publicity, the first thought that would occur to most people in such a shock wouldn't be *Call 911* but *Head to the lifeboat*? These lifeboats would have to be close enough for most people to get to and would have already been supplied with first-aid kits, water, and canned food, and—most important—local information; there would be people there who knew who owns generators, who is a ham radio operator, which neighbors are disabled and will need to be visited, which pharmacist can deliver prescription medicines, who can be put into service as couriers to check on other nearby lifeboats and encourage people to get to the nearest lifeboat. The key to keeping panic at bay is to put yourself among familiar faces, people who calmly, credibly take charge and answer your questions. Who should organize these? Not the government—too many people today are deeply suspicious of any government project. This would have to be a grassroots movement, self-organized by concerned citizens, your neighbors.

How many people could one panic-absorbing station protect? More than a hundred, maybe as many as a thousand. Where could we find three hundred thousand or four hundred thousand community centers to take care of over three hundred million people? Schools and libraries and fire stations would be likely buildings to serve as meeting places and provide storage for equipment and information, but a better plan would enlist the help of the roughly 380,000 churches in the country. There are, at latest count, also 3,727 synagogues and 2,769 mosques. Religious organizations properly take pride in their community spirit and their commitment to helping their neighbors and comforting the afflicted. These existing social networks would have a great way to "act locally and think globally," preparing their lifeboats for their communities. People all over the country could put together lists of things to do—and not to do—and hold lifeboat drills periodically, preserving and improving the best practices. The key to success is having almost everyone acquainted with a place to go *before* the internet goes down. You wouldn't have to be high tech to be a big help; if you know how to cook, run a mimeograph machine, fix a pump, keep children occupied with stories and games, you would be a valuable team member. We could all use the internet to communicate our best ideas, but we should *write everything down* in multiple hard copies, since our cell phones and laptops would be useless for a while.

This idea of panic absorbers is descended from a line of familiar institutions: volunteer fire brigades, soup kitchens, places of worship, and clubs, and these existing organizations could be the seeds from which local panic absorbers grow. I think we urgently need to scale up this great tradition of local help now, before it is too late.

So why did I ask TED not to put online my talk on this proposal? Because I was rushed and didn't articulate my plan C with the effectiveness I had hoped for, but also because I am not the right guy to be the spokesperson or leader of such a national effort. A bald, bearded, atheist philosophy professor? I didn't want to poison the well by associating this idea with such a dubious champion. So instead, I went around quietly spreading the word among people I thought might be in a better position to kindle this flame. There are in fact quite a few citizen groups that have committees looking into this and even putting their local versions in place. May there soon be many more.

Of course, there may never be a catastrophic internet collapse, thanks to Danny Hillis's plan B or some successor plan that makes our internet less fragile. Still, I feel obliged to raise the alarm, even if I get branded as an alarmist. Besides, I think it would be wonderful if we all got to know our neighbors better by participating in such projects. Think about it. But don't just think about it.

31.

WHY, OH WHY,
DO I LOVE . . .

. . . *Amsterdam*

How can a philosopher not love a country that has a magazine on philosophy available at most newsstands!

In 1993 the Dutch journalist Wim Kayzer produced his television program *A Glorious Accident.* I think few people thought it would work: a series of six ninety-minute introductions of individual thinkers, one each evening, followed by a "reunion" where all six thinkers met together with Wim, our host. When I was invited to be one of the talking heads, *I* certainly didn't think it would work, but it was a free trip to Amsterdam and a chance to interact at length with some interesting people: Oliver Sacks, Steve Gould, Freeman Dyson, the British philosopher Stephen Toulmin, and Rupert Sheldrake, the former Cambridge University chemist whose wild theory of "morphic resonances" was capturing the attention of many nonscientists and provoking the indignation and ridicule of most scientists who encountered him. (I learned that Richard Dawkins had been invited to participate but when he discovered that Rupert Sheldrake was one of the guests, he declined. Too bad, since he would have enjoyed the polite but merciless questioning the rest of us rained on Rupert and he missed as well a rare opportunity to converse directly with Steve Gould, his chief detractor in evolutionary biology.) Wim Kayzer, with his trademark eyepatch, was a famous figure on Dutch television, and he did an amazingly good job of shepherding his half-dozen talkers through the program, after interviewing each of us for *hours* in our homes or offices and then lodging us in separate hotels in Amsterdam so that we couldn't meet in advance of the "reunion" program, which was recorded in a single day's session—nine straight hours!—around a gigantic library table in a studio, with only brief bathroom breaks and a lunch break. This river of videotape was edited down expertly by Wim and his team, but still, the final program ran for more than four uninterrupted hours in its Dutch version (slightly telescoped further for its run on public TV in the US).

Would anybody watch it? Yes, as it turned out. Only the national speed-skating championships had a larger Dutch audience that year; they heard us in English, with subtitles provided. All of us were suddenly famous in the Netherlands, and not just for fifteen minutes; years later, riding a bicycle through Amsterdam, I was spotted and hailed by some fans who had seen the program.

A Glorious Accident demonstrated beyond all doubt that when you put the right talking heads together and let them speak at their own tempos and lengths, you can get unignorable television, better than documentaries tarted up with special effects and elaborate unusual backgrounds. For my interview, Susan had gone out of her way to spiff up our home interior for the cameras, but Kayzer's team mounted a single camera in our living room, and viewers had only a few fleeting glimpses of the house's exterior, in the final program. Yet the interview with Steve Gould had bits of scenes shot in Harvard Square (focused on a hammer dulcimer player seated on the sidewalk who happened to be the son of a dear friend of mine) and a tour of the Museum of Comparative Zoology, where Steve's Harvard office was. Why did he get all the cool surroundings, while I just got close-up shots of me sitting in my favorite chair? Wim later explained to Susan: "Steve didn't have much of anything to say, so I had to use a lot of padding. Dan had a lot to say, and I didn't want to cut any of it."

I was inspired by the program to try my hand at organizing a similar roundtable discussion at Tufts in 1995, filmed for television by a British documentary team, and testing my idea that when experts talk with other experts, the best way to keep them from underexplaining is to have a peripheral target audience of bright undergraduates, so that nobody will worry about insulting fellow experts by overexplaining. My chosen topic was the relation between artificial intelligence and evolution, and around the table I gathered Marvin Minsky, Seymour Papert, Sherry Turkle, David Haig, Pattie Maes, Oliver Selfridge, Hans Moravec, Rod Brooks, the physicist Murray Gell-Mann, the artificial life pioneers John Holland and Karl Sims, the historian Bruce Mazlish, and the futurist Kevin Kelly. I learned firsthand how hard it is to emulate Wim Kayzer and steer such a brilliant and opinionated gang into the topics I wanted them to discuss, but it worked well enough and was certainly a fine confrontation of different viewpoints among people who were all deeply involved in making sense of human minds. Although it was tentatively scheduled to run on Channel 4 in the UK, it was shelved for extraneous reasons and was finally issued in DVD format by Oxford University Press under the misleading title *Artificial Life: The Tufts Symposium*. It got one good review and disappeared. I have managed to disinter it and it is available to view, for the first time, on the supplementary archive for this book.

I suspect *A Glorious Accident* is largely responsible for having launched me so well in the Netherlands, leading to many lecture invitations over the years there, and, in 2012, the Erasmus Prize, the Netherlands' highest academic honor, presented with much ceremony by Prince Willem-Alexander, with his mother, Queen Beatrix, attending, shortly before she abdicated so that he could be crowned king.

And finally, there is the voyage of the *Stad Amsterdam*, a clipper ship that recreated the voyage of the *Beagle* during the bicentennial year of Darwin's birth, in 2009 and 2010. Ever since I was a boy, I had dreamed of sailing on a clipper ship, and for decades there were none still sailing, so I had relegated the desire to fantasy, but a few have been built recently, mostly as training ships. VPRO, the television company that created *A Glorious Accident*, chartered the

Dutch-built vessel to make a long series of programs about Darwin and invited me to be one of the talking heads. Susan and I were guests on the Melbourne-to-Adelaide leg, with albatrosses wheeling above us and whales breaching in our wake. I sang for my supper by doing a few video presentations on evolutionary theory and celestial navigation and got to spend hours studying the exquisite design of both the gear and the methods of the crew. I was unable to join them high above deck furling sails and replacing lines, but in almost every other regard my boyhood wish was granted, and we got to know another guest speaker—the botanist Sarah Darwin, great-great-granddaughter of the great man.

. . . Beirut

When I went off to graduate school in Oxford in 1963, Mother returned to her beloved Beirut to be the librarian at the American Community School attached to the American University of Beirut, and my younger sister, Charlotte, finished high school there. Susan and I joined them for a few weeks in the summer of 1964, along with my older sister, Cynthia, and enjoyed one of the happiest periods in Beirut's troubled history, when it was rightly called the Paris of the Middle East. Mother's apartment had a rooftop swimming pool, from which we could look down on the Mediterranean and the seaside amusement park where a traveling circus was summering and listen to lions roar and elephants trumpet while we sipped drinks on the balcony. We could also watch a dance group rehearsing the *dabke* and other Levantine dances to be performed at the Baalbeck festival later in the summer. Susan and Charlotte and I took a quick trip to Damascus, and then took a *service* (a fixed-route, scheduled taxi that takes multiple passengers) to Jerusalem (Jordan, not Israel). There are four passenger seats in a *service*, and I attempted to purchase the fourth seat, so we'd have the car to ourselves with a little more comfort, but the driver was strangely unwilling to consider this. The well-dressed man who insisted on joining us turned out to be Abu Nada, a Palestinian who had risen in the ranks of the government of Jordan. He took an instant liking to this trio of young Americans and was delighted to teach me a lot of Arabic words on the daylong journey, which included—at his direction—unscheduled stops at the ruins of Jerash and several other out-of-the-way points of interest. By the time we approached Jerusalem, he had promised a swim in the Dead Sea that evening and a *mensef* feast the next day with a Bedouin sheik who owed him a favor and was summering outside Jericho. At a *mensef*, with the guests seated on rugs around a huge copper tray piled with rice and lamb, the guest of honor is offered the lamb's eye to eat.

On the drive out beyond Jericho, I asked Abu Nada which would be worse etiquette: firmly declining the offer of the sheep's eye or trying *and failing* to gag the thing down? Neither would do, he replied, but we could try a diplomatic end run; I could make a flowery speech of thanks to the sheik, which Abu would translate, in which I asked permission to convey the honor of the lamb's eye to my dear friend Abu Nada, in gratitude for making this occasion possible. If the sheik accepted, Abu would happily eat the eye, as he had done on many occasions; if not, I was to take a deep breath and gulp the orb down one way or another. The sheik granted my request, so I have still never swallowed a lamb's eye. But I did witness the slaughtering of the lamb, at arm's length. A little lamb was brought out by the sheik's formally dressed chief servant, and after I had duly praised it for its beauty (*jamil ktir*), he took out his long curved knife and slit its throat, letting the blood spurt out at our feet. Then he cut a small slit in one of the lamb's hind legs near the hoof, hung it on a tent pole, and at lightning speed skinned the animal down to its head and shoulders, creating a bag into which, with a single deft stroke, he emptied the entrails, cutting off the lamb's head and front legs with a mighty swipe of his blade and handing the bag to his assistant. He left the rest of the butchering to his underlings, who carried off the clean carcass to be cut and prepared. Meanwhile Susan and my sisters were in the women's tent, helping to make the flatbreads, which were cooked on a metal dome over a wood fire. Then they got to try on the wedding dress and jewels of the sheik's latest wife, with cascades of gold coins covering their faces like a veil. Quite a day, and the rest of our visit was equally full of splendors.

Years passed, Mother died, Charlotte had an adventurous career as a journalist in Beirut, and I paid a brief visit there to give a talk at AUB, during a trip to Istanbul. Would I like to spend a semester at AUB? Absolutely. All my life, I had wanted to teach there, where my father had taught and met my mother, and where I had gone to nursery school in the '40s. (I amused my parents' friends when they visited us and asked if I, aged four or five, went to school. "Oh yes," I always replied. "I go to AUB.") So in 2011 Susan and I returned to Beirut for a spring semester, and part of my preparation was to remind myself that it couldn't be as grand an adventure as my parents' years in the '30s and '40s, or even our own adventures in the '60s. But it would still be fun. In fact the young faculty in the philosophy department and a few from other departments, mostly single and without children, adopted us immediately and took us on many adventures. We had a favorite taxi driver, who used to park within a block of our apartment in Ras Beirut just a few blocks from the university and seemed always to be ready on a minute's notice to take us wherever we wanted to go. (Sometimes he would warn us that where we wanted to go was dangerous. The troubles in Syria prevented us from making a return trip to Damascus, for instance, and the road to Baalbek was no longer safe.)

The students at AUB were intrepid and intellectually curious, and it was a joy to see young men and women from all over the Arabic-speaking world (a few women heavily veiled but others in miniskirts) learning together, living together, preparing to take their places in critical roles in their home countries as generations have done since the founding of AUB in 1866 by an American educator and missionary, Daniel Bliss. It's a beautiful campus overlooking the Mediterranean, and even in the most terrible times during the civil war of the 1980s, when one president of the university was kidnapped and another was murdered, it has kept going, and it continues to do so, with Lebanon in desperate financial shape following the large explosion and the continuing wars in the region, with refugee camps to maintain, and intermittent failures of the national infrastructure.

I went back to AUB for a philosophy conference in 2018 and returned in June of 2022 to accept an honorary doctorate and give the keynote speech. Lebanon, Beirut, and AUB are all bravely recovering from their recent catastrophes as they have always done in the past. Watching the hundreds of young doctors and engineers and economists—and yes, even philosophers—march proudly by me with their hard-won diplomas gives me hope for the future.

... *London*

In 2001 I was a Leverhulme Visiting Professor at the London School of Economics, which gave Susan and me our first opportunity to live in London for an extended period instead of staying in hotels or making day trips from elsewhere in England. We found a furnished apartment near Earl's Court, in the building where Diana Spencer lived before she married Prince Charles. There was a pleasant interior garden courtyard and good architectural details. My daily Tube trips to LSE and back were an interesting routine, and the best students at LSE were excellent. I did a seminar on free will, which led up to my 2003 book, *Freedom Evolves*. This was at a time when the UK was trying out a new scheme of quality assessment, tracking publications in peer-reviewed journals, and I learned to my amusement that one of the reasons I was invited to be a visiting professor was that the philosophy department at LSE got to list all my current publications in their record of accomplishments! It is more than difficult to measure academic achievement, and Goodhart's law rules: whenever a measure becomes a target, it ceases to be a good measure. LSE's philosophers were very productive but not above salting the mine with a few extra nuggets.

In 2013, I was invited to be on the faculty of the New College of the Humanities in London, philosopher Anthony Grayling's brave experiment in a private college—much like Tufts and so many famous colleges in the US—in a country that has frowned on the concept. Once I was assured that, just as at Tufts, there would be scholarship funding for worthy students who couldn't afford the tuition, I joined the faculty with the expectation that I would spend at least a week a year teaching there. There was an initial outcry among academics in the humanities in London against Grayling's proposal, partly inspired, I soon learned, by the fact that Grayling was luring excellent young people away from other London university departments with his better salaries and working conditions. "How could you agree to do this?" I was asked angrily by philosophy professors and graduate students in London, but I defended my decision; NCH, like Tufts, was privately funded, academically elite (like Oxbridge colleges), but not reserved for the rich. It had been arranged that NCH students would take the University of London examinations for their degrees, and the first proof of concept came in 2016, when NCH students were at the top of the listings.

NCH has been my London academic home now for almost a decade, and once COVID is firmly in retreat I hope to go back for some more lectures and seminars. Coming to London for a few weeks at a time is a great way of getting together with the dozens of academics in several fields whose work is of importance to me, and my dance card is always full when I'm in town, but we make sure to reserve some time for theater and music, going to Tom Stoppard's *The Hard Problem* as his guest one night, and David Benedictus's play, *The Happy Hypocrite*, based on a story by Max Beerbohm, on another.

. . . *Paris*

I've lost track of how many times I've been to Paris, as a speaker or as a tourist, and I've already mentioned several adventures, but a few more were life changing. In 1980, the Marxist philosopher Louis Althusser, a professor at the École normale supérieure, strangled his wife. He was declared insane and institutionalized, leaving a position open at that most prestigious institution. For several years, his chair was vacant, and Jean Khalfa, then one of my young philosopher fans in France (he's now at Trinity College, Cambridge), managed to persuade his elder colleagues there that they should give me a temporary visiting appointment while they continued their search for a permanent successor to Althusser. Needless to say, I accepted the invitation, especially since its requirement that I lecture in French would force me, finally, to achieve something approaching fluency in that language. For some reason that escapes me now, my visit had to be postponed for a year, and when I arrived at the storied edifice in rue d'Ulm in May 1985, Khalfa had left to take a position in Toulouse, and I had no natural hosts to show me the ropes. No matter, I would give my French lectures, in Jacques Derrida's acoustically treacherous round stone well of a classroom, to an audience that consisted of a few *normaliens* and a happy throng of cognitive scientists and philosophers from other Paris institutions, whose English was much, much better than my French, but I soldiered on gamely. I asked my official host, Bernard Pautrat, who attended my first lecture (only), for an assessment of my makeshift but enthusiastic French. It was, he said, "pittoresque mais très clair."

Academic French tends to be quite arch and flowery, and I was not even attempting to create such elegant sentences. The Princeton philosopher Richard Rorty and I once attended a UNESCO conference in Paris where simultaneous translation was provided and we both listened with the headphones providing English to one ear and the other ear free to listen to the French. The English translation was full of pauses along the lines of "And so . . . I think . . . there are three . . . issues . . . that need addressing . . . today . . . regarding . . . the challenges . . . facing democracy . . ." No content was being lost in this gappy translation, and at one point Dick leaned over and whispered in my ear, "They think they're thinking."

The ENS may well have been embarrassed, or at least inconvenienced, by my presence, since nobody in the philosophy department there was interested in cognitive science. They did nothing to advertise my lectures to other institutions in Paris. When Jean-Pierre Changeux, the silverback among French neuroscientists, learned of this, he wrote a ferocious letter to them, after which their relations with me improved somewhat. For one thing, people who phoned to ask about the time and place of my lectures were no longer told that the ENS knew nothing about them. This frosty reception didn't discourage me, since I was getting to know the gang at CREA, the Centre de recherche en épistémologie appliquée, where I later spent a happy few months in 1990, as well as the cognitive scientists at the Centre national de la recherche scientifique. Many of these researchers later formed the Institut Jean Nicod, where in 2001 I gave the Jean Nicod Lectures.

French philosophers have been slow to develop any interest in my work—aside from Pascal Engel, Jacques Bouveresse, Daniel Andler, and Pierre Jacob—but such cognitive neuroscientists as Changeux, Stanislas Dehaene, Claire Sergent, and others have more than filled that gap. I have been a friendly critic (or contributor) to the Global Workspace model of consciousness developed by them and Bernard Baars, the best articulation of something like my "fame in the brain" theory. When I published *Consciousness Explained* in 1991, I had lots of ideas, or at least hunches, about how the cognitive architecture of consciousness would work, but I didn't want to be prematurely dismissed if some of those hunches proved false, so I was deliberately noncommittal about a lot of details that have since been falling into place rather well, thanks to their work and the work of others. So far, so good.

On another pet theme of mine, the role of Dawkins's *memes* in creating our minds, I have had a running debate for three decades with my best French critic, Dan Sperber, and some of his colleagues about cultural evolution. I once presented something of a précis of my thinking on these topics (in French) to a group of French phenomenologists who were strangely defensive (and, I think, strangely offended) by my talk. Philosopher/engineer Jean-Pierre Dupuy scolded the audience for their closed-mindedness, and I said they reminded me of the wagon trains of settlers heading west in America and pulling their wagons into a defensive circle when they saw me coming. I told them not to worry: "I'm just moving through your territory. Soon I will be on the horizon, and you'll be in danger of running out of water."

32.

ONE MORE EDEN: THE
SANTA FE INSTITUTE

I'VE LEARNED MORE, AND LEARNED MORE ABOUT LEARN-
ing, at the Santa Fe Institute than at any of my other idyllic think
tanks. Now that I'm a professor on the SFI external faculty, Susan
and I make pilgrimages as often as we can arrange, and what draws
us back again and again (in addition to the glorious weather and
scenery) is how the institute's denizens uniquely combine open-
mindedness with a bracing insistence on clarity and rigor. One
innovation there will give you a sense of it. The young cognitive
scientist Simon DeDeo, when he was a fellow there, introduced a
Friday afternoon series he called the Dangerous Ideas Seminar. Fellows and faculty were invited to hold forth with a *half-baked* idea of
theirs, one not ready for peer review, let alone publication, and those
who showed up for the discussion were forbidden to use the word
"but"! (That was a joke, but it was a good way of insisting that criticism should be constructive, an effort to bake the target idea into
something sturdier and in sharper focus, so that everybody, not just
the inner coterie of would-be experts, could understand. Sniping was
discouraged.) These sessions were typically mind-bending, and they
epitomize the way SFI works. I've often praised the Dangerous Ideas
Seminar idea to colleagues around the world, and I think a few of
them have implemented versions of their own. Like the "X on Y" sessions I described in chapter 29, which has now been adopted by the
Tufts philosophy department colloquia, it is a good antidote to the
ever-present academic pressure to score points on one's rivals.

SFI was the incubator of artificial life, a collaborative enterprise by biologists and computer scientists to study evolution through attempts to create supersimple virtual life-forms that would evolve on their own by natural selection in computer-simulated worlds. My first visit to SFI was in 1996 to participate in a workshop on artificial life organized by Christopher Langton, who had coined the term and started the field in the late '80s at a Los Alamos meeting. Thomas Ray's Tierra, John Holland's Echo, Karl Sims's Evolved Virtual Creatures, and Richard Dawkins's Blind Watchmaker software were among the early fruits, and I had seen the field as a worthy companion to AI, in the new endeavor we might call computer-assisted thought experiments. These were like philosophers' thought experiments but much more demanding, in that you couldn't just wave your hands about vaporware; you had to have written the code. That is where I first met John Maynard Smith, who was not much impressed with this early work (in spite of the fact that his computer models had created the field of evolutionary game theory) because most of the modelers were not biologists and didn't seem to know much about actual, as opposed to virtual, organisms. But he was willing to give it a try, and he and I spent an instructive but fruitless day trying to model the Baldwin effect of learned behavior enhancing genetic evolution (discussed at some length in *Darwin's Dangerous Idea*) with the help of the great A-Life-hacker David Ackley (a Tufts alumnus, by the way). Later that day we got lost in the desert while trying to drive to a dinner party, which gave us some extra hours to talk about the subtleties of natural selection. He had supported my critique of Gould and Lewontin's "Spandrels" essay in a commentary in *BBS* in 1983, and later wrote his famous favorable review of *Darwin's Dangerous Idea* for the *New York Review of Books* (see chapter 34).

In recent years, I've put together workshops and working groups on cultural evolution, trying (unsuccessfully) to smooth out the disagreements between the French faction (Dan Sperber, Olivier Morin, and Nicolas Claidière), the American faction (Robert Boyd, Peter Richerson, and Joseph Henrich), the memes faction (Sue Blackmore and me), and the Australian philosophers of biology (Kim Sterelny and Peter Godfrey-Smith). The half-baked results of that working group can be found at Dan Sperber's website.

I hosted another working group that tried to get to the bottom of David Haig's intrepid venture into combining information theory, evolutionary theory, and philosophy of language (including Derrida!). This was also less successful than I had hoped, but, as always, SFI set ideas buzzing in my head that are still swarming around, hunting for solutions to the problems I encountered there. These sessions at SFI were my chief exploratory exercises while writing *From Bacteria to Bach and Back: The Evolution of Minds* (2017), which is, after all, the culmination of everything I've tried to get clear about in my career.

Part Four

ACADEMIC
BATTLES

33

THE HISTORY OF PHILOSOPHY; RICHARD RORTY

M Y FATHER WAS A HISTORIAN, AND I MADE SEVERAL valiant attempts as a student to follow in his footsteps but quickly discovered that my brain is not suited for historical scholarship: I forget the pivotal facts—names, places, dates, key phrases—within days of learning them, replacing them in my memory banks with gists, trends, themes, and impressions. For years I taught courses in the history of philosophy—huge surveys ("From Socrates to Russell") and specific courses on the British empiricists, Descartes and rationalism, Nietzsche, and twentieth-century analytic philosophy, for instance—and each year I would have to go back to my books and notes and relearn the details, which I had largely forgotten. It was always a chore for me, and I envy many of my colleagues for their fluent command of the details, which I do think are important. I have often been asked by scientists why philosophers need to study the history of philosophy. You can be a first-rate chemist or physicist or molecular biologist with only a sketchy introductory-textbook version of your field's history. Why should philosophy be different? Because, I say, the history of philosophy is largely the history of very tempting mistakes made by very smart people, and if you don't know the history, you are almost certain to make the same mistakes, because they're still very tempting. I find it both amusing and satisfying when a scientist leaps in, as they sometimes do when they have a free afternoon, and attempts to solve the mind-body problem or the free-will problem or the problem of causation and ends up, with gratifying regularity, remaking Plato's mistakes, Kant's mistakes, Hume's mistakes.

So I do believe all philosophers—myself included—should conscientiously study the history of philosophy, but I also believe, in disagreement with many philosophers, that it's quite all right to adopt a sort of smorgasbord approach to the literature, sampling a little bit here, taking a large serving there, helping myself—as I said at the outset, I'm a pack rat, a magpie—to slices of what strike *me* as the most exciting or thought-provoking tidbits and leaving the rest of the interpretation to the scholars. I think I have learned a lot from Husserl, but some distinguished Husserl scholars think my reading is irreparably ill-informed. I don't care. I turned to Husserl to figure out how the mind works and got some valuable help from that reading; if Husserl himself would be aghast at my construal, too bad for Husserl. I am happy to give him credit, but if Husserlians want to reject my gift, they are welcome to do so. I'm not going to spend days or weeks wrangling over hermeneutics. In the preface of one of my favorite books from my Oxford years, Peter Strawson's *The Bounds of Sense*, an ingenious interpretation of Kant's *Critique of Pure Reason*, he says much the same thing—more deferentially, but I've always counted on him as licensing my attitude. From his preface:

As any Kantian scholar who may read it will quickly detect, it is by no means a work of historical-philosophical scholarship. I have not been assiduous in studying the writings of Kant's lesser predecessors, his own minor works or the very numerous commentaries which two succeeding centuries have produced. I have written for those students of the *Critique* who, like myself, have read and re-read the work with a commingled sense of great insights and great mystification. I have tried to present a clear, uncluttered and unified interpretation, at least strongly supported by the text as it stands, of the system of thought which the *Critique* contains.

While on the subject of Peter Strawson's politeness just now, I cannot resist telling a story his devoted student Ruby Meager (who edited *The Bounds of Sense*) once told me. She was driving her hero and his wife back to Oxford on a foggy night and suddenly realized that the headlights of a lorry parked heading the wrong way were leading her off the road. She swerved and braked, but it was too late; they had a head-on collision with the lorry. As the three of them were having their minor injuries tended to in the hospital, they shared notes on what each had thought during that longish second or two when they all could foresee the crash. Ruby confessed that her thought had been that she was about to kill the world's greatest philosopher and his wife, and Mrs. Strawson said her thought was "I must cover my face," which she did in the nick of time, before her head went through the windshield. They turned to Peter, who allowed that he had had *two* thoughts. The first was "I shall be all right; I'm in the back seat." And the second was "That was not the thought of a gentleman!"

Philosophers are not always gentlemen—and women in the field are not always ladies. Times have changed dramatically during my half century in the field (we now turn to the history of *recent* philosophy), and for the first fifteen years of my philosophical questing the field was dominated (I use the word deliberately) by men, and in the Anglophone world by men who were "analytic philosophers"—as contrasted with the "Continental philosophers," who professed (and I use the word deliberately) from the dais in the university. The contrasts could be stark. Analytic philosophers tended to be dry, systematic, and sufficiently versed in logic to pepper their papers with formulae along the lines of

$$(\exists x)\ (\exists y)\ (x \text{ is an explosion \& } x \text{ is of the boiler \& } y \text{ is an explosion \& } y \text{ is of the boiler \& } x \neq y)$$

(Donald Davidson, "Eternal vs. Ephemeral Events,"
Noûs 5, no. 4 [November 1971])

—or—

Nob assumes that just one witch blighted Bob's mare, and Nob wonders whether (the following is the case:) just one witch is such that Nob assumes it to have blighted Bob's mare, and she killed Cob's sow.

(D. C. Dennett, "Geach on Intentional Identity," *Journal of Philosophy* 65, no. 11 [1968]; my reply to Peter Geach, Miss Anscombe's husband)

Yes, I could write like that, and still can, but choose not to do so. Analytic philosophers in the old days showed up with fully written-out papers to read, and perhaps handouts with dozens of numbered formulae to be discussed, and we expected to be challenged by whichever smart aleck had the quickest eye for a lurking infelicity or—god forbid!—covert contradiction. We were *serious*. By contrast, philosophers of the Continental tradition held forth in less structured and sometimes deliberately obscure language, daring their docile audiences to understand them and not expecting any impertinent challenges. I have often wondered how one got to be a *professor* of Continental philosophy; what initiation rite licensed one to declare one's *philosophy* from the dais without fear of contradiction?

The analytic-philosophy old-boys network ruled the field for decades, from the '50s through the '70s. I once challenged some of my colleagues to name an important living philosopher whose PhD was *not* from the Ivy League, Oxford or Cambridge, the University of Chicago, or Berkeley. First, it was interesting that most of those I asked knew where the famous philosophers did their graduate work, and second, it was interesting how long it took them to think of a counterexample. Hilary Putnam got his PhD from UCLA in 1951, working with Hans Reichenbach (after studying at Penn and Harvard). Offhand, I cannot think of another distinguished (analytic) philosopher of that era who had a similarly minor-league PhD.

Not all Ivy League philosophy departments were cut from the same cloth, though. In 1963 the University of Pittsburgh got a large gift that enabled them to raid the Yale philosophy department, luring Wilfrid Sellars and a bunch of brilliant logicians away, leaving behind a distinctly nonanalytic crew, who then made the serious mistake of hiring some of their own PhDs. The result was a department consisting of an inbred and isolated group of scholars that was, quite frankly, regarded as an embarrassment by most analytic philosophers and by many academics and administrators at Yale. Several Yale presidents in a row attempted to reform and rebuild the department, without success and with much rancor. My friend Bob Fogelin, himself a pre-raid PhD from Yale, was installed but was too junior to accomplish his task, and I can vividly remember him telling me, over a few beers around a pool table, how he dreamed of lining up all his senior colleagues and machine-gunning them in a St. Valentine's Day massacre. Another pre-raid Yale PhD, my friend Ruth Barcan Marcus, was brought in, and there was no feistier or cannier operator than Ruth, a superb logician and for many years the board chair of the American Philosophical Association. She was brought back to Yale's department to break heads, and did her best, but she too was defeated in the end. (At the Twentieth World Congress of Philosophy, in Boston in 1998, the Copley Place Hotel and conference center was overrun by thousands of philosophers from all over the world. The hotel is in the middle of an upscale shopping mall—Tiffany, Gucci, Jimmy Choo—so there were many well-to-do Bostonians mingling with the untidy crowd. I ran into Ruth, who came up to me laughing to tell me of the conversation she had just overheard in the elevator. "Who do you think all these strange people *are*?" asked one matron. "I don't know," her friend replied, "but I may have figured it out. I think it's a convention of the homeless!")

At Tufts, whenever we had a job opening in the philosophy department, we'd have hundreds of applications, and as a matter of informal policy we almost always decided to "make book" on Yale by interviewing one or two of their top candidates (by their lights). And with one exception I can recall, they all turned out to be the same: fatuous, supercilious prattlers who thought very highly of themselves for no reason that we could discern. Hugo Bedau and I coined a term for what they did: Yale Fancytalk. We hired the exception, the Nietzsche expert Michael Green, who could have received tenure had he stayed, but he left us after a few years to go to law school, telling me that on reflection he couldn't imagine spending his academic life dealing with the scholars in the Continental tradition. He eventually published an important book on Nietzsche but is now teaching at the law school at the College of William and Mary.

The hegemony of the analytic philosophers evaporated in 1979, at the Eastern Division meeting of the APA in Boston, when a coup d'état was staged by a group of mostly American but Continental philosophers who called themselves *pluralists* (let a thousand flowers bloom). I wonder how many of today's young philosophers and graduate students have ever heard about this. It was an academic earthquake at the time. Frustrated by the short shrift given them by members of the "analytic monolith," these philosophers studied the bylaws of the APA and discovered that although for decades the nominating committee had put forward a single candidate for vice president who was then elected by acclaim and would succeed as president the following year, the rules allowed nominations from the floor and actual elections! In secret, the pluralists put together their slate, prepared their challenges to the parliamentarian and other officers, and made sure their members were all set to descend en masse on the lightly attended business meeting and take over the APA Eastern Division. About half an hour before the meeting, their security broke down: a coup was rumored to be in the offing, and we monolith members were rounded up in the bar and hustled to the meeting to try to fend off the usurpation. Dick Rorty was president that year, and it was an irony (one of his favorite topics) that he—the most ecumenical and open-minded of the "analytic monolith" leaders—presided over the meeting, while Tom Nagel executed his duties as parliamentarian with aplomb. There were nominating speeches and rebuttals, the most memorable of which was by Ruth Marcus, whose Yale colleague John Smith, a philosopher of religion and a theologian, was the pluralists' candidate. She explicitly trashed his whole career, his character, his books. I had never heard a philosopher speak so ill of a colleague in public, and seldom in private.

We lost. The establishment had nominated Adolf Grünbaum, a Pittsburgh philosopher of science, to be the new vice president. Not wanting to offend innocent Adolf, the victorious pluralists nominated and elected him vice president the following year, so that in 1982 he finally got to deliver the presidential address he had expected to give earlier. He did not accept the olive branch with equanimity. Adolf was famous for his tirades against Freud as an unscientific poseur, and his address was vintage Grünbaum. I happened to follow a cluster of pluralists out of the hall at the close of his address and overheard the reply when a pluralist who had stayed away asked how Grünbaum's address had gone: "It was nasty, brutish and *long*."

Thereafter, the APA's programs were filled with papers on topics, and by philosophers, that would never have made the cut before the pluralist coup. Was this a good thing? Yes, said some monolith members, since it meant there was more guilt-free time to spend in the bar at conventions. Yes, said others, since the pluralists had justice on their side. My verdict is mixed. Still, the published programs of the APA meetings list dozens of talks whose titles are so ripe for parody that when I recently perused a few looking for likely examples to anonymize, I had difficulty "improving" on the actual candidates,

356 / I've Been Thinking

but ask yourself whether you are aching to go to the sessions where the following talks will be given:

"The Ineffability of History and the Problem of the Unitary Self"
"Dialectical Encroachment: Humiliation and Integrity"
"Can Relationalistic Ontology Avoid Incoherence through a Recursive Metatheory?"
"Art as War: The Resilience of Autonomy"

~

IT IS HARD TO OVERESTIMATE the support Dick Rorty gave my work since the day we met, at Princeton—on the occasion of my first invited talk (see chapter 7). Early in his career, when he was regarded as a leading philosopher of mind in the analytic tradition, he published several papers favorably discussing my theory of consciousness. We largely agreed on how philosophy of mind should proceed, except that he always tried to cajole me into adopting his more radical perspective, which I congenially resisted. I even made a joke of it, which I largely regret today. In a 1982 paper, "Contemporary Philosophy of Mind," Rorty wrote an enthusiastic account of the revolutionary "Ryle-Dennett tradition," and I responded mischievously, perhaps rudely. Was I really as radical a revolutionary as he said I was?

Since I, as an irremediably narrow-minded and unhistorical analytic philosopher, am always looking for a good excuse not to have to read Hegel or Heidegger or Derrida or those other chaps who don't have the decency to think in English, I am tempted by Rorty's performance on this occasion to enunciate a useful hermeneutical principle, the *Rorty Factor*: Take whatever Rorty says about anyone's views and multiply it by .742.

After all, if Rorty can find so much more in my own writing than I put there, he's probably done the same or better for

Heidegger—which means I can save myself the trouble of reading Heidegger; I can just read Rorty's *Philosophy and the Mirror of Nature* (Princeton University Press, 1979) and come out about 40% ahead while enjoying my reading at the same time.

I'm also a bit chagrined to acknowledge that the definition of *"a rortiori"* in my *Philosophical Lexicon* ("adj., true for even more obscure and fashionable Continental reasons") has probably contributed to a caricature of his work that is all too convenient: the analytic philosopher turned Continental belle-lettrist. At the same time, I really didn't want to join Dick in his postmodernist campaign, with its demotion of the concept of truth and facts. I have been harshly rebuked by some Rorty fans for "straw-manning" my friend in disagreeing with him over truth, but we did discuss it at length, for years, and I'm sure I got him right. As I wrote almost two decades later:

Richard Rorty deserves his large and enthralled readership in the arts and humanities, and in the "humanistic" social sciences, but when his readers enthusiastically interpret him as encouraging their postmodernist skepticism about truth, they trundle down paths he himself has refrained from traveling. When I press him on these points, he concedes that there is indeed a useful concept of truth that survives intact after all the corrosive philosophical objections have been duly entered. This serviceable, modest concept of truth, Rorty acknowledges, has its uses: when we want to compare two maps of the countryside for reliability, for instance, or when the issue is whether the accused did or did not commit the crime as charged.

Even Richard Rorty, then, acknowledges the gap, and the importance of the gap, between appearance and reality, between those theatrical exercises that may entertain us without pretense of truth-telling, and those that aim for, and often hit, the truth. He calls it a "vegetarian" concept of truth. Very well, then, let's all be vegetarians about the truth. Scientists never wanted to go the whole hog anyway.

Dick didn't always discourage the most radical (mis?)readings of his words, I think it is fair to say, and this attitude earned him some serious enemies in analytic philosophy. We often discussed this, most memorably at a sumptuous lunch in Buenos Aires when we slipped away from a pan-American philosophy conference to dine at what was claimed to be the finest restaurant in Argentina. Given the inflation then afflicting that country, our lunch cost roughly a month's salary of a university lecturer in Buenos Aires, and the power of our dollars gave the occasion a reflective seriousness that was not always our mood. At one point, I allowed that I cared more about maintaining the respect and interest of cognitive scientists than of most philosophers, and he responded by confessing that he didn't give a damn about his reputation among scientists—*or* philosophers; he coveted the esteem of poets! Why? His father, he said, had been the poetry editor of *Dissent*, that worthy left-wing magazine, and as a high school student Dick had tried his hand at writing a sonnet. (I too remember my high school sonnet—awful, but a fascinating exercise.) He showed his sonnet to his father, who read it briskly and handed it back with a single comment: "Doggerel."

Philosophy isn't just science—though some philosophers try to make it as scientific as possible—and it isn't just poetry. My favorite definition of the field is by Wilfrid Sellars: "The aim of philosophy, abstractly formulated, is to understand how things in the broadest possible sense of the term hang together in the broadest possible sense of the term." If this strikes you as comical or ludicrous, think again. Here are some of the different kinds of "things in the broadest possible sense of the term": thoughts, colors, smiles, songs, haircuts, opportunities, dollars, games, meanings, dangers, holes, numbers . . . as well as atoms, molecules, photons, quarks, cells, gravity. What are songs made of? Are colors real? What are opportunities made of? Don't ask a scientist—or don't expect a cogent and problem-free answer. One impatient answer is that nothing exists except atoms (or subatomic particles). Then what is the chemical composition of a song, a poem, an opportunity? "Those aren't real," comes the answer. Really? Attempts to *reduce* all the familiar things of life to the proper entities of science are all procrustean, but then what *is* the relationship between the various candidates for thinghood? How do they all hang together? Some people find these questions so annoyingly confusing that they block their ears and walk away. Fine. Philosophy isn't for everybody. But those who want to satisfy their curiosity will find that formal, systematic attempts to line up all the issues and knock them off one by one are doomed. Here is where philosophy is an art, an exercise in imagination-stretching, in dislodging the blockades set up by a host of semi-understood ideas. Dick Rorty wasn't always right, but he was always a fine philosopher.

34.

ACADEMIC BULLIES
AND ICONOCLASTS

IN EVERY ACADEMIC FIELD THERE ARE USUALLY A FEW
bullies—senior figures who terrorize the less established, especially nontenured faculty and graduate students, with their *obiter
dicta* and brusque dismissal of challenges. In the sciences, they also
often have considerable influence over who gets research funding;
getting on the wrong side of such a silverback can be an almost fatal
blow to one's career. Not needing federal or foundational grant support for my research, I have been in a particularly secure position to
bell a few cats, and I was eagerly encouraged to do so by colleagues
in both evolutionary biology and neuroscience when I took on Stephen Jay Gould and Gerald Edelman. I also had my encounters with
Noam Chomsky, but since I've described them elsewhere, I won't
repeat those stories here. I also want to tell a few tales about exemplary iconoclasts I have known and admired.

The bullies are almost always alpha-male primates, although there
are a few female bullies in my experience. Elizabeth Anscombe (see
chapter 5) was a bully, for instance, and I have dealt with a few others, but in private correspondence, not public challenge, so I will
pass over them in silence hoping they got the message. Most tough
women in philosophy stand as iconoclasts, not bullies, defending
initially derided views and weathering the blows with grace and
determination. Ruthless Ruth Millikan, ruthless Ruth Barcan Marcus, and the redoubtable Judith Jarvis Thomson come to mind.

In 1999, I got a phone call from the evolutionary biologist Lynn
Margulis, who said she would be happy to give a talk at Tufts. (She

was nearby at UMass Amherst and wanted an excuse to spend a weekend in Boston, as I recall.) I was only too pleased to invite her and decided to put together a series of talks, which I entitled "Iconoclasts on the Frontiers of Science." It featured four speakers. Lynn Margulis was rightly celebrated for championing—though she did not initiate the theory—the endosymbiotic origin of the eukaryotic cell. (I describe this in *Darwin's Dangerous Idea*.) Elizabeth Bates was a professor of psycholinguistics at UC San Diego and a stalwart critic of Chomsky and his hypothesis of an innate language acquisition device, or LAD, an idea that held back good work on the evolution of language for decades. Susan Blackmore is a British psychologist who (along with me) championed Richard Dawkins's memes and wrote *The Meme Machine* (1999). Elaine Morgan was a science journalist (not an official academic), who wrote *The Aquatic Ape* (1982), defending marine biologist Alister Hardy's theory that *H. sapiens* went through an evolutionary digression in the sea (following such other aquatic mammals as seals, whales, and dolphins) before returning to land with a variety of features that would be adaptive for shore-dwelling shellfish-eating primates. I had invited the psychologist Judith Rich Harris, author of *The Nurture Assumption* (1998), to be a speaker, but alas, she had to decline for health reasons.

All of these women had braved the brickbats and insults of their male colleagues and held the day—though many think the jury is still out on memes (while I persist in arguing for their importance, most recently and in great detail in *From Bacteria to Bach and Back*) and on the aquatic ape (about which I remain agnostic but hopeful). The motto of the series might well have been borrowed from Janis Joplin's "Me and Bobby McGee": "Freedom's just another word for nothing left to lose." While their male counterparts cautiously protected their positions in the old-boy network, these women decided that they might as well go all out.

All of them gave memorable, feisty talks to rapt audiences, but the best was by Elaine Morgan, who outlined the aquatic-ape theory and told us about the abuse heaped on her by the anthropological establishment. There were major figures in anthropology and evolutionary biology in the auditorium, and—even better—there was a young anthropologist of impeccable establishment credentials (and attitudes to match) who responded quite fiercely to Elaine's lively presentation. Nothing could have so strikingly illustrated and confirmed her account of the way she had been treated by the establishment than this fellow's badgering. She played him like a violin, calmly rebutting his claims, pointing out his overstatements, and responding cheerily to his ever more hostile retorts. It was obvious that she had thought harder and deeper about these issues than he had, and when she—always respectful, always friendly—was through with him, he was a snarling villain, and the entire audience was cheering her on. A week later, he showed up at my office abashed, acknowledged that he had "lost it," and apologized for making a scene, but I told him he had given us all a great demonstration of one of her major points, for which I was grateful. Elaine and I corresponded some over the years about her campaigns for the aquatic-ape theory, and when she told me she would like to defend it at the 2009 TED conference in Oxford, I recommended her vigorously to TED's curator, Chris Anderson, who found a slot for her. I was thrilled (but not surprised) when she stole the show at TED; I'd told Chris she would. I treasure her rhapsodic note of thanks after the event.

My conviction about women being the most likely innovators in science and philosophy has been quietly gaining strength in the meantime, and some of the best, most original thinkers I have worked with, besides Ruth Millikan and Kathleen Akins (see chapters 18 and 21), include philosophers Margaret Boden at Sussex, Carol Rovane at Columbia, Jenann Ismael at Johns Hopkins, Helena Cronin at the London School of Economics, Diana Raffman at Toronto, and Rosa Cao at Stanford; psychologists Claire Sergent in Paris, Cecilia Heyes at Oxford, Irene Pepperberg at Harvard, and Carolyn Ristau at Barnard; AI researchers Joanna Bryson at Bath and Cynthia Breazeal at MIT; evolutionary biologist Eva Jablonka at

Tel Aviv; and chemical engineer Frances Arnold at Caltech, whose work on directed enzyme evolution won her a Nobel Prize in chemistry. I have others coming along in the academic pipeline, but I don't want to jinx their chances by naming them here.

On to the bullies!

Stephen Jay Gould

I subscribed to *Natural History* magazine for a number of years back in the '80s and '90s just because I wanted to read Steve Gould's monthly essays, which were always fascinating and often provocative. Gould lived not far from Tufts, on a street in Cambridge that was walking distance from his office at Harvard, and I was delighted to be invited to lunch there with Doug Hofstadter (who turned out to be a distant cousin of Gould's) during one of Doug's visits to the Boston area while we were working on *The Mind's I*. I remember that one of the topics at our happy meeting was how to deal graciously with the flood of correspondence from readers that all three of us were receiving, though I'm sure mine was a trickle compared to Doug's and Steve's. So Gould and I got off to a good start, but the bonhomie didn't last long.

I had read Gould and Lewontin's notorious 1979 paper "The Spandrels of San Marco and the Panglossian Paradigm" soon after Jerry Fodor alerted me to it at the Dahlem meeting on cognitive ethology (see chapter 16), and I immediately saw through it. Since the paper was a highly influential storm cloud looming over the field, I decided to respond to it in my 1983 *BBS* target article, "Intentional Systems in Cognitive Ethology: The 'Panglossian Paradigm' Defended." I made a little insider joke in my essay, showing the striking parallels between their arguments and those of B. F. Skinner against "mentalism" and wondering if perhaps Gould and Lewontin had taken up the cudgels of their Harvard colleague Skinner and were the latest example of "Postpositivist Harvard Conservatism."

I knew that would boil their revolutionary blood. Was it wise of me to tease them? I was just fighting fire with fire; their paper is a disingenuous application of misleading rhetoric, and it has had tremendous impact that it didn't deserve. It unfairly tarnished the reputations of some exemplary researchers and, coupled with their ferocious political attack on their colleague E. O. Wilson's concept of sociobiology, was making it extremely difficult for young ethologists to find jobs if they adopted an evolutionary perspective in their fieldwork. As in any field, Sturgeon's law prevails—90 percent of everything is crap—but there were excellent ornithologists, ichthyologists, and entomologists who were being branded as *sociobiologists* and hence risky hires. In any case, my provocation worked. Dick Lewontin wrote a bristling commentary, tripping himself up in the process. Gould did not join his coauthor in this commentary, staying silent about my critique.

In 1989 there was a meeting at the Center for Cognitive Science at MIT at which Steve Pinker and his graduate student Paul Bloom defended their views about the evolution of language, with responses by Gould and my Italian friend Massimo Piattelli-Palmarini, a Chomsky acolyte and sailing buddy of Jerry Fodor's. At that meeting, I heard more misinformed assertions about evolution than I would expect to hear at a fundamentalist church service. As far as I could tell, no biologists at MIT were teaching about natural selection, and this seemed to open up a playground for would-be theorists in other disciplines to float silly theories. Pinker made a hilarious list of the actual claims made by tenured professors at MIT that he (and I) encountered in those days.

A baker's dozen from Steve Pinker

1. Color vision is useless; we could tell red from green apples using intensity cues.
2. Language is not designed for communication at all: it's not

like a watch, it's like a Rube Goldberg device with a stick in the middle that you can use as a sundial.

3. Any argument that language is functional could be made with equal plausibility and force when applied to writing in sand.

4. The structure of the cell is to be explained by physics, not evolution.

5. Having an eye calls for the same kind of explanation as having mass, because just as the eye lets you see, mass prevents you from floating into space.

6. Hasn't that stuff about insect wings refuted Darwin?

7. Language can't be useful; it's led to war.

8. Natural selection is irrelevant, because we now have chaos theory.

9. Language couldn't have evolved through selection pressure for communication because we can ask people how they feel without really wanting to know.

10. Everyone agrees that natural selection plays some role in the origin of the mind but that it cannot explain every aspect—thus there is nothing more to say.

11. One could describe any randomly constructed computer program or assortment of physical parts as adaptively complex.

12. If language is useful, how come chimps can't talk?

13. Language was designed for elegance, not for use.

A few years earlier, Gould had cotaught a seminar on evolution and cognition at Harvard with Massimo (later the coauthor with Jerry Fodor of that misbegotten 2010 book, *What Darwin Got Wrong*), and I was invited to attend. For a number of weeks, I sat there uncomfortably while Gould held forth, often misrepresenting the views of his targets: Robert Trivers, Richard Dawkins, William Hamilton, John Maynard Smith, and others. I played the quiet guest, watching the Harvard students dutifully taking notes as if they were listening to an oracle. Finally I could take it no longer, and after class one day I broached the subject privately with Gould. I told him I thought his claims about those he was attacking were often unfounded and urged him to reform his practice, but he just dismissed my concerns as the misconstruals of a philosopher who didn't know any better. I had to stop attending the seminar, because the thought of any of my students seeing me sitting there quietly without objecting was more than I could bear.

Gould and I were still on speaking terms in 1992, having just participated together in making Wim Kayzer's Dutch television program *A Glorious Accident* (see chapter 31), where he joined Oliver Sacks and me in giving the notorious Rupert Sheldrake a gentle but effective shakedown. I invited him to be a guest in my seminar on philosophy of evolutionary theory—just answering questions, not giving a talk—and he accepted. The class had read a lot of his essays, but also essays by Dawkins and Maynard Smith and others, and when my students began asking him tough questions, he suddenly stormed out of the classroom! I had to go retrieve him and talk him into returning to the class. He accused me of ambushing him, but I told him that my students—if not his at Harvard—were accustomed to challenging their professors. He returned, grumpily, to the seminar room and treated the rest of the session as a sort of antagonistic press conference. (My students were quite upset by Gould's reaction and asked me the following week if they had done something wrong. I told them I had never been prouder of Tufts students than I had been that day.)

As I was driving Steve home after the seminar, he asked me if I'd read Helena Cronin's new book, *The Ant and the Peacock*. I hadn't but had ordered it. Why had he asked? Because, he said, he planned to "trash" it in the *New York Review of Books*. Why? Because Richard Dawkins had published a stinging review in *Nature* of the ill-conceived book *Mystery Dance: On the Evolution of Human Sexuality* by Lynn Margulis and her son, Dorion Sagan. Dawkins's review was a mistake, made worse by the title chosen by the editors at *Nature*,

"Pornophilosophy." Dawkins excused Margulis, whom he admired, and blamed her postmodernist son for its flaws (never get between a mother bear and her cubs). But why trash Helena Cronin's book? Because, Gould told me, she had once been Richard Dawkins's girl-friend! When Steve's awful review came out, both John Maynard Smith and I independently wrote letters to the editor objecting to what Maynard Smith called Gould's "curiously ill-tempered" review, and I exposed and analyzed some of Gould's rhetorical tricks, includ-ing the "Gould two-step"—named by Robert Trivers in a congrat-ulatory note to me—in which you accuse your target of asserting something indefensible, then quote your target denying that very view and cite it as evidence that your target has conceded. Gould's response to our letters in the same issue (January 14, 1993) was remarkable; he claimed to be the victim of a "good-cop-bad-cop-grilling." Since he couldn't bring himself to slam the revered John Maynard Smith, describing him as "my dear colleague and good-cop," he then laid into me with a flurry of arrogant insults. John's nickname for me after Gould's outburst was "bad cop."

The 1989 MIT meeting was one of the provocations that led me to write *Darwin's Dangerous Idea*, to introduce the power of natural selection to the educated laypeople and nonbiologist academics who were in danger of being misled by Gould's strange brand of evolu-tionary thinking. I had realized that Gould's status as "evolutionist laureate" of the US was causing a lot of mischief, which I should try to undo. For instance, why hadn't Americans been shown the wonderful documentaries about evolution coming out of the UK? *Horizon*, the BBC's famous science documentary series, had a special relationship with WGBH (the flagship PBS station in Boston) such that it was a fairly normal expectation that a *Horizon* program would be taken by WGBH unless there was some good reason not to. In the mid-1980s, Richard Dawkins presented two *Horizon*s, "Nice Guys Finish First" (on evolutionary game theory) and "The Blind Watch-maker," which WGBH declined to purchase, to the deep puzzle-ment of people at the BBC, including Robin Brightwell, then head of *Horizon* (and the producer of my first dramatization of "Where Am I?"; see chapter 10). I learned from my sailing friend Henry Becton, then president of WGBH, that Gould, on the station's advisory board, had vetoed them because they had been presented by Richard Dawkins.

Darwin's Dangerous Idea wasn't just about Gould, of course; it's a wide-ranging exploration and recommendation of evolutionary thinking across academia, with a variety of novel proposals for extensions into psychology, anthropology, and economics, and even into ethics and epistemology. (One reviewer called it "the best single-author overview of all the implications of evolution by natural selection available.") I knew, though, that I was going to have to deal in it with Gould's misrepresentations, and I worked hard on the chapter "Bully for Brontosaurus" (the title of one of his collections of essays in *Natural History*), drafts of which I shared with a few knowledgeable philosophers of biology for comments, including a friend of Gould's who read it and urged me not to publish it—not because it was wrong but because it would drive Gould into a frenzy. I asked him if he could guarantee that Gould would not trash my book when it appeared if I left out the chapter. No, he couldn't, of course. Gould was going to hate the whole book, not just the chapter devoted to him, and since it would be worse than lame to respond to a Gould hatchet job with my list of Gould's sins, I had to mount a preemptive strike. I sent drafts of critical chapters to Gould more than a year in advance of the publication of *DDI* and got no response at all, not even an acknowledgment of receipt. Then in the summer of 1994, when the book was almost ready to be printed, I learned from John Brockman that Gould had decided he did want to discuss the "Brontosaurus" chapter with me and had asked John to arrange it. John suggested a house-party weekend at his retreat in Connecticut, Eastover Farm. Steve would be bringing his fiancée, Rhonda Shearer, a New York City sculptor; Marvin and Gloria Minsky would attend, and so would Nick Humphrey and his recently wed wife Ayla Kohn. Susan and I knew Ayla well but had been unable to attend the wedding, so this was our first time to celebrate with them.

We all assembled for drinks before dinner in the charming living room at Eastover Farm, and as champagne was poured from a fine magnum into ten glasses and passed around, John asked me to offer the toast. I was delighted to have the honor of toasting our dear friends Nick and Ayla and had a stirring speech percolating in my mind when John whispered in my ear, "Rhonda brought the champagne." Oh! I was expected to toast Steve and Rhonda, not the newlyweds Nick and Ayla! I somehow managed to shift my focus and declare some impromptu and threadbare wishes for future happiness to Steve and Rhonda, all the while conjuring up images of the social disaster I had narrowly avoided. Rhonda and I then had a lively conversation about her sculptures, particularly the technical details of the lost-wax bronze casting involved, and she invited me to come to New York and spend some time in her studio, an opportunity I never pursued.

The next day, Steve and I sat down under an ancient maple tree beside the farmhouse and spent several hours in intense discussion of my chapter. He had brought along a copy of his complete bibliography, which included articles I'd never come across, and complained that I had misrepresented him, misunderstood him, maligned him in various particulars. I took careful notes and asked him to send me copies of the papers he mentioned that I had not yet read. This he did within a couple of days after the weekend, and when I read the papers I found that it was he who had misremembered what he had written, not I who had misinterpreted him. I made a few minor adjustments to the wording of my chapter and sent it back to him with an explanation of why I was sticking to my guns. He never responded to that letter. When *DDI* came out, many people, journalists and others, asked him his opinion of it, and his response was that my book was a travesty beneath discussion. Two years later, he decided he had to attack it—throwing in an attack on Richard

Dawkins as well. His two-part diatribe in the *New York Review of Books*, and my response and his counterresponse, made for some exciting reading and inspired a dreadful book by the British journalist Andrew Brown, *The Darwin Wars* (1999), which included on the dust jacket a quote from an email of mine to a third party that Brown used without asking my permission: "I wouldn't admit it if Andrew Brown were my friend. What a sleazy bit of trash journalism." Which more or less proved my point. My tussle with Gould also inspired a gratifying response from major departments of evolutionary biology inviting me to give named lectures.

Thanks to my reputation as the mouse who belled the cat, over the years I have become something of a repository of tales about Gould's willingness to distort the truth. I have kept, and will keep, most of them to myself. I will, however, recount one incident that I witnessed directly, and let it stand for the rest. The Cognitive Science Society held its annual meeting at MIT in July 1990, and among the keynote speakers were Roger Schank and Steve Gould, invited by Massimo Piattelli-Palmarini, who was the local arrangements chair. Roger gave the first keynote address, a funny, informal synopsis of his new book, *Tell Me a Story: A New Look at Real and Artificial Memory*, and it included some in-jokes and barbs meant to taunt the Chomskyans, who abounded at MIT of course. (Chomsky himself was not present.) After Schank's talk, the first questioner was Kenneth Wexler, an ardent Chomskyan who had been my colleague at UC Irvine before moving to MIT. Ken's first mistake was to accuse Schank of dishonoring Kresge Auditorium (the MIT venue in which we met) with sexist and anti-Semitic jokes. Roger didn't miss a beat and replied that he didn't think this was what bothered Ken: "You just object to my criticizing your hero, Chomsky, on his own ground." Then Ken made his second mistake: he decided to poll the audience and—his third mistake—asked first for a show of hands by those who were offended by Roger's talk. No hands were raised! Ken slunk off without another word.

Gould was present in the audience for that remarkable confrontation but didn't say anything. In the afternoon, he gave his keynote address, and among his topics was the ignorance about evolution that had recently been exhibited in the well-publicized case of the transplantation of a baboon heart, instead of a chimpanzee heart, into "Baby Fae." One of the slides he used to illustrate his talk was a photograph of Baby Fae's gravestone, revealing her real name. After his talk, a young man rose to say he was shocked that Gould had shown the slide, since all the news media had agreed to maintain the anonymity of Baby Fae and her parents, an anonymity Gould had now breached. Besides, he went on, there were no available chimpanzee hearts for the emergency surgery, and the baboon heart was intended as a temporary measure until an infant human heart could be found. Gould's reaction was memorable: "Wow! Some society you have here!" But he didn't have any good response to the young man's charge. That is not the end of my tale. A few months later, I gave a talk at the New School for Social Research in New York City, and Gould was once again a keynote speaker. *He showed the same slide and made the same charges of ignorance.* Amazingly, the same young man was in the audience in New York, and he rose again to accuse Gould. It must have been a nightmare for Steve, who often seemed incapable of acknowledging error, but he deserved it.

I've often wondered if this was a sad side effect of his brush with cancer early in his career. He had contracted abdominal mesothelioma when he was just forty, and was thought to be dying, a tragic loss to the world of a brilliant young biologist. For several years, nobody wanted to criticize him, and perhaps he just got used to the idea that his opinions were sacrosanct, above criticism. The remission of his cancer put him back in the fray but without a shred of humility or a willingness to consider opposing views. There is no doubt that he was a scholar and often a wise theorist. His *Ontogeny and Phylogeny* (1977), his most technical book, played an important role in opening up imagination-space for evo-devo (evolutionary-developmental) biology, and some of his early essays in *Natural History* are brilliant explorations of adaptationist themes—themes he later disowned. His last book, *The Structure of Evolutionary Theory* (2002), published just before his death, is a gigantic book, including many tirades, but fortunately for his reputation it is almost unreadable, so it hasn't had much influence.

Gerald Edelman

In 1989–90, Peter Bieri, a Swiss philosopher and novelist, got a grant to support a yearlong workshop on mind and brain at ZiF, the Zentrum für interdisziplinäre Forschung (Center for Interdisciplinary Research) in Bielefeld, Germany. Bieri's taste in interdisciplinary researchers was excellent, and among those who spent weeks or months or semesters in the workshop that year were the American philosophers David Rosenthal and Jay Rosenberg, the German neurobiologist Hans Flohr, the German psychologist Eckart Scheerer, the Belgian psychologist Axel Cleeremans, the British psychologist Tony Marcel, the American neuroscientist and neurosurgeon Karl Pribram, and three of my gang of four: Marcel Kinsbourne, Nick Humphrey, and me. Many friendships and conclusions got established that year.

Karl Pribram, something of a legendary character in the field, was there for several months, and I got to know him well. He was famous for coauthoring, with George Miller and Eugene Galanter, one of the founding documents of cognitive science, *Plans and the Structure of Behavior* (1960), which valiantly attempted to take the fruits of behaviorism and exploit them in a model of internal control systems. (An old joke was that Miller thought it up, Galanter wrote it, and Pribram believed it.) He was also (in)famous for his typically imaginative theory that the brain stores information as *holograms*, a view that never quite came into focus. One day he handed me an advance copy he had just received of *The Remembered Present*, a book by the Nobel laureate Gerald Edelman, which he had been invited to review. He confessed that he had skimmed it and decided it was too much work. He wondered if I'd be interested. Yes indeed, but not to write a review, just to read. The title itself was slightly ominous to me, since it hinted that perhaps Edelman was about to scoop me on some of my ideas about time and the observer, which I was then trying to wrestle into shape. I had been on programs with Edelman a few times and had read his *Neural Darwinism: The Theory of Neuronal Group Selection* (1987), one of many attempts to apply evolutionary thinking to brain development and learning. I found Edelman abrasive and contentious, but certainly very smart, and overflowing with interesting claims and insights. He was scheduled to spend a week at the workshop in Bielefeld later in the spring, when I would be away at one of Umberto Eco's conferences at the University of San Marino, so I pushed my way through Edelman's book and wrote him a multipage letter explaining that I wouldn't be at ZiF when he visited, and commenting on his views and presentation, hoping he would thereby be alerted to some of the challenges that were under discussion in Bielefeld. I raised a number of criticisms and in particular charged him with failing to note that some of his ideas had been well prefigured by thinkers he dismissed unfairly—potential allies with whom he was picking gratuitous fights. He wrote me back a short note inviting me to visit his lab at Rockefeller University whenever I found myself in New York so we could discuss my letter.

That opportunity soon came up when I was giving some lectures at NYU and had a free Saturday in the city. I expected that he and I would sit down for a long, constructive chat, so I sent him the draft of the chapter of *Consciousness Explained* that presented my overview of the architecture of consciousness and contained a brief discussion of his views. When I got to his lab at Rockefeller, I found that he had ordered his team to spend the morning grilling me and objecting to the ideas in my draft chapter, which he had shared with them, although he hadn't shared my earlier letter, which would have provided a wealth of context. Giulio Tononi and Olaf Sporns led the attack in a sort of tag-team wrestling match, with Gerry egging them on. I was also obliged to sit through one of his multimedia slide lectures, which I had already heard two or three times. That he would require his brilliant young associates to spend a beautiful spring Saturday morning attacking me, without giving them the background of the occasion, was the first sign I had of his almost childish inability to listen to criticism. I took my pummeling and left unenlightened, and later wrote an email to Sporns and Tononi telling them about my letter.

A few years later, Edelman moved his Neurosciences Institute from Rockefeller to La Jolla, just a mile or so from Francis Crick's lab at UC San Diego. The two Nobel laureates were not friends, and Gerry was not invited to the afternoon "teas" that Francis presided over. One time I was invited to give a talk at the Crick lab, and several of Edelman's young associates came to hear my talk, staying afterward to question me (constructively!) at length. I noticed that they were somewhat nervously looking at their watches and asked them about it. They candidly replied that they had had to sneak out of Gerry's lab to come hear me and were quite sure they'd be fired if he got word of their betrayal. In 1992, Edelman and I were together with Oliver Sacks at a conference in Locarno, and when I tried to introduce Susan to the great man during a coffee break, he took one look at me, said, "Hello, fake!" and instead of shaking hands, turned abruptly and left the room, leaving us astonished. He then packed his bag and left the conference early. I had a long talk over dinner with Oliver, who had been swept up by Edelman into his posse, and soon thereafter Oliver drifted away from him.

If only Gerry had learned to treat others' views more sympathetically and had resisted the temptation to divide the world into Us versus Them, he could have had a lot more influence. He obliged his colleagues to sign loyalty oaths that forbade them to divulge what was happening in his lab. That level of secrecy is often an unfortunate feature of races for Nobel Prizes, and Gerry made no secret of his desire to beat out Linus Pauling, who had received two Nobel Prizes. Gerry was aiming for three! In addition to his prize in immunology, he figured he deserved one for his discovery of cell-adhesion molecules—and he was probably right—but he also wanted one for his theory of consciousness in the brain. Harboring such a desire is one thing and telling people about it is another. Gerry was sometimes remarkably obtuse in his interpersonal dealings, and it cost him greatly. It may well have cost him that second Nobel Prize.

Some years later, the Boston Society of Neurology, Neurosurgery, and Psychiatry, an ancient and distinguished organization headquartered at Harvard Medical School, invited Edelman to give a talk, and the host—not knowing of the bad blood between Gerry and me—invited me to be the impromptu commentator. I accepted. When I walked into the Harvard Club's private dining room for the dinner before the talk, Gerry looked like he'd seen a ghost. He hadn't been told I'd be the respondent, and it clearly bothered him. While he was setting up his multimedia show—with a carousel of slides and some videotapes in those days—I asked him politely if I might record the session. Since it was impromptu, I thought one of us might say something that would be worth reflecting on later. He glowered at me and responded, "I know what you're doing: you're just asking me in order to get me to refuse so you can say afterward that I refused, but you're not going to trap me that way. Do what you want!" Oh, Gerry, I thought at the time, you just gave me a much better story, didn't you? As it happened, Gerry's carousel presented him with a problem, since it contained slides that persisted in misrepresenting some of the views of his predecessors who had developed Darwinian models of the learning brain. When these came up, he went *click-click-click-click*, passing by the slides without comment but not too fast for me to glean what they said, and when it came time for my commentary, I praised Gerry for having *one* of the best of the *many* models that wisely applied Darwinian thinking to the problems of learning in the brain. Time had been too short for him to mention them in detail, so I filled in a few gaps for the audience. That was the last time I saw Gerry Edelman, though I have had many interactions with members of his team over the years, most of them positive.

Jerry Fodor

It took me years to figure out that Jerry Fodor's allegiance to science was narrow and conditional: science was wonderful as long as it supported his rather romantic vision of what minds must be. I spelled most of this out in "Granny's Campaign for Safe Science," my contribution to Barry Loewer and Georges Rey's *Meaning and Mind: Fodor and His Critics* (1991). Fodor often cited his "Granny," a supposedly no-nonsense source of everyday wisdom. It struck me that he was opposed to every promising development in the sciences of the mind. Skinnerian behaviorism was dead, of course, but he was also opposed to AI, connectionism, "new look" psychology (Jerome Bruner et al.), and—I eventually realized—any approach to the mind that exploited Darwinian evolutionary theory. My joke at the time, echoing Nancy Reagan's advice on drugs, was that Granny says if you can't do "classical" cognitive science, "just say no."

He certainly loved to provoke. I once described him as a human trampoline: "If I can see farther than others it is because I have been jumping on Jerry." (While I am paraphrasing that famous remark of Isaac Newton's, I have to add that I regret to say I was not the author, although I was once quoted as the author of another variation on that line: "If I can't see as far as others, it's because giants are standing on my shoulders!" I wish I'd said it, and I've said it now, but alas, I am not the author of it.)

Jerry loved to bite bullets. His great book, *The Language of Thought* (1975), had some arresting implications that he didn't disavow. Did his view imply that, say, Aristotle had the concept of a *Boeing 747 round-trip flight to Las Vegas* in his brain but just never got around to expressing it? Yes! He once assured me that neither Joseph Conrad nor Vladimir Nabokov spoke English, because English wasn't their native tongue. As you might expect, there is *something* to be said in support of this remarkable claim: every now and then, one finds a turn of phrase in these authors that a native speaker almost certainly wouldn't say. Are they tiny lacunas in the great authors' familiarity with English, or are they brilliant strokes of creativity? (This is actually a very good question to explore; native English speakers may be a little too habit bound in their choice of words, and nonnative speakers may well be major innovators in what soon *evolves* as acceptable English.)

Jerry insisted that our beliefs, as well as the beliefs of animals without language, were captured in our brains in Mentalese, the language of thought that permitted us to think rationally, drawing inferences and framing intentions to act. You would think then that he would be fascinated by the attempts by people in AI (in GOFAI—Good-Old-Fashioned Artificial Intelligence) to model just such a practical language of thought, but he had nothing but a contemptuous lack of interest in AI. He once claimed that the language of thought was like "machine language," the lowest level of coding in computers, but when my friend and former Tufts colleague David Israel, a philosopher turned AI researcher, asked him for details, it turned out that Jerry was just wildly wrong about what machine language is. David asked him where he got his misinformation, and Jerry nonchalantly replied, "I just asked myself, 'If I were a computer, what would my machine language be like?'" Jerry's concept of the language of thought turned out to be a brilliant way of *not* making scientific progress on the mysteries of the mind. His very influential book *The Modularity of Mind* (1983) described the mind as a collection of peripheral "modules" that feed their results to a central area of "belief fixation" that is *not* modular, and upon which no science has shed any light. All the progress, he claimed, has been in analyzing the structures and competences of the peripheral modules—the language parser, the face recognizer, and so forth. A more accurate title for the book would have been *The Nonmodularity of Mind*. The imagined "classical" cognitive science that Jerry endorsed was deeply Cartesian, anti-Darwinian, and nonbiological.

Zestful partisanship is one thing and bullying is another, and occasionally Jerry's zeal undid his sense of decorum and he lashed out at students or colleagues—sometimes with biting sarcasm, sometimes with ridicule. At times I felt reluctantly obliged to scold my old sailing and diving buddy in public. Almost anybody engaged in science takes for granted the basic tenets of Darwinian evolution—"Hey, the earth is round, water is H_2O, and organisms evolved by natural selection"—but I began to suspect that Jerry's adamant conviction that Gould and Lewontin had refuted adaptationism once and for all was the tip of an iceberg. Jerry was certainly no creationist, but his candid dislike of all Darwinian thinking was unsettling, and when I began commenting on this, his friends and colleagues sometimes said I was way off base and being unfair to Jerry. Was I? Jerry's fulminations were sometimes funny. About my views, he wrote (1990), "Teddy bears are artificial, but *real bears are artificial too*. We stuff the one and Mother Nature stuffs the other. Philosophy is *full* of surprises." It was after the publication of *Darwin's Dangerous Idea* in 1995 that our friendly relations became particularly strained. Jerry's review, in *Mind & Language*, was a masterpiece of sarcasm and caricature. It is true that my book exposed his distortions of evolutionary thinking and his zealous misreading of Gould and Lewontin's "Spandrels of San Marco" essay, so I wasn't surprised that he fought back, but I *was* surprised by the depths of his anti-Darwinism. His motto seemed to be "I don't know much about biology, but I know what I don't like: evolution by natural selection."

In 2007 Jerry published "Why Pigs Don't Have Wings" in the *London Review of Books*, making it clear that I had not been hallucinating his dislike of all things Darwinian. In 2009 I was in Arizona to give a lecture and staying with my old friends Massimo Piattelli-Palmarini and his wife Donata Vercelli, a world-class geneticist and immunologist. We didn't talk about evolution—by tacit agreement, I think—but as I was leaving, Massimo handed me a typescript of the book Jerry and he had written about evolution and asked if I could have a quick skim and give him some feedback. I read the thing on the plane back to Boston and decided that *probably* my friend Massimo wanted me to give him support in urging Jerry not to publish it. In any event, I decided that I would kick myself later if that had been Massimo's intent and I hadn't tumbled to it, so when I got home I took a leap and wrote him an email strongly recommending that the project be abandoned for the sake of our friend Jerry's reputation. I was wrong; Massimo was not inviting any such response, as his stony silence made clear. The book, *What Darwin Got Wrong*, was published in 2010 and is generally recognized (except by the Intelligent Design crowd, who loved it) as an embarrassment. Well, I gave it the old college try, and Massimo is still my friend—I hope—though I cannot fathom how he can cling to some of his wrongheaded views.

John Searle

When *Consciousness Explained* was published in 1991, Searle was invited to review it in the *New York Review of Books*, and he accepted. I know this because several people wrote to me saying they had volunteered to write a review for *NYRB* and were told that it had already been assigned to Searle. But no review appeared. Two years later he published his book *The Rediscovery of the Mind*, which refers to *Consciousness Explained* twice but does not discuss it at all. I reviewed John's new book in the *Journal of Philosophy* (April 1993), and I was certainly critical, largely because he was ostentatiously ignoring much of the work done in the field that undercut his own view. This raises a delicate issue: Haven't I done the same, over and over again? There are dozens of books and hundreds of articles by well-known philosophers of mind and language that I have never cited, never discussed. My *silence* on this score says loud and clear: "I do not consider these arguments worth discussing." Is there an important difference between Searle's silence and mine? Maybe only this: I've done a better job of choosing what to ignore! I don't know how conscientiously he has sampled the relevant literature, but I have been diligent enough to be comfortable with my own judgments. We all have to avoid the trap of taking *everybody* seriously, and we also have to avoid the meta-trap of taking seriously the task of defending all our judgments on this score. We pay a price for this: some good, intelligent, earnest people will feel unfairly ignored, and will, not surprisingly, decide not to take *us* seriously. If you ignore me, I'll ignore you. It is annoying to see growing mountains of work in philosophy that I consider clever but pointless, but I know better than to roll up my sleeves and try to set these folks straight. I have better things to do, and I count on others to do the required policing.

Two more years passed before John's review of *Consciousness Explained* appeared in the *New York Review of Books* (November 16, 1995). It appeared in the issue before John Maynard Smith's glowing review of *Darwin's Dangerous Idea* ("Genes, Memes and Minds," November 30, 1995), and I have often wondered if *NYRB* had to pressure him to get his review in after four years because they wanted to review my new book right away. In his review, he called my position "a form of intellectual pathology" and couldn't resist trotting out his Chinese Room argument and asking, "Now why does Dennett not face the actual argument as I have stated it? Why does he not tell us which of the three premises he rejects in the Chinese Room Argument?" Because, as I said in my reply, I had already done so:

> For instance, in "Fast Thinking" (way back in *The Intentional Stance*, 1987) I explicitly quoted his entire three premise argument and showed exactly why *all three of them* are false, when given the interpretation they need for the argument to go through! Why didn't I repeat that 1987 article in my 1991 book? Because, unlike Searle, I had gone on to other things. I did, however, cite my 1987 article prominently in a footnote (p. 436), and noted that Searle's only response to it had been simply to declare, without argument, that the points offered there were irrelevant.

In the exchange, John still ignored my challenge to show what was wrong with my criticism and went on to declare, without argument:

"To put it as clearly as I can: in his book, *Consciousness Explained*, Dennett denies the existence of consciousness." So even though I had devoted an entire early chapter of the book to explaining that what I was saying was that consciousness exists but it's not what you think it is, he was unable even to consider the hypothesis that I might be right.

In 2002 Susan and I and John and his wife, Dagmar, had a congenial lunch together in the courtyard of the Collegium Budapest, where I was a visiting fellow at the time. So, I thought that our relationship had been more or less repaired, and when I was invited to present a talk at a celebration of Searle's work at Santa Clara University in California in January 2010, I accepted. There were four speakers: Pat Churchland, Ned Block, Tyler Burge, and me. The other three went before me, and none of them talked about John's work at all; they talked about their own work and made some gracious passing reference to his work. Not I. I talked about Searle's work, in detail and with accurate quotations and explicit refutations. (If you invite me to a conference on X and I accept, you can expect me to talk about X.) My title was "Turing's Strange Inversion and John Searle's Failure of Imagination," which echoed a favorite theme of mine: philosophers and scientists who mistake a failure of imagination for an insight into necessity. It was actually a fairly lighthearted talk, poking a little fun at Tom Nagel and Jerry Fodor, both of whom had recently come out of the closet as Darwin doubters, and I pointedly noted that John had never to my knowledge said anything about evolution by natural selection. Did he agree with Fodor and Nagel or with me? Or did he have a view of his own that he might express on this occasion? I think my talk was a fair challenge, and it certainly put him in good company, since I compared his failure of imagination with similar lapses by Descartes, Leibniz, and William Bateson! But when I finished my talk Searle rose from his seat in the front row, turned his back on me, and proceeded to excoriate me in the most incendiary terms. He did not respond to my request for his opinion about evolution but instead scolded me for making fun of Tom and Jerry. (I had illustrated my quotations from their anti-evolution declarations with a PowerPoint slide of the cartoon cat and mouse looking at a book.)

He ignored the detailed critique I had offered of his Chinese Room argument and instead urged the audience to be deeply offended by my performance. When he finished his tirade, I told the audience, which seemed to be in a state of shock, that I didn't think I had crossed the line and I didn't think they thought I had crossed the line. They evidently agreed, since nobody raised any objections. Pat Churchland deftly put an end to this strange episode with a deflecting comment, and Searle sat down.

Immediately after the session, I asked the other participants if I had been impolite or worse, and they all said I had been fine; they were as puzzled by his outburst as I had been. Ned Block, who had been sitting behind the Searles, said that he heard Dagmar telling John that this was an outrageous attack on him and he should do something about it. So perhaps he was doing it all for Dagmar, who was apparently not accustomed to hearing any tough criticism of her husband. In any event, his attack on me spared him the task of telling the world what he thought about evolution by natural selection and the light it might shed on philosophical questions. This was in 2010, and by that time most of my talks at conferences were videotaped and later put online, but this one was not, so far as I know. It's the only time I've regretted not being able to look at an instant replay and see what all the fuss was about.

35.

REVERSE ENGINEERING ONE'S THINKING TOOLS

O NE OF DOUG HOFSTADTER'S BEST GIFTS TO ME WAS his suggestion that you should "turn all the knobs" on any thought experiment, to be sure you know what makes it work. This in turn gave birth to my concept of an *intuition pump*, and the idea that good thinkers should learn how their thinking tools work and why. I first used the term in print in my *BBS* commentary on Searle's Chinese Room. Searle's little fantasy is one of the most successful memes in cognitive science—but remember: a meme may flourish without being good for us, an irresistible bit of confusion that takes decades to expose and neutralize. Over the years, I have grown more and more comfortable with this perspective on philosophy: at its best, philosophy is intellectual reverse engineering, methodically dismantling bad habits of thought that sustain intellectual pandemics and replacing them with better thinking tools. One of the simplest good tools is also one of the best: the "surely" alarm: whenever you see the word "surely," a little bell should ring—*ding!*—and you should pause to scrutinize what follows, since this is typically the weakest spot in the author's case. It doesn't "go without saying," since the author feels the need to say it, but the author hopes a nudge ("surely") can take the place of a supporting argument. Sometimes it can, but often it can't. Try it, and you'll soon see how often this word papers over a big crack.

We are Gregorian creatures—our minds packed with thinking tools we didn't have to invent for ourselves but downloaded from our culture. This is the explanation of our brilliance compared with all other creatures, and it is obvious in retrospect. Its ramifications have recently been explored by, among others, Kim Sterelny (*The Evolved Apprentice*, 2012), Joe Henrich (*The Secret of Our Success*, 2015), and Cecilia Heyes (*Cognitive Gadgets*, 2018). Bo Dahlbom came up with the perfect aphorism on the topic: "You can't do much carpentry with your bare hands and you can't do much thinking with your bare brain."

Richard Feynman was so smart he didn't mind—in fact he enjoyed—revealing some of his tricks of the trade in *Surely You're Joking, Mr. Feynman!*, and this inspired me to follow his example. One of his best: when a speaker presents you with a theory you can't understand because of all the technical jargon in it, ask the speaker for the simplest example of the phenomenon in question. I had just two encounters with Feynman, and the first one gave me a fine example of his thinking tool in action. Steve Barney (creator of Aesop; see chapter 19) and I arrived late at a lunchtime session at Danny Hillis's legendary Thinking Machines Corporation. (Danny's company, originally called International Thinking Machines, built the first massive parallel computer, the Connection Machine, the fastest computer in the world in 1993, from which many thinking tools issued before the company went bankrupt. Their joke motto was "When we say Thinking we mean Business." Karl Sims's Evolved Virtual Creatures were the offspring that galvanized me, and for years I showed audiences the video Alan Alda made of them, still the most vivid demonstration of the creative power of natural selection that I know.) Stephen Grossberg, the Boston University neuroscientist, was giving a talk about his Adaptive Resonance Theory (too complicated to explain here, but worth some study if you're in the neuroscience field). I knew his work pretty well, having spent hours discussing it with him and having often heard him lecture on it. Stephen is not shy about telling the world how his ideas solve many of the outstanding problems in the field, but on this occasion, he was being remarkably accommodating to a fellow who kept interrupting with tough questions and asking for simple examples. This interlocutor clearly didn't know beans about neuroscience but was pushing Stephen hard, and Stephen was letting him do it! After the fourth or fifth interruption, Stephen said, "Well, Dr. Feynman, let me try to explain it this way . . . ," and I understood. I had just seen a live demonstration of Feynman's famous ability to cut to the core of an issue about which he was largely ignorant. The second encounter was also at Thinking Machines, where Feynman spent many of his last days with his old friend Danny Hillis exploring the power of massive computation to solve problems in physics that were otherwise intractable. Feynman had contempt for philosophers, which he didn't bother concealing from me on this occasion, but he humored me with some tales about his few encounters with philosophers when he was at Cornell in the '50s. The philosophy department at Cornell then was very eminent, but philosophers often present themselves in self-defeating ways to people in other disciplines, and Feynman's description of their combination of arrogance and ignorance of science rang true to me. Ah me, philosophers, if the only folks you talk to are other philosophers, you will perpetuate the stereotype of smarty-pants know-nothings!

Thinking tools work. Whether you use them to nibble away at a problem until it gradually takes on a new and valuable shape (my usual method, philosophical whittling, you might say) or to blow bad assumptions to smithereens, you should frequently stand back to see how it's going and adjust course as necessary. Here's my advice to would-be philosophers: don't worry too much about your IQ or how fast you can compose an objection; add a few more tools to your kit and learn how to use them, and you'll soon be able to avoid digging yourself deeper into the trenches your warring colleagues are stuck in. You do take a risk when you stay out of the trenches: you tend to appear a mere amateur, someone who can be safely ignored, a popularizer or journalist, not a specialist. It sometimes frustrates me to watch other philosophers "making a meal" (as the Brits say) of an issue when I have already shown them a sound escape route if only they'd take it seriously. By their lights, I am a party pooper, dissolving the swell challenges they have trained themselves to tackle.

Intuition Pumps offers advice ("the higher-order truths of chmess") about how these philosophical traps arise and how to avoid them. I treasure the thank-you notes I've received from students who have followed it.

Aside from saving myself from years of intellectual scut work on trivia, what good has come from all my thinking tools? What have I managed to construct with them? A sturdy framework consilient with the scientific progress we have achieved so far and a suggestive wellspring of ideas about how to make further progress on three of the great philosophical problems: meaning (or content), consciousness, and free will. The solutions I have sketched over the years to all three problems fit together beautifully, each reinforcing the others. Things with minds are intentional systems, discernible from the intentional stance; minds are composed of parts, some of which are themselves intentional systems, tiny agents with agendas and also composed of parts, whose design is discernible from the design stance, which shows them to be mechanisms obeying the laws of physics, visible from the physical stance. The patterns visible at each stance are real, in that they are reliably projectable, permitting prediction and explanation, construction and manipulation at many levels. No "real magic," no "wonder tissue," is required. I've been building on my initial account, *Content and Consciousness* (1969), for half a century, and the latest details of the framework are spelled out in *From Bacteria to Bach and Back*.

Meaning, consciousness, and free will are entirely natural achievements, robust features of the manifest image that is the product of billions of years of natural selection. I can finally see how to display their main points in a few paragraphs, thanks to recent conversations I've been having with Keith Frankish, in Crete, off the coast of Greenland, and on Zoom. Think of a drone, remotely controlled by a (human) drone pilot. The user interface is brilliantly designed to make literally thousands of tiny adjustments to the motors and effectors that are conveniently beneath the notice of the pilot. That design work has to come from somewhere; it is the fruit of hundreds of thousands of hours of intelligent design by specialist engineers. The pilot takes advantage of the user interface provided, but the pilot's know-how is also brilliantly designed, and that design work doesn't come for free either; it takes thousands of hours of practice, much of it brute trial and error but also hastened by wise self-manipulation that is itself a product of special training. That training is conveyed to the pilot with the help of language, which is itself brilliantly designed to permit explanations to be shared.

Where does all this design come from? From evolution by natural selection, of several kinds: genetic, intracranial, cultural. First, life evolved and refined itself over several billion years of natural selection. Single-celled organisms—archaea and bacteria—solved the fundamental problem of reproduction, creating and optimizing the genetic code of DNA, the copy-machine ribosomes, the motor proteins, and other elegantly designed mechanisms. Then the eukaryotic revolution gave birth to specialized cells, of greater complexity, the first and most important instance of "technology transfer," which multiplied the talents of single cells by orders of magnitude, permitting them to come together in multicellular organisms that could discover, through evolution in their own brains, still further good tricks for surviving and thriving in an ever more complicated world, leading eventually to a species, the well-named *Homo sapiens*, that wasn't just competent but capable of (imperfect but growing) comprehension of the sources and explanations of its own competences. Our species was able not only to notice its own noticings but also eventually to analyze them and share the analyses with conspecifics, thanks to language. And how did language arise? It too is brilliantly designed and almost all of that design must have come from R & D processes over millions of years by agents who did not *yet* understand what they were doing and why. Cultural evolution by natural selection of memes added a faster, more bountiful generator of design, which gave human beings more *degrees of freedom* than were enjoyed by any other living things—along with the problem of how to control those degrees of freedom. Dealing with that problem turns into the problem of what to think about next, and that is what generates the stream of consciousness. There is no Boss, no Traffic Cop, to keep all the ideas in proper order. There is no general, algorithmic solution to this control problem because each innovation creates further degrees of freedom to cope with, and the natural result is a control architecture in human brains that is freewheeling, composed of competitive and collaborative semi-agents—"active symbols," as Doug Hofstadter puts it—generating our streams of consciousness. How do we know about this stream of consciousness? The question betrays the fundamental error that traces back at least to Descartes: what you *are* is not some separate soul or self, sitting in the Cartesian Theater, but that very control architecture, with the designed competence to tell others—and itself—*some* of the wonderful things it is doing. As Doug says, *I Am a Strange Loop*. Put the emphasis on "am"; not "I *watch* a strange loop" or "I *experience* a strange loop," but "I *am* a strange loop." Or as I put it in *Consciousness Explained*:

> How do I get to know all about this? How come I can tell you all about what was going on in my head? The answer to the puzzle is simple: *Because that is what I am.* Because a knower and reporter of such things in such terms is what is me. *My* existence is explained by the fact that there are these capacities in this body. (p. 410)

The first step the engineers would take to build a truly autonomous drone with onboard, not remote, control would be to throw away the LED screen with all the colors, since those were designed for an agent with eyes and color vision. There is no movie in your head; there are only the myriad discernments of content you rely on to control your expectations and actions. And then what about free will? It is an achievement, not a metaphysical feature, of normal human beings who have learned how to control their many degrees of freedom—and to keep others from remotely controlling them—by developing such habits of self-stimulation as imagining and reflecting on the outcomes of possible actions. Initiation into adulthood (securing the right to make legally binding promises and move freely around in the world) is itself a wonderful social mechanism and it too was designed by natural selection of memes, refined over thousands of years of civilization. All the glories of life depend on design, and designs can be destroyed or damaged; a brain tumor can destroy your free will, other brain pathologies can render you unconscious or unable to discern the meaning of the words you hear or say or read or write.

It takes vigilant thinking to avoid falling into the trap of imagining a Central Meaner that is the source of meaning, a Self that is the evaluator and enjoyer of consciousness, a Soul that defies physics and makes your decisions. These ideas are familiar and all but irresistible, and many thinkers find the prospect of abandoning them utterly repugnant. If you balk at relinquishing any of them, you are in good company, but just remind yourself that such ideas are all part of the largely benign user illusion that has been cobbled together over the eons by the various kinds of natural selection.

Life is what brings reasons and meaning into existence, and in our neck of the universe only human beings have the thinking tools—based on language—to figure this out. We are the only *reasoners*—in the strong sense of *explainers*—on the planet. *Reasons* predated reasoners by billions of years in the same way *numbers* predated mathematicians. It took *two* hydrogen atoms to unite with *one* oxygen atom to make a water molecule long before anybody could count, and the *reason* that living things have membranes isolating them (under controlled conditions) from the rest of the world is that living things need to protect themselves from succumbing to the second law of thermodynamics and can't afford to protect the whole world, a reason that wasn't *appreciated* until very, very recently in the history of life on this planet. Every living thing is composed of parts that are the way they are *for reasons*, but only we human beings *represent* reasons. Evolution has gifted us, and all living things, with brilliantly designed mechanisms that make life easier than it otherwise would be, but this gives living things competence without com-prehension. Trees cope brilliantly under many conditions without a shred of comprehension; so do rabbits and foxes and elephants, who do many wise things without needing to know *why* these are wise things to do or when to do them. It is our human capacity to frame why-questions and evaluate candidate answers that sets us apart from the rest of nature, not some apparently magical soul that does the understanding and the feeling, the loving and fearing.

Isn't this terribly anthropocentric? No, it is properly centered on what matters. Control is the key to life and everything that matters. The more things you can control, the more things can matter to you. Chimpanzees and dolphins are at risk from, but oblivious to, the problems of climate change, economic inequality, pollution, and war, but we alone can think that these problems matter enough to devote our energy to solving them. Noblesse oblige. Descartes was right to insist that human beings are profoundly different from other animals; he just made the mistake of trying to isolate that difference in an immaterial and unfathomable lump of mind-stuff. Reverse engineering that fantastic array of competences is the great intellec-tual adventure we are now embarked on, and it has been my extraor-dinary good fortune to be in the thick of it for my whole adult life.

We seem to be getting closer and closer to a stable solution to a lot of the problems I've been working on for more than half a century. First, materialism reigns, and the major philosophical problems of consciousness, meaning, and free will all have accounts that owe more to biology than to physics. The beginning of life is the begin-ning of reasons and meaning and information (in one of its most important senses); human brains have been turned into minds by the products of *cultural* evolution, of memes, not genes; and conscious-ness creates the user illusion of a Self or Central Meaner, which is not a part of the brain (and certainly not an immaterial soul playing the brain's keyboard, as Sir John Eccles would have it!) but better seen as a useful abstraction: the Center of Narrative Gravity. We ask one another questions—which the members of no other species can do—and the answers we give are not infallible or perfectly available in introspection, but as close as *anyone* can get to what we "really mean." Quine is right to insist that radical translation is not guaranteed to find a single correct interpretation, and Millikan is right to insist that we don't have privileged access to what or even whether we mean, and Haig is right—along with Derrida—to insist that there are only interpretations and further interpretations of interpretations and no good reason to call any of them Absolute Truth. So we will have to settle, with science, on a "vegetarian" concept of truth, which is good enough to reveal the real patterns that have guided us to the moon and back and will soon take us to the planets.

36.

WHAT IF I'M WRONG?

I USED TO BE A MUCH MORE CONSCIENTIOUS SCHOLAR than I am now. I would encounter a journal article or book that was relevant to my interests but forbiddingly technical (or, if the author was a philosopher, just forbiddingly badly written, convoluted, and jargon packed), and I would beat my head against it for hours and hours, running down and checking out all the references—a time-consuming library job in the old days before internet links. I made it something of a point of honor to arrive at a state of confident understanding; I kept at it until I *owned* that argument. Now I give such candidates for my attention a quick skim, remembering that life is short and if this novelty is worth understanding, somebody I trust will soon explain it to me in terms I can readily digest. These days I almost always outsource the hard work of comprehension when I encounter difficulties, and the policy works wonders—for me. Distributed understanding is a real phenomenon, but you have to get yourself into a community of communicators that can effectively summon the relevant expertise. I don't know if other philosophers have the same policy; many of them seem to me to spend their whole careers working largely alone and grappling with a few narrow issues, voluntarily giving themselves tunnel vision. Perhaps, I think, they cannot do otherwise, given their training. After all, many scientists are in similar trenches. I once asked a promising young neuroscientist, after I'd spent hours watching him run experiments on monkeys with chronically implanted electrodes, what he thought the implications of his research might be, and his answer was "Oh Dan, I don't have time to think!"

All my early due diligence was probably good for me. It got me to confront the difficulty of the questions, seeing with my own eyes the pitfalls that trap many very smart and conscientious thinkers. This injected a small dose of modesty into my growing confidence that I had found—and partly invented—a prodigious explanation-device that reliably devoured difficulties, day after day. The insights (if that is what they were) that I had struggled so hard to capture in my dissertation and my first book have matured and multiplied, generating answers to questions, solutions to problems, rebuttals to objections, and—most important—suggestions for further questions to ask with gratifying consilience. I just turn the crank and out they pour, falling into place like the last pieces in a jigsaw puzzle. Perhaps my whole perspective is a colossal mistake—some of my critics think so—and perhaps its abundant fruits are chimeras.

What if I'm wrong? Good thinkers frequently ask themselves this question, the way good doctors frequently check their practices against the Hippocratic oath they swore, and not just as a formulaic ritual. I once asked an evangelical pastor who was interviewing me on his radio program if he ever asked himself that question, and he proudly announced that he had no need to ask it. In other words, he considered his faith foolproof. Right there, I submit, lies one of the greatest dangers to civilization. As I have said, religious faith gives people a gold-plated excuse to stop thinking. Anybody who has been persuaded that it is their *religious duty* not to question their faith has been partially disabled. It is sometimes effective, when people play this faith card, to reply, with genuine concern, "I apologize. I hadn't realized you have a cognitive disability; I'll bear that in mind and not burden or embarrass you with questions you are not equipped to consider." Excuse them from the discussion and carry on without them, but don't scorn or humiliate them; they cannot help it. St. Augustine, of course, had a bold retort to this suggestion: *credo ut intelligam*. I believe in order to understand. This would be more impressive if there weren't so many instances of religious believers who manifestly fail to understand many of the theories and facts that the rest of us can accept and exploit with gratifying success.

My favorite chapter of Mark Twain's *Adventures of Tom Sawyer* tells of Tom's brilliant stunt of getting his friends to *pay him* for the privilege of whitewashing the fence in front of his house, not just saving him a chore but enriching him. This inspired me to adopt the same strategy with my books: I invite Tufts students to help me write my books by sharing the penultimate draft with them in a seminar, where they are all encouraged to point out errors, challenge arguments, demand more clarity, and in general complain about anything that strikes them as amiss. They don't get paid for this excellent editorial service—in fact they are paying one of the highest rates of tuition in the country—but they do get thanked in the preface by name, and they get an autographed copy of the book when it's published. I believe everyone involved has been quite content with this arrangement.

I particularly cherish the intrepid naysayers who force me to expand, revise, or drop what I had thought were good points. Students often come to my office to discuss their term-paper projects in my courses, and a familiar combination of ambition and anxiety is the enthusiastic student who has a Big Idea—a Refutation of some well-regarded claim of mine or of some other writer we have read. They're itching to go for it, but *"What if I'm wrong?"* I have some not-quite-foolproof advice: take courage and set out to write up the Great Discovery; if after many hours of red-hot thinking and writing you discover to your dismay a fatal flaw, something that you overlooked or underestimated, all is not lost. Go back to the first paragraph and write something along the lines of "It is tempting to think that . . . , because there seems to be a powerful argument to the effect that . . . , but as we shall see, this is an error." Then make a few minor adjustments to the rest of the paper, pointing carefully to the error that you almost made, and you're ready to submit it. If your Big Idea was tempting to you, it might well be tempting to others. Showing the field that this is a cul-de-sac to be avoided is a genuine contribution. The same strategy, writ large, is good advice for a whole career. Try your Big Hunch out on a few knowledgeable people; if nobody can knock it down right away, then take a leap, make a major investment of your time (bearing in mind the large cost of lost opportunities if you make a bad choice) and hope for the best. You may at least be able to salvage a definitive refutation of your hunch, all the more credible for having been composed by somebody who was initially a partisan.

The Discovery Institute is the well-funded propaganda site for Intelligent Design, as creationism is now called. I have often scoffed publicly at the dismal ratio of propaganda to peer-reviewed science in its output and urged its directors to put their money into some real science that might, conceivably, prove them right. So when they announced in 2005 that they were setting up a serious research facility, the Biologic Institute, to do experiments aiming to refute the theory of evolution by natural selection, they asked me to express my opinion of this innovation. I wrote back that I applauded this move, since there are scads of unasked questions in evolutionary biology that are neglected by biologists simply because they're sure they already know the answer: How did species X with feature Y come to be? It evolved, of course, but we don't know the details. Nobody wants to sic a graduate student or postdoc on any of those questions, because the reaction among the influential workers in the field to the results would be along the lines of "Ho hum, what else is new?"—not a good way to start a career. If, however, the Biologic Institute wants to fund young scientists who are passionately committed to disproving evolution, this will harness their energy and training without our having any scruples about encouraging them to waste their precious time. They will see themselves as crusaders on a divine mission, and what could be more glorious than that? They will try to find hidden among these unasked questions embarrassing examples of "irreducible complexity" that couldn't have evolved gradually. They will eventually discover that they're wrong, and we will have yet further examples of evolution's devious paths. In my terminology, their dogged search for skyhooks will uncover heretofore unimagined cranes. And precisely because their conclusions will be the opposite of what they hoped to discover, we will take them seriously. Good theories thrive on serious attempts to refute them that fail in instructive ways.

What, though, if *my* supposed insights are just generated by a prodigiously fertile mistake? It's worth remembering that this has happened before, on a cosmic scale. Descartes wrote his retrospectively preposterous books—*Le Monde* (eventually published in full in 1667) and *Principia Philosophiae* (1644)—presenting the first detailed TOE (theory of everything). He had deduced (he claimed) the truth about everything under the sun and beyond the sun, including starlight and planets, tides, volcanoes, magnets, and much, much more, most of it dead wrong. It was Newton's majestic *Principia* (1687) that decisively refuted Descartes. Descartes's theory of everything is, even in hindsight, remarkably coherent and persuasive. It is hard to imagine a *different* equally coherent and equally false theory! He was wrong, and so of course I may well be wrong, but enough other thinkers I respect have come to see things my way that when I ask myself, "What if *we* are wrong?" I can keep this skeptical murmur safely simmering on a back burner.

ACKNOWLEDGMENTS

THIS BOOK IS THE WORK OF MANY MINDS. FIRST, ALL the people whose interactions with me are recounted in this book deserve to be considered coauthors of sorts (like the hundreds of authors on physics papers these days, none of them responsible for residual errors that remain). No doubt a few errors will still be found, in spite of the wonderful editing, first by Sara Lippincott, and then by Sarah Johnson and Brendan Curry at Norton. So many typos and thinkos caught and removed! Luca Del Baldo looked hard into my mind and not just at my face before painting his portrait of me on the cover. My agents, John Brockman and Katinka Matson, did their usual superb job shaping and shepherding my writing into a finished book.

The book is long, but I could happily have written a dozen more chapters, telling of my discussions and tutorials with Maarten Boudry, Joanna Bryson and Will Lowe, Tom Clark, Norm Daniels, Marc Hauser, Bryce Huebner, Wyn Kelley and Dale Peterson, Erin Kelly, Enoch Lambert, Dan Lloyd, Ryan McKay, Amber Ross, Evan Thompson, Chris Viger, Chris Westbury, and Chris Wood—and many others. Love to our dear sailing, skiing, singing, and adventuring friends who grew old with us and to their kids who grew up with our kids, sharing adventures that could fill another book: Tom and Gina, Ross and Gail, A and Ricky, Sue and Taz, Dick and Lolli, Jeff and Paula, and our goddaughter Emily.

NOTES

Part One: OFF TO A FAST START

xxi   **supersmart people into my orbit:** Anyone in cognitive science will be green with envy to see who my advisors, critics, and collaborators have been. Among them, in roughly the order they entered my life: Donald MacKay, Michael Arbib, Michael Gazzaniga, Richard Gregory, Marvin Minsky, Steven Pinker, Allen Newell, John McCarthy, Douglas Hofstadter, Oliver Selfridge, Richard Dawkins, George Williams, John Holland, Lynn Margulis, Anthony Marcel, Marcel Kinsbourne, Nicholas Humphrey, Ray Jackendoff, Owen Flanagan, Patricia and Paul Churchland, Dan Lloyd, Ulric Neisser, Jonathan Miller, David Premack, Rodney Brooks, Ruth Millikan, Kim Sterelny, Stanislas Dehaene, Jean-Pierre Changeux, Dan Sperber, David Haig, Terrence Deacon, Deb Roy, Thomas Metzinger, Adrian Owen, Michael Levin, Anil Seth, Sean Carroll, and the whole gang at the Santa Fe Institute. Then there were the people who came to work with me at Tufts' Center for Cognitive Studies— Kathleen Akins, Cecilia Heyes, Evan Thompson, Alva Noë, Ryan McKay, Diana Raffman, Rosa Cao, Bryce Huebner, and Krys Dolega, among others. If you can't pick up something ultra-interesting from this company, you aren't paying attention!

xxi   **check out my repairs:** In addition to these endnotes, there is a searchable archive of links to over thirty video interviews I conducted with Enoch Lambert, my postdoc, going deeper into episodes and themes in my work, mainly of interest to philosophers and cognitive scientists. The website (https://sites.tufts .edu/cogstud/ive-been-thinking-archive/) also provides links to:

> The never-aired documentary I made, the Tufts symposium on AI and evolution, with Marvin Minsky, Seymour Papert, Murray Gell-Mann, David Haig, John Holland, Karl Sims, Pattie Maes, Sherry Turkle, Kevin Kelly, Rodney Brooks, Oliver Selfridge, and Bruce Mazlish (see chapter 31)
> "Moonlight Waltz" (my country-western version of Brahms; see chapter 2)
> Dozens of videos of talks and interviews
> All my twenty-first-century published articles

> (In addition to the rest of my published work, my correspondence, both mail and email, from 1965 to the present, is archived at Tufts and is accessible by researchers with my permission.)

xxii **exactly one possible future:** Peter van Inwagen, *An Essay on Free Will* (Oxford, UK: Clarendon Press, 1983), 3.

xxiv   **"chmess":** Dennett, *Intuition Pumps and Other Tools for Thinking* (New York: W. W. Norton, 2013), chap. 76.

26   **copy of the DAT:** This recording is available on the book's website.

27   *Mind out of Matter:* Tzadik Records, Cat. #4021; released February 2018.

29   **"a belief in some fundamental":** Quine, "Two Dogmas of Empiricism," in *From a Logical Point of View* (Cambridge, MA: Harvard University Press, 1953), 20.

53   **"what we would say":** J. L. Austin, *Philosophical Papers*, 2nd ed., ed. J. O. Urmson and G. J. Warnock (Oxford: Oxford University Press, 1970), 273.

63   **our paper** Christopher Taylor and Daniel C. Dennett, "Who's Afraid of Determinism: Rethinking Causes and Possibilities," in *The Oxford Handbook of Free Will*, ed. Robert H. Kane (Oxford: Oxford University Press, 2002), 257–77.

63   **Default Responsibility Principle:** Alfred Mele, *Autonomous Agents: From Self-Control to Autonomy* (Oxford: Oxford University Press, 1995).

64   **"Minds and Machines":** In *Dimensions of Minds*, ed. Sidney Hook (New York: New York University Press, 1960), 138–64.

65   **a paper on free will:** D. M. MacKay, "On the Logical Indeterminacy of Free Choice," *Mind* 69, no. 273 (1960): 31–40.

67   **voice-throat problem:** Daniel C. Dennett, *Content and Consciousness* (London: Routledge & Kegan Paul, 1969), 9.

68   **"Critical Notice":** Daniel C. Dennett, "A Cure for the Common Code," *Brainstorms* (Cambridge, MA: MIT Press, 1978).

78   **"Beliefs about Beliefs":** "Beliefs about Beliefs," *Behavioral and Brain Sciences* 1, no. 4 (December 1978): 568–70.

Part Two: OTHER MINDS

91   **the Tuned Deck:** Daniel C. Dennett, "Explaining the 'Magic' of Consciousness," in *Sweet Dreams: Philosophical Obstacles to a Science of Consciousness* (Cambridge, MA: MIT Press, 2005).

96   **"Large legacy? Sixteen bears":** See my "The Interpretation of Texts, People and Other Artifacts," *Philosophy and Phenomenological Research* 1, Supplement (Fall 1990).

98   **"Intentional Systems":** In *Journal of Philosophy* 68, no. 4 (February 25, 1971): 87–106.

99   **Gottlob Frege's pioneering work:** *Grundgesetze der Arithmetik*, Band I (1893); Band II (1903) (Jena, Germany: Verlag Hermann Pohle). In English (translation of selected sections), "Translation of Part of Frege's *Grundgesetze der Arithmetik*," in *Translations from the Philosophical Writings of Gottlob Frege*, trans. and ed. Peter Geach and Max Black (New York: Philosophical Library, 1952), 137–158.

100   *spell my name right*: See chapter 74, "A Faustian Bargain," in *Intuition Pumps and Other Tools for Thinking* (New York: W. W. Norton, 2014).

101   **eighth edition:** See the Philosophical Lexicon website, http://www.philosophicallexicon.com.

109   **Sellars's view of qualia:** See *Consciousness Explained* (Boston: Little, Brown,

1991), 383ff; and *Sweet Dreams: Philosophical Obstacles to a Science of Consciousness* (Cambridge, MA: MIT Press, 2005).

110   **because it was humorous:** "Comment on Wilfrid Sellars," *Synthese* 27 (July/August 1974): 439–44.

117   **Norbert Wiener:** See my essay "What Can We Do?" in *Possible Minds*, ed. John Brockman (New York: Penguin, 2019).

118   **I certainly learned a lot about computers:** See chapter 12, "What Is a Deepity?" in *Intuition Pumps*.

120   *The Language of Thought*: See my Critical Notice, in *Mind*, April 1977, reprinted as "A Cure for the Common Code?" in *Brainstorms*.

Part Three: MY ODYSSEY

171   **"Beyond Belief":** In *Thought and Object: Essays on Intentionality*, ed. Andrew Woodfield (Oxford, UK: Clarendon Press, 1982).

172   **café wall:** R. L. Gregory and P. Heard, "Border Locking and the Cafe Wall Illusion," *Perception* 8, no. 4 (1979): 365–80, fig. 17, https://doi.org/10.1068/p080365..

172   *tools make you smarter*: See R. L. Gregory, *Mind in Science: A History of Explanations in Psychology and Physics* (Cambridge: Cambridge University Press, 1981); and my review, "The Well-Furnished Mind," in *Contemporary Psychology* 27, no. 8 (1982).

172   **Tower of Generate and Test:** The basic ideas were sketched in "Why the Law of Effect Will Not Go Away," *Journal for the Theory of Social Behaviour* 5 (October 1975): 169–87; but the labels "Popperian" and "Gregorian" were added in *Darwin's Dangerous Idea* (New York: Simon and Schuster, 1995).

188   *New York Review of Books*: Douglas R. Hofstadter, "Who Am I Anyway?," *New York Review of Books*, May 29, 1980.

188   **Geoffrey Hinton:** Review in *Contemporary Psychology* 24 (1979): 746–48.

192   **Searle reviewed:** John R. Searle, "The Myth of the Computer," *New York Review of Books*, April 29, 1982.

192   **a response to Searle's diatribe:** *New York Review of Books*, June 24, 1982.

192   **Robert French:** To get a good sense of French's project, see my foreword to his book *The Subtlety of Sameness* (Cambridge, MA: MIT Press, 1995); reprinted in my *Brainchildren: Essays on Designing Minds* (Cambridge, MA: MIT Press, 1998).

200   **"The Social Function of Intellect":** Nicholas Humphrey, "The Social Function of Intellect," in *Growing Points in Ethology*, ed. P. P. G. Bateson and R. A. Hinde (Cambridge: Cambridge University Press, 1979).

202   **"The Absurd":** Thomas Nagel, "The Absurd," *Journal of Philosophy* 68, no. 20 (1971): 716–27.

209   **When her book was published:** Ruth Garrett Millikan, *Language, Thought, and Other Biological Categories* (Cambridge, MA: MIT Press, 1984).

215   **a simulated register machine in Logo:** My introduction to register machines, "The Seven Secrets of Computer Power Revealed," is chapter 24 of *Intuition Pumps*.

215   *imagination prostheses*: Daniel C. Dennett, "Notes on Prosthetic Imagination," *New Boston Review* 7 (June 1982): 3–7.

219 **yielded some impressive results:** See, for example, Brian Skyrms, *The Evolution of the Social Contract* (Cambridge: Cambridge University Press, 1996); Chris Eliasmith, *How to Build a Brain* (Oxford: Oxford University Press, 2013); Kun Zhang, Joseph D. Ramsey, and Clark Glymour, "The Evaluation of Discovery: Models, Simulation and Search through 'Big Data,'" *Open Philosophy* 2 (2019): 39–48, https://doi.org/10.1515/opphil-2019-0005.

220 **"Descartes's Argument from Design":** *Journal of Philosophy* 105, no. 7 (2008): 333–45.

221 **"free will inflation":** "Herding Cats and Free Will Inflation," Romanell Lecture delivered at the 117th annual Central Division meeting of the American Philosophical Association, Chicago, February 28, 2020.

223 **the frame problem:** A good introductory essay on the frame problem by Ed Yalta can be found in the (online) Stanford Encyclopedia of Philosophy, https://plato.stanford.edu/entries/frame-problem/.

224 **monkey research:** "Out of the Armchair and into the Field," *Poetics Today* 9 (1988): 205–21; reprinted in *Brainchildren*, 289–306.

229 **Kathleen Akins:** K. A. Akins and M. Hahn, "More Than Mere Colouring: The Role of Spectral Information in Human Vision," *British Journal for the Philosophy of Science* 65, no. 1 (2014): 125–71, http://doi.org/10.1093/bjps/axt060; K. A. Akins, "A Bat without Qualities," in *Consciousness*, ed. M. Davies and G. Humphreys (Oxford, UK: Blackwells, 1993), 258–73; K. A. Akins, "Of Sensory Systems and the 'Aboutness' of Mental States," *Journal of Philosophy* 93, no. 7 (July 1996): 337–72.

231 *center of narrative gravity:* "The Self as the Center of Narrative Gravity," in *Self and Consciousness: Multiple Perspectives*, ed. F. Kessel, P. Cole, and D. Johnson (Hillsdale, NJ: Erlbaum, 1992).

233 **we published it elsewhere:** Nicholas Humphrey and Daniel C. Dennett, "Speaking for Our Selves," *Raritan: A Quarterly Review* 9 (Summer 1989): 68–98; reprinted in *Brainchildren*, 31–58.

236 **Julie Christie problem:** Daniel C. Dennett, "Commentary on Newell: Is There an Autonomous 'Knowledge Level'?," in *Meaning and Cognitive Structure*, ed. Z. Pylyshyn and W. Demopoulos (Norwood, NJ: Elsevier, 1986), 51–54; reprinted in *Brainchildren*, 282.

237 **Shakespeare and Newton:** Nicholas Humphrey, "Scientific Shakespeare," Edge, accessed December 7, 2022, https://www.edge.org/3rd_culture/humphrey/shakespeare.html.

239 **Anthony Marcel and Edoardo Bisiach:** See A. J. Marcel and E. Bisiach, *Consciousness in Contemporary Science* (Oxford: Oxford University Press, 1988).

243 **See my review:** *Journal of Philosophy* 76 (1979): 91–97.

250 **"the silliest claim ever made":** Galen Strawson, "The Consciousness Deniers," *New York Review of Books*, March 13, 2018.

250 **he has persisted undaunted:** Galen Strawson, "A Hundred Years of Consciousness: 'A Long Training in Absurdity,'" *Estudios de Filosofía* (Medellín, Colombia) 59 (January/June 2019).

250 **Keith Frankish:** Keith Frankish, "Illusionism as a Theory of Consciousness," *Journal of Consciousness Studies* 23, nos. 11/12 (2016): 11–39; Keith Frankish,

"Not Disillusioned: Reply to Commentators," *Journal of Consciousness Studies* 23, nos. 11/12 (2016): 256–89; Keith Frankish, *Illusionism as a Theory of Consciousness* (Exeter, UK: Imprint Academic, 2017).

251 **no movie in the head:** See Tim Adams, "Neuroscientist Anil Seth: 'We Risk Not Understanding the Central Mystery of Life,'" *Guardian*, August 21, 2021.

251 **Michael Graziano:** Michael S. A. Graziano, *Rethinking Consciousness: A Scientific Theory of Subjective Experience* (New York: W. W. Norton, 2019); Michael S. A. Graziano, Arvid Guterstam, Branden J. Bio, and Andrew I. Wilterson, "Toward a Standard Model of Consciousness: Reconciling the Attention Schema, Global Workspace, Higher-Order Thought, and Illusionist Theories," *Cognitive Neuropsychology* 37, nos. 3–4 (May–June 2020): 155–72; Daniel C. Dennett, "On Track to a Standard Model," *Cognitive Neuropsychology* 37, nos. 3–4 (May–June 2020): 173–75.

251 **Eccles:** Karl R. Popper and John C. Eccles, *The Self and Its Brain* (New York: Springer, 1977), 364.

251 **a memorable exchange:** Patricia Churchland, "On the Alleged Backwards Referral of Experiences and Its Relevance to the Mind-Body Problem," *Philosophy of Science* 48 (1981): 165–81; Patricia Churchland, "The Timing of Sensations: Reply to Libet," *Philosophy of Science* 48 (1981): 492–97.

251 **Occam's broom:** For more on this term, see chapter 6 in my *Intuition Pumps*.

255 **John Murray:** David McClay, "Darwin and His Publisher," *Science Progress* 92, nos. 3/4 (2009): 211–40.

259 **The Grimes effect:** See Odegaard et al.'s poster at the Vision Sciences Society, https://www.davidrosenthal.org/Odegaard-poster_VSS2022_CDDS-final.pdf.

261 **Arthur Danto:** Arthur C. Danto, "Age of Innocence," *Nation*, December 20, 2001.

264 **that is an illusion:** See Michael A. Cohen, Daniel C. Dennett, and Nancy Kanwisher, "What Is the Bandwidth of Perceptual Experience," *Trends in Cognitive Sciences* 20, no. 5 (May 2016): 324–35.

265 **partisan misrepresentations:** This sad fact is well exposed by Jared Warren in "This Quintessence of Dust—*Consciousness Explained*, at Thirty," *Philosophical Papers* 50, no. 4 (2021): 1–28.

266 **critiques to which I responded:** Ned Block, "Begging the Question against Phenomenal Consciousness," *Behavioral and Brain Sciences* 15, no. 2 (1992): 205–6; Ned Block, Review of *Consciousness Explained*, *Journal of Philosophy* 90, no. 4 (1993): 181–93; Ned Block, "On a Confusion about a Function of Consciousness," *Behavioral and Brain Sciences* 18, no. 2 (1995): 227–47; Ned Block, "What Is Dennett's Theory a Theory Of?," *Philosophical Topics* 22, nos. 1/2 (1994): 23–40. My responses include "The Path Not Taken," *Behavioral and Brain Sciences* 18, no. 2 (1995): 252–53; and the aptly titled (thanks to Susan) "Get Real," *Philosophical Topics* 22, nos. 1/2 (1994): 505–68, which included my identification of what I later called the "surely" alarm, noting that very often the word "surely" points to the weakest point in anybody's argument.

266 **"mental paint":** Ned Block, "Mental Paint," in *Reflections and Replies: Essays on the Philosophy of Tyler Burge*, ed. M. Hahn and B. Ramberg (Cambridge, MA: MIT Press, 2003).

267   **"relational neural property":** Ned Block, "Attention and Mental Paint," *Philosophical Issues* 20 (2010): 23–63, n2.

267   ***virtual* paint:** See my review article "Facing Up to the Hard Question of Consciousness" in *Philosophical Transactions of the Royal Society B* (2018) for a detailed look at virtual properties of virtual machines.

267   **Michael A. Cohen . . . Nancy Kanwisher:** Michael A. Cohen and Daniel C. Dennett, "Consciousness Cannot Be Separated from Function," *Trends in Cognitive Sciences* 15, no. 8 (2011): 358–64; Cohen, Dennett, and Kanwisher, "What Is the Bandwidth."

274   **Strasser . . . Schwitzgebel:** Eric Schwitzgebel, "Results: The Computerized Philosopher: Can You Distinguish Daniel Dennett from a Computer?," *The Splintered Mind* (blog), July 25, 2022, https://schwitzsplinters.blogspot.com/2022/07/results-computerized-philosopher-can.html.

275   **Bender as a "stochastic parrot":** Emily Bender et al., "On the Dangers of Stochastic Parrots: Can Language Models Be Too Big?," *FAccT '21: Proceedings of the 2021 ACM Conference on Fairness, Accountability, and Transparency* (March 2021): 610–23, https://doi.org/10.1145/3442188.3445922.

275   **David Cope:** David Cope, *Virtual Music: Computer Synthesis of Musical Style* (Cambridge, MA: MIT Press, 2001).

277   **"Fast, Cheap and Out of Control":** Rodney A. Brooks and Anita M. Flynn, "Fast, Cheap and Out of Control: A Robot Invasion of the Solar System," *Journal of the British Interplanetary Society* 42 (1989): 478–85.

284   **photos of Tati:** There they still reside, at https://sites.tufts.edu/cogstud/tati-photos/.

294   **Richard Dawkins:** Richard Dawkins, "The Future Looks Bright," *Guardian*, June 21, 2003.

294   **Brights:** The Brights' website: http://www.the-brights.net.

295   ***New York Times*:** Daniel C. Dennett, "The Bright Stuff," *New York Times*, July 12, 2003.

297   **Four Horsemen:** Christopher Hitchens, Richard Dawkins, Sam Harris, and Daniel C. Dennett, *The Four Horsemen: The Conversation That Sparked an Atheist Revolution* (New York: Random House, 2019).

301   **Joseph Henrich:** See my review of Henrich's *The Weirdest People in the World*, *New York Times*, September 12, 2020.

303   **excellent reviews:** *The Unbelieving* reviews include Laura Collins-Hughes, " 'The Unbelieving' Review: Life After Faith," *New York Times*, Nov. 1, 2022, https://www.nytimes.com/2022/11/01/theater/the-unbelieving-review.html; Marina Kennedy, "THE UNBELIEVING at 59E59 Theaters—Compelling Play Presents a Meaningful Discussion of Religious Faith," Broadway World, Oct. 28, 2022, https://www.broadwayworld.com/off-off-broadway/article/Review-THE-UNBELIEVING-at-59E59-Theaters-A-Compelling-Play-that-Presents-a-Meaningful-Discussion-of-Religious-Faith-20221028; Sandy Mac-Donald, "The Unbelieving: Agnostics Anonymous—Renegade Preachers Confess Their Doubts," New York Stage Review, Oct. 27, 2022, https://nystagereview.com/2022/10/27/the-unbelieving-agnostics-anonymous-renegade-preachers-confess-their-doubts/; Helen Shaw, "The Unbelieving," Goings On About Town, *New Yorker*, https://www.newyorker.com/goings-on-about-town/theatre/the-unbelieving-11-07-22; and "The Unbelieving NYC Reviews and Tickets,"

Show-Score, https://www.show-score.com/off-broadway-shows/the-unbelieving. For inquiries about future productions contact Megan Kingery (megan@ megankingery.com) or Marin Gazzaniga (maringazz@gmail.com).

303 **Clergy Project:** You can learn about them on their website (https://clergyproject .org), but you can't get in unless you can prove that you are indeed a clergy person who has lost the faith.

307 **Norman Cousins:** Norman Cousins, *Anatomy of an Illness* (New York: W. W. Norton, 1979).

309 **available in a small book:** Daniel C. Dennett and Alvin Plantinga, *Science and Religion: Are They Compatible?* (Oxford: Oxford University Press, 2010).

314 **intentionality:** Daniel C. Dennett, "Intentionality," reprinted in *The Opened Curtain: A U.S.-Soviet Philosophy Summit,* ed. Keith Lehrer and Ernest Sosa (Boulder, CO: Westview Press, 1991), 44–54.

320 ***Zombie from Boston:*** D. B. Volkov, *The Zombie from Boston: D. Dennett and His Theory of Consciousness* [in Russian] (Moscow: URSS Press, 2011).

321 **mental representation:** Hugh Clapin, ed., *Philosophy of Mental Representation* (Oxford, UK: Clarendon Press, 2002).

322 **vigorous but constructive discussion:** The video team recorded all the discussions, which can be found on Dmitry's website, https://www.youtube .com/c/MoscowCenterforConsciousnessStudies/videos. (David Chalmers's photos of the trip are excellent: http://consc.net/pics/greenland.html.)

327 **Danny Hillis . . . TED talk:** See https://www.ted.com/talks/danny_hillis_ the_internet_could_crash_we_need_a_plan_b/.

334 ***Tufts Symposium:*** https://sites.tufts.edu/cogstud/ive-been-thinking-archive/.

334 **Erasmus Prize:** "Erasmus: Sometimes a Spin Doctor Is Right," *Praemium Erasmianum Essay 2012,* essay written for the Praemium Erasmianum Foundation on the occasion of the award of the Erasmus Prize, Amsterdam, November 2012.

334 **voyage of the *Beagle*:**

> *In het kielzog van Darwin* (English: *Beagle: In Darwin's wake*) was a Dutch-Flemish television series from 2009 and 2010 initiated by the VPRO in collaboration with Teleac (Dutch educational broadcaster) and Canvas, to commemorate the 150th anniversary of Charles Darwin's ground-breaking book *On the Origin of Species.* The series is centered on an 8-month voyage around the world on board the clipper *Stad Amsterdam,* which follows the route of the five-year-long voyage of Charles Darwin on board of the ship HMS *Beagle* between 1831 and 1836. The *Stad Amsterdam* departed from the English port of Plymouth on September 1, 2009.
>
> (Wikipedia, s.v. *"Beagle: In Darwin's Wake,"*
> last modified November 9, 2022, 07:12,
> https://en.wikipedia.org/wiki/Beagle:_In_
> Darwin%27s_wake)

https://www.vpro.nl/programmas/beagle-in-het-kielzog-van-darwin.html#/ talen/item/12/; Hans Fels, dir., *One Small Step for Man—The Beagle,* VPRO World Stories, posted on YouTube November 9, 2017, https://www.youtube .com/watch?v=8YPkxxMPshc.

345 **results of that working group:** "SFI Cultural Evolution Workshop," International Cognition & Culture Institute, http://cognitionandculture.net/webinars/sfi-cultural-evolution-workshop/.

Part Four: ACADEMIC BATTLES

354 **Michael Green:** Michael Steven Green, *Nietzsche and the Transcendental Tradition* (Urbana: University of Illinois Press, 2002).

356 **discussing my theory of consciousness:** See, e.g., Richard Rorty, "Dennett on Awareness," *Philosophical Studies* 23, no. 3 (1972): 153–62; and his "Functionalism, Machines, and Incorrigibility," *Journal of Philosophy* 69, no. 8 (1972): 203–20.

356 **"Contemporary Philosophy of Mind":** Richard Rorty, "Contemporary Philosophy of Mind," *Synthese* 53, no. 2 (November 1982): 323–48.

356 **I responded mischievously:** Daniel C. Dennett, "Comments on Rorty," *Synthese* 53, no. 2 (November 1982): 349–56.

357 **"vegetarian" concept of truth:** "Postmodernism and Truth," https://tufts.box.com/s/q5gyng1tlfdpmz5sjhf6y1m2gigob4jl.

358 **"The aim of philosophy":** Wilfrid Sellars, "Philosophy and the Scientific Image of Man," in *Frontiers of Science and Philosophy*, ed. Robert Colodny (Pittsburgh, PA: University of Pittsburgh Press, 1962), 35.

360 **encounters with Noam Chomsky:** See *Darwin's Dangerous Idea* (New York: Simon and Schuster, 1995), 381–93, 397–400; *Intuition Pumps and Other Tools for Thinking* (New York: W. W. Norton, 2014), 29–30; and *From Bacteria to Bach and Back* (New York: W. W. Norton, 2017), 276–81, 374–76.

364 **Sturgeon's law:** See *Intuition Pumps*, chapter 4.

364 **Lewontin wrote a bristling commentary:** Richard C. Lewontin, "Elementary Errors about Evolution," *Behavioral and Brain Sciences* 6, no. 3 (1983): 367–68.

366 **Dawkins's review:** Richard Dawkins, "Pornophilosophy," *Nature*, 354 (1991): 442–43.

367 **Steve's awful review:** Stephen Jay Gould, "The Confusion over Evolution," *New York Review of Books*, November 19, 1992.

368 **One reviewer called it:** John Gribbin, *Sunday Times* (London), June 12, 1996.

370 **two-part diatribe . . . and my response:** Stephen Jay Gould, "Darwinian Fundamentalism," *New York Review of Books*, June 12, 1997; Stephen Jay Gould, "Evolution: The Pleasures of Pluralism," *New York Review of Books*, June 26, 1997; Daniel C. Dennett, reply by Stephen Jay Gould, "'Darwinian Fundamentalism': An Exchange," *New York Review of Books*, August 14, 1997.

376 **human trampoline:** Daniel C. Dennett, "Not Just a Fine Trip Down Memory Lane," in *Content and Consciousness Revisited*, ed. Carlos Muñoz-Suárez and Felipe De Brigard (New York: Springer, 2015), 199–220.

378 **"Philosophy is *full* of surprises":** Jerry A. Fodor, *A Theory of Content and Other Essays* (Cambridge, MA: MIT Press, 1990), 87.

378 **Jerry's review:** Jerry Fodor, "Deconstructing Dennett's Darwin," *Mind & Language* 11, no. 3 (1996): 246–62. See my rebuttal, same issue, "Granny versus Mother Nature—No Contest."

380 **I said in my reply:** "The Mystery of Consciousness: An Exchange," *New York Review of Books*, December 21, 1995.

384 **Adaptive Resonance Theory:** See Grossberg's *Conscious Mind, Resonant Brain: How Each Brain Makes a Mind* (Oxford: Oxford University Press, 2021).

386 **The patterns visible at each stance are real:** Daniel C. Dennett, "Real Patterns," *Journal of Philosophy*, 88, 27–51, January 1991. Reprinted in *Brainchildren*.

395 **Biologic Institute:** Daniel C. Dennett, "The Hoax of Intelligent Design and How It Was Perpetrated," in *Intelligent Thought*, ed. John Brockman (New York: Vintage, 2006), 33–49.

INDEX